AF675573

Advanced Research in Pure and Applied Algebra

Advanced Research in Pure and Applied Algebra

Guest Editor

Xiaomin Tang

MDPI

Basel • Beijing • Wuhan • Barcelona • Belgrade • Novi Sad • Cluj • Manchester

Guest Editor
Xiaomin Tang
School of Mathematical
Science
Heilongjiang University
Harbin
China

Editorial Office
MDPI AG
Grosspeteranlage 5
4052 Basel, Switzerland

This is a reprint of the Special Issue, published open access by the journal *Mathematics* (ISSN 2227-7390), freely accessible at: https://www.mdpi.com/journal/mathematics/special_issues/0NA58QLJ0L.

For citation purposes, cite each article independently as indicated on the article page online and as indicated below:

Lastname, A.A.; Lastname, B.B. Article Title. *Journal Name* **Year**, *Volume Number*, Page Range.

ISBN 978-3-7258-7486-6 (Hbk)
ISBN 978-3-7258-7487-3 (PDF)
https://doi.org/10.3390/books978-3-7258-7487-3

© 2026 by the authors. Articles in this reprint are Open Access and distributed under the Creative Commons Attribution (CC BY) license. The reprint as a whole is distributed by MDPI under the terms and conditions of the Creative Commons Attribution-NonCommercial-NoDerivs (CC BY-NC-ND) license (https://creativecommons.org/licenses/by-nc-nd/4.0/).

Contents

About the Editor . . . . **vii**

Xiaomin Tang
Preface to the Special Issue "Advanced Research in Pure and Applied Algebra"
Reprinted from: *Mathematics* **2025**, *13*, 2934, https://doi.org/10.3390/math13182934 . . . . **1**

Ho Yun Jung
Minimal Polynomials of Some Eta-Quotients Evaluated at CM Points
Reprinted from: *Mathematics* **2025**, *13*, 3127, https://doi.org/10.3390/math13193127 . . . . **3**

Aftab Hussain Shah, Bana Al Subaiei, Shariq Ali Attari and Dilawar Juneed Mir
On Group-like Properties of Left Groups
Reprinted from: *Mathematics* **2025**, *13*, 3109, https://doi.org/10.3390/math13193109 . . . . **16**

Huber Nieto-Chaupis
Canonical Commutation Relation Derived from Witt Algebra
Reprinted from: *Mathematics* **2025**, *13*, 1910, https://doi.org/10.3390/math13121910 . . . . **32**

Nawaf L. Alsowait, Mohammed Al-Shomrani, Radwan M. Al-omary and Zakia Z. Al-Amery
On a Quotient Ring That Satisfies Certain Identities via Generalized Reverse Derivations
Reprinted from: *Mathematics* **2025**, *13*, 870, https://doi.org/10.3390/math13050870 . . . . **48**

Ali Yahya Hummdi, Zeliha Bedir, Emine Koç Sögütcü, Öznur Gölbaşıand Nadeem ur Rehman
Lie Ideals and Homoderivations in Semiprime Rings
Reprinted from: *Mathematics* **2025**, *13*, 548, https://doi.org/10.3390/math13040548 . . . . **60**

Yanliang Cheng
The Equivalent Standard Forms of a Class of Tropical Matrices and Centralizer Groups
Reprinted from: *Mathematics* **2025**, *13*, 399, https://doi.org/10.3390/math13030399 . . . . **73**

Muhammad Saad, Usama A. Aburawash, Ahmed M. A. El-Sayed and Nour Nabil
An Introduction to i-Commutative Rings
Reprinted from: *Mathematics* **2025**, *13*, 253, https://doi.org/10.3390/math13020253 . . . . **85**

Rahmah Al Omari and Mohammed Al Shomrani
The Category $\mathfrak{G}$-GrR-Mod and Group Factorization
Reprinted from: *Mathematics* **2024**, *12*, 3344, https://doi.org/10.3390/math12213344 . . . . **99**

Yongyue Zhong and Xiaomin Tang
The Connection between $\mathrm{Der}(\mathrm{U}_{\mathrm{q}}^{+}(\mathrm{g}))$ and $\mathrm{Der}(\mathrm{U}_{\mathrm{r,s}}^{+}(\mathrm{g}))$
Reprinted from: *Mathematics* **2024**, *12*, 2517, https://doi.org/10.3390/math12162517 . . . . **113**

Nawaf Alsowait, Radwan M. Al-omary, Zakia Al-Amery, Mohammed Al-Shomrani
Exploring Commutativity via Generalized (α, β)-Derivations Involving Prime Ideals
Reprinted from: *Mathematics* **2024**, *12*, 2325, https://doi.org/10.3390/math12152325 . . . . **127**

Fuyang Zhu and Wen Teng
Cohomology and Crossed Modules of Modified Rota–Baxter Pre-Lie Algebras
Reprinted from: *Mathematics* **2024**, *12*, 2260, https://doi.org/10.3390/math12142260 . . . . **137**

Hua Sun, Yuyan Zhang, Ziliang Jiang, Mingyu Huang and Jiawei Hu
The Ribbon Elements of the Quantum Double of Generalized Taft–Hopf Algebra
Reprinted from: *Mathematics* **2024**, *12*, 1802, https://doi.org/10.3390/math12121802 . . . . **154**

About the Editor

Xiaomin Tang

Xiaomin Tang is affiliated with the School of Mathematical Science at Heilongjiang University, Harbin, China. His main research interests focus on Lie theory, cluster algebra and brace, which are important research directions in modern pure algebra with extensive applications in mathematical physics and combinatorics. He has long been engaged in the in-depth research of the structural theory of Lie algebras, the combinatorial properties of cluster algebras and the algebraic structure of braces, and has achieved a series of important research results in these fields. As a Guest Editor, he successfully organized the Special Issue "Advanced Research in Pure and Applied Algebra" of the international journal *Mathematics*, gathering thirteen high-quality research papers from domestic and foreign algebraic researchers and promoting academic exchange and cooperation in the field of pure and applied algebra. He is committed to the research and teaching of algebra, and has cultivated a number of young researchers engaged in algebraic research. His research work has provided valuable theoretical references for the development of related algebraic research fields, and he is actively engaging in academic exchange and cooperation with many well-known international algebraic research teams.

mathematics

MDPI

Editorial

Preface to the Special Issue "Advanced Research in Pure and Applied Algebra"

Xiaomin Tang

School of Mathematical Science, Heilongjiang University, Harbin 150080, China; x.m.tang@163.com

MSC: 11E81; 13A02; 15A80; 16W22; 16W25; 16N60; 16U40; 17A01; 17B3; 20B99; 81R50

This is a continuation of the work initiated with a previous Special Issue entitles "Advanced Research in Pure and Applied Algebra" published in the MDPI journal Mathematics. Among the 48 submissions received for this Special Issue, the editors selected ten articles that successfully passed the peer-review process, and were then published in the journal in the period from March 2024 to November 2025. The selected contributions delve into the intricate structures of rings, algebras, and their representations, exploring deep interconnections with quantum mechanics, group theory, and topological algebra.

The works presented in this volume reflect a broad spectrum of contemporary algebraic research. A significant theme is the exploration of various types of derivations and their impact on the structure of rings. For instance, Alsowait et al. in (Contributions 2), in their two contributions, investigate how generalized reverse derivations and generalized (α, β)-derivations influence the commutativity of quotient rings modulo a prime ideal, providing essential conditions under which these structures become commutative. Complementing this, Hummdi et al. in (Contributions 3) present a comprehensive study on homoderivations in semiprime rings, establishing several conditions that force these maps to act as commuting maps on Lie ideals, thus generalizing several classical results in this area. Another prominent thread is the study of non-commutative and deformed algebraic structures. Zhu and Teng offer a sophisticated treatment of the cohomology and crossed modules of modified Rota–Baxter pre-Lie algebras, linking their findings to infinitesimal deformations and extension theory. In a similar way, Zhong and Tang bridge the gap between one- and two-parameter quantum groups by elucidating the precise connections between their derivation algebras, providing a valuable tool for parallel development in both theories. Furthermore, Sun et al. undertake a detailed analysis of the ribbon elements in the quantum double of a generalized Taft–Hopf algebra, offering a complete classification based on the parity of the parameters involved. The special issue also features novel algebraic constructions. Saad et al. in (Contributions 5) introduce the intriguing concept of i-commutative rings, a new class defined by idempotent-driven commutativity conditions, and explore their fundamental properties with illustrative matrix examples. Cheng contributes to tropical algebra by establishing equivalent standard forms for a class of tropical matrices and describing the structure of their centralizer groups, revealing new insights into their algebraic symmetry. The connection between algebra and quantum physics is powerfully demonstrated by Nieto-Chaupis, who derives the canonical commutation relation of quantum mechanics from the Witt algebra (Virasoro algebra with null central charge). This groundbreaking work suggests a profound and previously unexplored link between fundamental quantum observables and this infinite-dimensional Lie algebra. Finally, Al-Omari and Al-Shomrani advance graded module theory by introducing and studying G-weak graded rings and modules, proving a Maschke-type equivalence of categories for strongly graded rings in this generalized setting.

The Guest Editor wishes to express their deepest gratitude to all the authors for their excellent contributions, which have significantly enriched this Special Issue. We are also profoundly indebted to the numerous anonymous reviewers for their rigorous peer review, insightful comments, and invaluable suggestions that greatly enhanced the quality of the manuscripts. Furthermore, we acknowledge the excellent collaboration with the publisher, the constant assistance provided by the MDPI associate editors in bringing this project to the end, and the great support of the Managing Editor of this Special Issue, Ms. Jialin Su.

Conflicts of Interest: The guest editors declare no conflicts of interest.

List of Contributions:

1. Nieto-Chaupis, H. Canonical Commutation Relation Derived from Witt Algebra. *Mathematics* **2025**, *13*, 1910. https://doi.org/10.3390/math13121910.
2. Alsowait, N.L.; Al-Shomrani, M.; Al-omary, R.M.; Al-Amery, Z.Z. On a Quotient Ring That Satisfies Certain Identities via Generalized Reverse Derivations. *Mathematics* **2025**, *13*, 870. https://doi.org/10.3390/math13050870.
3. Hummdi, A.Y.; Bedir, Z.; Koç Sögütcü, E.; Gölbaşı, Ö.; ur Rehman, N. Lie Ideals and Homoderivations in Semiprime Rings. *Mathematics* **2025**, *13*, 548. https://doi.org/10.3390/math13040548.
4. Cheng, Y. The Equivalent Standard Forms of a Class of Tropical Matrices and Centralizer Groups. *Mathematics* **2025**, *13*, 399. https://doi.org/10.3390/math13030399.
5. Saad, M.; Aburawash, U.A.; El-Sayed, A.M.A.; Nabil, N. An Introduction to i-Commutative Rings. *Mathematics* **2025**, *13*, 253. https://doi.org/10.3390/math13020253.
6. Al-Omari, R.; Al-Shomrani, M. The Category G-GrR-Mod and Group Factorization. *Mathematics* **2024**, *12*, 3344. https://doi.org/10.3390/math12213344.
7. Zhong, Y.; Tang, X. The Connection between Der(U^+_q(g)) and Der($U^+_{r,s}$(g)). Mathematics **2024**, *12*, 2517. https://doi.org/10.3390/math12162517.
8. Alsowait, N.; Al-omary, R.M.; Al-Amery, Z.; Al-Shomrani, M. Exploring Commutativity via Generalized (α, β)-Derivations Involving Prime Ideals. *Mathematics* **2024**, *12*, 2325. https://doi.org/10.3390/math12152325.
9. Zhu, F.; Teng, W. Cohomology and Crossed Modules of Modified Rota–Baxter Pre-Lie Algebras. *Mathematics* **2024**, *12*, 2260. https://doi.org/10.3390/math12142260.
10. Sun, H.; Zhang, Y.; Jiang, Z.; Huang, M.; Hu, J. The Ribbon Elements of the Quantum Double of Generalized Taft–Hopf Algebra. *Mathematics* **2024**, *12*, 1802. https://doi.org/10.3390/math12121802.

Disclaimer/Publisher's Note: The statements, opinions and data contained in all publications are solely those of the individual author(s) and contributor(s) and not of MDPI and/or the editor(s). MDPI and/or the editor(s) disclaim responsibility for any injury to people or property resulting from any ideas, methods, instructions or products referred to in the content.

mathematics

MDPI

Article

Minimal Polynomials of Some Eta-Quotients Evaluated at CM Points

Ho Yun Jung

Department of Mathematics, Dankook University, Cheonan-si 31116, Republic of Korea;
hoyunjung@dankook.ac.kr

Abstract

We study certain eta-quotients of weight zero evaluated at CM points of imaginary quadratic orders. Using the theory of extended form class groups, we show that these special values generate the corresponding ring class fields and we provide explicit descriptions of their minimal polynomials. Finally, we apply these results to certain Diophantine problems.

Keywords: class field theory; form class groups; ideal class groups; modular functions

MSC: 11R37; 11E12; 11F03; 11R65

1. Introduction

Let $\mathbb{H}$ denote the complex upper half-plane, namely,

$$\mathbb{H} = \{\tau \in \mathbb{C} \mid \mathrm{Im}(\tau) > 0\}.$$

The *Dedekind eta-function* on $\mathbb{H}$ is defined by the infinite product

$$\eta(\tau) = q^{1/24} \prod_{m=1}^{\infty} (1 - q^m) \quad (\tau \in \mathbb{H},\ q = e^{2\pi \mathrm{i} \tau}). \tag{1}$$

For a positive integer N, a function of the form

$$\prod_{d \mid N} \eta(d\tau)^{m_d} \quad (m_d \in \mathbb{Z})$$

is called an *eta-quotient*, whose modularity was investigated by Newman [1,2] and Gordon-Sinor [3]. Such eta-quotients can be used to construct bases for certain spaces of modular forms for the congruence subgroup

$$\Gamma_0(N) = \left\{ \gamma = \begin{bmatrix} a & b \\ c & d \end{bmatrix} \in \mathrm{SL}_2(\mathbb{Z}) \mid c \equiv 0 \pmod{N} \right\}$$

(see [4–6]).

The aim of this paper is to enrich the explicit class field theory for imaginary quadratic fields in terms of eta-quotients. More precisely, we consider eta-quotients of weight 0 evaluated at CM points and study their minimal polynomials.

Let K be an imaginary quadratic field with the ring of integers $\mathcal{O}_K$, and let $\mathcal{O}$ be an order in K with conductor $\ell_{\mathcal{O}}$ and discriminant $D_{\mathcal{O}}$. Define the element $\tau_{\mathcal{O}}$ in $\mathbb{H}$ by

$$\tau_{\mathcal{O}} = \begin{cases} \dfrac{-1+\sqrt{D_{\mathcal{O}}}}{2} & \text{if } D_{\mathcal{O}} \equiv 1 \pmod 4, \\ \dfrac{\sqrt{D_{\mathcal{O}}}}{2} & \text{if } D_{\mathcal{O}} \equiv 0 \pmod 4 \end{cases} \tag{2}$$

so that $\mathcal{O} = \mathbb{Z}\tau_{\mathcal{O}} + \mathbb{Z}$. Eum et al. proved that if $N \equiv 0 \pmod 4$ and η_N is the eta-quotient given by

$$\eta_N(\tau) = 4^4 \frac{\eta(N\tau)^8}{\eta((N/4)\tau)^8} \quad (\tau \in \mathbb{H}),$$

then the special value $\eta_N(\tau_{\mathcal{O}_K})$ is a real algebraic integer and generates the ring class field of the order of conductor N over K ([7], Theorem 4.5) (see also [8]). In this paper, we extend this result to CM points associated with arbitrary quadratic orders and we further describe the Galois actions concisely by means of the extended form class group. Our main theorem is as follows.

Theorem 1 (Theorem 3). *Assume that $N \equiv 0 \pmod 4$.*

(i) *The special value $\eta_N(\tau_{\mathcal{O}})$ is a real algebraic integer.*
(ii) *It generates the ring class field of the order of conductor $N\ell_{\mathcal{O}}$ over K.*
(iii) *Let $Q_1, Q_2, \ldots, Q_s$ be all the reduced binary quadratic forms of discriminant $D_{\mathcal{O}}$. Furthermore, let $\gamma_1, \gamma_2, \ldots, \gamma_t$ be a complete set of representatives for the left cosets of $\Gamma_0(N)$ in $\mathrm{SL}_2(\mathbb{Z})$. If $D_{\mathcal{O}} \neq -3, -4$, then the minimal polynomial of $\eta_N(\tau_{\mathcal{O}})$ over K is given by*

$$\prod_{(i,k)\in S_{\mathcal{O},N}} \left(x - \eta_N(\widehat{\gamma_k}(-\overline{\omega_{Q_i}})) \right) \quad (\in \mathbb{Z}[x]),$$

where

$$S_{\mathcal{O},N} = \left\{ (i,k) \in \mathbb{Z}\times\mathbb{Z} \mid 1 \le i \le s,\ 1 \le k \le t,\ Q_i\left(\gamma_k \begin{bmatrix} x \\ y \end{bmatrix}\right) \in \mathcal{Q}(D_{\mathcal{O}}, N) \right\}.$$

For the extended form class group $\mathcal{Q}(D_{\mathcal{O}}, N)/\sim_{\Gamma_0(N)}$, developed in [9,10], see Section 3. Furthermore, for $\gamma = \begin{bmatrix} a & b \\ c & d \end{bmatrix} \in \mathrm{SL}_2(\mathbb{Z})$, we denote by $\widehat{\gamma} = \begin{bmatrix} d & b \\ c & a \end{bmatrix}$. We note that Theorem 1 (iii) can be viewed as a refinement of ([11], Section 6). We then present a couple of examples illustrating Theorem 1 (iii) and conclude with an application of our results to the primes of the form $x^2 + ny^2$.

2. Class Fields for Orders

Throughout this paper, we use the following notation:

- K: An imaginary quadratic field.
- $\mathcal{O}$: An order in K.
- $\ell_{\mathcal{O}}$: The conductor of $\mathcal{O}$.
- $D_{\mathcal{O}}$: The discriminant of $\mathcal{O}$.
- N: A positive integer.

In this section, we shall introduce class fields for $\mathcal{O}$ and their construction.

Let $I(\mathcal{O})$ be the group of proper fractional $\mathcal{O}$-ideals, and let $P(\mathcal{O})$ be its subgroup consisting of principal fractional $\mathcal{O}$-ideals (cf. [12], Section 7.A). For each subgroup G of $(\mathbb{Z}/N\mathbb{Z})^*$, we define

$$\mathcal{C}_G(\mathcal{O}, N) = I(\mathcal{O}, N)/P_G(\mathcal{O}, N)$$

where $I(\mathcal{O}, N)$ and $P_G(\mathcal{O}, N)$ are subgroups of $I(\mathcal{O})$ and $P(\mathcal{O})$, respectively, given by

$$I(\mathcal{O}, N) = \langle \mathfrak{a} \mid \mathfrak{a} \text{ , a nontrivial proper } \mathcal{O}\text{-ideal prime to } N\rangle;$$
$$P_G(\mathcal{O}, N) = \langle \nu\mathcal{O} \mid \nu \in \mathcal{O}\setminus\{0\} \text{ and } \nu \equiv t \pmod{N\mathcal{O}} \text{ for some } t \in \mathbb{Z} \text{ satisfying } t + N\mathbb{Z} \in G\rangle.$$

As shown in ([9], Corollary 2.8), the group $\mathcal{C}_G(\mathcal{O}, N)$ is isomorphic to a generalized ideal class group of K modulo $N\ell_{\mathcal{O}}\mathcal{O}_K$. Thus, by the existence theorem of class field theory (cf. [13], V.8), there exists a unique abelian extension $K_{\mathcal{O},G}$ of K such that

(i) Every prime of K ramified in $K_{\mathcal{O},G}$ divides $\ell_{\mathcal{O}}N\mathcal{O}_K$;
(ii) $\mathrm{Gal}(K_{\mathcal{O},G}/K)$ is isomorphic to the generalized ideal class group via the Artin map for the modulus $\ell_{\mathcal{O}}N\mathcal{O}_K$.

In particular, if $N = 1$ (so $G = (\mathbb{Z}/\mathbb{Z})^*$), then $\mathcal{C}_G(\mathcal{O}, N)$ is the usual $\mathcal{O}$-ideal class group $I(\mathcal{O})/P(\mathcal{O})$. Note further that

$$I(\mathcal{O})/P(\mathcal{O}) \simeq I(\mathcal{O}_K, \ell_{\mathcal{O}})/P_{(\mathbb{Z}/\ell_{\mathcal{O}}\mathbb{Z})^*}(\mathcal{O}_K, \ell_{\mathcal{O}}) \tag{3}$$

(cf. [12], Proposition 7.22). In this case, $K_{\mathcal{O},G}$ is called the *ring class field* of the order $\mathcal{O}$, simply denoted by $K_{\mathcal{O}}$. Let j be the elliptic modular function with Fourier expansion

$$j(\tau) = \frac{1}{q} + 744 + 196884q + 21493760q^2 + \cdots \quad (\tau \in \mathbb{H}).$$

As a consequence of the first main theorem of the theory of complex multiplication, we obtain the following.

Proposition 1. *With $\tau_{\mathcal{O}}$ as in (2), the singular modulus $j(N\tau_{\mathcal{O}}) = j(N\ell_{\mathcal{O}}\tau_{\mathcal{O}_K})$ generates $K_{\mathcal{O}'}$ over K, where $\mathcal{O}'$ is the order of conductor $N\ell_{\mathcal{O}}$ in K.*

Proof. Observe that

$$\mathbb{Z}(N\tau_{\mathcal{O}}) + \mathbb{Z} = \mathbb{Z}(N\ell_{\mathcal{O}}\tau_{\mathcal{O}_K}) + \mathbb{Z} = \mathcal{O}'.$$

The proposition follows from ([14], Theorem 5 in Chapter 10). □

Remark 1. *Note that $j(N\tau) \in \mathcal{F}_{\Gamma_0(N),\mathbb{Q}}$ (cf. [12], Theorem 11.9).*

For a congruence subgroup Γ of $\mathrm{SL}_2(\mathbb{Z})$, let $\mathcal{F}_{\Gamma,\mathbb{Q}}$ denote the field of meromorphic modular functions for Γ with rational Fourier coefficients (cf. [15], Section 2.1). Define

$$\Gamma_G = \left\{ \gamma \in \mathrm{SL}_2(\mathbb{Z}) \mid \gamma \equiv \begin{bmatrix} t & * \\ 0 & * \end{bmatrix} \pmod{NM_2(\mathbb{Z})} \text{ for some } t \in \mathbb{Z} \text{ such that } t + N\mathbb{Z} \in G \right\}.$$

Here, for matrices $\gamma, \delta \in M_2(\mathbb{Z})$, the notation $\gamma \equiv \delta \pmod{NM_2(\mathbb{Z})}$ means that $\gamma - \delta \in NM_2(\mathbb{Z})$.

Using the theory of Shimura's canonical models ([15], Chapter 6), we obtain the following.

Proposition 2. *We have*

$$K_{\mathcal{O},G} = K(f(\tau_{\mathcal{O}}) \mid f \in \mathcal{F}_{\Gamma_G,\mathbb{Q}} \text{ is finite at } \tau_{\mathcal{O}}).$$

Proof. See ([9], Theorem 3.5). □

3. Extended Form Class Groups

Following [9,10], we shall review explicit class field theory via extended form class groups.

Let D be a negative integer such that $D \equiv 0$ or $1 \pmod 4$. Define

$$\mathcal{Q}(D, N) = \left\{ Q(x, y) = Q\left(\begin{bmatrix} x \\ y \end{bmatrix}\right) = ax^2 + bxy + cy^2 \in \mathbb{Z}[x, y] \;\middle|\; \begin{array}{l} \gcd(a, b, c) = 1, \\ b^2 - 4ac = D,\ a > 0, \\ \gcd(a, N) = 1 \end{array} \right\}.$$

The congruence subgroup Γ_G naturally acts on the set $\mathcal{Q}(D, N)$, inducing the equivalence relation $\sim_{\Gamma_G}$ defined by the following:
For $Q, Q' \in \mathcal{Q}(D, N)$,

$$Q \sim_{\Gamma_G} Q' \quad \Longleftrightarrow \quad Q'\left(\begin{bmatrix} x \\ y \end{bmatrix}\right) = Q\left(\begin{bmatrix} x \\ y \end{bmatrix}\right)^{\gamma} = Q\left(\gamma \begin{bmatrix} x \\ y \end{bmatrix}\right) \text{ for some } \gamma \in \Gamma_G.$$

For $Q(x, y) = ax^2 + bxy + cy^2 \in \mathcal{Q}(D, N)$, let ω_Q be the root of the quadratic polynomial $Q(x, 1) = ax^2 + bx + c$ lying in $\mathbb{H}$, i.e.,

$$\omega_Q = \frac{-b + \sqrt{D}}{2a}.$$

Proposition 3. *The set of equivalence classes $\mathcal{Q}(D_{\mathcal{O}}, N)/\sim_{\Gamma_G}$ can be endowed with a group structure such that the map*

$$\begin{aligned} \mathcal{Q}(D_{\mathcal{O}}, N)/\sim_{\Gamma_G} &\to \mathrm{Gal}(K_{\mathcal{O},G}/K) \\ [Q] &\mapsto (f(\tau_{\mathcal{O}}) \mapsto f(-\overline{\omega_Q}) \mid f \in \mathcal{F}_{\Gamma_G,\mathbb{Q}} \text{ is finite at } \tau_{\mathcal{O}}) \end{aligned}$$

is a well-defined isomorphism. Here, $\overline{\cdot}$ denotes the complex conjugation.

Proof. See Proposition 2 and ([9], Corollary 5.5). □

We call the group $\mathcal{Q}(D_{\mathcal{O}}, N)/\sim_{\Gamma_G}$ in Proposition 3 an *extended form class group* of discriminant $D_{\mathcal{O}}$ and level N, which extends the classical form class group $\mathcal{Q}(D_{\mathcal{O}}, 1)/\sim_{\mathrm{SL}_2(\mathbb{Z})}$ due to Gauss (cf. [12], Section 7.B).

Remark 2. *(i)* *Moreover, the map*

$$\begin{aligned} \mathcal{Q}(D_{\mathcal{O}}, N)/\sim_{\Gamma_G} &\to \mathcal{C}_G(\mathcal{O}, N) \\ [Q] &\mapsto [\mathbb{Z}\omega_Q + \mathbb{Z}] \end{aligned}$$

is a well-defined isomorphism ([9], Theorem 5.4).

(ii) *Let $f \in \mathcal{F}_{\Gamma_G,\mathbb{Q}}$ be finite at $\tau_{\mathcal{O}}$. By Proposition 3, we have*

$$\mathrm{irr}(f(\tau_{\mathcal{O}}), K) = \prod_{i=1}^{h} (x - f(-\overline{\omega_{Q_i}})),$$

where $Q_1, Q_2, \ldots, Q_h \in \mathcal{Q}(D_{\mathcal{O}}, N)$ form a complete set of representatives for the elements of the extended form class group $\mathcal{Q}(D_{\mathcal{O}}, N)/\sim_{\Gamma_G}$. Since $e^{2\pi i \tau_{\mathcal{O}}}$ is real, $f(\tau_{\mathcal{O}})$ is real as well. Hence $\mathrm{irr}(f(\tau_{\mathcal{O}}), K)$ has coefficients in $\mathbb{Q}$.

4. Representatives for the Elements of an Extended Form Class Group

Using the argument of ([16], Section 6), we shall present a complete set of representatives for the elements of the extended form class group $\mathcal{Q}(D_{\mathcal{O}}, N)/\sim_{\Gamma_G}$ under the assumption that $D_{\mathcal{O}} \neq -3, -4$.

Lemma 1. *If $D_{\mathcal{O}} \neq -3, -4$, then the isotropy group of $Q \in \mathcal{Q}(D_{\mathcal{O}}, 1)$ in $\mathrm{SL}_2(\mathbb{Z})$ is $\{\pm I_2\}$.*

Proof. See ([17], Proposition 1.5 (c)). □

Theorem 2. *Let $Q_1, Q_2, \ldots, Q_s$ be all the reduced binary quadratic forms of discriminant $D_{\mathcal{O}}$. Furthermore, let $\gamma_1, \gamma_2, \ldots, \gamma_t$ be a complete set of representatives for the left cosets of the subgroup $\pm\Gamma_G$ in $\mathrm{SL}_2(\mathbb{Z})$, i.e.,*

$$\mathrm{SL}_2(\mathbb{Z}) = \gamma_1\Gamma \uplus \gamma_2\Gamma \uplus \cdots \uplus \gamma_t\Gamma \quad \text{with } \Gamma = \pm\Gamma_G. \tag{4}$$

If $D_{\mathcal{O}} \neq -3, -4$, then the forms

$$Q_i^{\gamma_k} \quad (1 \le i \le s,\ 1 \le k \le t \text{ such that } Q_i^{\gamma_k} = Q_i(\gamma_k \begin{bmatrix} x \\ y \end{bmatrix}) \text{ belongs to } \mathcal{Q}(D_{\mathcal{O}}, N)) \tag{5}$$

represent all distinct elements of the extended form class group $\mathcal{Q}(D_{\mathcal{O}}, N)/\sim_{\Gamma_G}$.

Proof. Let $C \in \mathcal{Q}(D_{\mathcal{O}}, N)/\sim_{\Gamma_G}$. Then

$$C = [Q] \quad \text{for some } Q \in \mathcal{Q}(D_{\mathcal{O}}, N). \tag{6}$$

Since

$$\mathcal{Q}(D_{\mathcal{O}}, 1)/\sim_{\mathrm{SL}_2(\mathbb{Z})} = \{[Q_1], [Q_2], \ldots, [Q_s]\} \quad \text{of order } s \tag{7}$$

(cf. [12], Theorem 2.8), we have

$$Q = Q_i^{\alpha} \quad \text{for some } \alpha \in \mathrm{SL}_2(\mathbb{Z}). \tag{8}$$

From the left coset decomposition (4) of $\mathrm{SL}_2(\mathbb{Z})$, it follows that

$$\alpha = \gamma_k\beta \quad \text{for some } 1 \le k \le t \text{ and } \beta \in \Gamma = \pm\Gamma_G. \tag{9}$$

By (6), (8), and (9), we obtain

$$C = [Q_i^{\gamma_k\beta}] = [(Q_i^{\gamma_k\beta})^{\beta^{-1}}] = [Q_i^{\gamma_k}].$$

Hence every element of $\mathcal{Q}(D_{\mathcal{O}}, N)/\sim_{\Gamma_G}$ can be represented by a form of the type given in (5).

On the other hand, suppose that in the form class group $\mathcal{Q}(D_{\mathcal{O}}, N)/\sim_{\Gamma_G}$

$$[Q_i^{\gamma_k}] = [Q_{i'}^{\gamma_{k'}}] \quad \text{for some } 1 \le i, i' \le s \text{ and } 1 \le k, k' \le t \text{ such that } Q_i^{\gamma_k}, Q_{i'}^{\gamma_{k'}} \in \mathcal{Q}(D_{\mathcal{O}}, N).$$

Then

$$Q_{i'}^{\gamma_{k'}} = (Q_i^{\gamma_k})^{\gamma} \quad \text{for some } \gamma \in \Gamma_G.$$

This forces—by (7)—that $i' = i$, and hence,

$$Q_i^{\gamma_{k'}} = Q_i^{\gamma_k \gamma}.$$

Since the isotropy group of Q_i in $\mathrm{SL}_2(\mathbb{Z})$ is $\{\pm I_2\}$ by Lemma 1, we obtain

$$\gamma_{k'} = \gamma_k \gamma \quad \text{or} \quad \gamma_{k'} = -\gamma_k \gamma.$$

Therefore, $\gamma_{k'}\Gamma = \gamma_k\Gamma$ with $\Gamma = \pm\Gamma_G$. By (4), it follows that $k' = k$, which shows that no two forms in (5) represent the same element of $\mathcal{Q}(D_{\mathcal{O}}, N)/\sim_{\Gamma_G}$. □

Remark 3. *(i)* *Recall that a form $Q(x, y) = ax^2 + bxy + cy^2 \in \mathcal{Q}(D_{\mathcal{O}}, 1)$ is said to be reduced if*

$$|b| \le a \le c \quad \text{and} \quad b \ge 0 \text{ if either } |b| = a \text{ or } a = c.$$

One sees that if $Q(x, y)$ is reduced, then $a \le \sqrt{\frac{|D_{\mathcal{O}}|}{3}}$.

(ii) *Consider the case where $G = (\mathbb{Z}/N\mathbb{Z})^*$. Then we have $\pm\Gamma_G = \Gamma_0(N)$. Let $\mathrm{SL}_2(\mathbb{Z})/\Gamma_0(N)$ denote the set of left cosets of $\Gamma_0(N)$ in $\mathrm{SL}_2(\mathbb{Z})$. There is a well-known bijection ([15], Proposition 1.43):*

$$\begin{aligned}\{(c, d) \in \mathbb{Z}^2 \mid \gcd(N, c, d) = 1\}/\sim &\to \mathrm{SL}_2(\mathbb{Z})/\Gamma_0(N)\\ [(c, d)] &\mapsto [\text{any } \gamma \in \mathrm{SL}_2(\mathbb{Z}) \text{ satisfying } \gamma \equiv \begin{bmatrix} * & * \\ c & d \end{bmatrix} \pmod{NM_2(\mathbb{Z})}],\end{aligned}$$

where $\sim$ is the equivalence relation defined by

$$(c, d) \sim (c', d') \iff (c, d) \equiv u(c', d') \pmod{N\mathbb{Z}^2} \text{ for some } u \in (\mathbb{Z}/N\mathbb{Z})^*.$$

Thus, we have $[\mathrm{SL}_2(\mathbb{Z}) : \Gamma_0(N)] = N\prod_{p|N}\left(1 + \frac{1}{p}\right)$.

5. Special Values of Some Eta-Quotients

In this section, we shall prove our main theorem concerning special values of eta-quotients.

Lemma 2. *If $\{m_d\}_{d|N}$ is a family of integers such that*

(i) $\sum_{d|N} m_d = 0$,

(ii) $\sum_{d|N} dm_d \equiv \sum_{d|N}(N/d)m_d \equiv 0 \pmod{24}$,

(iii) $\prod_{d|N} d^{m_d}$ *is a rational square,*

then the associated eta-quotient $\prod_{d|N} \eta(d\tau)^{m_d}$ is a weakly holomorphic modular function for $\Gamma_0(N)$ with rational Fourier coefficients.

Proof. See [2] or [18]. □

We focus on the specific eta-quotient

$$\eta_N(\tau) = 4^4 \frac{\eta(N\tau)^8}{\eta((N/4)\tau)^8} \quad (\tau \in \mathbb{H}) \tag{10}$$

when $N \equiv 0 \pmod 4$. It is a weakly holomorphic modular function for $\Gamma_0(N)$ with rational Fourier coefficients by the definition (1) and Lemma 2.

Lemma 3. *If $N \equiv 0 \pmod 4$, then there is a pair of polynomials $A(x),\ B(x) \in \mathbb{Q}[x]$ satisfying*

(i) $j(N\tau) = A(\eta_N(\tau))/B(\eta_N(\tau))$,

(ii) $B(\eta_N(\tau_{\mathcal{O}})) \neq 0$.

Proof. (i) Note that if we set $g(\tau) = 4^4\eta(4\tau)^8/\eta(\tau)^8$, then the field $\mathcal{F}_{\Gamma_0(4),\mathbb{Q}} = \mathbb{Q}(g(\tau))$ (see [7], Lemma 3.5). Since $j(4\tau) \in \mathcal{F}_{\Gamma_0(4),\mathbb{Q}}$, there exist relatively prime polynomials $A(x), B(x) \in \mathbb{Q}[x]$ such that

$$j(4\tau) = \frac{A(g(\tau))}{B(g(\tau))}.$$

By substituting $(N/4)\tau$ for τ, we obtain the assertion.

(ii) From Proposition 2, we know that $\eta_N(\tau_{\mathcal{O}}) \in K_{\mathcal{O},(\mathbb{Z}/N\mathbb{Z})^*}$. If $B(\eta_N(\tau_{\mathcal{O}})) = 0$, then $A(\eta_N(\tau_{\mathcal{O}})) = 0$, since $j(N\tau)$ is weakly holomorphic. However, this would imply that the minimal polynomial of $\eta_N(\tau_{\mathcal{O}})$ over $\mathbb{Q}$ divides both $A(x)$ and $B(x)$, which is impossible.

See also ([7], Lemmas 3.5 and 4.3). □

Lemma 4. *If M is a positive integer and $\tau_0 \in \mathbb{H}$ is an imaginary quadratic argument, then the special value $M\eta(M\tau_0)^2/\eta(\tau_0)^2$ is an algebraic integer dividing M.*

Proof. See ([14], Theorem 4 in Chapter 12). □

Theorem 3. *Assume that $N \equiv 0 \pmod 4$:*

(i) *The special value $\eta_N(\tau_{\mathcal{O}})$ is a real algebraic integer.*

(ii) *It generates the ring class field of the order of conductor $N\ell_{\mathcal{O}}$ over K.*

(iii) *Let $Q_1, Q_2, \ldots, Q_s$ be all the reduced binary quadratic forms of discriminant $D_{\mathcal{O}}$. Furthermore, let $\gamma_1, \gamma_2, \ldots, \gamma_t$ be a complete set of representatives for the left cosets of $\Gamma_0(N)$ in $\mathrm{SL}_2(\mathbb{Z})$. If $D_{\mathcal{O}} \neq -3, -4$, then the minimal polynomial of $\eta_N(\tau_{\mathcal{O}})$ over K is given by*

$$\prod_{(i,k)\in S_{\mathcal{O},N}} \left(x - \eta_N(\widehat{\gamma_k}(-\overline{\omega_{Q_i}}))\right) \quad (\in \mathbb{Z}[x]),$$

where

$$S_{\mathcal{O},N} = \left\{ (i,k) \in \mathbb{Z}\times\mathbb{Z} \mid 1 \le i \le s,\ 1 \le k \le t,\ Q_i\left(\gamma_k \begin{bmatrix} x \\ y \end{bmatrix}\right) \in \mathcal{Q}(D_{\mathcal{O}}, N) \right\}.$$

Proof. (i) From Remark 2 (ii), we observe that the special value $\eta_N(\tau_{\mathcal{O}})$ is a real number. Moreover, since $(N/4)\tau_{\mathcal{O}} \in \mathbb{H}$, the special value

$$4\eta(4\cdot(N/4)\tau_{\mathcal{O}})^2/\eta((N/4)\tau_{\mathcal{O}})^2$$

is an algebraic integer by Lemma 4. Consequently, by the definition (10), $\eta_N(\tau_{\mathcal{O}})$ is a real algebraic integer.

(ii) We deduce that

$$\begin{aligned} K_{\mathcal{O},(\mathbb{Z}/N\mathbb{Z})^*} &= K(f(\tau_{\mathcal{O}}) \mid f \in \mathcal{F}_{\Gamma_0(N),\mathbb{Q}} \text{ is finite at } \tau_{\mathcal{O}}) \text{ by Proposition 2} \\ &= K(f([\begin{smallmatrix} 1 & u \\ 0 & 1 \end{smallmatrix}](\ell_{\mathcal{O}}\tau_{\mathcal{O}_K})) \mid f \in \mathcal{F}_{\Gamma_0(N),\mathbb{Q}} \text{ is finite at } \tau_{\mathcal{O}}) \end{aligned}$$

$$
\begin{aligned}
& \quad \text{where } u \text{ is an integer satisfying } \tau_{\mathcal{O}} = \ell_{\mathcal{O}}\tau_{\mathcal{O}_K} + u \\
&= K(f(\ell_{\mathcal{O}}\tau_{\mathcal{O}_K}) \mid f \in \mathcal{F}_{\Gamma_0(N),\mathbb{Q}} \text{ is finite at } \tau_{\mathcal{O}}) \quad \text{because } \left[\begin{smallmatrix} 1 & u \\ 0 & 1 \end{smallmatrix}\right] \in \Gamma_0(N) \\
&\subseteq K(g(\tau_{\mathcal{O}_K}) \mid g \in \mathcal{F}_{\Gamma_0(N\ell_{\mathcal{O}}),\mathbb{Q}} \text{ is finite at } \tau_{\mathcal{O}}) \\
& \quad \text{since } f(\ell_{\mathcal{O}}\tau) = f(\left[\begin{smallmatrix} \ell_{\mathcal{O}} & 0 \\ 0 & 1 \end{smallmatrix}\right](\tau)) \in \mathcal{F}_{\Gamma_0(N\ell_{\mathcal{O}}),\mathbb{Q}} \text{ for all } f \in \mathcal{F}_{\Gamma_0(N),\mathbb{Q}} \\
&= K_{\mathcal{O}_K,(\mathbb{Z}/N\ell_{\mathcal{O}}\mathbb{Z})^*} \quad \text{by Proposition 2} \\
&= K_{\mathcal{O}'} \quad \text{where } \mathcal{O}' \text{ is the order of conductor } N\ell_{\mathcal{O}} \text{ in } K \\
&= K(j(N\tau_{\mathcal{O}})) \quad \text{by Proposition 1} \\
&\subseteq K(\eta_N(\tau_{\mathcal{O}})) \quad \text{by Lemma 3} \\
&\subseteq K_{\mathcal{O},(\mathbb{Z}/N\mathbb{Z})^*} \quad \text{by Lemma 2 and Proposition 2.}
\end{aligned}
$$

This argument yields the following chain of inclusions:

$$K_{\mathcal{O},(\mathbb{Z}/N\mathbb{Z})^*} \subseteq K_{\mathcal{O}'} \subseteq K(\eta_N(\tau_{\mathcal{O}})) \subseteq K_{\mathcal{O},(\mathbb{Z}/N\mathbb{Z})^*}.$$

Since the two ends of this chain coincide, we obtain that

$$K(\eta_N(\tau_{\mathcal{O}})) = K_{\mathcal{O},(\mathbb{Z}/N\mathbb{Z})^*} = K_{\mathcal{O}'}. \tag{11}$$

(iii) The result follows by (i), (ii), (11), Remark 2 (ii), Theorem 2 and the observation

$$-\overline{\omega_{Q_i^{\gamma_k}}} = \widehat{\gamma_k}(-\overline{\omega_{Q_i}})((i,k) \in S_{\mathcal{O},N}).$$

□

In the next section, we present several examples. The computations were carried out using the MAPLE software (Version 2025.1). The procedures for finding reduced quadratic forms and coset representatives were based on Remark 3. From a computational perspective, eta-quotients are advantageous because they are defined by relatively simple q-products and are classical modular functions in number theory with rational Fourier coefficients. In our computations with MAPLE, we truncate the product expansion of the eta function up to $m = 500$ and determine the minimal polynomial of $\eta_N(\tau_{\mathcal{O}})$ over K by combining the approximate values with the theoretical fact that the coefficients are integers.

6. Examples

In this section, we shall present a couple of examples of Theorem 3 (iii).

Example 1. *Let $K = \mathbb{Q}(\sqrt{-2})$, $\mathcal{O}$ be the order of conductor 3 in K, N $= 4$. There are two reduced forms of discriminant $D_{\mathcal{O}} = -72$:*

$$Q_1 = x^2 + 18y^2, \quad Q_2 = 2x^2 + 9y^2.$$

By Remark 3 (iii), we determine a complete set of representatives for the left cosets of $\Gamma_0(4)$ in $\mathrm{SL}_2(\mathbb{Z})$ as follows:

$$\gamma_1 = \begin{bmatrix} 1 & 0 \\ 0 & 1 \end{bmatrix}, \quad \gamma_2 = \begin{bmatrix} 0 & -1 \\ 1 & 0 \end{bmatrix}, \quad \gamma_3 = \begin{bmatrix} 1 & -1 \\ 1 & 0 \end{bmatrix},$$
$$\gamma_4 = \begin{bmatrix} 1 & 0 \\ 2 & 1 \end{bmatrix}, \quad \gamma_5 = \begin{bmatrix} 1 & 0 \\ 3 & 1 \end{bmatrix}, \quad \gamma_6 = \begin{bmatrix} 2 & -1 \\ 1 & 0 \end{bmatrix}.$$

By using these representatives, we compute

$$
\begin{aligned}
&Q_1^{\gamma_1} = x^2 + 18y^2, && Q_1^{\gamma_2} = 18x^2 + y^2, && Q_1^{\gamma_3} = 19x^2 - 2xy + y^2,\\
&Q_1^{\gamma_4} = 73x^2 + 72xy + 18y^2, && Q_1^{\gamma_5} = 163x^2 + 108xy + 18y^2, && Q_1^{\gamma_6} = 22x^2 - 4xy + y^2,\\
&Q_2^{\gamma_1} = 2x^2 + 9y^2, && Q_2^{\gamma_2} = 9x^2 + 2y^2, && Q_2^{\gamma_3} = 11x^2 - 4xy + 2y^2,\\
&Q_2^{\gamma_4} = 38x^2 + 36xy + 9y^2, && Q_2^{\gamma_5} = 83x^2 + 54xy + 9y^2, && Q_1^{\gamma_6} = 17x^2 - 8xy + 2y^2.
\end{aligned}
$$

From this computation, we obtain

$$S_{\mathcal{O},4} = \{(1,1), (1,3), (1,4), (1,5), (2,2), (2,3), (2,5), (2,6)\}.$$

Applying Theorem 3 (iii), we deduce that the minimal polynomial of $\eta_4(\tau_{\mathcal{O}}) = \eta_4(\sqrt{-18})$ *over K is*

$$
\begin{aligned}
&\prod_{(i,k)\in S_{\mathcal{O},4}} \left(x - \eta_4(\widehat{\gamma_k}(-\overline{\omega_{Q_i}}))\right)\\
&= \left(x - \eta_4\left(\left[\begin{smallmatrix}1&0\\0&1\end{smallmatrix}\right]\left(\sqrt{-18}\right)\right)\right)\left(x - \eta_4\left(\left[\begin{smallmatrix}0&-1\\1&1\end{smallmatrix}\right]\left(\sqrt{-18}\right)\right)\right)\left(x - \eta_4\left(\left[\begin{smallmatrix}1&0\\2&1\end{smallmatrix}\right]\left(\sqrt{-18}\right)\right)\right)\\
&\times \left(x - \eta_4\left(\left[\begin{smallmatrix}1&0\\3&1\end{smallmatrix}\right]\left(\sqrt{-18}\right)\right)\right)\left(x - \eta_4\left(\left[\begin{smallmatrix}0&-1\\1&0\end{smallmatrix}\right]\left(\tfrac{\sqrt{-18}}{2}\right)\right)\right)\left(x - \eta_4\left(\left[\begin{smallmatrix}0&-1\\1&1\end{smallmatrix}\right]\left(\tfrac{\sqrt{-18}}{2}\right)\right)\right)\\
&\times \left(x - \eta_4\left(\left[\begin{smallmatrix}1&0\\3&1\end{smallmatrix}\right]\left(\tfrac{\sqrt{-18}}{2}\right)\right)\right)\left(x - \eta_4\left(\left[\begin{smallmatrix}0&-1\\1&2\end{smallmatrix}\right]\left(\tfrac{\sqrt{-18}}{2}\right)\right)\right)\\
&= x^8 + 64x^7 + 616160x^6 + 29518336x^5 + 500985984x^4 + 3441954816x^3 - 370278512640x^2\\
&\quad - 6042786430976x + 4096.
\end{aligned}
$$

Example 2. *Let* $K = \mathbb{Q}(\sqrt{-15})$*,* $\mathcal{O}$ *be the order of conductor 2 in K,* $N = 12$*. There are two reduced forms of discriminant* $D_{\mathcal{O}} = -60$*:*

$$Q_1 = x^2 + 15y^2, \quad Q_2 = 3x^2 + 5y^2.$$

A complete set of the left coset representatives of $\Gamma_0(12)$ *in* $\mathrm{SL}_2(\mathbb{Z})$ *is given by*

$$
\begin{aligned}
&\gamma_1 = \begin{bmatrix}1&0\\0&1\end{bmatrix}, \gamma_2 = \begin{bmatrix}0&-1\\1&0\end{bmatrix}, \gamma_3 = \begin{bmatrix}1&-1\\1&0\end{bmatrix}, \gamma_4 = \begin{bmatrix}1&0\\2&1\end{bmatrix}, \gamma_5 = \begin{bmatrix}1&0\\3&1\end{bmatrix}, \gamma_6 = \begin{bmatrix}1&0\\4&1\end{bmatrix},\\
&\gamma_7 = \begin{bmatrix}1&0\\5&1\end{bmatrix}, \gamma_8 = \begin{bmatrix}1&0\\6&1\end{bmatrix}, \gamma_9 = \begin{bmatrix}1&0\\7&1\end{bmatrix}, \gamma_{10} = \begin{bmatrix}1&0\\8&1\end{bmatrix}, \gamma_{11} = \begin{bmatrix}1&0\\9&1\end{bmatrix}, \gamma_{12} = \begin{bmatrix}1&0\\10&1\end{bmatrix},\\
&\gamma_{13} = \begin{bmatrix}1&0\\11&1\end{bmatrix}, \gamma_{14} = \begin{bmatrix}2&-1\\1&0\end{bmatrix}, \gamma_{15} = \begin{bmatrix}2&-1\\3&-1\end{bmatrix}, \gamma_{16} = \begin{bmatrix}2&-1\\5&-2\end{bmatrix}, \gamma_{17} = \begin{bmatrix}3&-1\\1&0\end{bmatrix}, \gamma_{18} = \begin{bmatrix}3&1\\2&1\end{bmatrix},\\
&\gamma_{19} = \begin{bmatrix}3&-1\\4&-1\end{bmatrix}, \gamma_{20} = \begin{bmatrix}3&-1\\7&-2\end{bmatrix}, \gamma_{21} = \begin{bmatrix}4&-1\\1&0\end{bmatrix}, \gamma_{22} = \begin{bmatrix}4&1\\3&1\end{bmatrix}, \gamma_{23} = \begin{bmatrix}4&-1\\5&-1\end{bmatrix}, \gamma_{24} = \begin{bmatrix}6&-1\\1&0\end{bmatrix}.
\end{aligned}
$$

From these, one can compute that

$$
\begin{array}{lll}
Q_1^{\gamma_1} = x^2 + 15y^2, & Q_1^{\gamma_2} = 15x^2 + y^2, & Q_1^{\gamma_3} = 16x^2 - 2xy + y^2, \\
Q_1^{\gamma_4} = 61x^2 + 60xy + 15y^2, & Q_1^{\gamma_5} = 136x^2 + 90xy + 15y^2, & Q_1^{\gamma_6} = 241x^2 + 120xy + 15y^2, \\
Q_1^{\gamma_7} = 376x^2 + 150xy + 15y^2, & Q_1^{\gamma_8} = 541x^2 + 180xy + 15y^2, & Q_1^{\gamma_9} = 736x^2 + 210xy + 15y^2, \\
Q_1^{\gamma_{10}} = 961x^2 + 240xy + 15y^2, & Q_1^{\gamma_{11}} = 1216x^2 + 270xy + 15y^2, & Q_1^{\gamma_{12}} = 1501x^2 + 300xy + 15y^2, \\
Q_1^{\gamma_{13}} = 1816x^2 + 330xy + 15y^2, & Q_1^{\gamma_{14}} = 19x^2 - 4xy + y^2, & Q_1^{\gamma_{15}} = 139x^2 - 94xy + 16y^2, \\
Q_1^{\gamma_{16}} = 379x^2 - 304xy + 61y^2, & Q_1^{\gamma_{17}} = 24x^2 - 6xy + y^2, & Q_1^{\gamma_{18}} = 69x^2 + 66xy + 16y^2, \\
Q_1^{\gamma_{19}} = 249x^2 - 126xy + 16y^2, & Q_1^{\gamma_{20}} = 744x^2 - 426xy + 61y^2, & Q_1^{\gamma_{21}} = 31x^2 - 8xy + y^2, \\
Q_1^{\gamma_{22}} = 151x^2 + 98xy + 16y^2, & Q_1^{\gamma_{23}} = 391x^2 - 158xy + 16y^2, & Q_1^{\gamma_{24}} = 51x^2 - 12xy + y^2, \\
Q_2^{\gamma_1} = 3x^2 + 5y^2, & Q_2^{\gamma_2} = 5x^2 + 3y^2, & Q_2^{\gamma_3} = 8x^2 - 6xy + 3y^2, \\
Q_2^{\gamma_4} = 23x^2 + 20xy + 5y^2, & Q_2^{\gamma_5} = 48x^2 + 30xy + 5y^2, & Q_2^{\gamma_6} = 83x^2 + 40xy + 5y^2, \\
Q_2^{\gamma_7} = 128x^2 + 50xy + 5y^2, & Q_2^{\gamma_8} = 183x^2 + 60xy + 5y^2, & Q_2^{\gamma_9} = 248x^2 + 70xy + 5y^2, \\
Q_2^{\gamma_{10}} = 323x^2 + 80xy + 5y^2, & Q_2^{\gamma_{11}} = 408x^2 + 90xy + 5y^2, & Q_1^{\gamma_{12}} = 503x^2 + 100xy + 5y^2, \\
Q_2^{\gamma_{13}} = 608x^2 + 110xy + 5y^2, & Q_2^{\gamma_{14}} = 17x^2 - 12xy + 3y^2, & Q_2^{\gamma_{15}} = 57x^2 - 42xy + 8y^2, \\
Q_2^{\gamma_{16}} = 137x^2 - 112xy + 23y^2, & Q_2^{\gamma_{17}} = 32x^2 - 18xy + 3y^2, & Q_2^{\gamma_{18}} = 47x^2 + 38xy + 8y^2, \\
Q_2^{\gamma_{19}} = 107x^2 - 58xy + 8y^2, & Q_2^{\gamma_{20}} = 272x^2 - 158xy + 23y^2, & Q_2^{\gamma_{21}} = 53x^2 - 24xy + 3y^2, \\
Q_2^{\gamma_{22}} = 93x^2 + 54xy + 8y^2, & Q_2^{\gamma_{23}} = 173x^2 - 74xy + 8y^2, & Q_1^{\gamma_{24}} = 113x^2 - 36xy + 3y^2.
\end{array}
$$

In this case, the set $S_{\mathcal{O},12}$ is given precisely by

$$
\begin{aligned}
S_{\mathcal{O},12} = \{ & (1,1), (1,4), (1,6), (1,8), (1,10), (1,12), (1,14), (1,15), \\
& (1,16), (1,21), (1,22), (1,23), (2,2), (2,4), (2,6), (2,10), \\
& (2,12), (2,14), (2,16), (2,18), (2,19), (2,21), (2,23), (2,24) \}.
\end{aligned}
$$

By Theorem 3 (iii), the minimal polynomial of $\eta_{12}(\tau_{\mathcal{O}}) = \eta_{12}(\sqrt{-15})$ over K is

$$
\begin{aligned}
& \prod_{(i,k)\in S_{\mathcal{O},12}} \left(x - \eta_{12}(\widehat{\gamma_k}(-\overline{\omega_{Q_i}}))\right) \\
&= \left(x - \eta_{12}\left(\left[\begin{smallmatrix}1&0\\0&1\end{smallmatrix}\right]\left(\sqrt{-15}\right)\right)\right)\left(x - \eta_{12}\left(\left[\begin{smallmatrix}1&0\\2&1\end{smallmatrix}\right]\left(\sqrt{-15}\right)\right)\right)\left(x - \eta_{12}\left(\left[\begin{smallmatrix}1&0\\4&1\end{smallmatrix}\right]\left(\sqrt{-15}\right)\right)\right) \\
&\times \left(x - \eta_{12}\left(\left[\begin{smallmatrix}1&0\\6&1\end{smallmatrix}\right]\left(\sqrt{-15}\right)\right)\right)\left(x - \eta_{12}\left(\left[\begin{smallmatrix}1&0\\8&1\end{smallmatrix}\right]\left(\sqrt{-15}\right)\right)\right)\left(x - \eta_{12}\left(\left[\begin{smallmatrix}1&0\\10&1\end{smallmatrix}\right]\left(\sqrt{-15}\right)\right)\right) \\
&\times \left(x - \eta_{12}\left(\left[\begin{smallmatrix}0&-1\\1&2\end{smallmatrix}\right]\left(\sqrt{-15}\right)\right)\right)\left(x - \eta_{12}\left(\left[\begin{smallmatrix}-1&-1\\3&2\end{smallmatrix}\right]\left(\sqrt{-15}\right)\right)\right)\left(x - \eta_{12}\left(\left[\begin{smallmatrix}-2&-1\\5&2\end{smallmatrix}\right]\left(\sqrt{-15}\right)\right)\right) \\
&\times \left(x - \eta_{12}\left(\left[\begin{smallmatrix}0&-1\\4&1\end{smallmatrix}\right]\left(\sqrt{-15}\right)\right)\right)\left(x - \eta_{12}\left(\left[\begin{smallmatrix}1&1\\3&4\end{smallmatrix}\right]\left(\sqrt{-15}\right)\right)\right)\left(x - \eta_{12}\left(\left[\begin{smallmatrix}-1&-1\\5&4\end{smallmatrix}\right]\left(\sqrt{-15}\right)\right)\right) \\
&\times \left(x - \eta_{12}\left(\left[\begin{smallmatrix}0&-1\\1&0\end{smallmatrix}\right]\left(\tfrac{\sqrt{-15}}{3}\right)\right)\right)\left(x - \eta_{12}\left(\left[\begin{smallmatrix}1&0\\2&1\end{smallmatrix}\right]\left(\tfrac{\sqrt{-15}}{3}\right)\right)\right)\left(x - \eta_{12}\left(\left[\begin{smallmatrix}1&0\\4&1\end{smallmatrix}\right]\left(\tfrac{\sqrt{-15}}{3}\right)\right)\right) \\
&\times \left(x - \eta_{12}\left(\left[\begin{smallmatrix}1&0\\8&1\end{smallmatrix}\right]\left(\tfrac{\sqrt{-15}}{3}\right)\right)\right)\left(x - \eta_{12}\left(\left[\begin{smallmatrix}1&0\\10&1\end{smallmatrix}\right]\left(\tfrac{\sqrt{-15}}{3}\right)\right)\right)\left(x - \eta_{12}\left(\left[\begin{smallmatrix}0&-1\\1&2\end{smallmatrix}\right]\left(\tfrac{\sqrt{-15}}{3}\right)\right)\right) \\
&\times \left(x - \eta_{12}\left(\left[\begin{smallmatrix}-2&-1\\5&2\end{smallmatrix}\right]\left(\tfrac{\sqrt{-15}}{3}\right)\right)\right)\left(x - \eta_{12}\left(\left[\begin{smallmatrix}1&1\\2&3\end{smallmatrix}\right]\left(\tfrac{\sqrt{-15}}{3}\right)\right)\right)\left(x - \eta_{12}\left(\left[\begin{smallmatrix}-1&-1\\4&3\end{smallmatrix}\right]\left(\tfrac{\sqrt{-15}}{3}\right)\right)\right) \\
&\times \left(x - \eta_{12}\left(\left[\begin{smallmatrix}0&-1\\1&4\end{smallmatrix}\right]\left(\tfrac{\sqrt{-15}}{3}\right)\right)\right)\left(x - \eta_{12}\left(\left[\begin{smallmatrix}-1&-1\\5&4\end{smallmatrix}\right]\left(\tfrac{\sqrt{-15}}{3}\right)\right)\right)\left(x - \eta_{12}\left(\left[\begin{smallmatrix}0&-1\\1&6\end{smallmatrix}\right]\left(\tfrac{\sqrt{-15}}{3}\right)\right)\right) \\
&= x^{24} + 192x^{23} - 7122306993261792x^{22} - 1253526030816147968x^{21} - 91383204195139439529x^{20} \\
&\quad - 3389719435105910475168x^{19} - 494012418500132696728 16x^{18} \\
&\quad + 12284733219874386689640 96x^{17} + 868401323558758894871453 49x^{16} \\
&\quad + 2457144449583692060476097152x^{15} + 44234812305221946123591380928x^{14}
\end{aligned}
$$

$$
\begin{aligned}
&+ 5527358761823792328229994588 10x^{13} + 48417998816531005839643779788 42x^{12} \\
&+ 2830828122234420158148780471 2803x^{11} + 9014181055032507691267952125 9347x^{10} \\
&- 3703739216878745957796365230 3623x^{9} - 1550236147193962873251193610 591518x^{8} \\
&- 3639162775938143122457492966 909150x^{7} + 1882161335822216052941940224 0943524x^{6} \\
&+ 1363327389158179348647324505 27911904x^{5} + 2988723425137814681688832050 86012077x^{4} \\
&+ 2296419700325238554605756075 7637927x^{3} + 1694808824718030833349954509 125564x^{2} \\
&- 1981533472909728482257942510 04x + 1
\end{aligned}
$$

Additionally, we observe that $\eta_{12}(\tau_{\mathcal{O}}) = \eta_{12}(\sqrt{-15})$ *is a unit.*

Remark 4. *The computations in the above examples were carried out with the MAPLE software, using 100 significant digits for numerical approximations. For instance, in Example 1, the approximate value of the coefficient of* x^7 *is*

$$63.999\ldots 9760481790273634068827$$

from which the corresponding integer coefficient is determined to be 64. For all other coefficients, the error between the approximate value and the corresponding integer is less than 10^{-60}.

7. Application to Primes of the Form $x^2 + ny^2$

Let n be a positive integer. In this final section, we present our recent joint work with Koo, Shin and Yoon [9], which extends Cho's study ([12], Theorem 15.19) on primes of the form $x^2 + ny^2$ under the additional conditions $x \equiv 1 \pmod{N}$ and $y \equiv 0 \pmod{N}$. We further apply these results to the minimal polynomial of $\eta_N(\tau_{\mathcal{O}})$ over K.

It is worth noting that the study of primes of this type has a long history. In his two-squared theorem, Gauss showed that class field theory is useful:

$$p = x^2 + y^2 \iff p = 2 \text{ or } p \text{ splits completely in } \mathbb{Q}(\sqrt{-1}).$$

Here, $\mathbb{Q}(\sqrt{-1})$ is a class field (an abelian extension) of $\mathbb{Q}$. Later, Weber, Hilbert, and Artin extended this idea to primes of the form $x^2 + ny^2$ for positive integers n (see [7]).

For a prime p, we let $\left(\frac{\cdot}{p}\right)$ be the Kronecker symbol.

Proposition 4. *Let* n *be a positive integer,* $K = \mathbb{Q}(\sqrt{-n})$ *and* $\mathcal{O} = \mathbb{Z}[\sqrt{-n}]$. *Let* $\mathfrak{p}$ *be a real algebraic integer which generates* $K_{\mathcal{O},G}$ *over* K *and* $f(X) \in \mathbb{Z}[X]$ *be its minimal polynomial over* K. *If* p *is a prime dividing neither* $2nN$ *nor the discriminant of* $f(X)$, *then*

$$
\begin{aligned}
& p \text{ splits completely in } K_{\mathcal{O},G} \\
\iff\; & p = x^2 + ny^2 \text{ for some } x,\ y \in \mathbb{Z} \text{ such that } x + N\mathbb{Z} \in G \text{ and } y \equiv 0 \pmod{)}N \\
\iff\; & \left(\frac{-n}{p}\right) = 1 \text{ and } f(X) \equiv 0 \pmod{p} \text{ has an integer solution.}
\end{aligned}
$$

Example 3. *Let* $n = 18$ *and* $N = 4$. *In this case,* $K = \mathbb{Q}(\sqrt{-18}) = \mathbb{Q}(\sqrt{-2})$ *and* $\mathcal{O} = \mathbb{Z}[\sqrt{-18}]$ *is the order of conductor 3 in* K *as in Example 1. By Theorem 3 (ii), the special value* $\eta_4(\tau_{\mathcal{O}})$ *generates the field* $K_{\mathcal{O},(\mathbb{Z}/4\mathbb{Z})^*}$ *over* K.

Now, let $F_1(X)$ *denote the minimal polynomial of* $\eta_4(\tau_{\mathcal{O}})$ *computed in Example 1. The discriminant of* $F_1(X)$ *is*

$$2^{140} \times 3^4 \times 5^{24} \times 7^{24} \times 13^4 \times 23^2 \times 29^4 \times 31^4 \times 47^2 \times 53^4 \times 61^4 \times 71^2$$

By Proposition 4, we obtain that if p is a prime dividing neither $2 \times 18 \times 4 = 2^4 \times 3^2$ *nor the discriminant of* $F_1(X)$*, then*

$$\begin{aligned} & p = x^2 + 18y^2 \text{ for some } x,\ y \in \mathbb{Z} \text{ such that } x + 4\mathbb{Z} \in (\mathbb{Z}/4\mathbb{Z})^* \text{ and } y \equiv 0 \pmod{)}4 \\ \Longleftrightarrow\ & \left(\frac{-18}{p}\right) = \left(\frac{-2}{p}\right) = 1 \text{ and } F_1(X) \equiv 0 \pmod{p} \text{ has an integer solution.} \end{aligned}$$

Example 4. *Now suppose that* $n = 15$ *and* $N = 12$*. In this setting,* $K = \mathbb{Q}(\sqrt{-15})$ *and* $\mathcal{O} = \mathbb{Z}[\sqrt{-15}]$ *is the order of conductor* 2 *in K as in Example 2. According to Theorem 3 (ii), the special value* $\eta_{12}(\tau_{\mathcal{O}})$ *generates the field* $K_{\mathcal{O},(\mathbb{Z}/12\mathbb{Z})^*}$ *over K.*

Let $F_2(X)$ *be the minimal polynomial of* $\eta_{12}(\tau_{\mathcal{O}})$ *obtained in Example 2. Its discriminant is*

1632307284832228718158746061289157482137253227993306249138258190141743
4443886904187699419233968544129371609537666746058020201645256459023316
1450976209285388060263902555546664209814035196870467272938837811559698
4646777031790006030223836505343256035536977578802290009208146418232314
7207023344755523235848212080602604501510776930718153742770446681908313
1121066322695831455501223560962300752968883605012639239629618085337152
4135622077689093458736503200226802006277447862764466920648473690147947
8838276826852283173788448512760066665196740033344822814786500932531274
3066197568526166959058190073392084856601495255137071381658875036689443
7316416266743663550022019921472794570589619274430792993430690949100309
3301211813098054734935429130659739199585880351314003697305749253438887
8125460909721029258210543309243456065960236418896059032355518538069598
8769704753247909041266437556413094470271294756321425909670008432149825
6632191525267779790953881718905128776564373037893414184701110326854965
3620150694730593478351814158637819770323066261877876743430503705793406
9288576995423061523788622204848624863398597089386590680850993070553066
1367202403986980935658276679478281327479417523238889.

Proposition 4 implies that if p is a prime dividing neither $2 \times 15 \times 12 = 2^3 \times 3^2 \times 5$ *nor the discriminant of* $F_2(X)$*, then*

$$\begin{aligned} & p = x^2 + 15y^2 \text{ for some } x,\ y \in \mathbb{Z} \text{ such that } x + 12\mathbb{Z} \in (\mathbb{Z}/12\mathbb{Z})^* \text{ and } y \equiv 0 \pmod{12} \\ \Longleftrightarrow\ & \left(\frac{-15}{p}\right) = 1 \text{ and } F_2(X) \equiv 0 \pmod{p} \text{ has an integer solution.} \end{aligned}$$

Funding: This research was supported by the National Research Foundation of Korea (NRF) grant funded by the Korea government (MSIT) (No. RS-2023-00252986).

Data Availability Statement: No new data were created or analyzed in this study. Data sharing is not applicable to this article.

Conflicts of Interest: The author declare no conflicts of interest.

References

1. Newman, M. Construction and application of a class of modular functions. *Proc. Lond. Math. Soc.* **1957**, *7*, 334–350. [CrossRef]
2. Newman, M. Construction and application of a class of modular functions. II. *Proc. Lond. Math. Soc.* **1959**, *9*, 373–387. [CrossRef]

3. Gordon, B.; Sinor, D. *Multiplicative Properties of η-Products*; Lecture Notes in Math. 1395; Springer: Berlin, Germanry, 1989; pp. 173–200.
4. Bhattacharya, S. Finiteness of simple holomorphic eta quotients of a given weight. *Adv. Math.* **2017**, *308*, 879–895. [CrossRef]
5. Choi, D. Spaces of modular forms generated by eta-quotients. *Ramanujan J.* **2007**, *14*, 69–77. [CrossRef]
6. Soumya, B. Holomorphic eta quotients of weight 1/2. *Adv. Math.* **2017**, *320*, 1185–1200. [CrossRef]
7. Eum, I.S.; Koo, J.K.; Shin, D.H. Some applications of eta-quotients. *Proc. Roy. Soc. Edinburgh Sect. A* **2016**, *146*, 565–578. [CrossRef]
8. Koo, J.K.; Shin, D.H.; Yoon, D.S. Generation of ring class fields by eta-quotients. *J. Korean Math. Soc.* **2018**, *55*, 131–146.
9. Jung, H.Y.; Koo, J.K.; Shin, D.H.; Yoon, D.S. Class fields and form class groups for solving certain quadratic Diophantine equations. *J. Number Theory* **2025**, *275*, 1–34. [CrossRef]
10. Jung, H.Y.; Koo, J.K.; Shin, D.H.; Yoon, D.S. Arithmetic properties of orders in imaginary quadratic fields. *Indian J. Pure Appl. Math.* 2025, *in press*. [CrossRef]
11. Stevenhagen, P. Hilbert's 12th problem, complex multiplication and Shimura reciprocity. In *Class Field Theory—Its Centenary and Prospect)*; Mathematical Society of Japan: Tokyo, Japan, 1998; pp. 161–176.
12. Cox, D.A. *Primes of the Form $x^2 + ny^2$–Fermat, Class Field Theory, and Complex Multiplication*, 3rd ed.; With Solutions, with Contributions by Roger Lipsett; AMS Chelsea Publishing: Providence, RI, USA, 2022.
13. Janusz, G.J. *Algebraic Number Fields*, 2nd ed.; Graduate Studies in Mathematics Series 7; American Mathematical Society: Providence, RI, USA, 1996.
14. Lang, S. *Elliptic Functions*, 2nd ed.; With an Appendix by J. Tate; Graduate Texts in Mathematics Volume 112; Springer: New York, NY, USA, 1987.
15. Shimura, G. *Introduction to the Arithmetic Theory of Automorphic Functions*; Iwanami Shoten and Princeton University Press: Princeton, NJ, USA, 1971.
16. Koo, J.K.; Shin, D.H.; Yoon, D.S. A simplified algorithmic realization of Galois actions on special values of modular functions. *arXiv* **2025**, arXiv:2506.14139. [CrossRef]
17. Silverman, J.H. *Advanced Topics in the Arithmetic of Elliptic Curves*; Graduate Texts in Mathematics Volume 151; Springer: New York, NY, USA, 1994.
18. Savitt, D. An elementary proof of Newman's eta-quotient theorem. *arXiv* **2025**, arXiv:2507.16225. [CrossRef]

Disclaimer/Publisher's Note: The statements, opinions and data contained in all publications are solely those of the individual author(s) and contributor(s) and not of MDPI and/or the editor(s). MDPI and/or the editor(s) disclaim responsibility for any injury to people or property resulting from any ideas, methods, instructions or products referred to in the content.

mathematics
MDPI

Article

On Group-like Properties of Left Groups

Aftab Hussain Shah [1], Bana Al Subaiei [2,*], Shariq Ali Attari [1] and Dilawar Juneed Mir [3]

1 Department of Mathematics, Central University of Kashmir, Ganderbal 191201, Jammu and Kashmir, India
2 Department of Mathematics and Statistics, College of Science, King Faisal University, P.O. Box 400, Al-Ahsa 31982, Saudi Arabia
3 Department of Mathematics, University Institute Sciences, Chandigarh University, Mohali 140413, Punjab, India
* Correspondence: banajawid@kfu.edu.sa

Abstract

A left group is a semigroup that is the direct product of a left zero semigroup and a group. In this paper, we investigate some group-like properties of left groups. In particular, we characterise monogenic left group monoids and prove some fundamental results on left group morphisms. We also characterise Green's equivalences on left groups and, analogously to groups, establish a correspondence between congruences and normal sub-left groups. Finally, we characterise DSC left groups.

Keywords: left group; left zero semigroup; group

MSC: 06A06; 20M20

1. Introduction and Preliminaries

A non-empty set S together with an associative binary operation is called a *semigroup*. An element a of a semigroup S is called a *left zero* element if $ab = a$ for all b in S. A semigroup consisting entirely of left zero elements is called a *left zero semigroup*. A *right zero* semigroup is defined analogously. A semigroup S is called *left simple* if $S = Sa$ for all $a \in S$. If for all a, b, c in $S, ac = bc$ implies $a = b$, we say that S is a *right-cancellative semigroup*. Dually, one can define a *right simple* semigroup and a *left-cancellative* semigroup.

A semigroup S is called a *left group* if it is left simple and right cancellative. Every group is a left group, but the converse is not true (see [1]). In Exercises 2.6 (5(b)) of [1], the Bear–Levi semigroup is not a left group. Following Clifford and Preston [2] (Theorem 1.27), a semigroup S is a left group if, and only if, $S = L \times G$, where L is a left zero semigroup and G is a group. If S is a left group, then the following are true: the set $E(S)$ of idempotents of S is non-empty and is a left zero subsemigroup of S; every idempotent is a left identity of S; and eS is a subgroup of S for every $e \in E(S)$ (see Exercise 2.6 (6) of [1]). Analogously, a semigroup S is called a *right group* if it is right simple and left cancellative. Alternatively, by [2] (Theorem 1.27), S is a right group if, and only if, $S = R \times G$, where R is a right zero semigroup and G is a group. The analogue of the above-mentioned facts about left groups also holds for right groups. For more details on left (right) groups, the reader is referred to [2] (Section 1.11, pp. 37–40) and [1] (Exercises 2.6 (5–6)). In this paper, we shall only consider the study of left groups. The analogous results for right groups can be proven in a similar way and shall not be a part of this paper.

Left groups are peculiar in the sense that, on one hand, they behave like groups, but on the other hand, they fail in some of the basic algebraic properties which hold in a group. For example, a non-trivial left group has no identity element, and no element has a two-sided inverse. Left groups play a foundational role in semigroup theory, particularly within the study of regular semigroups and their structural properties. They provide a structural foundation for decomposing more complex semigroups. Specifically, a semigroup is a left group if, and only if, it is left simple and contains at least one idempotent element. The idempotent theory for left regular bands of groups has been developed by researchers. This structure generalises group algebras of finite groups and left regular band algebras, showing how concepts from left groups are used in the representation theory of more complex algebraic structures. The study of left groups has led to the generalisation of semigroup regularities. For instance, concepts such as left regular elements and left magnifying elements are important in studying regular semigroups, which have applications in other areas of mathematics and theoretical computer science.

Semigroups have applications in automata theory, coding theory and formal languages, where concepts such as left and right ideals and Green's relations are used to understand the structure and behaviour of automata. In short, left groups serve as fundamental building blocks in the structural theory of semigroups, providing a deep understanding of regularity and the decomposition of more complex semigroups into simpler, group-like components.

This motivated the first and third author [3] to consider studying left groups, where weaker notions such as *L-identity* and *L-inverse* have been introduced. They also characterised all morphisms between any two left groups, and a characterisation of congruences on a left group is also provided, besides investigating various properties of the monoid of endomorphisms of a left group S. In [4], these authors further investigated the structure and endomorphisms of a strong semilattice of left groups.

This paper is a sequel to [3,4] and aims to investigate the *group-like* properties of left groups. Cyclic groups play a central role in group theory, and the analogous notion of a monogenic semigroup exists for semigroups. In Section 2, we explore monogenic left group monoids and provide some necessary and sufficient conditions for a left group monoid to be a monogenic monoid. In Section 3, we exhibit group-like properties for left group homomorphisms. We extend the notion of the kernel of group homomorphism to a left group homomorphism, which we call the *L-kernel* of a left group homomorphism, and prove that some of the basic properties of the kernel hold for the L-kernel.

Green's equivalences are very important relations defined on a semigroup. Exploring them provides deep insight into the structure of semigroups. This motivates us to explore these equivalences of left groups. In Section 4, we characterise Green's equivalences on left groups. It is a well-known result that for a group G, the notion of a congruence relation is equivalent to that of a normal subgroup. This motivates us to see the analogy for a left group. In Section 4, we introduce the concept of a *normal sub-left group* of a left group and prove a similar equivalence between a congruence and a normal sub-left group. Finally, in Section 5, we study the relation between a diagonal subsemigroup and a congruence on a left group.

In summary, since this paper explores the basic structure of a left group, it will open up new dimensions for further research on this important algebraic object. In the future, we intend to apply our expertise on automorphism groups of semigroups (see [5]) and epimorphisms, dominions and amalgams (see [6,7]) to left groups and their strong semilattices in order to produce some exciting and fruitful research.

If a semigroup S does not contain the identity element, then $S^1 = S \cup \{1\}$ denotes the *monoid obtained by adjoining the identity element* 1 *to* S, where the extended operation on S^1 is defined as $1s = s = s1$ for all $s \in S$ and $11 = 1$. Note that the element 1 does not have the left zero property, so a left zero semigroup L cannot contain 1. Thus, a left group $S = L \times G$ cannot be a monoid. This prompts us to consider the monoid L^1 obtained by adjoining the element 1 to the left zero semigroup L and the monoid $S^1 = L^1 \times G$ with the identity element $(1, e)$, where e is the identity of the group G. We call L^1 a *left zero monoid* and S^1 a *left group monoid*. In this paper, the terms 'left group' and 'left group monoid' shall be distinct and shall be mentioned explicitly.

Suppose S is a left group. Then, the element $(1, e)$ is not in S. In this case, for each $a = (l, g) \in S$, there exists a unique element $a_e = (l, e) \in S$ such that $aa_e = a_e a = a$. We call a_e the *L-identity* for a. Also, there exists a unique element $a^\perp = (l, g^{-1})$ for each $a = (l, g) \in S$ such that $aa^\perp = a^\perp a = (l, e) = a_e$, and we call it the *L-inverse* of a (see [3] for details).

An element a of a semigroup S is said to be an idempotent if $a^2 = a$. Note that every element of a left zero semigroup L is idempotent. Let $a = (l, g)$ be an idempotent element of a left group S. Then, $a^2 = a$ implies $(l, g^2) = (l, g)$. As $g^2 = g$ in a group G if, and only if, $g = e$, it follows that $a = (l, e) = a_e$. Hence, if $E(S)$ denotes the set of idempotents of the left group S, then $E(S) = \{a_e : a \in S\}$. Before we move on to the next sections, we want to end this section by presenting some simple but nontrivial examples to clarify the definitions introduced so far.

Example 1. *Let L be any element left zero semigroup and let $G = \mathbb{Z}_2 = \{0, 1\}$ be the cyclic group of order 2. Consider the left group $S = L \times G$. Then,*

$$S = \{(l, 0), (l, 1) : l \in L\}.$$

The set $E(S)$ of L-identities (idempotents) is $E(S) = \{(l, 0) : l \in L\}$. This semigroup possesses very nice algebraic properties.

(i) For each $l \in L$, $(l, 1)_e = (l, 0)$, i.e., $(l, 0)$ is the L-identity of $(l, 1)$.
(ii) For each $x \in S$, $x^\perp = x$, i.e., every element of S is a self L-inverse.
(iii) For any $x, y \in S \setminus E(S)$, we have $xy = x_e$ and $yx = y_e$, i.e., the product of any two non-idempotent elements is an idempotent element and is the L-identity of the element appearing on the left in the product.

Example 2. *Let L be any left zero semigroup and $G = K_4 = \{1, a, b, c\}$ be the Klein 4-group, the non-cyclic abelian group of order 4. Consider the left group $S = L \times G$. Then,*

$$S = \{(l, 1), (l, a), (l, b), (l, c) : l \in L\}.$$

Some important properties of S are as follows:

(i) The set of L-identities of S is $E(S) = \{(l, 1) : l \in L\}$.
(ii) For each $x \in S$, $x^\perp = x$, every element of S is a self L-inverse.
(iii) For each fixed $l \in L$, the subset $S_l = \{(l, 1), (l, g) : g \in G\}$ of S is a group and $S_l \cong G$.

2. Monogenic Left Group Monoids

Cyclic groups are important objects in the theory of groups and equally important is the structure of a monogenic semigroup in semigroup theory. Since a left group is a direct product of a left zero semigroup and a group, it is important to investigate how the cyclic structure in the second component affects the monogenic part of the first component and vice versa. Also worth investigating are cases in which a left group is monogenic. In this section, we answer these questions.

Let S be a semigroup and $a \in S$. Then, $< a > = \{a^n : n \in \mathbb{N}\}$ is called the *monogenic subsemigroup* of S generated by a. If S is a monoid with identity 1 and $a \in S$, then the *monogenic submonoid* of S generated by a will contain 1 and thus it is $< a >^* = \{a^n : n \in \mathbb{N}^0\}$. The semigroup S is said to be monogenic if $S =< a >$ for some $a \in S$. A monogenic monoid can be defined similarly. We begin by proving a very basic result on monogenic left group monoids.

Proposition 1. *Let $S^1 = L^1 \times G$ be a left group monoid. S is a monogenic monoid if, and only if, $L^1 = \{l\}^1 = \{l\} \cup \{1\}$ and G is a monogenic monoid.*

Proof. Suppose that S^1 is a monogenic monoid. Then, $S^1 =< a >^*$ for some $a = (l, g) \in S$. For any $x \in S$, there exists $k \in \mathbb{N}^0$ such that $x = a^k$. If $x = (1, e)$, then by taking $k = 0$, we have $a^0 = (l, g)^0 = (1, e)$. Suppose now that $x = (l', g') \neq (1, e)$. Then, $k \in \mathbb{N}$ with $(l', g') = (l, g)^k = (l^k, g^k) = (l, g^k)$. This means $l' = l$ and $g' = g^k$. Hence, $L^1 = \{l\}^1$ and $G =< g >^*$ is a monogenic monoid. Conversely assume that these two conditions are satisfied. Take any $x = (l', g') \in S^1$. If $x = (1, e)$, then for any $a = (l, g) \in S$, $x = a^0$. On the other hand, if $x \neq (1, e)$, then $l' = l$ and $g' = g^r$ for some $r \in \mathbb{N}$, where $G =< g >$. Therefore, $x = (l', g') = (l, g^r) = (l, g)^r$, where $r \in \mathbb{N}^0$. Hence, S^1 is a monogenic monoid with identity $1 = (1, e)$, as required. □

From the proof of the proposition above, one sees that a left zero monoid L^1 is monogenic if, and only if, $L^1 = \{l\}^1$. Therefore, we have:

Corollary 1. *A left group monoid $S^1 = L^1 \times G$ is a monogonic monoid if, and only if, L^1 and G are monogenic monoids.*

Next, we prove that the terms 'cyclic' and 'monogenic' are equivalent in the case of finite groups. We also illustrate with an example that the same is not true for all infinite groups.

Proposition 2. *Let G be a finite group. G is a monogenic monoid if, and only if, it is a cyclic group.*

Proof. Let $|G| = m$. Suppose that $G =< a >$ is a cyclic group. Then, m is the least positive integer such that $a^m = 1 = a^0$ and $a^0, a^1, a^2, \ldots, a^{m-1}$ are all distinct. Since all elements of G are obtained as non-negative powers of a, it follows that $G =< a >= \{1, a, a^2, \ldots, a^{m-1}\}$ is a monogenic monoid. Conversely, assume that $G =< a >$ is a monogenic monoid of order m. Since G is a group, it must be a cyclic group of order m. □

Remark 1. *The above proposition is not valid if we take G as an infinite group. Take $G = (\mathbb{Z}, +)$. Then, G is an infinite cyclic group generated by both 1 and -1, respectively. However, it is not a monogenic monoid since for any negative integer k, we have $k \neq m.1$ for any positive integer m. A similar argument applies when 1 is replaced by -1 and k is a positive integer. Also, as every infinite cyclic group is isomorphic to $(\mathbb{Z}, +)$, the above proposition is not valid for all infinite groups G.*

Recall that a finite cyclic group of order n is isomorphic to Z_n, the group of integers modulo n. This enables us to deduce a very important result regarding left groups.

Corollary 2. *A finite left group monoid $S^1 = L^1 \times G$ is a monogenic monoid if, and only if, $L = \{l\}^1$ and G is Z_n for some positive integer n.*

The connection between monogenic semigroups and homomorphisms is fundamental to understanding the structure of these semigroups. For monogenic semigroups, this relationship allows for a complete classification of their structure and reveals a direct link to a special class of quotient semigroups and cyclic groups. Let F be the free monogenic semigroup, which is isomorphic to $(\mathbb{Z}^+, +)$. This semigroup consists of all formal powers of a single generator, x, with no relations imposed. For any monogenic semigroup $S = \langle a \rangle$, a canonical surjective homomorphism $f : F \to S$ can be defined by mapping the generator of F to the generator of S: $f(x^n) = a^n$. The properties of this homomorphism f directly reflect the structure of S. If S is infinite, f is an isomorphism, mapping F bijectively to S. If S is finite with index m and period r, the homomorphism f is many-to-one. The equality $a^k = a^l$ in S means that the corresponding powers x^k and x^l in F map to the same element, a^k, in S. The kernel of a finite monogenic semigroup is the minimal ideal, which is a cyclic group.

This cyclic group is one of the congruence classes of a canonical homomorphism, illustrating how the homomorphism's kernel reveals key structural components of the monogenic semigroup. In the next section, we explore the group-like properties of left group homomorphisms.

3. Homomorphisms of Left Groups

Homomorphisms play a central and unifying role in algebra. They are structure-preserving maps between algebraic structures that respect the operations defined on those structures. Some of the well-known important properties of a *group homorphism* f between the groups G and H are that it preserves the identity, preserves inverses and preserves integer powers. Also its kernel, $kerf$, is a normal subgroup of G and its image, and Imf is a subgroup of H. The homomorphism f is injective if, and only if, $kerf$ is trivial. The preimage of a subgroup is a subgroup, and the image of a cyclic group is a cyclic group. Not all of these properties are necessarily satisfied by a *semigroup homomorphism*. As left groups are a special kind of semigroup, we shall try to investigate which of these properties can be generalised to a left group homomorphism.

If S and T are any two semigroups (groups), by $Hom(S, T)$, we mean the set of all semigroup (group) homomorphisms from S into T. The next lemma is an important result from [3], which characterises the set $Hom(S, T)$, where S and T are left groups.

Lemma 1 ([3] Theorem 4.1). *Let $L_1 \times G$ and $L_2 \times H$ be two left groups. Take $t \in Hom(G, H)$ and $s \in Hom(L_1, L_2)$. Define $f : L_1 \times G \to L_2 \times H$ by*

$$(l, x)f = ((l)s, (x)t)$$

for every $(l, x) \in L_1 \times G$. Then, f is a homomorphism, and conversely, every homomorphism from $L_1 \times G$ into $L_2 \times H$ can be so constructed. Moreover, f is bijective if, and only if, s and t are bijective.

We can now adopt the notation for a homomorphism f between the left groups $S = L_1 \times G$ and $T = L_2 \times H$ as $f = (s, t)$, where s and t are given in Lemma 1.

In the next proposition, we show that some of the crucial properties of a group homomorphism listed at the beginning of this section can be extended to a left group homomorphism.

Proposition 3. *Let $S = L_1 \times G$ and $T = L_2 \times H$ be two left groups and $f = (s, t) \in Hom(S, T)$. Then, the following statements are true.*

(i) $(a^{\perp})f = [(a)f]^{\perp}$ $\forall\, a \in S$, *i.e., a left group homomorphism preserves the L-inverse of an element.*

(ii) $(E(S))f \subseteq E(T)$, *i.e., a left group homomorphism carries the set idempotents of S into the set of idempotents of T. The equality holds if s is onto.*

(iii) $(a_e)f$ *is the L-identity of* $(a)f$ $\forall\, a \in S$, *i.e., f preserves the L-identity of an element.*

(iv) *For each $n \in \mathbb{N}^0$ and each $(l, g) \in S$,* $((l, g)^n)f = ((l, g)f)^n$.

Proof. Let $S = L_1 \times G$ and $T = L_2 \times H$ be two left groups and $f = (s,t) \in Hom(S,T)$.

(i) Let $a = (l,g)$ be any element of $L_1 \times G$. Then,
$(a)f = (l,g)f = ((l)s,(g)t) = (l^{'},k)$, where $l' = (l)s$ and $k = (g)t$.
Now,

$$\begin{aligned}(a^{\perp})f &= (l,g^{-1})f \\ &= ((l)s,(g^{-1})t) \\ &= (l^{'},[(g)t]^{-1}) \text{ (as } t \in Hom(G,H)). \\ &= (l^{'},k^{-1}) \\ &= [(a)f]^{\perp}.\end{aligned}$$

(ii) Let $(l,e) \in E(S)$. Then, $(l,e)f = ((l)s,(e)t) = (l',e') \in E(T)$ for some $l' \in L_2$ and e' is the identity of H; thus, $(E(S))f \subseteq E(T)$.
Take any $(l',e') \in E(T)$, as s is onto $l' = (l)s$ for some $l \in L_1$ and t being in $Hom(G,H)$ implies $e' = (e)t$. Therefore, $(l',e') = ((l)s,(e)t) = (l,e)f$. This implies $E(T) \subseteq (E(S))f$, and so we have the desired equality.

(iii) Take any $a \in S$. As already noted, $aa_e = a = a_e a = a$. Therefore, $(af)(a_e f) = (aa_e)f = (a)f$. Similarly, $(a_e f)(af) = (a)f$. Thus, $(a_e)f$ is the L-identity of $(a)f$.

(iv) This is straightforward.

□

Part (ii) of Proposition 3 motivates us to investigate cases in which elements other than idempotent elements of S are mapped to idempotent elements of T. For this, let $S = L_1 \times G$ and $T = L_2 \times H$ be two left groups and $f \in Hom(S,T)$. The *L-kernel* of f, denoted by $L - Ker(f)$, is the set of elements $a \in S$ such that $(a)f \in E(T)$, i.e.,

$$L - Ker(f) = \{(l,g) \in S : (l,g)f = (l^{'},e^{'}) \text{ where } l^{'} \in L' \text{ and } e^{'} \text{ is the identity of } H\}.$$

Equivalently,

$$L - ker(f) = \{(l,g) \in S : (l)s = l^{'} \text{ and } g \in Ker(t)\}.$$

Clearly, $E(S) \subseteq L - ker(f)$, so it is non-empty. We say that $L - ker(f)$ is *trivial* if $L - ker(f) = E(S)$. Also, we note that if the left group S is trivial, then $L - ker(f)$ reduces to the kernel of a group homomorphism.

Following [3], a non-empty subset U of a left group S is said to be the *sub-left group* of S if U itself is a left group under the operation of S. The next two results from [3] give the criteria for a subsemigroup of a left group to be a sub-left group.

Lemma 2 ([3] Lemma 2.6). *Let $S = L_1 \times G$ be a left group and T be a subset of S. Then, T is a sub-left group of S if, and only if, $T = L_2 \times H$, where L_2 is a subsemigroup of L_1 and H is a subgroup of G.*

Lemma 3 ([3] Proposition 2.8). *A subset T of a left group $S = L_1 \times G$ is a sub-left group of S if, and only if, $ab^{\perp} \in T$ for all $a,b \in T$.*

A sub-left group T of a left group S is said to be a *normal sub-left group* of S if for each $a \in S$ and $b \in T$, we have $aba^{\perp} \in T$.

The next proposition gives a characterisation of a normal sub-left group of a left group.

Proposition 4. *Let $S = L \times G$ be a left group and $T = L' \times H$ be a sub-left group of S. T is a normal sub-left group of S if, and only if, $L' = L$ and H is a normal subgroup of G.*

Proof. Suppose that T is a normal sub-left group of G. Then, for each $a = (l, g) \in S$ and $b = (k, h) \in T$, we have $aba^{\perp} \in T$. This means that $(l, ghg^{-1}) \in L' \times H$. Therefore, $l \in L'$ and $ghg^{-1} \in H$. Thus, $L' = L$ and H is a normal subgroup of G. Conversely, suppose that $L' = L$ and H is normal in G. Take any $a = (l, g) \in S$ and $b = (k, h) \in T$. Now, $aba^{\perp} = (l, ghg^{-1})$, and from the given conditions, we have $l \in L'$, $ghg^{-1} \in H$. Thus, $aba^{\perp} \in T$, proving that T is a normal sub-left group of G. □

The next two examples illustrate how to construct sub-left groups and normal sub-left groups of well-known left groups.

Example 3. *Consider the left group $S = L \times \mathbb{Z}_2$. The only subgroups of $\mathbb{Z}_2$ are $\mathbb{Z}_2$ and the trivial subgroup $\{0\}$, which are clearly normal in $\mathbb{Z}_2$. Thus, the sub-left groups of S are of the form $L' \times \mathbb{Z}_2$ and $L' \times \{0\}$, where L' is a subsemigroup of L. There are only two normal sub-left groups, namely, S itself and $L \times \{0\}$.*

Example 4. *Consider the left group $S = L \times K_4$. The subgroups of K_4 are $\{1\}$, $\{1, a\}$, $\{1, b\}$, $\{1, c\}$ and K_4 itself. All the subgroups of K_4 are normal in K_4. Any sub-left group of S will be of any of the following types:*

(i) $L' \times K_4$;
(ii) $L' \times \{1\}$;
(iii) $L' \times \{1, a\}$;
(iv) $L' \times \{1, b\}$;
(v) $L' \times \{1, c\}$;

where L' is a subsemigroup of L. On the other hand, by taking $L' = L$ in these cases, we obtain all the 5 normal sub-left groups of S.

The next theorem is the main result of this section, where we generalise some of the properties being preserved by a group homomorphism to a left group homomorphism.

Theorem 1. *Let $S = L_1 \times G$ and $T = L_2 \times H$ be two left groups, R be any sub-left group of S and $f \in Hom(S, T)$. The following statements are true.*

(i) *$(R)f$ is a sub-left group of T.*
(ii) *$L - ker(f)$ is trivial if, and only if, t is one-to-one.*
(iii) *$L - ker(f)$ is a normal sub-left group of S.*
(iv) *$(L - ker(f))f \subseteq E(T)$. Moreover $(L - ker(f))f = E(T)$ if s is onto, and in this case, the former is a normal sub-left group of T.*

Proof.

(i) By Lemma 2, $R = L_1' \times K$, where L_1' is a subsemigroup of L_1 and K is a subgroup of G. Let $x = (l_2, h), y = (l_2', h') \in (R)f$. Then, there exist $l_1, l_1' \in L_1'$, $g, g' \in K$ such that $(l_2, h) = (l_1, g)f$ and $(l_2', h') = (l_1', g')f$. Now, $xy^{\perp} = (l_1, g)f((l_1', g')f)^{\perp} = (l_1, g)f(l_1', g')^{\perp}f$ (by Proposition 3 (ii)). Since $f \in Hom(S, T)$, we have $(l_1, g)f(l_1', g')^{\perp}f = ((l_1, g)(l_1', g')^{\perp})f$. Since R is a sub-left group of S, by Lemma 3, we have $(l_1, g)(l_1', g')^{\perp} \in R$. Thus, $xy^{\perp} \in (R)f$ as required.

(ii) We have to show that $L - ker(f) \subseteq E(S)$. Take any $(l, g) \in L - ker(f)$. Then, $(l, g)f = (l', e')$, so $((l)s, (g)t) = (l', e')$, where $l' = (l)s$ and e' is the identity of H. Now, $(g)t = e'$ if, and only if, $g \in ker(t)$. As t is one-to-one, $ker(t) = \{e\}$, and therefore, $g = e$. Thus, $(l, g) \in E(S)$, as required.

(iii) Note that $L - ker(f) = L_1 \times ker(t)$. Since $ker(t)$ is a normal subgroup of G, using Lemma 2, we have that $L - ker(f)$ is a normal sub-left group of S, as required.

(iv) Clearly, $(L - ker(f))f \subseteq E(T)$. For the last statement, as $E(S) \subseteq L - ker(f)$, this implies that $(E(S))f \subseteq (L - ker(f))f$. as s is onto according to Proposition 3 (ii) $(E(S))f = E(T)$. Therefore, $E(T) \subseteq (L - ker(f))f$, showing the reverse inclusion. As s is onto, $(kert)t$ is a normal subgroup of H. Now, $(L - ker(f))f = (L_1 \times ker(t))f = (L_1)s \times (ker(t))t = L_2 \times H'$, where $L_2 = (L_1)s$ is a subsemigroup of L_2 and $H' = (ker(t))t$ is a normal subgroup of H. Thus, $(L - ker(f))f$ is a normal subgroup of T, as required.

□

In the next example, we exhibit a non-trivial left group homomorphism of an infinite left group where the L-kernel is normal but not trivial.

Example 5. *Let L be a non-trivial left zero semigroup and $G = \mathbb{Z}$ be the group of integers. Suppose $H = \frac{\mathbb{Z}}{n\mathbb{Z}}$ with $n \geq 2$. Consider the left groups $S = L \times G$ and $T = L \times H$. Let $f : S \longrightarrow T$ be a homomorphism given by $f(l,k) = (l, k(mod n))$. Then, $L - ker(f) = L \times ker(t) = L \times n\mathbb{Z}$. As $n\mathbb{Z}$ is a normal subgroup of $\mathbb{Z}$ by Proposition 4 $L - ker(f)$ is a normal sub-left group of S and is clearly non-trivial.*

In a semigroup, the relationship between homomorphisms and Green's equivalences is complex, providing insight into the semigroup's internal structure. Homomorphisms do not necessarily preserve the fine structure of Green's classes, but they do map principal ideals to ideals. That is, if $f : S \to T$ is a homomorphism, then $f(S^1a) = f(S)^1 f(a)$. The Green's classes in the image of a homomorphism, $f(S)$, are often smaller than their corresponding Green's classes in S. For example, a single $\mathcal{L}$ class in S may be mapped to multiple $\mathcal{L}$ classes in T by a homomorphism. Specialised semigroups called 'transformation semigroups' are defined by maps that explicitly preserve a given equivalence relation. These are a good example of how homomorphisms can be constructed to uphold a specific Green's relation. In regular semigroups, homomorphisms can have a well-defined relationship with Green's relations. For instance, in an inverse semigroup, which is a special type of regular semigroup, each $\mathcal{L}$ class and $\mathcal{R}$ class contains a unique idempotent. Studies on specific semigroup classes, such as completely regular semigroups, have shown that homomorphisms can facilitate the decomposition of these semigroups based on Green's relations.

Like any other algebraic structure, homomorphisms are well behaved with congruences in semigroups. For any homomorphism $f : S \to T$, the kernel of f is a semigroup congruence on S. This congruence, denoted by $kerf$, relates elements that map to the same image in T, i.e., $(a,b) \in kerf$ if, and only if, $f(a) = f(b)$. A homomorphism $f : S \to T$ also induces an isomorphism between the quotient semigroup $S/\ker f$ and the image $f(S)$. This means the structure of the image can be understood by examining the congruence classes of the kernel. In the next section, we further explore these relations in the case of left groups.

4. Green's Equivalences and Congruences on Left Groups

Green's equivalences (or Green's relations) are fundamental tools in semigroup theory. They partition a semigroup S into classes that reveal its internal structure, especially regarding ideals, principal ideals and factorisation properties. For a group G, Green's equivalences simplify drastically because every element is invertible. This forces every group into a single Green's class and thus there is no finer partition because invertibility collapses the distinctions.

Congruences are central to semigroup theory because they provide the primary mechanism for decomposing and analysing semigroups. In semigroup theory, a congruence is the analogue of a normal subgroup in group theory. It is a way to define a quotient structure that remains a semigroup and enables the factorisation of a semigroup into simpler components, analogous to factor groups.

In this section, we characterise Green's equivalences in the case of left groups. We also generalise some well-known results regarding congruences from groups to left groups.

Let $S = L \times G$ be a left group and let

$$\rho = \{((l_1, g_1), (l_2, g_2)) : l_1, l_2 \in L, g_1, g_2 \in G\}$$

be a binary relation on S. Then, ρ gives rise to binary relations σ and τ on L and G, respectively, given by $((l, g), (l', g')) \in \rho$ if, and only if, $(l, l') \in \sigma$ and $(g, g') \in \tau$. Conversely, every binary relation σ on L and τ on G gives a binary relation ρ on S. Therefore, ρ can be viewed as the pair (σ, τ).

Let S be a semigroup and $a, b \in S$, S^1a (aS^1, S^1aS^1) denotes, respectively, the principal left (right, two-sided) ideal of S generated by a. The five Green's equivalences are defined in terms of principal ideals as follows:

$$\begin{aligned} a\mathcal{L}b &\text{ if, and only if, } S^1a = S^1b \\ a\mathcal{R}b &\text{ if, and only if, } aS^1 = bS^1 \\ a\mathcal{J}b &\text{ if, and only if, } S^1aS^1 = S^1bS^1 \\ a\mathcal{H}b &\text{ if, and only if, } a\mathcal{L}b \text{ and } a\mathcal{R}b \\ \mathcal{D} &= \mathcal{L} \circ \mathcal{R} = \mathcal{R} \circ \mathcal{L} = \mathcal{L} \vee \mathcal{R} \end{aligned}$$

One can easily check that $\mathcal{H} = \mathcal{L} \cap \mathcal{R}$, $\mathcal{L} \subseteq \mathcal{J}$ and $\mathcal{R} \subseteq \mathcal{J}$ since $\mathcal{D}$ is the join of $\mathcal{L}$ and $\mathcal{R}$, $\mathcal{D} \subseteq \mathcal{J}$. If the semigroup S is a group G, then all reduce to the universal relation on G, i.e., $\mathcal{L} = \mathcal{R} = \mathcal{D} = \mathcal{J} = G \times G$.

A relation ρ on a semigroup is considered left compatible if for all $a, b, t \in S$, we have $(a, b) \in S$ implies $(ta, tb) \in S$ and *right compatible* if $\forall\, a, b, t \in S, (a, b) \in S$ implies $(at, bt) \in S$. It is called *compatible* if it is both left compatible and right compatible. A compatible equivalence relation on S is called a *congruence* on S.

Remark 2. *It is easy to verify that, if $\rho = (\sigma, \tau)$ is an equivalence on a left group $S = L \times G$, then ρ is a congruence on S if, and only if, σ is a congruence on L and τ is a congruence on G.*

Further details on Green's equivalences and congruences can be found in any standard text on semigroup theory. In particular, the reader is referred to Howie [1] and Clifford and Preston [2].

Next, we first characterise Green's equivalences on left groups. Unlike groups, it turns out that not all the Green's relations on a left group are universal. However, like in a group G, each of the Green's equivalence is proven as a congruence on a left group S. First, we characterise Green's equivalences on a left zero semigroup L. This, together with the results on groups, provides a characterisation of left groups.

For any semigroup S, I^S denotes the identity relation on S.

Proposition 5. *Let L be a left zero semigroup. Then, the following statements are true.*

(i) $\mathcal{R} = \mathcal{H} = I^L$.

(ii) $\mathcal{L} = \mathcal{J} = \mathcal{D} = L \times L$.

Proof. Let L be a left zero semigroup.

(i) Take any $a,b \in L$ such that $a\mathcal{R}b$. Then, there exists $u,v \in L^1$ such that $au = b, bv = a$. By the left zero property of L, $a = b$. This implies $\mathcal{R} = I^L$. Since $\mathcal{H} = \mathcal{L} \cap \mathcal{R} = \mathcal{L} \cap I^L = I^L$; therefore, $\mathcal{R} = \mathcal{H} = I^L$.

(ii) For any $(a,b) \in L \times L$ by the left zero property of L, we have $ab = a$ and $ba = b$. This implies $a\mathcal{L}b$, and thus $L \times L = \mathcal{L}$. Now, $L \times L = \mathcal{L} \subseteq \mathcal{J} \subseteq L \times L = \mathcal{L}$, so it follows that $\mathcal{L} = \mathcal{J} = L \times L$. Finally, as $\mathcal{D} = \mathcal{L} \circ \mathcal{R} = \mathcal{R} \circ \mathcal{L}$; therefore, $\mathcal{D} = \mathcal{L} \circ I^L = I^L \circ \mathcal{L} = \mathcal{L}$. Hence, $\mathcal{L} = \mathcal{J} = \mathcal{D} = L \times L$, as required.

□

Note that the identity relation I^S and the universal relation $S \times S$ are easily seen as compatible on any semigroup S, so the next corollary is immediate.

Corollary 3. *Let S be a left zero semigroup. Then, all the Green's equivalences are congruences on S.*

If $S = L \times G$ is a left group and $\rho \in \{\mathcal{L}, \mathcal{R}, \mathcal{H}, \mathcal{J}, \mathcal{D}\}$ on S, then we denote it by ρ^S, and so $\rho^S = (\rho^L, \rho^G)$, where ρ^L and ρ^G denote the corresponding relations on L and G, respectively. We are now in a position to characterise Green's equivalences on the left group S.

Theorem 2. *Let $S = L \times G$ be a left group. Then, the following statements are true.*

(i) $\mathcal{L}^S = \mathcal{J}^S = \mathcal{D}^S = S \times S$.

(ii) $\mathcal{R}^S = \mathcal{H}^S = (I^L, G \times G) = I^L \times (G \times G)$

Proof. Let $S = L \times G$ be a left group and $\rho^S = (\rho^L, \rho^G) \in \{\mathcal{L}, \mathcal{R}, \mathcal{H}, \mathcal{J}, \mathcal{D}\}$.

(i) Let $\rho = \mathcal{L}$. Then, $\mathcal{L}^S = (\mathcal{L}^L, \mathcal{L}^G)$. By Proposition 5 $\mathcal{L}^L = L \times L$, and as already mentioned above (see [1]), $\mathcal{L}^G = G \times G$. Therefore, $\mathcal{L}^S = (L \times L, G \times G) = (L \times G) \times (L \times G) = S \times S$. Since $\mathcal{D}^G = \mathcal{J}^G = G \times G$, we can apply a similar argument to prove that $\mathcal{J}^S = \mathcal{D}^S = S \times S$.

(ii) By Proposition 5 $\mathcal{H}^L = \mathcal{R}^L = I^L$, and as mentioned above, $\mathcal{H}^G = \mathcal{R}^G = G \times G$. Now, $\mathcal{R}^S = (\mathcal{R}^L, \mathcal{R}^G) = (I^L, G \times G) = I^L \times (G \times G)$. Since, $\mathcal{H}^G = G \times G$, we can apply a similar argument to prove that $\mathcal{H}^S = I^L \times (G \times G)$.

□

The equalities established in the above theorem may not hold for non-left group semigroups. By Exercise 2.6 (1) of [1], if C is a cancellative semigroup without identity, then $\mathcal{L} = \mathcal{R} = \mathcal{D} = I^C$, but there is a cancellative semigroup S without identity such that $\mathcal{J} = S \times S$. Again, by Exercise 2.6 (2) of [1], in the bicyclic semigroup, $\mathbb{B} = \mathbb{N}^0 \times \mathbb{N}^0$, $\mathcal{L} \subset \mathcal{D} = \mathcal{J} = \mathbb{B} \times \mathbb{B}$. Thus, it would be interesting for future research to explore the non-left group semigroup classes in which the equalities established in the above theorem are true.

Corollary 4. *Let $S = L \times G$ be a left group and $\rho^S \in \{\mathcal{L}^S, \mathcal{R}^S, \mathcal{H}^S, \mathcal{J}^S, \mathcal{D}^S\}$. Then, ρ^S is a congruence on S.*

Proof. We complete the proof in the form of two cases. Suppose first that $\rho^S \in \{\mathcal{L}^S, \mathcal{J}^S, \mathcal{D}^S\}$. By part (i) of Theorem 2, $\rho^S = S \times S$ so trivially is a congruence on S. Suppose next that $\rho^S = \mathcal{R}^S$ and take any $a,b,s \in S$ such that $(a,b) \in \rho^S$. Let $a = (l,g), b = (l',g')$ and $s = (l'',g'')$. Now, $(a,b) \in \rho^S$ implies $(l,l') \in \rho^L$ and $(g,g') \in \rho^G$. By part (ii) of Theorem 2, $\rho^L = I^L$ and $\rho^G = G \times G$ are congruences on L and G, respectively. Thus,

$\rho^S = \mathcal{R}^S = (\mathcal{R}^L, \mathcal{R}^G)$ is a congruence on G. By the similar argument $\mathcal{H}^S$ is a congruence on S. □

In group theory, every congruence on a group G corresponds to a unique normal subgroup and vice versa. This fundamental correspondence allows us to translate problems on congruences into normal subgroups, which are more familiar and easy to handle. It is natural to expect a similar kind of correspondence in the case of left groups. We are able to provide such a correspondence on left groups. We first prove a basic lemma, which is required to prove the main result.

Lemma 4. *Let $S = L \times G$ be a left group. Then, for any $a = (l, g), b = (l', g') \in S$, $(ab)^{\perp} = b^{\perp}a^{\perp}$.*

Proof. Let $a = (l, g), b = (k, h) \in S$. Then,

$$(ab)b^{\perp}a^{\perp}(ab) = (l, ghh^{-1}g^{-1}gh) = (l, gh) = (l, g)(k, h) = ab.$$

Similarly, $b^{\perp}a^{\perp}(ab)b^{\perp}a^{\perp} = b^{\perp}a^{\perp}$. Therefore, we get $(ab)^{\perp} = b^{\perp}a^{\perp}$, as required. □

Now, we prove the main result of this section.

Theorem 3. *Let $S = L \times G$ be a left group. The following statements hold.*

(i) For any normal sub-left group T of S,

$$\rho_T = \{(x, y) \in S \times S : xy^{\perp} \in T\}$$

is a congruence on S.

(ii) Let $\rho = (\sigma, \tau)$ be a congruence on S. For each idempotent (l, e) in S, the set $T = (l, e)\rho$ is a normal sub-left group of S if, and only if, $l\sigma = L$, and so $\rho = \rho_T$.

(iii) If T, U are normal sub-left groups of S, then $\rho_T \cap \rho_U = \rho_{T \cap U}$ and $\rho_T \circ \rho_U = \rho_{TU}$.

Proof.

(i) Let T be a normal sub-left group of a left group S. By Proposition 4, $T = L \times H$, where H is a normal subgroup of G. First, we show ρ_T is an equivalence on S.

- *Reflexive*: Take any $a = (l, g) \in S$. As T is a normal sub-left group of S, it follows that $aa^{\perp} = (l, gg^{-1}) = (l, e) \in T$. This implies $(a, a) \in \rho_T$.
- *Symmetric*: Take any $a = (l, g), b = (k, h) \in S$. Let $(a, b) \in \rho_T$. Then, $ab^{\perp} = (l, gh^{-1}) \in T$. Again, as S is a normal sub-left group of S, we have $ba^{\perp} = (k, hg^{-1}) = (k, (gh^{-1})^{-1}) \in T$. Thus, $(b, a) \in \rho_T$.
- *Transitive*: Let (a, b) and $(b, c) \in \rho_T$. Then, $ab^{\perp}$ and $bc^{\perp} \in T$. Now $bb^{\perp} = b_e$ and $ab_e = a$, so T being a sub-left group implies $ab^{\perp}bc^{\perp} = ac^{\perp} \in T$. Thus, $(a, c) \in \rho_T$.

Now, it remains to be shown that ρ_T is left and right compatible. Take any $a = (l, g)$, $b = (k, h)$ and $s = (m, n) \in S$. Suppose that $(a, b) \in \rho_T$ and so $ab^{\perp} \in T$. By Lemma 4, $sa(sb)^{\perp} = sab^{\perp}s^{\perp}$, and as $ab^{\perp} \in T$ and T is a normal sub-left group, it follows that $sa(sb)^{\perp} = s(ab^{\perp})s^{\perp} \in T$. Thus, $(sa, sb) \in \rho_T$, proving the left compatibility of ρ_T. Again, using Lemma 4, we get $as(bs)^{\perp} = ass^{\perp}b^{\perp} = as_eb^{\perp} = ab^{\perp} \in T$. Thus, $(as, bs) \in \rho_T$, proving the right compatibility. Hence, ρ_T is a congruence on S.

(ii) Take any congruence $\rho = (\sigma, \tau)$ on $S = L \times G$ and let $T = (l, e)\rho$, where (l, e) is an idempotent in S. Now, as $(l, e)\rho = l\sigma \times e\tau$, we have to show that $l\sigma \times e\tau$ is a normal sub-left group, which, by Proposition 4, is equivalent to showing that $l\sigma = L$ and $e\tau$ is a normal subgroup of G. By Proposition 1.8.2 of [1] $e\tau$ is a normal subgroup of G. Therefore, the statement holds if, and only if, $l\sigma = L$.

Next, we have to prove that $\rho = (\sigma, \tau) = \rho_T = \rho_{(l,e)} = (\sigma_l, \tau_e)$, and this happens if, and only if, $\sigma = \sigma_l$ and $\tau = \tau_e$. Since $l\sigma = l$, it follows that $\sigma_l = L \times L$, so $\sigma \subseteq \sigma_l$. On the other hand, if $(l_1, l_2) \in \sigma_l$, then $(l_1, l) \in \sigma$ and $(l, l_2) \in \sigma$, and because σ is transitive, it follows that $(l_1, l_2) \in \sigma$. This proves the reverse inclusion, and thus $\sigma = \sigma_l$. For the remaining case, $(g, h) \in \tau$ if, and only if, $(gh^{-1}, hh^{-1}) \in \tau$ if, and only if, $(gh^{-1}, e) \in \tau$ if, and only if, $gh^{-1} \in e\tau$ if, and only if, $(g, h) \in \tau_e$. Thus, $\tau = \tau_e$ as required.

(iii) Finally, if T and U are normal sub-left groups of S, then

$$\begin{aligned} & (a,b) \in \rho_T \cap \rho_U \\ \Leftrightarrow\ & ab^{\perp} \in T \text{ and } ab^{\perp} \in U \\ \Leftrightarrow\ & ab^{\perp} \in T \cap U \\ \Leftrightarrow\ & (a,b) \in \rho_{T\cap U}. \end{aligned}$$

Next, take any $(a, b) \in \rho_T \circ \rho_U$ there exists some $c \in S$ such that $(a, c) \in \rho_T$ and $(c, b) \in \rho_U$. This implies $ac^{\perp} \in T$ and $cb^{\perp} \in U$, and so $ab^{\perp} = ac^{\perp}cb^{\perp} \in TU$. Thus, $(a, b) \in \rho_{TU}$, proving that $\rho_T \circ \rho_U \subseteq \rho_{TU}$. For the reverse inclusion, assume that $(a, b) \in \rho_{TU}$, which implies $ab^{\perp} \in TU$. Thus, $ab^{\perp} = tu$ for some $t \in T$ and $u \in U$. Take $c = ub$. Then, $ac^{\perp} = a(ub)^{\perp} = ab^{\perp}u^{\perp} = tuu^{\perp} = t \in T$, and so $(a, c) \in \rho_T$. Also, $cb^{\perp} = ubb^{\perp} = u \in U$, proving that $(c, b) \in \rho_U$. Thus, $(a, b) \in \rho_T \circ \rho_U$, as required.

Hence, $\rho_T \cap \rho_U = \rho_{T\cap U}$ and $\rho_T \circ \rho_U = \rho_{TU}$. This completes the proof of the theorem. □

This correspondence between normal sub-left groups and congruences cannot be extended to more general classes of semigroups because one cannot exploit the existence of L-inverses, L-identities and idempotents in a general semigroup. For example, if S is a commutative semigroup, then there exists a congruence η on S such that the quotient semigroup S/η is a semilattice. Since a semilattice is not a left group, this congruence cannot correspond to a normal sub-left group.

In a semigroup S, a congruence is a special type of equivalence relation that can be characterised as a diagonal subsemigroup of the direct product $S \times S$ with additional properties. The connection reveals how a congruence can be understood as an algebraic substructure of the larger semigroup product. The connection is established by showing that a congruence on S is precisely a diagonal subsemigroup of $S \times S$ that is also a reflexive, symmetric and transitive relation. For a group G, the connection becomes simpler. In this case, every diagonal subgroup of $G \times G$ is automatically a congruence on G. The equivalence between diagonal subsemigroups and congruences does not hold for general semigroups, showing a key difference from groups. This difference motivated the definition of a DSC semigroup—a semigroup where every diagonal subsemigroup is necessarily a congruence. In the next section, we explore the DSC property in the case of left groups.

5. Diagonal Subsemigroups and Left Groups

Let S be a semigroup and $\rho \subseteq S \times S$. Then, ρ is said to be a *diagonal subsemigroup* of $S \times S$ if ρ is a subsemigroup of $S \times S$ containing the identity relation I^S on S. It is natural to then determine for which semigroups S a congruence ρ on S corresponds to a diagonal subsemigroup of $S \times S$ and vice versa. This study has been undertaken in [8], and this motivated us to investigate this interesting question for a left group S. The next lemma is immediate, but for completeness, we include its proof.

Lemma 5. *If ρ is a congruence on a semigroup S, then it is a diagonal subsemigroup of $S \times S$.*

Proof. Let ρ be a congruence on S. Since ρ is reflexive, it follows that $I^S \subseteq \rho$. Take any (a,b) and (c,d) in ρ. Since ρ is compatible, it follows that $(a,b)(c,d) = (ac,bd) \in \rho$. This proves that ρ is a diagonal subsemigroup of $S \times S$. □

It is important to determine when the converse of the above lemma holds. In particular, is the converse true if $S = L \times G$ is a left group? In this section, we shall answer this question.

Lemma 6. *Let $S = L \times G$ be a left group and $\rho = (\sigma, \tau) \subseteq S \times S$. Then, ρ is a diagonal subsemigroup of $S \times S$ if, and only if, σ is a diagonal subsemigroup of $L \times L$ and τ is a diagonal subsemigroup of $G \times G$.*

Proof. Observe that $\sigma \subseteq L \times L$ and $\tau \subseteq G \times G$. Also, $\rho^2 \subseteq \rho$ if, and only if, $\sigma^2 \subseteq \sigma$ and $\tau^2 \subseteq \tau$. Thus, ρ is a subsemigroup of $S \times S$ if, and only if, σ is a subsemigroup of $L \times L$ and τ is a subsemigroup of $G \times G$. Finally, as $I^S = (I^L, I^G)$, it follows that $I^S \subseteq \rho$ if, and only if, $I^L \subseteq \sigma$ and $I^G \subseteq \tau$. Hence, we conclude that ρ is a diagonal subsemigroup of $S \times S$ if, and only if, σ is a diagonal subsemigroup of $L \times L$ and τ is a diagonal subsemigroup of $G \times G$. □

The next result shows that for a group G, the notions of a diagonal subgroup and a congruence are equivalent.

Proposition 6. *Let G be a group and τ be a diagonal subgroup of $G \times G$. Then, τ is a congruence on G.*

Proof. As τ is a subgroup of $G \times G$, the compatibility follows automatically. So, we only need to show that τ is an equivalence on G.

(i) Reflexive: Since $I^S \subseteq \tau$, clearly τ is reflexive.

(ii) Symmetric: Let $(g,h) \in \tau$. As $(h^{-1},h^{-1}) \in \tau$ and τ is a subgroup of $G \times G$, it follows that $(g,h)(h^{-1},h^{-1}) = (gh^{-1},e) \in \tau$. Again, as $(g^{-1},g^{-1}) \in \tau$, by the same argument, we have $(g^{-1},g^{-1})(gh^{-1},e) = (h^{-1},g^{-1}) \in \tau$. Since τ is a subgroup, $(h,g) = (h^{-1},g^{-1})^{-1} \in \tau$, as required.

(iii) Transitive: Let (g,h) and $(h,k) \in \tau$. As $(h^{-1},h^{-1}) \in \tau$ and τ is a subgroup of $G \times G$, we get $(g,k) = (g,h)(h^{-1},h^{-1})(h,k) \in \tau$. This shows that τ is transitive.

Hence, τ is a congruence on G. □

By Example 1.3 of [8], for a 2-element left zero semigroup L, it is not true in general that a diagonal subsemigroup of $L \times L$ is a congruence on L. The next example illustrates that the same holds for a 3-element left zero semigroup.

Example 6. *Consider the left zero semigroup $L = \{l, m, n\}$ and take*

$$\sigma = \{(l,l), (l,m), (m,m), (l,n), (n,n)\}.$$

Clearly, σ is a diagonal subsemigroup of $L \times L$, but it is not a congruence on L, as it is not symmetric.

Following [8], a semigroup S is said to be *DSC* if every diagonal subsemigroup of $S \times S$ is a congruence on S. Thus, by the above examples, any 2-element and 3-element left zero semigroup is not DSC. The next proposition allows us to extend it to any left zero semigroup.

Proposition 7. *A 3-element left zero semigroup can be embedded into any left zero semigroup T such that $|T| \geq 3$.*

Proof. Let $S = \{a_1, a_2, a_3\}$ be a 3-element left zero semigroup and let $T = \{b_1, b_2, b_3, \ldots\}$ be any left zero semigroup, where $|T| \geq 3$. Since $|T| \geq 3$, we can select three distinct elements from T to be the images of the elements of S. Let us define a map $\phi : S \to T$ as follows: $\phi(a_1) = b_1, \phi(a_2) = b_2$ and $\phi(a_3) = b_3$. The map ϕ is clearly injective, as it maps distinct elements of S to distinct elements of T. For any $x, y \in S$, we have $\phi(xy) = \phi(x)$ and $\phi(x)\phi(y) = \phi(x)$. Since $\phi(xy) = \phi(x)\phi(y)$, the map is a homomorphism and thus an embedding. □

The next proposition is important in deciding the DSC property for the case of left groups.

Proposition 8. *Let $S = L \times G$ be a left group. Then, S is DSC if, and only if, both L and G are DSC.*

Proof. By Remark 2, an equivalence $\rho = (\sigma, \tau)$ is a congruence on S if, and only if, σ is a congruence on L and τ is a congruence on G. By Lemma 6, $\rho = (\sigma, \tau)$ is a diagonal subsemigroup of $S \times S$ if, and only if, σ is a diagonal subsemigroup of $L \times L$ and τ is a diagonal subsemigroup of $G \times G$. This completes the proof of the lemma. □

Thus, through Propositions 7 and 8, we conclude the following important results regarding the DSC property of left zero semigroups and left groups.

Corollary 5. *A left zero semigroup L is DSC if, and only if, it is trivial.*

By Corollary 2.5 of [8], a finite semigroup S is DSC if, and only if, it is a group. In particular, it implies that every finite group G is DSC. The next example illustrates that an infinite group is not necessarily DSC.

Example 7 ([8] Example 1.5). *Let $\mathbb{Z}$ denote the infinite cyclic group. Then, the relation $\tau = \{(x, y) : x \leq y\}$ is a diagonal subsemigroup of $\mathbb{Z} \times \mathbb{Z}$ but not a congruence on $\mathbb{Z}$.*

Corollary 6. *If $S = L \times G$ is a non-trivial left group (finite or infinite), then S is not necessarily DSC.*

In fact, we have a stronger result.

Corollary 7. *A left group $S = L \times G$ is DSC if, and only if, $|L| = 1$ and G is a finite group.*

Proof. Suppose that $S = L \times G$ is a DSC semigroup. Then, by Lemma 6, both L and G must be DSC. If $|L| \geq 2$, then by Example 6 and [8], Example 1.3 L cannot be DSC. Thus, $|L|$ must be 1. Also by Example 7 and Corollary 2.5 of [8], G must be a finite group. Conversely, if these two conditions are satisfied, then $S = \{l\} \times G$ is a finite semigroup isomorphic to G. As G being a finite group is DSC, it follows that S is DSC, as required. □

Next, we illustrate the above corollary with the help of an example.

Example 8. *Consider the left group S of Example 1 with $L = \{l_1, l_2\}$. Let $\sigma = \{(l_1, l_1), (l_1, l_2), (l_2, l_2)\}$. Then, σ is a diagonal subsemigroup of $L \times L$ but not a congruence on L. Take any diagonal subsemigroup τ of $G \times G$. Then, τ is a congruence on G. By Lemma 8, S cannot be DSC.*

We end this section by observing whether or not the DSC property is preserved under the common construction of left groups, such as direct products or strong semilattices of left groups. By Corollary 7, a left group is DSC if, and only if, it is isomorphic to a finite group G. As any finite direct product of finite groups is again a finite group, it must be DSC. Thus, we get an important result.

Corollary 8. *Let $S_1, S_2, \ldots, S_n$ be DSC left groups and let $S = S_1 \times S_2 \times \cdots \times S_n$ be their finite direct product. Then, S is DSC.*

By Theorem 4.2.1 of [1], a semigroup S is a strong semilattice of groups if, and only if, S is a Clifford semigroup; that is, if, and only if, S is regular and the idempotents of S are central. A finite strong semilattice of finite groups is not necessarily a finite group and so cannot be DSC. The simplest example is the two-element semigroup $S = \{0, 1\}$ with usual multiplication of integers. It is clearly a regular semigroup with two central idempotents 0 and 1. Thus, S is a finite non-group Clifford semigroup, as 0 has no inverse in S. Hence, we conclude that a strong semilattice of DSC left groups may not be a DSC semigroup.

6. Conclusions

In this paper, we explored the group-like properties of left groups. We considered the study of monogenic left group monoids and proved that a left group monoid is monogenic if, and only if, the left zero monoid component,and the group component are monogenic. We extended properties of group homorphisms to that of left group homomorphisms. In particular, we introduced the notion of the L-kernel, which extends the kernel of a group homomorphism and forms a normal sub-left group. We also characterised Green's equivalences and congruences on left groups. The major contribution of this characterisation is the establishment of a correspondence between congruences and normal sub-left groups, analogous to a well-known correspondence between congruences and normal subgroups in groups. Finally, we explored the DSC property for left groups and proved that a non-trivial group fails to satisfy the DSC property. Basic but non-trivial examples have been provided to the reader to explain the new concepts and to justify the analogous results. Detailed counter examples have been provided for certain results that do not hold. The impacts of the results on their applications have been highlighted in the introduction. Overall, the paper has achieved its goal of exploring group-like properties for left groups. However, this paper has opened a new direction for future research. Specifically, one may explore the deep structure of left groups, their endomorphisms and their automorphisms by taking some well-known groups. One could also explore these properties for rectangular groups, strong semilattices of left groups and strong semilattices of rectangular groups (see [9–15]).

Author Contributions: Conceptualization, A.H.S., B.A.S., S.A.A. and D.J.M.; Methodology, A.H.S., B.A.S., S.A.A. and D.J.M.; Software, A.H.S., B.A.S., S.A.A. and D.J.M.; Validation, A.H.S., B.A.S., S.A.A. and D.J.M.; Formal analysis, A.H.S., B.A.S., S.A.A. and D.J.M.; Investigation, A.H.S., B.A.S., S.A.A. and D.J.M.; Resources, A.H.S., B.A.S., S.A.A. and D.J.M.; Data curation, A.H.S., B.A.S., S.A.A. and D.J.M.; Writing—original draft, A.H.S., B.A.S., S.A.A. and D.J.M.; Writing—review & editing, A.H.S., B.A.S., S.A.A. and D.J.M.; Visualization, A.H.S., B.A.S., S.A.A. and D.J.M.; Supervision, A.H.S., B.A.S., S.A.A. and D.J.M.; Project administration, A.H.S., B.A.S., S.A.A. and D.J.M.; Funding acquisition, A.H.S. and B.A.S. All authors have read and agreed to the published version of the manuscript.

Funding: This work was supported by the Deanship of Scientific Research, Vice Presidency for Graduate Studies and Scientific Research, King Faisal University, Saudi Arabia [Grant No. KFU253327].

Data Availability Statement: The original contributions presented in this study are included in the article. Further inquiries can be directed to the corresponding author.

Conflicts of Interest: The authors declare no conflicts of interest.

References

1. Howie, J.M. *Fundamentals of Semigroup Theory*; The Clarendon Press: Oxford, UK; Oxford University Press: Oxford, UK, 1995.
2. Clifford, A.H.; Preston, G.B. *The Algebraic Theory of Semigroups*; American Mathematical Society: Providence, RI, USA, 1961; Volume 1.
3. Shah, A.H.; Attari, S.A.; Khan, N.M. On left groups and their Endomorphisms. *Asian-Eur. J. Math.* **2024**, *17*, 2450021. [CrossRef]
4. Shah, A.H.; Attari, S.A. Structure and endomorphisms of a strong semilattice of left groups. *Ric. Mat.* **2025**, 1–15. [CrossRef]
5. Shah, A.H.; Mir, D.J.; Gregson, T.Q. Inner automorphisms of Clifford monoids. *Hacet. J. Math. Stat.* **2024**, *53*, 1060–1074. [CrossRef]
6. Shah, A.H.; Subaiei, B.A. Epimorphisms Amalgams And Po-Unitary Pomonoids. *Axioms* **2025**, *14*, 87. [CrossRef]
7. Khan, N.M.; Shah, A.H. Epimorphisms, dominions and permutative semigroups. *Semigroup Forum* **2010**, *80*, 181–190. [CrossRef]
8. Barber, C.; Ruskuc, N. Semigroup Congruences and Subsemigroups of the Direct Square. *Bull. Aust. Math. Soc.* **2025**, 1–12. [CrossRef]
9. Jende, A.; Kopitz, J. A characterization of strong semilattices of periodic groups and rectangular bands by disjunctions of identities. *Asian-Eur. J. Math.* **2022**, *15*, 2250196. [CrossRef]
10. Ayık, G.; Ayık, H.; Unlu, Y. Presentations and word problem for strong semilattices of semigroups. *Algebra Discret. Math.* **2005**, *4*, 28–35.
11. Koch, R.J.; Madison, B.L. Notes on congruences on regular semigroups I. *J. Austral. Math. Soc.* **1985**, *39*, 146–158. [CrossRef]
12. Elagan, S.K. Some remarks on strong semilattices of monoids. *Ann. Fuzzy Math. Inform.* **2011**, *1*, 13–23.
13. Wanj, Z.-P. Fundamental Semilattices of Semigroups. *Acta Math. Hungar.* **2015**, *146*, 22–39. [CrossRef]
14. Worawiset, S. The Structure of Endomorphism Monoids of Strong Semilattices of Left Simple Semigroups. Doctoral Dissertation, University of Oldenburg, Oldenburg, Germany, 2011.
15. Zang, J.; Yang, Y.; Shen, R. The Strong Semilattice of π Groups. *Eur. J. Pure Appl. Math.* **2018**, *11*, 589–597. [CrossRef]

Disclaimer/Publisher's Note: The statements, opinions and data contained in all publications are solely those of the individual author(s) and contributor(s) and not of MDPI and/or the editor(s). MDPI and/or the editor(s) disclaim responsibility for any injury to people or property resulting from any ideas, methods, instructions or products referred to in the content.

mathematics MDPI

Article

Canonical Commutation Relation Derived from Witt Algebra

Huber Nieto-Chaupis

Faculty of Engineering, Universidad Autónoma del Perú, Lima 15842, Peru; hubernietochaupis@gmail.com

Abstract: From an arbitrary definition of operators inspired by oscillators of Virasoro, an algebra is derived. It fits the structure of Virasoro algebra with null central charge or Witt algebra. The resulting formalism has yielded commutators with a dependence on integer numbers, and it follows the Witt-like algebra. Also, the quantum mechanics evolution operator for the case of the quantum harmonic oscillator was identified. Furthermore, the Schrödinger equation was systematically derived under the present framework. When operators are expressed in the framework of Hilbert space states, the resulting Witt algebra seems to be proportional to the well-known canonical commutation relation. This has demanded the development of a formalism based on arbitrary and physical operators as well as well-defined rules of commutation. The Witt-like was also redefined through the direct usage of the uncertainty principle. The results of the paper might suggest that Witt algebra encloses not only quantum mechanics' fundamental commutator but also other unexplored relations among quantum mechanics observables and Witt algebra.

Keywords: Witt algebra; Virasoro algebra; quantum mechanics; commutators

MSC: 11E81; 7B68; 18M40

1. Introduction

1.1. Motivation

It is well known the role of string theories in the direct development of mathematical physics and in the theory of elementary particles. String theories have influenced us to gain a deep understanding of cosmology and gravitation, black holes, for example, and other areas of theoretical physics. Although it has not been experimentally probed so far, a noteworthy strength and well-known capability of string theories constitutes its theoretical formalism exhibiting a robust mathematical structure. On the other hand, it is fair to wonder if such mathematical technology might have direct application to tangible quantum theory and solve realistic problems. For instance, abstract theories based on algebra applied to tangible QM are seen in the work of Girving et al. [1]. There, the density operator has been used in the study of variational estimates for the excitation energy of the quantum Hall effect. This operator has fulfilled the Lie algebra. P. Ginsparg [2], under the context of conformal field theory, has applied Laurent expansion to the stress-energy tensor to derive Virasoro's algebra, which was discovered inside the framework of string theories. J. Ellis et al. [3] have concluded that the whole string theory is quantum mechanics (QM) according to their results, by which it was found that massive string states are related to quantum light states. In the same way, S. Katagiri et al. [4] have tried to close the gap between abstract string theory formalism and QM observables. In fact, they have reformulated Virasoro's generators to address the modeling of Nth-order squeezing with operators' position and momentum. Indeed, the well-known quantum time-dependent

Mathematics **2025**, *13*, 1910

https://doi.org/10.3390/math13121910

harmonic oscillator was treated with Virasoro's oscillators. The spirit of this paper just goes over the avenue characterized by the lack of a direct link between string theory and quantum mechanics. This paper just explores this lack by using new definitions based on Virasoro's generators.

1.2. Background

In the context of the Veneziano model [5], new gauge conditions were formulated, giving origin to what is known as string theory. In this context emerged the so-called Virasoro algebra [6] with central charge c, and this algebra can be written below as follows:

$$[\mathcal{L}_m, \mathcal{L}_n] = (m-n)\mathcal{L}_{m+n} + \frac{c}{12}(m^3 - m)\delta_{m+n,0}. \tag{1}$$

It is evident that $\delta_{m,-n}$ is well-known as the delta of Krönecker. Operators $\mathcal{L}_m$, also called oscillators of Virasoro, defined as a sum of products between no-commutative modes, can be written as

$$\mathcal{L}_n = \frac{1}{2}\sum_{p \in Z} \alpha_{n-p}\alpha_p. \tag{2}$$

The Operators written above have played a critical role in the formulation of dual models that express the covariant form of harmonic oscillator containing infinite modes satisfying $[\alpha_p^\mu, \alpha_q^\nu]{=}\delta_{p,q}g^{\mu,\nu}$ as seen in the work of R. C. Brower in [7]. Virasoro algebra from Lie generators and its link to Lie group because the $c-$number was studied by P. V. Alstine in [8], where it was also analyzed as to its direct relation to QM Jacobi theory, yielding interesting relationships involving the oscillators as new representations of $c-$number. In [9] R. Akhoury and Y. Okada have investigated the role of Virasoro oscillators as a function of classical variables inside the framework of Hamiltonian such as $H = \sum_i \pi_i \dot{q}_i - L(X^\mu, X^\nu)$ with the Lagrangian enclosing the action of closed bosonic string theory. The resulting oscillators have yielded a copy of Virasoro algebra at the flat space. Here, it was also reformulated oscillators that have been defined in order to annihilate ghosts, a fact that demanded the construction of a series of commutation relations (not like Virasoro algebra). Y. Saito in [10] has investigated the action of Virasoro oscillators inside the Becchi–Rouet–Stora (BRS) formalism in the form of subsidiary conditions specifically as seen in the action of them onto the Fock's space for $n > 0$:

$$(\mathcal{L}_n + \alpha_0\delta_{n,0})\,|\text{phys}\rangle = 0. \tag{3}$$

Indeed, Saito observed that under conditions dictated by Virasoro algebra, they do not eliminate the negative states of a squeezed string. Such conditions have derived the redefinition of Virasoro oscillators in a new version, this being a kind of extension from the standard structure of algebra. In addition, complex forms in accordance with the ones obtained by Scherk, as seen in [11], were found. Variations on the Virasoro oscillators have been obtained in [12] through the modifications of Kac–Moody algebra, arriving at modified Virasoro oscillators containing also Kac–Moody generators and yielding other classes of Virasoro algebra (Equation (2.7), Ref. [11]). Here, it was seen the role of the central charge to interpret some properties of oscillators to some extent (see [13] for example).

1.3. Contribution of Paper

As mentioned above in [4], S. Katagiri and collaborators have postulated the idea that Virasoro generators, despite the fact that they are dimensionless entities in string theories, can be expressed as linear combinations of momentum and position operators (see in [4] Section 4.1, Equation (1), for instance). In the context of Katagiri's work the generators can be written as $\mathcal{L}_i = -\frac{i}{2}(\hat{\mathbf{x}}^{i+1}\hat{\mathbf{p}} - \hat{\mathbf{p}}\hat{\mathbf{x}}^{i+1})$ with an i integer number and $\mathcal{L}_i$ satisfying algebra Equation (1). It is interesting to find possible links between dimensionless operators (Virasoro oscillators) and QM observables since it might yield important implications that cross an unproven string theory and tested QM theory [14]. As it is well-known, QM is based on a sophisticated mathematical formulation of physics operators acting on wave functions, in full agreement with QM postulates [15]. The central equation of QM theory, known as the Schrödinger equation, is written as

$$\mathbf{H}(\hat{\mathbf{x}}, \hat{\mathbf{p}}) \left|\Psi(\mathbf{r}, t)\right\rangle = \mathcal{E} \left|\Psi(\mathbf{r}, t)\right\rangle, \tag{4}$$

being $\mathbf{H}$ is the Hamiltonian operator [16–19] often depending on $\hat{\mathbf{x}}$ and $\hat{\mathbf{p}}$, the position and momentum operators, respectively, satisfying the well-known canonical commutation relation that can be written as

$$[\hat{\mathbf{x}}, \hat{\mathbf{p}}] = i\hbar, \tag{5}$$

and $\hbar$ the Planck constant [20–23]. This relation constitutes the main piece in the formulation of quantum theory. Moreover, other relations can be derived from it. An important aspect linked to Equation (5) is the unknown mathematical procedure that yields that. Some attempts have been performed in the past [24,25]. In this manner, it is interesting to identify a clear link (if any) between Equation (5) and the so-called Witt's algebra (or also centerless Virasoro algebra) [26–29] that is defined as

$$[\Xi_m, \Xi_n] = (m - n)\Xi_{m+n}, \tag{6}$$

with Ξ_q Virasoro oscillators that have played a noteworthy role in the development of string theory. While m and n are integer numbers, Equation (6) is also called Virasoro algebra without central extension [30–35] or Witt's algebra that can be rewritten again as

$$[\mathcal{L}(u, m), \mathcal{L}(u, n)] = g(m, n)\mathcal{A}(u, \Xi_q), \tag{7}$$

with $g(m, n)$ a function of integer numbers, and $\mathcal{A}(u, \Xi_q)$ a function of commutators such as the ones of Equation (5), and u being a physical observable. Therefore, this paper has as its central objective to demonstrate that there exists an alternative way that would allow us to arrive at the Canonical Commutation Relation (CCR) in a closed form from Witt algebra in a direct or indirect way. (By which new types of Virasoro oscillators $\mathcal{L}_q$ are proposed.) To accomplish this, it is argued that $\mathcal{L}_q(s)$ is proportional to the QM momentum operator defined as

$$\hat{\mathbf{p}} = \frac{\hbar}{i}\frac{d}{ds}, \tag{8}$$

in the sense that ($\mathcal{L}_q(s) \propto \mathbf{p}Y(s)$, with operator operating onto $Y(s)$ being an arbitrary integration as shall be seen below). Thus, all of the above allows us to write down the oscillator $\mathcal{L}_q(s)$ as

$$\mathcal{L}_q(s) = \frac{d}{ds}\int \delta(w - s) f(w) g_q(s, w) dw. \tag{9}$$

It should be noted that the derivative in Equation (8) comes from Equation (8), and the quantity $\frac{\hbar}{i}$ is absorbed by integration (only for pedagogical reasons). With respect to Equation (9), the derivative $\frac{d}{ds}$ with s having units of distance with q integer number and "$\delta(w-s)$" Dirac delta function and $g_q(s,w)$ arbitrary function. In this manner the hypothesis would consist that these oscillators are fulfilling the algebra:

$$[\mathcal{L}_p, \mathcal{L}_q] = (p-q)\mathcal{L}_{p+q}. \tag{10}$$

Therefore, the proposal of this paper is to establish that the left side of Equation (10) follows the rule:

$$[\mathcal{L}_p, \mathcal{L}_q] \equiv \mathcal{A}([\hat{\mathbf{x}}, \hat{\mathbf{p}}]), \tag{11}$$

by which one can see that Witt algebra might be an explicit function of CCR through the $\mathcal{A}(\cdot)$ function of QM commutators $[\hat{\mathbf{x}}, \hat{\mathbf{p}}]$. As shall be demonstrated in the next sections, $\mathcal{L}_q(s)$ is a pure QM expression in the sense that it has an imminent ground based on wave function and physical observables. Because of this, one would expect a set of QM relations such as CCR, for example. Indeed, extra commutators can also be derived, but without physics meaning.

Thus, oscillator Equation (9) can be seen as a kind of arbitrary expression instead of being perceived as one belonging to QM or having a well-defined physics profile. When $\frac{\hbar}{i}$ is restored into Equation (9):

$$\mathcal{L}_q(s) = \frac{\hbar}{i}\frac{d}{ds}\cdot\int \delta(w-s)f(w)g_q(s,w)dw. \tag{12}$$

One can see that while $\int \delta(w-s)f(w)g_q(s,w)dw$ the whole integration is dimensionless, oscillator $\mathcal{L}_q(s)$ from Equation (12) is proportional to momentum operator $\mathcal{L}_q(s) \approx \mathbf{p}$, since $\hbar$ has units of momentum times distance. The rest of the paper is as follows: The second section presents the proposal of redefining Virasoro oscillators as a kind of Witt operator. Here are described the key pieces of paper. In the third section, the QM interpretation of Witt operators is explored by means of the derivation of the QM evolution operator as well as the Schrödinger equation. In the fourth section, the results of the paper are explicitly presented, and finally, the conclusion of the paper is given.

2. Definition and Properties of Witt Operators

We begin the present debate with the consideration of arbitrary operators: $\mathcal{A}_m$ and $\mathcal{A}_n$ with m and n integer numbers, then it is said that both satisfy Witt algebra [36–40] if

$$[\mathcal{A}_m, \mathcal{A}_n] = (m-n)\mathcal{A}_{m+n}. \tag{13}$$

From above it is clear that commutator is understood to follow the rule:

$$[\mathcal{A}_m, \mathcal{A}_n] = \mathcal{A}_m\mathcal{A}_n - \mathcal{A}_n\mathcal{A}_m, \tag{14}$$

so that it is obvious that

$$\mathcal{A}_m\mathcal{A}_n - \mathcal{A}_n\mathcal{A}_m = m\mathcal{A}_{m+n} - n\mathcal{A}_{m+n}. \tag{15}$$

So far, no information about operators $\mathcal{A}_m$ and $\mathcal{A}_n$ has been explicitly manifested. In other words, these operators are not necessarily to be subjected to being a real or complex quantity. Nevertheless, in virtue of Equation (12), one can see its complex character (although it can also be defined as pure real expression). It is important to observe that such operators are arbitrary entities without any concrete role. Based on the structure shown in Equation (12) with $\hbar = 1$, one can define a kind of Witt operator (being them complex quantities) as

$$\mathcal{L}_K = x_\ell\left(\frac{i}{\sqrt{2}}\right)\delta^m_\ell \frac{d}{dx}\int_{-\infty}^{\infty}\delta(x - x_m)x^K_m dx_m, \tag{16}$$

and its corresponding "partner" (essentially follows the change $K \to L$) in the sense that

$$\mathcal{L}_L = x_\ell\left(\frac{i}{\sqrt{2}}\right)\delta^m_\ell \frac{d}{dx}\int_{-\infty}^{\infty}\delta(x - x_m)x^L_m dx_m. \tag{17}$$

It should be noted that subindices K and L are seen inside integration through polynomials x^K_m and x^L_m. Now, written in that way, $\mathcal{L}_K$ and $\mathcal{L}_L$ are exhibiting their dimensionless character. Indeed, it is seen in both the presence of the delta of Krönecker as well as the Dirac delta function [41–43]. Indeed, it should be noted that $\frac{1}{\sqrt{2}}$ plays the role of a kind of normalization constant, although it is not exactly its genuine function, as shall be seen later. Because of the complex numbers, one can claim at first instance that both operators are pure complex entities. The reader can be aware that when Equations (16) and (17) are solved independently, $[\mathcal{L}_K, \mathcal{L}_L]$=$\mathcal{L}_K\mathcal{L}_L - \mathcal{L}_L\mathcal{L}_K = 0$. Nevertheless, the case when we are operating on each other and vice versa, the commutator yields $[\mathcal{L}_K\mathcal{L}_L - \mathcal{L}_L\mathcal{L}_K] \neq 0$.

In this manner and by following the order seen in Equation (14), the next step is to calculate $[\mathcal{L}_K, \mathcal{L}_L] = \mathcal{L}_K \otimes \mathcal{L}_L - \mathcal{L}_L \otimes \mathcal{L}_K$, that demands to calculate the products:

$$\mathcal{L}_K \otimes \mathcal{L}_L, \tag{18}$$

$$\mathcal{L}_L \otimes \mathcal{L}_K, \tag{19}$$

with $\otimes$ denoting the product of operators. In this manner one can carry out the products firstly in Equation (18) as follows:

$$\mathcal{L}_K \otimes \mathcal{L}_L = x_\ell\left(\frac{i}{\sqrt{2}}\right)\delta^m_\ell \frac{d}{dx}\int_{-\infty}^{\infty}\delta(x - x_m)x^K_m dx_m \otimes x_\ell\left(\frac{i}{\sqrt{2}}\right)\delta^m_\ell \frac{d}{dx}\int_{-\infty}^{\infty}\delta(x - x_m)x^L_m dx_m. \tag{20}$$

This can be also written as

$$\left[x_\ell\delta^m_\ell\left(\frac{i}{\sqrt{2}}\right)\frac{d}{dx}\int_{-\infty}^{\infty}\delta(x - x_m)x^K_m dx_m x_\ell\delta^m_\ell\right] \otimes \left(\frac{i}{\sqrt{2}}\right)\frac{d}{dx}\int_{-\infty}^{\infty}\delta(x - x_m)x^L_m dx_m. \tag{21}$$

Also that product $x_\ell\delta^m_\ell$ has passed to be inside the bracket on the left side. Further operations will do the direct usage of delta of Krönecker by affecting the quantity x_ℓ in both extremes, yielding for them $\delta^m_\ell x_\ell = x^m$, so that subsequently ℓ opts for m in the whole Equation (21). Thus, one obtains

$$\mathcal{L}_K \otimes \mathcal{L}_L = \left[\left(\frac{i}{\sqrt{2}}\right)\frac{d}{dx}\int_{-\infty}^{\infty}\delta(x - x_m)x^{K+2}_m dx_m\right] \otimes \left(\frac{i}{\sqrt{2}}\right)\delta^m_\ell \frac{d}{dx}\int_{-\infty}^{\infty}\delta(x - x_m)x^L_m dx_m. \tag{22}$$

The same operation as done to the left-side bracket is applied to the right side. On the other side, it is obvious that $\left(\frac{i}{\sqrt{2}}\right)\left(\frac{i}{\sqrt{2}}\right) = -\frac{1}{2}$ by which the product $\mathcal{L}_K \otimes \mathcal{L}_L$ is flipping to real space. In this manner, one arrives at

$$\mathcal{L}_K \otimes \mathcal{L}_L = \left(-\frac{1}{2}\right)\left[\frac{d}{dx}\int_{-\infty}^{\infty}\delta(x - x_m)x^{K+2}_m dx_m\right] \otimes \delta^m_\ell \frac{d}{dx}\int_{-\infty}^{\infty}\delta(x - x_m)x^L_m dx_m. \tag{23}$$

From above it is clear that polynomial x^m was absorbed by integrations in both sides, so that one has below that

$$\mathcal{L}_K \otimes \mathcal{L}_L = \left(-\frac{1}{2}\right)\frac{d}{dx}\int_{-\infty}^{\infty}\delta(x-x_m)x_m^{K+2}dx_m\frac{d}{dx}\int_{-\infty}^{\infty}\delta(x-x_m)x_m^L dx_m. \tag{24}$$

Integrations containing the Dirac delta functions and their subsequent derivatives are solved in a straightforward manner. For the right side, one obtains

$$\frac{d}{dx}\int_{-\infty}^{\infty}\delta(x-x_m)x_m^L dx_m = \frac{d}{dx}x^L = Lx^{L-1}. \tag{25}$$

The same procedure is applied to the left side as follows:

$$\frac{d}{dx}\int_{-\infty}^{\infty}\delta(x-x_m)x_m^{K+2}dx_m = \frac{d}{dx}x^{K+2} = (K+2)x^{K+1}, \tag{26}$$

so that one arrives at

$$\mathcal{L}_K \otimes \mathcal{L}_L = \left(-\frac{1}{2}\right)(K+2)x^{K+1}Lx^{L-1} = \left(-\frac{1}{2}\right)L(K+2)x^{K+L}. \tag{27}$$

In order to solve product $\mathcal{L}_L \otimes \mathcal{L}_K$, the reader should be aware that it follows as done to $\mathcal{L}_K \otimes \mathcal{L}_L$. With this view, one can write down

$$\mathcal{L}_L \otimes \mathcal{L}_K = \left(-\frac{1}{2}\right)x^m\frac{d}{dx}\int_{-\infty}^{\infty}\delta(x-x_m)x_m^L dx_m x^m\frac{d}{dx}\int_{-\infty}^{\infty}\delta(x-x_m)x_m^K dx_m. \tag{28}$$

Therefore, one arrives at

$$\mathcal{L}_L \otimes \mathcal{L}_K = \left(-\frac{1}{2}\right)(L+2)x^{L+1}Kx^{K-1} = \left(-\frac{1}{2}\right)K(L+2)x^{K+L}. \tag{29}$$

Equations (27) and (29) allow us to calculate the commutator $[\mathcal{L}_K, \mathcal{L}_L] = \mathcal{L}_K \otimes \mathcal{L}_L - \mathcal{L}_L \otimes \mathcal{L}_K$. Therefore, by putting them altoobtainher, one can demonstrate that $[\mathcal{L}_K, \mathcal{L}_L]$ is in full agreement with Witt algebra $\mathcal{L}_K \otimes \mathcal{L}_L - \mathcal{L}_L \otimes \mathcal{L}_K =$

$$\left(-\frac{1}{2}\right)L(K+2)x^{K+L} - \left(-\frac{1}{2}\right)K(L+2)x^{K+L} = \left(-\frac{1}{2}\right)(LK+2L-KL-2K)x^{K+L}$$
$$= \left(-\frac{1}{2}\right)(2L-2K)x^{K+L}\mathcal{L}_K \otimes \mathcal{L}_L - \mathcal{L}_L \otimes \mathcal{L}_K = (K-L)x^{K+L} \Rightarrow [\mathcal{L}_K, \mathcal{L}_L] = (K-L)x^{K+L}, \tag{30}$$

that satisfies the Witt-like algebra:

$$[\mathcal{L}_K, \mathcal{L}_L] = (K-L)x^{K+L}. \tag{31}$$

One can note that Equation (31) fits exactly to Witt algebra if the following proposal holds:

$$x^{K+L} \Rightarrow \mathcal{L}_{K+L}, \tag{32}$$

that can be validated through the usage of Equation (16), for example, with the substitution $K \to K+L$

$$\mathcal{L}_{K+L} = x_\ell\left(\frac{i}{\sqrt{2}}\right)\delta_\ell^m \frac{d}{dx}\int_{-\infty}^{\infty}\delta(x - x_m)x_m^{K+L}dx_m \tag{33}$$

$$= \left(\frac{i}{\sqrt{2}}\right)\frac{d}{dx}\int_{-\infty}^{\infty}\delta(x - x_m)x_m^{K+L+1}dx_m = \left(\frac{i}{\sqrt{2}}\right)(K + L + 1)x^{K+L+1} \tag{34}$$

$$\Rightarrow \mathcal{L}_{K+L} = \left(\frac{i}{\sqrt{2}}\right)(K + L)x^{K+L+1} + \left(\frac{i}{\sqrt{2}}\right)x^{K+L+1}. \tag{35}$$

Aside, while Equation (35) is divided by $\frac{ix}{\sqrt{2}}$ one obtains

$$\Rightarrow \frac{\mathcal{L}_{K+L}}{\frac{ix}{\sqrt{2}}} = (K + L)x^{K+L} + x^{K+L} \Rightarrow \frac{\mathcal{L}_{K+L}}{\frac{ix}{\sqrt{2}}} - x^{K+L} = (K + L)x^{K+L}, \tag{36}$$

and one can see from above right-side Equation (36) one obtains directly the following:

$$\frac{\mathcal{L}_{K+L}}{\frac{ix}{\sqrt{2}}} = (K + L + 1)x^{K+L}. \tag{37}$$

Yielding that Equation (32) is satisfied under the condition derived above, written as

$$x = \frac{\sqrt{2}}{i(K + L + 1)}, \tag{38}$$

establishing the fact that under the proposal given by Equation (32), $K + L \neq 1$. One can see that if this inequality is violated, therefore, one can see in a straightforward manner inside Witt algebra the following:

$$[\mathcal{L}_K, \mathcal{L}_L]\Big|_{K+L=1} = (K - L)x^{K+L}\Big|_{K+L=1} \Rightarrow [\mathcal{L}_{1-L}, \mathcal{L}_L] = (1 - 2L)x, \tag{39}$$

yielding another type of algebra differing notably from Witt algebra. It is easy to check that the commutation is null only when $L = \frac{1}{2}$, which cannot be sustained in a scenario of Witt or Virasoro algebra that depends only on integer numbers.

Interestingly, the Witt commutator in the last term of Equation (29) can also be derived in a straightforward manner through the assumption that symmetry exists between operators, in the sense that when Equation (27) opts for $K \to L$ and $L \to K$, one obtains Equation (29). Thus, has that

$$\mathcal{L}_K \otimes \mathcal{L}_L = \left(-\frac{1}{2}\right)L(K + 2)x^{K+L}, \tag{40}$$

$$K \to L$$

$$L \to K$$

$$\mathcal{L}_L \otimes \mathcal{L}_K = \left(-\frac{1}{2}\right)K(L + 2)x^{L+K}, \tag{41}$$

yielding directly $[\mathcal{L}_K, \mathcal{L}_L] = (K - L)x^{K+L}$ providing the fulfilling of Witt algebra. Aside, one can argue that this operation of symmetry might be considered a sufficient condition to arrive at Witt algebra in a straightforward manner.

3. Role of Witt Operators in Non-Relativistic QM

3.1. Identification of QM Structures

Since DeWitt operators Equations (16) and (17) exhibit the same structure, then one can carry out kind of "mathematical radiography" in order to interpret them inside QM territory. Thus, for example, one can rewrite Equation (16) as

$$\mathcal{L}_K = x_\ell\left(\frac{i}{\sqrt{2}}\right)\delta_\ell^m \frac{d}{dx}\int_{-\infty}^{\infty}\delta(x-x_m)x_m^K dx_m, \tag{42}$$

moreover, by taking into account these definitions through the usage of bra and kets as states of Hilbert space, one obtains below:

$$\delta(x-x_m) = \langle x|x_m\rangle\,, \tag{43}$$

$$x_m^K = \langle x_m|K\rangle\,. \tag{44}$$

In virtue to properties of brat and ket of Dirac's formalism, $\Phi_K(x_m) = \langle x_m|K\rangle = x_m^K$, indicating now braket $\langle x_m|K\rangle$ is defined as a polynomial of Kth order, so that one can rewrite Equation (42) as

$$\mathcal{L}_K = x_\ell\left(\frac{i}{\sqrt{2}}\right)\delta_\ell^m \frac{d}{dx}\int_{-\infty}^{\infty}\langle x|x_m\rangle\,\langle x_m|K\rangle\,,dx_m. \tag{45}$$

Here, it should be noted that one can appeal to the well-known completeness relationship as commonly used in QM:

$$\int_{-\infty}^{\infty}|x_m\rangle\,\langle x_m|\,dx_m = \mathbb{I}, \tag{46}$$

that applies to integration Equation (45) as follows:

$$\mathcal{L}_K = x_\ell\left(\frac{i}{\sqrt{2}}\right)\delta_\ell^m \frac{d}{dx}\int_{-\infty}^{\infty}\langle x|\,|x_m\rangle\,\langle x_m|\,dx_m\,|K\rangle\,, = x_\ell\left(\frac{i\delta_\ell^m}{\sqrt{2}}\right)\frac{d}{dx}\langle x|\left[\int_{-\infty}^{\infty}|x_m\rangle\,\langle x_m|\,dx_m\right]|K\rangle\,. \tag{47}$$

In this way, operator can again be rewritten as

$$\mathcal{L}_K = x_\ell\left(\frac{i\delta_\ell^m}{\sqrt{2}}\right)\frac{d}{dx}\langle x|\,\mathbb{I}\,|K\rangle = \left(\frac{i\delta_\ell^m}{\sqrt{2}}\right)x_\ell\frac{d}{dx}\langle x|K\rangle\,. \tag{48}$$

With the definition of function $\langle x|K\rangle = \Phi_K(x)$, it allows to arrive to a form of operator as

$$\mathcal{L}_K = \left(\frac{i\delta_\ell^m}{\sqrt{2}}\right)x_\ell\frac{d}{dx}\Phi_K(x), \tag{49}$$

in conjunction with its partner, given by

$$\mathcal{L}_L = \left(\frac{i\delta_\ell^m}{\sqrt{2}}\right)x_\ell\frac{d}{dx}\Phi_L(x). \tag{50}$$

Subsequently, when we incorporate the Planck's constants in both Equations (49) and (50), we arrive at

$$\mathcal{L}_K = \left(-\frac{\delta_\ell^m}{\sqrt{2}\hbar}\right)x_\ell\frac{\hbar}{i}\frac{d}{dx}\Phi_K(x), \tag{51}$$

$$\mathcal{L}_L = \left(-\frac{\delta_\ell^m}{\sqrt{2}\hbar}\right)x_\ell\frac{\hbar}{i}\frac{d}{dx}\Phi_L(x). \tag{52}$$

It is easy to observe above that the momentum operator $\mathbf{p} = \frac{\hbar}{i}\frac{d}{dx}$ has been identified. With this, one can rewrite Equations (51) and (52) as follows:

$$\mathcal{L}_K = \left(-\frac{\delta_\ell^m}{\sqrt{2}\hbar}\right) x_\ell \mathbf{p} \Phi_K(x), \tag{53}$$

$$\mathcal{L}_L = \left(-\frac{\delta_\ell^m}{\sqrt{2}\hbar}\right) x_\ell \mathbf{p} \Phi_L(x). \tag{54}$$

Consider for example, Equation (53), so that both sides are multiplied by $\frac{\mathbf{p}}{M\sqrt{2}}$; in this manner, one obtains

$$\frac{\mathbf{p}}{M\sqrt{2}}\mathcal{L}_K = \left(-\frac{\delta_\ell^m}{\hbar}\right) x_\ell \frac{\mathbf{p}^2}{2M}\Phi_K(x) = \left(-\frac{x_m}{\hbar}\right)\frac{\mathbf{p}^2}{2M}\Phi_K(x), \tag{55}$$

the right side exhibits the form of kinetic energy. This fact can be harnessed in order to address quantum properties that presumably would emerge Witt operators in a direct manner.

3.2. Quantization of Harmonic Oscillator

One can write again Equation (55) under the argumentation of eigenvalue equations such as

$$\frac{\mathbf{p}^2}{2M}\Phi_K(x) = -\frac{\hbar \mathbf{p}}{M\sqrt{2}x_m}\mathcal{L}_K. \tag{56}$$

Thus, one can claim that Equation (56) is a kind of Schrödinger equation established for a harmonic oscillator whose Hamiltonian is operating onto $\Phi_K(x)$. Therefore, by incorporating the potential energy in the left side above, one obtains

$$\mathbf{H}\Phi_K(x) = \left[\frac{\mathbf{p}^2}{2M} + \frac{M\omega^2 x_m^2}{2}\right]\Phi_K(x). \tag{57}$$

From Equation (56), one arrives at

$$\mathbf{H}\Phi_K(x) = -\frac{\hbar \mathbf{p}}{M\sqrt{2}x_m}\mathcal{L}_K. \tag{58}$$

It can be noted that on the right side of Equation (58), a frequency emerges in the sense that

$$\frac{\mathbf{p}}{M\sqrt{2}x_m} \equiv \omega, \tag{59}$$

by encompassing the balance of physical units on both sides of Equation (58). Thus, one obtains below that

$$\mathbf{H}\Phi_K(x) = -\hbar\omega\mathcal{L}_K. \tag{60}$$

Equation (60) offers an interesting scenario to speculate about the physical meaning of that equation. Thus, while it is assumed, for instance, (It is allowed in virtue of the polynomial character of Equations (16) and (17).) $\Phi_K(x) = x^{-(\frac{K}{2}+1)}$ and guided by main definitions Equations (16) and (17) (having a derivative), then one can also assume the relationship:

$$\mathcal{L}_K = \frac{d}{dx}\Phi_K(x), \tag{61}$$

fact that allows us to arrive at quantized energies of harmonic oscillator given by

$$\mathbf{H}\Phi_K(x) = \hbar\omega(\frac{K}{2}+1)\Phi_K(x). \quad (62)$$

3.3. Derivation of Schrödinger Equation

Despite the fact that to some extent the procedures above have been done inside a purely arbitrary scheme, some noteworthy aspects associated with tangible physics, such as the harmonic oscillator (e.g., Equation (62) presented above), might be consistently derived. For example, consider the case that states are canceling each other:

$$\mathcal{L}_K + \Phi_K(x) = 0, \quad (63)$$

implying the triviality $\mathcal{L}_K \Rightarrow -\Phi_K(x)$, then from Equation (58) one arrives at

$$\mathbf{H}\Phi_K(x) = \frac{\hbar\mathbf{p}}{M\sqrt{2}x_m}\Phi_K(x). \quad (64)$$

In this way one should be guaranteed that $\frac{\hbar\mathbf{p}}{M\sqrt{2}x_m}$ must be consistent with units of energy. It can be so only if

$$\frac{\mathbf{p}}{Mx_m\sqrt{2}} = \frac{1}{t} \equiv \omega, \quad (65)$$

having units of frequency. In this way, one can multiply by the left side of both terms of Equation (59) by $Mx_m^2\omega$, yielding

$$\sqrt{\frac{1}{8}}\omega x_m\mathbf{p} = \frac{1}{2}Mx_m^2\omega^2 = \mathcal{E}_{\mathrm{HAR}}, \quad (66)$$

the classical energy of the harmonic oscillator again, and units are checked on both sides. In addition, from Equation (53), for example, one has again that

$$\mathcal{L}_K = \Big(-\frac{\delta_\ell^m}{\sqrt{2}\hbar}\Big)x_\ell\mathbf{p}\Phi_K(x) = \Big(-\frac{1}{\sqrt{2}\hbar}\Big)x_m\mathbf{p}\Phi_K(x). \quad (67)$$

With the usage of Equations (65) and (66) one arrives at

$$\mathcal{L}_K = \Big(-\frac{2}{\hbar\omega}\Big)\sqrt{\frac{1}{8}}\omega x_m\mathbf{p}\Phi_K(x). \quad (68)$$

Now one can see that now operator is proportional to the energy of the harmonic oscillator, so that one can write down that

$$\mathcal{L}_K = \Big(-\frac{2}{\hbar\omega}\Big)\mathcal{E}_{\mathrm{HAR}}\Phi_K(x). \quad (69)$$

Based on the approximation Equation (65),

$$\omega = \frac{1}{\Delta t}. \quad (70)$$

Additionally, one can extend the meaning of Equation (63) so that one has two roots:

$$(\Phi_K(x) - \mathcal{L}_K)\Big(\Phi_K(x) - \frac{i}{2}\Psi_K(x)\Big) = 0, \quad (71)$$

by allowing to arrive in the reformulation of field $\Phi_K(x)$ as

$$\Phi_K(x) \Rightarrow \frac{i}{2}\Psi_K(x), \tag{72}$$

then, operator Equation (69) can be written as

$$\mathcal{L}_K = \left(-\frac{i\mathcal{E}_{\text{HAR}}\Delta t}{\hbar}\right)\Psi_K(x). \tag{73}$$

From above, if Δt passes to the left side, then one has the below:

$$\frac{\mathcal{L}_K}{\Delta t} = \left(-\frac{i\mathcal{E}_{\text{HAR}}}{\hbar}\right)\Psi_K(x). \tag{74}$$

In this way, the mathematical structure of the above Equation (74) is suggesting to accept that term in brackets on the right side is the outcome of the time-derivative of the well-known QM evolution operator given by $\mathbf{U}(t-t_0) = \text{Exp}\left[-i\frac{i\mathcal{E}_{\text{HAR}}(t-t_0)}{\hbar}\right]$. Thus from Equation (74) follows that

$$\frac{\mathcal{L}_K}{\Delta t} \equiv \left\{\frac{\partial}{\partial t}\mathbf{U}(t-t_0)\right\}\Psi_K(x) = \left\{\frac{\partial}{\partial t}\text{Exp}\left[-i\frac{i\mathcal{E}_{\text{HAR}}(t-t_0)}{\hbar}\right]\right\}\Psi_K(x) = \left(-\frac{i\mathcal{E}_{\text{HAR}}}{\hbar}\right)\Psi_K(x), \tag{75}$$

by which it was assumed $\Delta = t - t_0$. By taking into account the first and last terms of Equation (75) (from left to right), it can also be written in a more familiar manner as

$$i\hbar\frac{1}{\Delta t}\mathcal{L}_K = \mathcal{E}_{\text{HAR}}\Psi_K(x). \tag{76}$$

Since the kinetic part is missing, then it might be associated with the approximation under the assumption (That can also be understood as the inequality: $x_m \gg \frac{\mathbf{P}}{M\omega}$ in the classical limit applying systems with a large amplitude of oscillation) of $\frac{\mathcal{E}_{\text{KI}}}{\mathcal{E}_{\text{HAR}}} \approx 0$

$$\mathcal{E}_{\text{HAR}} \approx \mathcal{E}_{\text{HAR}}\left(1 + \frac{\mathcal{E}_{\text{KI}}}{\mathcal{E}_{\text{HAR}}}\right) \Rightarrow \mathcal{E}_{\text{HAR}} + \mathcal{E}_{\text{KI}}. \tag{77}$$

For infinitesimal times (commonly expected in quantum systems), one can approximate $\frac{1}{\Delta} \rightarrow \frac{\partial}{\partial t}$ so that one can employ the time derivative on the left side of Equation (57); therefore one arrives at

$$i\hbar\frac{\partial}{\partial t}\mathcal{L}_K = (\mathcal{E}_{\text{HAR}} + \mathcal{E}_{\text{KI}})\Psi_K(x) = \mathcal{E}\Psi_K(x). \tag{78}$$

Also, one can see that if operator $\mathcal{L}_K$ coincides with field $\Psi_K(x)$ (or $\mathcal{L}_K = \Psi_K(x)$), then, because of this, one can write down the Schrödinger equation:

$$i\hbar\frac{\partial}{\partial t}\Psi_K(x) = \mathcal{E}\Psi_K(x). \tag{79}$$

It should be noted that under the equality $\mathcal{L}_K = \Psi_K(x)$ and Equation (72), one also arrives at

$$(\mathcal{L}_K - \Psi_k)(\mathcal{L}_K - \frac{i}{2}\Psi_k) = 0, \tag{80}$$

leading to quadratic equation:

$$\mathcal{L}_K^2 - \left(\frac{i}{2}+1\right)\Psi_K\mathcal{L}_K - \frac{i}{2}\Psi_K^2 = 0. \tag{81}$$

by which holds the commutation $[\mathcal{L}_K, \Psi_K] = 0$, clearly not necessarily to be fulfilled.

4. Main Result

As shown above, both the evolution operator and the Schrödinger equation might be revealing some aspects that are not evident from Witt algebra as well as from the operators initially defined by Equations (13) and (14). In this manner, one can argue that these central operators and involved algebra would be more intrinsically associated with the aspects of quantum mechanics than being simple abstract operators belonging to unphysical Witt algebra. Under this view, Equations (49) and (50) can be harnessed to be used directly, with $\mathbf{p} = \frac{\hbar}{i}\frac{d}{dx}$, in commutators such as $[\mathcal{L}_K, \mathcal{L}_L] = \mathcal{L}_K \otimes \mathcal{L}_L - \mathcal{L}_L \otimes \mathcal{L}_K =$

$$[\mathcal{L}_K, \mathcal{L}_L] = \left[\frac{-\delta_\ell^m x_\ell}{i\sqrt{2}}\frac{d}{dx}\Phi_K(x)\right] \otimes \left[\frac{-\delta_\ell^m x_\ell}{i\sqrt{2}}\frac{d}{dx}\Phi_L(x)\right] - \left[\frac{-\delta_\ell^m x_\ell}{i\sqrt{2}}\frac{d}{dx}\Phi_L(x)\right]\left[\frac{-\delta_\ell^m x_\ell}{i\sqrt{2}}\frac{d}{dx}\Phi_K(x)\right] \tag{82}$$

$$= \left[\frac{\delta_\ell^m x_\ell}{i\sqrt{2}}\frac{\delta_\ell^m x_\ell}{i\sqrt{2}}\right] \otimes \left[\frac{d}{dx}\Phi_K(x)\frac{d}{dx}\Phi_L(x)\right] - \left[\frac{\delta_\ell^m x_\ell}{i\sqrt{2}}\frac{\delta_\ell^m x_\ell}{i\sqrt{2}}\right] \otimes \left[\frac{d}{dx}\Phi_L(x)\frac{d}{dx}\Phi_K(x)\right] \tag{83}$$

$$= \left[\frac{x_m^2}{2}\right] \otimes \left[\frac{d}{dx}\Phi_L(x)\frac{d}{dx}\Phi_K(x)\right] - \left[\frac{x_m^2}{2}\right] \otimes \left[\frac{d}{dx}\Phi_K(x)\frac{d}{dx}\Phi_L(x)\right] \tag{84}$$

$$= \left[\frac{x_m^2}{2}\right]\left(\frac{d}{dx}\Phi_L(x)\frac{d}{dx}\Phi_K(x) - \frac{d}{dx}\Phi_K(x)\frac{d}{dx}\Phi_L(x)\right). \tag{85}$$

Clearly while, not any rule of commutation between $\Phi_K(x)$ and $\Phi_L(x)$ has been explicitly established, then it is assumed that $[\Phi_K(x), \Phi_L(x)] \neq 0$.

On the other side, one can employ the momentum-based definitions as seen in Equation (67) for both cases: $\mathcal{L}_K = \frac{-\delta_\ell^m x_\ell}{\sqrt{2}\hbar}\mathbf{p}\Phi_K(x)$ and $\mathcal{L}_L = \frac{-\delta_\ell^q x_\ell}{\sqrt{2}\hbar}\mathbf{p}\Phi_L(x)$) inside Equation (82) so that one obtains

$$[\mathcal{L}_K, \mathcal{L}_L] = \frac{-\delta_\ell^m x_\ell}{\sqrt{2}\hbar}\mathbf{p}\Phi_K(x)\frac{-\delta_\ell^q x_\ell}{\sqrt{2}\hbar}\mathbf{p}\Phi_L(x) - \frac{-\delta_\ell^q x_\ell}{\sqrt{2}\hbar}\mathbf{p}\Phi_L(x)\frac{-\delta_\ell^m x_\ell}{\sqrt{2}\hbar}\mathbf{p}\Phi_K(x) \tag{86}$$

$$= \frac{x_m}{\sqrt{2}\hbar}\mathbf{p}\Phi_K(x)\frac{x_q}{\sqrt{2}\hbar}\mathbf{p}\Phi_L(x) - \frac{x_q}{\sqrt{2}\hbar}\mathbf{p}\Phi_L(x)\frac{x_m}{\sqrt{2}\hbar}\mathbf{p}\Phi_K(x) \tag{87}$$

$$= \frac{1}{2\hbar^2}\left[x_m\mathbf{p}x_q\mathbf{p}\Phi_K(x)\Phi_L(x) - x_q\mathbf{p}x_m\mathbf{p}\Phi_L(x)\Phi_K(x)\right]. \tag{88}$$

It should be remarked that the change of Equation (86) to Equation (87) has demanded to accept the validity of these commutators:

$$[\Phi_K, x_q] = 0, \tag{89}$$

$$[\Phi_L, x_m] = 0. \tag{90}$$

From above, one can argue that Equation (88) might also be written as (By which it was added and subtracted the term $x_q\mathbf{p}x_m\mathbf{p}\Phi_K(x)\Phi_L(x)$.):

$$[\mathcal{L}_K, \mathcal{L}_L] = \frac{1}{2\hbar^2}[x_m\mathbf{p}x_q\mathbf{p}\Phi_K(x)\Phi_L(x) - x_q\mathbf{p}x_m\mathbf{p}\Phi_K(x)\Phi_L(x) + x_q\mathbf{p}x_m\mathbf{p}\Phi_K(x)\Phi_L(x) - x_q\mathbf{p}x_m\mathbf{p}\Phi_L(x)\Phi_K(x)] \tag{91}$$

$$= \frac{1}{2\hbar^2}\left[[x_m\mathbf{p}, x_q\mathbf{p}]\Phi_K(x)\Phi_L(x) + x_q\mathbf{p}x_m\mathbf{p}[\Phi_K(x), \Phi_L(x)]\right]. \tag{92}$$

Clearly, from $[x_m\mathbf{p}, x_q\mathbf{p}]$ in Equation (92), it is needed the usage of identity $[AB, CD] = A[B, C]D + [A, C]BD + CA[B, D] + C[A.D]B$. By applying this in a straightforward manner, one obtains the following:

$$[\mathcal{L}_K, \mathcal{L}_L] = \frac{1}{2\hbar^2}\big[(x_q[x_m, \mathbf{p}]\mathbf{p} - x_m[x_q, \mathbf{p}]\mathbf{p})\Phi_K(x)\Phi_L(x) + x_q\mathbf{p}x_m\mathbf{p}\{\Phi_K(x), \Phi_L(x)\}\big], \quad (93)$$

demonstrating the validity of the hypothesis formulated in Equation (7). Equation (93) becomes the main result of this paper. The general formulation of CCR given by $[x_I, p_J] = i\hbar\delta_{I,J}$ stops us from going through commutators in Equation (93), essentially because neither $x_{m,q}$ nor $\mathbf{p}$ have been explicitly specified. In this way, various scenarios might emerge for the choice of a concrete component of $\mathbf{p}$, as well as for x_m and x_q. The particular case when $m = q$ reduces Equation (93) to

$$[\mathcal{L}_K, \mathcal{L}_L] = \frac{1}{2}\left(\frac{x_m\mathbf{p}}{\hbar}\right)^2[\Phi_K(x), \Phi_L(x)]. \quad (94)$$

Because commutator $[\mathcal{L}_K, \mathcal{L}_L]$ has now acquired a certain physical meaning because the position and momentum operators, then Equation (94) can also be rewritten as a function of observables measurements such as

$$[\mathcal{L}_K, \mathcal{L}_L] = \frac{1}{2}\left(\frac{\Delta x_m\Delta\mathbf{p}}{\hbar}\right)^2[\Phi_K(x), \Phi_L(x)]. \quad (95)$$

Inspired at the uncertainty principle, one can impose the following restriction:

$$\Delta x_m\Delta\mathbf{p} \geq \sqrt{2}\hbar, \quad (96)$$

yielding an alternative redefinition of Witt algebra through new operators $\Phi_K(x)$ and $\Phi_L(x)$ as

$$[\mathcal{L}_K, \mathcal{L}_L] = [\Phi_K(x), \Phi_L(x)], \quad (97)$$

entering into a total contradiction with Equation (63). This suggests keeping Equation (96) as $\Delta x_m\Delta\mathbf{p} \geq \hbar$, which allows writing Equation (95) down as

$$[\mathcal{L}_K, \mathcal{L}_L] = \left[-i\frac{\Phi_K(x)}{\sqrt{2}}, i\frac{\Phi_L(x)}{\sqrt{2}}\right], \quad (98)$$

by which emerges the complex version of Equation (63) in the sense of

$$\mathcal{L}_K + i\frac{\Phi_K(x)}{\sqrt{2}} = 0, \quad (99)$$

$$\mathcal{L}_L - i\frac{\Phi_L(x)}{\sqrt{2}} = 0. \quad (100)$$

5. Discussion

Along the paper, it was employed the so-called Witt operators, essentially Equations (16) and (17), constructed in an artificial manner to demonstrate that they fulfill the Witt algebra or Virasoro centerless algebra. Although the whole procedure has been merely operative, it has planted the idea that these formulations have implications in a tangible QM. It is remarked on the role of integrals whose form has been relevant to deriving the QM evolution operator and the Schrödinger equation. The polynomial term Equation (44) has been crucial to claiming quantization of harmonic oscillators, even though no annihilation or creation operators have been considered. Because of this, one can wonder if all structures that fulfill Witt algebra can be seriously considered as unexplored territories and ends in a QM arena. Or results can be seen as fortuitous derivations that can also be ambiguities of a single formalism? The only fact that commutators of Witt operators yield the CCR is proof that Virasoro-like schemes might also be open windows to a general usage of string theories in concrete QM applications. As seen in [4], the Virasoro algebra has served to build a model of N-th order squeezing based on Virasoro oscillators through the definition of oscillators as functions of annihilation and creation operators as an indirect way to link the algebra to momentum and position operators. In the present paper, instead of opting for intermediate derivations involving extra operators, it was assumed the integral form as given at Equations (16) and (17), whose structure has been harnessed to derive QM energies (quantization of harmonic oscillator). For example, in [44], ideas about string theory as dissipative QM based at symmetries have yielded interesting similarities (both might be the same theory), far from common considerations as done in field theories. The proposal of this paper clearly is going in a novel direction with robust redefinitions of Virasoro oscillators that allow it to pass over the QM area without appealing to quantum symmetries or incorporating extra structures based on QM operators. On the other side, the spirit of this paper is to some extent inclined to view [45] in the sense that association of QM and general relativity can be only consistent through an inclusion of all spectrum of topological string states. The fact that Equations (16) and (17) have turned out to be fulfilling Witt algebra and are also a robust scheme for the derivation of QM relations and equations is, to some extent, comparable to the work of Bars and Rychkov [46] since they have taken advantage of Moyal string field theory formalism to derive commutators of operators' position and momentum. Indeed, Equation (57) of this paper might be aligned with the idea that the Moyal product yields products of string fields that finally can be recognized as ordinary QM Hamiltonians. Furthermore, Equation (44), which introduces the polynomial profile to Witt operators, would be in agreement with recent work [47], where Lie algebra based on polynomial algebra structures offers a new path to be applied in QM and related areas.

6. Conclusions

In this paper, it was presented a mathematical methodology that allows demonstrating that schemes based on Witt algebra are consistently linked to quantum mechanics canonical commutation relation (CCR), despite the fact that not any assumption associated with quantum variables or quantum mechanics formalism was deeply considered. As seen in Equations (16) and (17), operators have been defined built on the basis of the Krönecker delta and Dirac delta function, as well as the operations of derivative and integration. After closed form operations, as seen in previous sections, these operators have turned out to fulfill the Witt algebra. Although some abstract procedures have been applied, it was seen that all that have acquired sense when quantum mechanics definitions were shortly applied. Particularly, the momentum operator emerged in a spontaneous manner. It has played a noteworthy role, as noted in the last section of the paper. In this manner, based rigorously on the presented formalism (by which it might be extended and improved), Witt algebra has turned out to be proportional to well-known CCR. Certainly, more formalism and operations would have to be added in order to claim a robust proportionality between the DeWitt (Virasoro central charge [48]) algebra and the quantum mechanics canonical commutation relation.

Funding: This research received no external funding.

Data Availability Statement: No new data were created or analyzed in this study.

Conflicts of Interest: The author declares no conflicts of interest.

References

1. Girvin, S.M.; MacDonald, A.H.; Platzman, P.M. Magneto-roton theory of collective excitations in the fractional quantum Hall effect. *Phys. Rev. B* **1986** , *33*, 2481–2986. [CrossRef] [PubMed]
2. Ginsparg, P. Lectures given at Les Houches summer session, 28 June–5 August 1988. *arXiv* **1989**. [CrossRef]
3. Ellis, J.R.; Mavromatos, N.E.; Nanopoulos, D.V. String theory modifies quantum mechanics. *Phys. Lett. B* **1992**, *293*, 37–48. [CrossRef]
4. Katagiri, S.; Sugamoto, A.; Yamaguchi, K.; Yumibayashi, T. Beyond squeezing à la Virasoro algebra. *Prog. Theor. Exp. Phys.* **2019**, *2019*, 123B04 . [CrossRef]
5. Veneziano, G. Construction of a crossing-simmetric, Regge-behaved amplitude for linearly rising trajectories. *Nuovo Cimento A (1965–1970)* **1968**, *57*, 190–197. [CrossRef]
6. Virasoro, M.A. Subsidiary Conditions and Ghosts in Dual-Resonance Models. *Phys. Rev. D* **1970**, *1*, 2933. [CrossRef]
7. Brower, R.C. Spectrum-Generating Algebra and No-Ghost Theorem for the Dual Model. *Phy. Rev. D* **1972**, *6*, 1655. [CrossRef]
8. Van Alstine, P. Remark on the c-number anomaly in the Virasoro algebra. *Phy. Rev. D* **1975**, *12*, 1834. [CrossRef]
9. Akhoury, R.; Okada, Y. String in curved space-time: Virasoro algebra in the classical and quantum theory. *Phy. Rev. D* **1987**, *35*, 1917. [CrossRef]
10. Saito, Y. Nonexistence of a ground state and breaking of the no-ghost theorem on a squeezed string. *Phy. Rev. D* **1987**, *36*, 3178. [CrossRef]
11. Scherk, J. An introduction to the theory of dual models and string. *Rev. Mod. Phys.* **1975**, *47*, 123. [CrossRef]
12. Sakai, N.; Suranyi, P. Modification of Virasoro Generators by Kac-Moody Generators. *Nucl. Phys. B* **1989**, *318*, 655–668. [CrossRef]
13. Dotsenko, V.S.; Fateev, V. Conformal algebra and multipoint correlation functions in 2D statistical models. *Nucl. Phys. B* **1984**, *240*, 312. [CrossRef]
14. Chaichian, M.; Presnajder, P. Discrete-time quantum field theory and the deformed super-Virasoro algebra. *Phys. Lett. A* **2004**, *322*, 156–165. [CrossRef]
15. Sakurai, J.J.; Tuan, S.F. *Modern Quantum Mechanics*; Chap-II, Revised Edition; Pearson Education: London, UK, 1994.
16. Chinmoy, S.; Aniruddha, C. Exact results for the Schrödinger equation with moving localized potential. *Phys. Lett. A* **2021**, *408*, 127485.
17. Band, Y.B. Quantum Mechanics with Applications to Nanotechnology and Information Science. In *The Formalism of Quantum Mechanics*; Avishai, Y., Ed.; Academic Press: Cambridge, MA, USA, 2013; pp. 61–104.
18. Ray, J.R. Exact solutions to the time-dependent Schrödinger equation. *Phys. Rev. A* **1982**, *26*, 729. [CrossRef]
19. Newton, R.G. Representation of the Potential in the Schrödinger Equation. *Phys. Rev. Lett.* **1984**, *53*, 1863. [CrossRef]
20. Caballar, R.C.F.; Ocampo, L.R.; Galapon, E.A. Characterizing multiple solutions to the time-energy canonical commutation relation via internal symmetries. *Phys. Rev. A* **2010**, *81*, 062105. [CrossRef]
21. Shapiro, M. Derivation of the coordinate-momentum commutation relations from canonical invariance. *Phys. Rev. A* **2006**, *74*, 042104. [CrossRef]
22. Pikovski, I.; Vanner, M.; Aspelmeyer, M.; Kim, M.S.; Brukner, Č. Probing Planck-scale physics with quantum optics. *Nat. Phys.* **2012**, *8*, 393–397. [CrossRef]
23. Maggiore, M. A generalized uncertainty principle in quantum gravity. *Phys. Lett. B* **1993**, *304*, 65–69. [CrossRef]
24. Gil Gat, O.W.; Greenberg, M. Canonical commutation relations in the Schwinger model. *Phys. Lett. B* **2006**, *328*, 119–122. [CrossRef]
25. Dirac, P.A.M. *The Principles of Quantum Mechanics*, 4th ed.; Oxford University Press: Oxford, UK, 1958.
26. Chaichian, M.; Isaev, A.P.; Lukierski, J.; Popowicz, Z.; Prešnajder, P. q-deformations of Virasoro algebra and conformal dimensions. *Phys. Lett. B* **1991**, *262*, 32–38. [CrossRef]
27. Frenkel, E.; Reshetikhin, N. Quantum affine algebras and deformations of the Virasoro and W-algebras. *Comm. Math. Phys.* **1996**, *178*, 237–264. [CrossRef]
28. Strade, H. Representations of the Witt algebra. *J. Algebra* **1977**, *49*, 595–605. [CrossRef]
29. Blattner, R.J. Induced and produced representations of Lie algebras. *Trans. Am. Math. Sot.* **1969**, *114*, 457–474. [CrossRef]
30. Veneziano, G. An introduction to dual models of strong interactions and their physical motivations. *Phys. Rep.* **1974**, *9*, 199–242. [CrossRef]
31. Redlich, A.N. When is the central charge of the Virasoro algebra in string theories in curved space-time not a numerical constant? *Phys. Rev. D* **1986**, *33*, 1094. [CrossRef]
32. Bagger, J.; Nemeschansky, D.; Yankielowicz, S. Virasoro algebras with central charge c>1. *Phys. Rev. Lett.* **1988**, *60*, 389. [CrossRef]
33. Banados, M. Embeddings of the Virasoro Algebra and Black Hole Entropy. *Phys. Rev. Lett.* **1999**, *82*, 2030. [CrossRef]
34. Johnson, C.V. Supersymmetric Virasoro minimal string. *Phys. Rev. D* **2024**, *110*, 066016. [CrossRef]
35. Johnson, C.V. Random matrix model of the Virasoro minimal string. *Phys. Rev. D* **2024**, *110*, 066015. [CrossRef]
36. Sakamoto, R. Explicit formula for singular vectors of the Virasoro algebra with central charge less than 1. *Chaos Solitons Fractals* **2005**, *25*, 147–151. [CrossRef]

37. Fortin, J.-F.; Quintavalle, L.; Skiba, W. Casimirs of the Virasoro algebra. *Phys. Lett. B* **2024**, *858*, 139080. [CrossRef]
38. Iohara, K.; Koga, Y. *Representation Theory of the Virasoro Algebra Springer Monographs in Mathematics*; Springer: London, UK, 2011.
39. Dong, C.; Zhang, W. On classification of rational vertex operator algebras with central charges less than 1. *J. Algebra* **2008**, *320*, 86–93. [CrossRef]
40. Curtright, T.L.; Fairlie, D.B.; Zachos, C.K. Ternary Virasoro–Witt algebra. *Phys. Lett. B* **2008**, *666*, 386–390. [CrossRef]
41. Arfken, G.B.; Weber, H.J. *Mathematical Methods for Physicists*, 4th ed.; Academic Press: San Diego, CA, USA, 1995.
42. Butkov, E. *Mathematical Physics*; Addison-Wesley: Reading, UK, 1968.
43. Mathews, J.; Walker, R.L. *Mathematical Methods of Physics*, 2nd ed.; W. A. Benjamin: New York, NY, USA, 1970.
44. Callan, C.G.; Thorlacius, L. Open String Theory as Dissipative Quantum Mechanics. *Nucl. Phys. B* **1990**, *329*, 117–138. [CrossRef]
45. Ellis, J.; Mavromatos, N.E.; Nanopoulos, D.V. Quantum mechanics and black holes in four-dimensional string theory. *Phys. Lett. B* **1992**, *278*, 246–256. [CrossRef]
46. Bars, I.; Rychkov, D. Is string interaction the origin of quantum mechanics? *Phys. Lett. B* **2014**, *739*, 451–456. [CrossRef]
47. Marquette, I.; Zhang, J.; Zhang, Y.-Z. Algebraic structures and Hamiltonians from the equivalence classes of 2D conformal algebras. **2025**, *477*, 169998. [CrossRef]
48. Fidelis, C.; Diniz, D.; Koshlukov, P. Z-graded identities of the Virasoro algebra. *J. Algebra* **2024**, *640*, 401–431. [CrossRef]

Disclaimer/Publisher's Note: The statements, opinions and data contained in all publications are solely those of the individual author(s) and contributor(s) and not of MDPI and/or the editor(s). MDPI and/or the editor(s) disclaim responsibility for any injury to people or property resulting from any ideas, methods, instructions or products referred to in the content.

mathematics

MDPI

Article

On a Quotient Ring That Satisfies Certain Identities via Generalized Reverse Derivations

Nawaf L. Alsowait [1], Mohammed Al-Shomrani [2], Radwan M. Al-omary [3,*] and Zakia Z. Al-Amery [4]

1 Department of Mathematics, College of Science, Northern Border University, Arar 73213, Saudi Arabia; nawaf.lazzam@nbu.edu.sa
2 Department of Mathematics, Faculty of Science, King Abdulaziz University, Jeddah 21589, Saudi Arabia; malshamrani@kau.edu.sa
3 Department of Mathematics, Ibb University, Ibb 70270, Yemen
4 Department of Mathematics, Aden University, Aden 5243, Yemen; alameryzakia@gmail.com
* Correspondence: raradwan959@gmail.com

Abstract: In this article, for a prime ideal ρ of an arbitrary ring $\Re$, we study the commutativity of the quotient ring $\Re/\rho$, whenever $\Re$ admits a generalized reverse derivation ϑ associated with a reverse derivation ∂ that satisfies certain identities in ρ. Additionally, we show that, for some cases, the range of the generalized reverse derivation ϑ lies in the prime ideal ρ. Moreover, we explore several consequences and special cases. Throughout, we provide examples to demonstrate that various restrictions in the assumptions of our results are essential.

Keywords: prime ideal; integral domain; generalized reverse derivation; quotient ring

MSC: 16W25; 16N60; 16U80

1. Introduction

The study of derivations on rings plays an important role and has many applications in other areas of mathematics, such as analysis, algebraic geometry, and the properties of algebraic systems. These applications are outside the scope of current study.

In this article, $\Re$ is an associative ring and $Z(\Re)$ is its center. A proper ideal ρ of $\Re$ is prime if, for each pair of elements ξ and η in $\Re$, the condition $\xi\Re\eta \subseteq \rho$ implies that either ξ belongs to ρ or η belongs to ρ. A ring $\Re$ is prime if and only if the set $\{0\}$ is a prime ideal of $\Re$. A domain is a ring that does not have any non-zero divisors.

An additive mapping $\partial : \Re \to \Re$ is called a derivation if it satisfies the equation $\partial(\xi\eta) = \partial(\xi)\eta + \xi\partial(\eta)$ for all $\xi, \eta \in \Re$. An additive mapping $\vartheta : \Re \to \Re$ is a generalized derivation associated with the derivation ∂ if the equation $\vartheta(\xi\eta) = \vartheta(\xi)\eta + \xi\partial(\eta)$ is satisfied for all $\xi, \eta \in \Re$. For a fixed $r \in \Re$, a mapping $\partial_r : \Re \to \Re$ such that $\partial_r(\xi) = [r, \xi]$ for any $\xi \in \Re$ is a derivation, which is called the inner derivation induced by r. For a non-trivial example of a derivation on a non-commutative ring, the reader can refer to [1] (Example 2.2).

The concept of a reverse derivation was initially defined by Herstein in [2] when he proved that the prime ring $\Re$ is a commutative integral domain whenever the imposed derivation is a Jordan derivation. It was defined to be an additive mapping $\partial : \Re \to \Re$ that satisfies the equation $\partial(\xi\eta) = \partial(\eta)\xi + \eta\partial(\xi)$ for any $\xi, \eta \in \Re$. It can be noted that, in the case of Lie algebras, the concept of a reverse derivation is analogy to the concept of the antiderivation. According to this fact, several authors have studied the reverse derivation on algebra and subalgebra (see, for example [3–5]). In ref. [6], a study was conducted by Samman et al. on the reverse derivation of the semiprime ring.

In [7], Aboubakr et al. discussed the correlation between a generalized reverse derivation and a generalized derivation on a semiprime ring. A generalized reverse derivation is defined as an additive map ϑ that satisfies the equation $\vartheta(\xi\eta) = \vartheta(\eta)\xi + \eta\partial(\xi)$ for all ξ and η in $\Re$, where ∂ is a reverse derivation of $\Re$. In the previous literature, there are numerous non-trivial examples of generalized reverse derivations on non-commutative rings. For example, please see reference [8]. Furthermore, we will provide several concrete examples of generalized reverse derivations on non-commutative rings at the end of this article. It is known that every generalized reverse derivation is a reverse derivation. However, it is important to note that the converse is not always true. The concepts of generalized reverse derivations are related to generalizations of generalized derivations. It is clear that if $\Re$ is commutative, then both generalized reverse derivations and generalized derivations are the same. However, the converse may not be true in general, as shown in [9] (Example 1).

In a study by Ibraheem [10], it was proven that a prime ring is commutative, if $[\vartheta(\xi), \xi] \in Z(\Re)$ for all ξ belonging to a right ideal $\aleph$ of a ring, given that the right ideal $\aleph \cap Z(\Re) \neq 0$. Here, ϑ represents a generalized reverse derivation associated with a nonzero reverse derivation ∂. In a related study by Bulak et al. [11], further exploration of generalized reverse derivations was conducted. The first part of the study focused on the commutativity of prime rings under the influence of differential identities provided by two generalized reverse derivations. The second part examined the relationships between r-generalized reverse derivations and l-generalized derivations, as well as l-generalized reverse derivations and r-generalized derivations, in a non-central square closed Lie ideal in a semiprime ring

Building upon prior findings, many researchers have achieved multiple outcomes regarding commutativity across diverse algebraic structures, including prime and semiprime rings. These outcomes have been attained through the utilization of suitable mappings, such as derivations, generalized derivations, and generalized reverse derivations, which adhere to specific identities when operating on suitable subsets of $\Re$. The interested readers can be referred to [1,8,9,12].

Recently, in continuation of the above studies, several authors have discussed the situation of a quotient ring $\Re/\rho$ and the way it behaves under derivation or generalized derivation that satisfies certain identities involving a prime ideal (for more details, refer to [13–20]).

In [21], the concept of the generalized derivation ϑ was replaced by a generalized reverse derivation, and the commutativity of $\Re/\rho$ was studied whenever the proposed algebraic identities contained in a prime ideal were concerned with ϑ.

The main aim of this article is to study further in this direction. More precisely, assuming that $\Re$ is an arbitrary ring that admits a generalized reverse derivation ϑ associated with a reverse derivation ∂, we prove that if ϑ satisfies certain identities involving a prime ideal ρ, then the quotient ring $\Re/\rho$ is a commutative integral domain. In some cases, it comes out that the range of the generalized reverse derivation ϑ is in a prime ideal ρ, i.e., $\vartheta(\Re) \subseteq \rho$. Moreover, some consequences as well as special cases are obtained. Examples that illustrate the necessity of the assumptions stated in our theorems are provided.

2. Preliminary Results

We begin this section by recalling the following basic concepts: Let $\xi, \eta \in \Re$. We may define the commutator $[\xi, \eta]$ as the difference between $\xi\eta$ and $\eta\xi$, and the anticommutator $\xi \circ \eta$ as the sum of $\xi\eta$ and $\eta\xi$. The following identities will be used extensively throughout this article to facilitate access to the proofs of our theorems, which are satisfied for all $\xi, \eta, \zeta \in \Re$:

$$[\xi\eta, \zeta] = \xi[\eta, \zeta] + [\xi, \zeta]\eta,$$
$$[\xi, \eta\zeta] = \eta[\xi, \zeta] + [\xi, \eta]\zeta,$$
$$\xi \circ (\eta\zeta) = (\xi \circ \eta)\zeta - \eta[\xi, \zeta] = \eta(\xi \circ \zeta) + [\xi, \eta]\zeta,$$
$$(\xi\eta) \circ \zeta = \xi(\eta \circ \zeta) - [\xi, \zeta]\eta = (\xi \circ \zeta)\eta + \xi[\eta, \zeta].$$

For the purpose of developing our proofs, we will present the following important remark and lemmas: The proof of Remark 1 is based on the fact that a group cannot be written as the set-theoretic union of its two proper subsets, and the proof of Lemma 1 can be found in [20].

Remark 1. *Let ρ be a prime ideal of an arbitrary ring $\Re$, and let $\aleph$ be an additive subgroup of $\Re$. Let $\ell, \wp : \aleph \to \Re$ be additive functions such that $\ell(s)\Re\wp(s) \subseteq \rho$ for all $s \in \aleph$. Then, either $\ell(s) \in \rho$ for all $s \in \aleph$, or $\wp(s) \in \rho$ for all $s \in \aleph$.*

Lemma 1 ([20], Lemma 1.2). *Let $\Re$ be a ring and let ρ be a prime ideal of $\Re$. If $[\xi, \eta] \in \rho$ for all $\xi, \eta \in \Re$, then $\Re/\rho$ is a commutative integral domain.*

The following lemma is an expansion of ([21], Lemma 2.5).

Lemma 2. *Let ρ be a prime ideal of an arbitrary ring $\Re$. If $\Re$ admits a generalized reverse derivation ϑ associated with a reverse derivation ∂ such that $[\xi, \vartheta(\xi)] \in \rho$ for all $\xi \in \rho$, then either $\partial(\Re) \subseteq \rho$ or $\Re/\rho$ is a commutative integral domain.*

Proof. From the hypothesis, we have

$$[\xi, \vartheta(\xi)] \in \rho, \quad \text{for all } \xi \in \Re. \tag{1}$$

By linearizing Equation (1), which simply means replacing ξ by $\xi + \eta$, we obtain

$$[\xi, \vartheta(\eta)] + [\eta, \vartheta(\xi)] \in \rho, \quad \text{for all } \xi, \eta \in \Re. \tag{2}$$

By replacing η by $\eta\xi$ in (2) and utilizing (1), we get

$$\vartheta(\xi)[\xi, \eta] + \xi[\xi, \partial(\eta)] + [\eta, \vartheta(\xi)]\xi \in \rho, \quad \text{for all } \xi, \eta \in \Re. \tag{3}$$

Setting $\xi = \eta$ in (3) and using (1) again, we obtain $\xi[\xi, \partial(\xi)] \in \rho$, for all $\xi \in \Re$. Replacing $\partial(\xi)$ by $\partial(\xi)\tau$ in the previous equation and using it, we get $\xi\partial(\xi)[\xi, \tau] \in \rho$ for all $\xi, \tau \in \Re$. Placing $\tau\nu$ instead of τ in the previous equation and using it, we get $\xi\partial(\xi)\tau[\xi, \nu] \in \rho$ for all $\xi, \tau, \nu \in \Re$. In other words, $\xi\partial(\xi)\Re[\xi, \nu] \subseteq \rho$ for all $\xi, \nu \in \Re$. Since ρ is prime, considering Remark 1, we find that either $\xi\partial(\xi) \in \rho$ or $[\xi, \nu] \in \rho$ for all $\xi, \nu \in \Re$. If $[\xi, \nu] \in \rho$ for all $\xi, \nu \in \Re$, we deduce that $\Re/\rho$ is a commutative integral domain, by Lemma 1. In the alternative scenario, we have $\xi\partial(\xi) \in \rho$ for all $\xi \in \Re$. Linearizing the previous expression, we obtain $\xi\partial(\eta) + \eta\partial(\xi) \in \rho$ for all $\xi, \eta \in \Re$. By replacing ξ by $\nu\xi$ in the previous equation and using it we find, after appropriate treatment, that $\eta\partial(\xi)\nu - \nu\eta\partial(\xi) + \eta\xi\partial(\nu) \in \rho$ for all $\xi, \eta, \nu \in \Re$. Again, placing $\tau\eta$ instead of η in the last relation and using it, we find $[\tau, \nu]\eta\partial(\xi) \in \rho$ for all $\xi, \tau, \nu, \eta \in \Re$. This results in $[\tau, \nu]\Re\partial(\xi) \subseteq \rho$ for all $\xi, \tau, \nu \in \Re$. By employing the assumption that ρ is prime along with Remark 1, we conclude that either $\partial(\xi) \in \rho$ or $[\tau, \nu] \in \rho$ for all $\xi, \tau, \nu \in \Re$. Therefore, we can infer that the first case leads to $\partial(\mathfrak{R}) \subseteq \rho$, and for the second case, we use Lemma 1 to obtain that $\mathfrak{R}/\rho$ is a commutative integral domain. □

Corollary 1. *Let ρ be a prime ideal of an arbitrary ring $\mathfrak{R}$. If $\mathfrak{R}$ admits a reverse derivation ∂, such that $[\xi, \partial(\xi)] \in \rho$ for all $\xi \in \mathfrak{R}$, then either $\partial(\mathfrak{R}) \subseteq \rho$ or $\mathfrak{R}/\rho$ is a commutative integral domain. Moreover, if $\rho = \{0\}$, then either $\mathfrak{R}$ is commutative or ∂ turns out to be zero.*

Remark 2. *In Lemma 2, if $\mathfrak{R}$ is commutative, then ϑ becomes a generalized derivation, and thus we obtain ([20], Proposition 1.3).*

3. Main Results

In [14] (Theorem 2.5), Bouchannafa et al. proved that either the ring $\mathfrak{R}/\rho$ is a commutative integral domain or $\partial(\mathfrak{R})$ is a subset of ρ, whenever the ring $\mathfrak{R}$ has a generalized derivation ϑ such that $\vartheta(\xi \circ \eta) - \vartheta(\xi) \circ \eta$ belongs to the center $Z(\mathfrak{R}/\rho)$ for all ξ and η in $\mathfrak{R}$, where ρ is a prime ideal of $\mathfrak{R}$. In the next theorem, our objective is to achieve the same outcome by substituting the generalized derivation ϑ from the previous theorem with the notion of a generalized reverse derivation, which is associated with a reverse derivation ∂ that fulfills the condition $\vartheta(\xi) \circ \eta - \vartheta(\xi \circ \eta) \in \rho$, for all $\xi, \eta \in \mathfrak{R}$.

Theorem 1. *Consider a prime ideal ρ in a ring $\mathfrak{R}$, where $\mathfrak{R}$ can be any ring. If $\mathfrak{R}$ admits a generalized reverse derivation ϑ that is associated with a reverse derivation ∂, and satisfies the condition $\vartheta(\xi) \circ \eta - \vartheta(\xi \circ \eta) \in \rho$ for all ξ and η in $\mathfrak{R}$, then either $\partial(\mathfrak{R})$ is a subset of ρ or the quotient ring $\mathfrak{R}/\rho$ is a commutative integral domain.*

Proof. Suppose that

$$\vartheta(\xi) \circ \eta - \vartheta(\xi \circ \eta) \in \rho, \quad \text{for all } \xi, \eta \in \mathfrak{R}. \tag{4}$$

Placing $\eta\xi$ instead of ξ in (4) yields

$$(\vartheta(\xi) \circ \eta)\eta + (\xi \circ \eta)\partial(\eta) + \xi[\partial(\eta), \eta] - \vartheta(\xi \circ \eta)\eta - (\xi \circ \eta)\partial(\eta) \in \rho, \text{ for all } \xi, \eta \in \mathfrak{R}. \tag{5}$$

By multiplying (4) by η from the right and comparing it with (5), we obtain

$$\xi[\partial(\eta), \eta] \in \rho, \quad \text{for all } \xi, \eta \in \mathfrak{R}.$$

The last equation is simplified as follows: $\xi\mathfrak{R}[\partial(\eta), \eta] \subseteq \rho$, where ξ and η are elements of $\mathfrak{R}$. Given that $\rho \neq \mathfrak{R}$ and ρ is a prime, the last equation implies that $[\partial(\eta), \eta]$ belongs to ρ for every η in $\mathfrak{R}$. Therefore, according to Corollary 1, either $\mathfrak{R}/\rho$ is a commutative integral domain or $\partial(\mathfrak{R})$ is a subset of ρ. □

When $\mathfrak{R}$ is a prime ring and $\vartheta = \partial$, respectively, the following corollaries can be immediately obtained from Theorem 1.

Corollary 2. *Consider a ring $\mathfrak{R}$, which is prime. If $\mathfrak{R}$ admits a generalized reverse derivation ϑ associated with a reverse derivation ∂, satisfying the equation $\vartheta(\xi) \circ \eta - \vartheta(\xi \circ \eta) = 0$ for all $\xi, \eta \in \mathfrak{R}$, then either ∂ is equal to zero or $\mathfrak{R}$ is a commutative ring.*

Corollary 3. *Consider a prime ideal ρ in a ring $\mathfrak{R}$, where $\mathfrak{R}$ can be any ring. If $\mathfrak{R}$ admits a reverse derivation ∂, and satisfies the condition $\partial(\xi) \circ \eta - \partial(\xi \circ \eta) \in \rho$ for all ξ and η in $\mathfrak{R}$, then either $\partial(\mathfrak{R})$ is a subset of ρ or the quotient ring $\mathfrak{R}/\rho$ is a commutative integral domain.*

Theorem 2. *Consider a prime ideal ρ of a ring $\Re$. If $\Re$ admits a generalized reverse derivation ϑ associated with a reverse derivation ∂, such that $\vartheta(\xi)\circ\eta+\vartheta(\xi\circ\eta)\in\rho$, for all $\xi,\eta\in\Re$, then either $\partial(\Re)\subseteq\rho$ or $\Re/\rho$ is a commutative integral domain of $char(\Re/\rho)=2$.*

Proof. The given identity states that

$$\vartheta(\xi)\circ\eta+\vartheta(\xi\circ\eta)\in\rho,\quad \text{for all }\xi,\eta\in\Re. \tag{6}$$

Replacing ξ by $\eta\xi$ in (6), gives

$$(\vartheta(\xi)\circ\eta)\eta+(\xi\circ\eta)\partial(\eta)+\xi[\partial(\eta),\eta]+\vartheta(\xi\circ\eta)\eta+(\xi\circ\eta)\partial(\eta)\in\rho,\ \text{for all }\xi,\eta\in\Re. \tag{7}$$

By multiplying (6) by η from the right-hand side and comparing it with (7), we obtain

$$2(\xi\circ\eta)\partial(\eta)+\xi[\partial(\eta),\eta]\in\rho,\quad \text{for all }\xi,\eta\in\rho. \tag{8}$$

Now, we discuss the following two cases:

Case (i): If $char(\Re/\rho)=2$, then (8) becomes $\xi[\partial(\eta),\eta]\in\rho,\quad \text{for all }\xi,\eta\in\rho$. Following the same arguments as above, we find either $\partial(\Re)$ is a subset of ρ or $\Re/\rho$ is a commutative integral domain.

Case (ii): If $char(\Re/\rho)\neq 2$, then replacing ξ by $\tau\xi$ in (8) results in

$$2\tau(\xi\circ\eta)\partial(\eta)-2[\tau,\eta]\xi\partial(\eta)+\tau\xi[\partial(\eta),\eta]\in\rho,\ \text{for all }\xi,\eta,\tau\in\rho. \tag{9}$$

Now, multiplying (8) by τ from the left-hand side and comparing with (9), yields $2[\tau,\eta]\xi\partial(\eta)\in\rho$ for all $\xi,\eta,\tau\in\Re$. Our assumption that $char(\Re/\rho)\neq 2$ leads to $[\tau,\eta]\xi\partial(\eta)\in\rho$ for all $\xi,\eta,\tau\in\Re$, and hence $[\tau,\eta]\Re\partial(\eta)\subseteq\rho$ for all $\eta,\tau\in\Re$. Thus, the primeness of ρ together with Remark 1 lead to either $[\tau,\eta]\in\rho$ for all $\tau,\eta\in\Re$ or $\partial(\Re)\subseteq\rho$. If $\partial(\Re)$ is not a subset of ρ, then $[\tau,\eta]$ belongs to ρ for every elements τ and η in $\Re$. Using Lemma 1 shows that the quotient ring $\Re/\rho$ is a commutative integral domain. By utilizing the commutativity of $\Re/\rho$ with the identity (8), we can easily deduce that $2(\xi\circ\eta)\partial(\eta)$ belongs to ρ for all ξ and η in $\Re$. The statement $4\xi\eta\partial(\eta)\in\rho$ holds for all $\xi,\eta\in\Re$ because $char(\Re/\rho)\neq 2$. This implies that $\xi\eta\partial(\eta)\in\rho$ for all $\xi,\eta\in\Re$, due to the commutativity of $\Re$. Furthermore, the previous expression is equivalent to $\eta\xi\partial(\eta)\in\rho$ for all $\xi,\eta\in\Re$, which may be written as $\eta\Re\partial(\eta)\subseteq\rho$ for all $\eta\in\Re$. However, our hypothesis that $\partial(\Re)\nsubseteq\rho$ and ρ is a prime ideal of $\Re$ forces $\xi\in\rho$, which eventually implies that $\Re=\rho$. This contradicts our basic hypothesis about ρ being a proper ideal of $\Re$. Therefore, we can deduce that $\partial(\Re)\subseteq\rho$. □

If the ring $\Re$ imposed in Theorem 2 is prime, meaning $\rho=\{0\}$, then the following corollary results immediately:

Corollary 4. *Consider a prime ring $\Re$. If $\Re$ admits a generalized reverse derivation ϑ associated with a reverse derivation ∂ such that $\vartheta(\xi)\circ\eta+\vartheta(\xi\circ\eta)=0$ for all ξ and η in $\Re$, then either $\partial(R)=0$ or $\Re$ is commutative of $char(\Re)=2$.*

When we consider $\vartheta=\partial$ in Theorem 2, the following corollary is immediately obtained.

Corollary 5. *Consider a prime ideal ρ of a ring $\Re$. If $\Re$ admits a reverse derivation ∂ such that $\partial(\xi)\circ\eta+\partial(\xi\circ\eta)\in\rho$ for all $\xi,\eta\in\Re$, then either $\partial(\Re)\subseteq\rho$ or $\Re/\rho$ is a commutative integral domain of $char(\Re/\rho)=2$.*

In ref. [20], Rehman et al. established a result stating that if $\Re$ is a ring and ρ is a prime ideal of it, such that $\Re$ admits a generalized derivation ϑ associated with ∂ and meets the condition $\vartheta(\xi)\vartheta(\eta) - [\xi,\eta] \in \rho$ for all $\xi,\eta \in \Re$, then either $\partial(\Re) \subseteq \rho$ or $\Re/\rho$ is a commutative integral domain.

This result prompts us to investigate the properties of the ring $\Re/\rho$ when we replace the assumption that ϑ is a generalized derivation by a generalized reverse derivation associated with a reverse derivation ∂. For this purpose, we introduce the following theorem:

Theorem 3. *Consider ρ as a prime ideal in any ring $\Re$. If $\Re$ admits a generalized reverse derivation ϑ which is associated with a reverse derivation ∂ and satisfies the condition $\vartheta(\xi)\vartheta(\eta) \pm [\xi,\eta] \in \rho$ for all ξ and η in $\Re$, then $\partial(\Re)$ is a subset of ρ and the quotient ring $\Re/\rho$ is a commutative integral domain.*

Proof. The given identity states that

$$\vartheta(\xi)\vartheta(\eta) - [\xi,\eta] \in \rho, \text{ for all } \xi,\eta \in \Re. \tag{10}$$

By replacing η with $\xi\eta$ in (10), we obtain

$$\vartheta(\xi)\vartheta(\eta)\xi + \vartheta(\xi)\eta\partial(\xi) - \xi[\xi,\eta] \in \rho, \text{ for all } \xi,\eta \in \Re. \tag{11}$$

Multiplying (10) by ξ on the right gives

$$\vartheta(\xi)\vartheta(\eta)\xi - [\xi,\eta]\xi \in \rho, \text{ for all } \xi,\eta \in \Re. \tag{12}$$

By comparing Equations (11) and (12), we obtain

$$\vartheta(\xi)\eta\partial(\xi) - \xi[\xi,\eta] + [\xi,\eta]\xi \in \rho, \text{ for all } \xi,\eta \in \Re. \tag{13}$$

Again, by replacing η by $\xi\eta$ in the previous equation, we obtain

$$\vartheta(\xi)\xi\eta\partial(\xi) - \xi^2[\xi,\eta] + \xi[\xi,\eta]\xi \in \rho, \text{ for all } \xi,\eta \in \Re. \tag{14}$$

Multiplying (13) from the left by ξ and comparing it with (14) yield

$$\vartheta(\xi)\xi\eta\partial(\xi) - \xi\vartheta(\xi)\eta\partial(\xi) \in \rho, \text{ for all } \xi,\eta \in \Re.$$

It follows that $[\vartheta(\xi),\xi]\Re\partial(\xi) \subseteq \rho$ for all $\xi \in \Re$. Hence, the primeness of ρ together with Remark 1 forces that either $[\vartheta(\xi),\xi] \in \rho$ for all $\xi \in \Re$ or $\partial(\xi) \in \rho$ for any $\xi \in \Re$. If $[\vartheta(\xi),\xi] \in \rho$ for all $\xi \in \Re$, then, according to Lemma 2, $\Re/\rho$ is a commutative integral domain or $\partial(\Re) \subseteq \rho$.

Let $\Re/\rho$ be a commutative integral domain. Then, (10) can be reduced to $\vartheta(\xi)\Re\vartheta(\eta) \subseteq \rho$ for all $\xi,\eta \in \Re$. That is $\vartheta(\xi) \in \rho$, for all $\xi \in \Re$. Now, we replace ξ by $\eta\xi$ in the previous expression and use it to conclude that $\partial(\Re) \subseteq \rho$. On the other hand, if we assume $\partial(\Re) \subseteq \rho$, then (13) can be simplified to

$$[\xi,[\xi,\eta]] \in \rho, \text{ for all } \xi,\eta \in \Re. \tag{15}$$

By setting $\xi = \xi + \zeta$ in the previous equation and using it, we can easily find $[\xi,[\zeta,\eta]] + [\zeta,[\xi,\eta]] \in \rho$ for all $\xi,\eta,\zeta \in \Re$. Replacing ζ by $\eta\zeta$ in the last relation and using it, we obtain $[\xi,\eta][\zeta,\eta] + [\eta,[\xi,\eta]]\zeta \in \rho$ for all $\xi,\eta,\zeta \in \Re$. By replacing ζ by $\zeta\xi$ in the last expression and using it, we deduce that $[\xi,\eta]\Re[\xi,\eta] \subseteq \rho$ for all $\xi,\eta \in \Re$. The primeness of ρ implies that $[\xi, \eta] \in \rho$ for all $\xi, \eta \in \Re$. Therefore, once again, $\Re/\rho$ is a commutative integral domain, by using Lemma 1.

By applying similar arguments to those shown earlier, with only slight adjustments, the same result can be obtained for the case $\vartheta(\xi)\vartheta(\eta) + [\xi, \eta] \in \rho$, for all ξ and η in $\Re$. □

In Theorem 3, if $\Re$ is assumed to be prime, the following corollary can be immediately obtained.

Corollary 6. *Consider $\Re$ is a prime ring admits a generalized reverse derivation ϑ, which is associated with a nonzero reverse derivation ∂ and satisfies the condition $\vartheta(\xi)\vartheta(\eta) \pm [\xi, \eta] = 0$ for all ξ and η in $\Re$, then the ring $\Re$ a commutative.*

By setting $\vartheta = \partial$ in Theorem 3, we promptly obtain the subsequent corollary.

Corollary 7. *Consider a prime ideal ρ in any ring $\Re$. Suppose that $\Re$ admits a reverse derivation d such that $\partial(\xi)\partial(\eta) \pm [\xi, \eta]$ belongs to ρ for all $\xi, \eta \in \Re$. In this case, $\partial(\Re)$ is a subset of ρ and $\Re/\rho$ is a commutative integral domain.*

Proof. The proof can be directly obtained from Equation (10) in Theorem 3, by setting $\vartheta = \partial$ and following the same arguments and techniques of its proof. □

Theorem 4. *Let ρ be a prime ideal in any ring $\Re$. If $\Re$ admits a generalized reverse derivation ϑ that is associated with a reverse derivation ∂ and satisfies the condition $\vartheta(\xi\eta) \pm \partial(\xi)\vartheta(\eta) \in \rho$ for all $\xi, \eta \in \Re$, then $\vartheta(\Re) \subseteq \rho$.*

Proof. The given assumption states that

$$\vartheta(\xi\eta) + \partial(\xi)\vartheta(\eta) \in \rho \text{ for all } \xi, \eta \in \Re. \tag{16}$$

Replacing η by $\xi\eta$ in (16) gives

$$\vartheta(\xi\eta)\xi + \xi\eta\partial(\xi) + \partial(\xi)\vartheta(\eta)\xi + \partial(\xi)\eta\partial(\xi) \in \rho, \text{ for all } \xi, \eta \in \Re. \tag{17}$$

Multiplying Equation (16) by ξ from the right and comparing it with (17) yield $\partial(\xi)\eta\partial(\xi) + \xi\eta\partial(\xi) \in \rho$ for all $\xi, \eta \in \Re$. That is, $(\partial(\xi) + \xi)\Re\partial(\xi) \subseteq \rho$ for all $\xi \in \Re$. By using the primeness of ρ together with Remark 1, we get either $\partial(\xi) \in \rho$ for all $\xi \in \Re$ or $(\partial(\xi) + \xi) \in \rho$ for all $\xi \in \Re$. If $\partial(\xi) \in \rho$ for all $\xi \in \Re$, (16) can be reduced to $\vartheta(\eta)\xi \in \rho$ for all $\xi, \eta \in \Re$. Hence, we have $\vartheta(\Re) \subseteq \rho$. On the other hand, for

$$\partial(\xi) + \xi \in \rho, \text{ for all } \xi \in \Re, \tag{18}$$

we substitute $\eta\xi$ in the place of ξ in (18) to obtain $\partial(\xi)\eta + \xi\partial(\eta) + \eta\xi \in \rho$ for all $\xi, \eta \in \Re$. Multiplying (18) by η from the right and comparing it with the last relation, we get

$$\xi\partial(\eta) + [\eta, \xi] \in \rho, \text{ for all } \xi, \eta \in \Re. \tag{19}$$

Now, placing $\tau\xi$ instead of ξ in Equation (19), we get

$$\tau\xi\partial(\eta) + \tau[\eta, \xi] + [\eta, \tau]\xi \in \rho, \text{ for all } \xi, \eta, \tau \in \Re. \tag{20}$$

Left-multiplying (19) by τ and comparing it with (20) yields $[\eta, \tau]\xi \in \rho$ for all $\xi, \eta, \tau \in \Re$. Again, replacing τ by $\nu\tau$ in the last equation and using it gives $[\eta, \nu]\Re\xi \subseteq \rho$ for all $\xi, \eta, \nu \in \Re$. Since ρ is a prime ideal, either $\xi \in \rho$ for all $\xi \in \Re$ or $[\eta, \nu] \in \rho$ for all $\eta, \nu \in \Re$. If $\xi \in \rho$ for all $\xi \in \Re$, then it implies that $\rho = \Re$, which contradicts the fact that ρ is a proper ideal. If $[\eta, \nu] \in \rho$ for all $\eta, \nu \in \mathfrak{R}$, then, according to Lemma 1, $\mathfrak{R}/\rho$ is a commutative integral domain. In this case, (19) can be simplified to $\xi\partial(\eta) \in \rho$ for all $\xi, \eta \in \mathfrak{R}$, which is leading to $\partial(\mathfrak{R}) \subseteq \rho$. So, we can conclude, as above, that $\vartheta(\mathfrak{R}) \subseteq \rho$.

By following the exact techniques as described previously, we can prove the same conclusion in the case of the identity $\vartheta(\xi\eta) - \partial(\xi)\vartheta(\eta) \in \rho$ for all $\xi, \eta \in \mathfrak{R}$. □

By equating ϑ to ∂ in the prior theorem, we can obtain the following conclusion as a similar version of ([16], Theorem 4(1)).

Corollary 8. *Let ρ be a prime ideal in any ring $\mathfrak{R}$. If $\mathfrak{R}$ admits a reverse derivation ∂ such that $\partial(\xi\eta) \pm \partial(\xi)\partial(\eta) \in \rho$ for all $\xi, \eta \in \mathfrak{R}$, then $\partial(\mathfrak{R}) \subseteq \rho$.*

Corollary 9. *Let $\mathfrak{R}$ be a prime ring that admits a generalized reverse derivation ϑ that is associated with a reverse derivation ∂ and satisfies the condition $\vartheta(\xi\eta) \pm \partial(\xi)\vartheta(\eta) = 0$ for all $\xi, \eta \in \mathfrak{R}$, then $\vartheta(\mathfrak{R}) = 0$.*

Theorem 5. *Consider ρ as a prime ideal in any ring $\mathfrak{R}$. If $\mathfrak{R}$ admits a generalized reverse derivation ϑ, which is associated with a reverse derivation ∂, and satisfies the condition $\vartheta(\xi\eta) \pm \partial(\eta)\vartheta(\xi) \in \rho$ for all $\xi, \eta \in \mathfrak{R}$, then $\vartheta(\mathfrak{R}) \subseteq \rho$.*

Proof. The given assumption states that

$$\vartheta(\xi\eta) - \partial(\eta)\vartheta(\xi) \in \rho, \text{ for all } \xi, \eta \in \mathfrak{R}. \tag{21}$$

We replace ξ by $\tau\xi$ in (21) and use it to obtain

$$\xi\eta\partial(\tau) - \partial(\eta)\xi\partial(\tau) \in \rho, \text{ for all } \xi, \eta, \tau \in \mathfrak{R}. \tag{22}$$

If we replace ξ by $\nu\xi$ in the previous equation, we obtain $\nu\xi\eta\partial(\tau) - \partial(\eta)\nu\xi\partial(\tau) \in \rho$ for all $\xi, \eta, \tau, \nu \in \mathfrak{R}$. By left multiplying Equation (22) by ν and comparing it with the last equation, we find $\nu\partial(\eta)\xi\partial(\tau) - \partial(\eta)\nu\xi\partial(\tau) \in \rho$ for all $\xi, \eta, \tau, \nu \in \mathfrak{R}$. This implies that $[\nu, \partial(\eta)]\xi\partial(\tau) \in \rho$ for all $\xi, \eta, \tau, \nu \in \mathfrak{R}$. In other words, $[\nu, \partial(\eta)]\mathfrak{R}\partial(\tau) \subseteq \rho$ for all $\eta, \tau, \nu \in \mathfrak{R}$. Using the primeness of ρ together with Remark 1 yield either $[\nu, \partial(\eta)] \in \rho$ for all $\eta, \nu \in \mathfrak{R}$ or $\partial(\mathfrak{R}) \subseteq \rho$. In the second case, (21), becomes $\vartheta(\eta)\xi \in \rho$ for all $\xi, \eta \in \mathfrak{R}$ and therefore, $\vartheta(\mathfrak{R}) \subseteq \rho$. For the case of $[\nu, \partial(\eta)] \in \rho$ for all $\eta, \nu \in \mathfrak{R}$, we have, in particular, that $[\eta, \partial(\eta)] \in \rho$ for all $\eta \in \mathfrak{R}$. We use Corollary 1 to obtain that either $\mathfrak{R}/\rho$ is a commutative integral domain or $\partial(\mathfrak{R}) \subseteq \rho$. If $\mathfrak{R}/\rho$ is a commutative integral domain, then (22) can be rewritten as $(\eta - \partial(\eta))\xi\partial(\tau) \in \rho$ for all $\xi, \eta, \tau \in \mathfrak{R}$. That is, $(\eta - \partial(\eta))\mathfrak{R}\partial(\tau) \subseteq \rho$ for all $\eta, \tau \in \mathfrak{R}$. Again, using the primeness of ρ together with Remark 1 give that either $(\eta - \partial(\eta)) \in \rho$ for all $\eta \in \mathfrak{R}$ or $\partial(\mathfrak{R}) \subseteq \rho$. When $(\eta - \partial(\eta)) \in \rho$ for all $\eta \in \mathfrak{R}$, we replace η by $\xi\eta$ in the last relation and use it to get $[\xi, \eta] - \eta\partial(\xi) \in \rho$ for all $\xi, \eta \in \mathfrak{R}$. For the other case, the commutativity of $\mathfrak{R}/\rho$ leads to $\eta\partial(\xi) \in \rho$ for all $\xi, \eta \in \mathfrak{R}$, and hence, $\partial(\mathfrak{R}) \subseteq \rho$. Thus, (21) becomes $\vartheta(\eta)\xi \in \rho$ for all $\xi, \eta \in \mathfrak{R}$. Therefore, $\vartheta(\mathfrak{R}) \subseteq \rho$.

By following the exact techniques as described previously, we can prove the same conclusion for the case of the identity $\vartheta(\xi\eta) + \partial(\eta)\vartheta(\xi) \in \rho$ for all $\xi, \eta \in \mathfrak{R}$. □

Corollary 10. *Consider $\mathfrak{R}$ is a prime ring that admits a generalized reverse derivation ϑ associated with a reverse derivation ∂ and satisfies the condition $\vartheta(\xi\eta) \pm \partial(\eta)\vartheta(\xi) = 0$ for all $\xi, \eta \in \mathfrak{R}$, then $\vartheta(\mathfrak{R}) = 0$.*

Corollary 11. *Consider ρ as a prime ideal in any ring $\mathfrak{R}$. If $\mathfrak{R}$ admits a reverse derivation ∂ and satisfies the condition $\partial(\xi\eta) \pm \partial(\eta)\partial(\xi) \in \rho$ for all $\xi, \eta \in \mathfrak{R}$, then $\partial(\mathfrak{R}) \subseteq \rho$.*

In [20] (Theorem 1.5(iii)), Rehman et al. showed that the quotient ring $\mathfrak{R}/\rho$ is a commutative integral domain, where ρ is a prime ideal of $\mathfrak{R}$, if $\mathfrak{R}$ admits a generalized derivation ϑ associated with a derivation ∂ that satisfies $\vartheta(\xi)\vartheta(\eta) \pm \xi\eta \in \rho$, for every $\xi, \eta \in \mathfrak{R}$.

The following theorem aims to generalize the above identity to $\vartheta(\xi)\vartheta(\eta) + \partial(\xi)\partial(\eta) \in \rho$ for every $\xi, \eta \in \mathfrak{R}$ and prove that $\vartheta(\mathfrak{R})$ is a subset of ρ when $char(\mathfrak{R}/\rho) \neq 2$ and the imposed ϑ is a generalized reverse derivation associated with a reverse derivation ∂.

Theorem 6. *Consider a prime ideal ρ in a ring $\mathfrak{R}$ with a characteristic not equal to 2. If $\mathfrak{R}$ admits a generalized reverse derivation ϑ that is associated with a reverse derivation ∂, and if $\vartheta(\xi)\vartheta(\eta) + \partial(\xi)\partial(\eta) \in \rho$ for all ξ and η in $\mathfrak{R}$, then $\vartheta(\mathfrak{R})$ is a subset of ρ.*

Proof. The given hypothesis states that

$$\vartheta(\xi)\vartheta(\eta) + \partial(\xi)\partial(\eta) \in \rho, \text{ for all } \xi, \eta \in \mathfrak{R}. \tag{23}$$

By replacing η with $\tau\eta$ in (23), we obtain

$$\vartheta(\xi)\vartheta(\eta)\tau + \vartheta(\xi)\eta\partial(\tau) + \partial(\xi)\partial(\eta)\tau + \partial(\xi)\eta\partial(\tau) \in \rho, \text{ for all } \xi, \eta, \tau \in \mathfrak{R}. \tag{24}$$

Now, by multiplying Equation (23) by τ from the right and comparing it with (24), we obtain

$$(\vartheta(\xi) + \partial(\xi))\eta\partial(\tau) \in \rho, \text{ for all } \xi, \eta, \tau \in \mathfrak{R}. \tag{25}$$

That is, $(\vartheta(\xi) + \partial(\xi))\mathfrak{R}\partial(\tau) \subseteq \rho$. Hence, the condition of ρ being prime, together with Remark (1), forces either $\vartheta(\xi) + \partial(\xi) \in \rho$ for all $\xi \in \mathfrak{R}$ or $\partial(\tau) \in \tau$ for all $\tau \in \mathfrak{R}$. Let us consider the first case and replace ξ with $\eta\xi$. This yields $\vartheta(\xi)\eta + \xi\partial(\eta) + \partial(\xi)\eta + \xi\partial(\eta) \in \rho$ for all $\xi, \eta \in \mathfrak{R}$. By multiplying the first equation by η from the right and comparing it with the second equation, we obtain $\xi\partial(\eta) + \xi\partial(\eta) \in \rho$ for all $\xi, \eta \in \mathfrak{R}$, which in turn means that $2\xi\partial(\eta) \in \rho$ for every $\xi, \eta \in \mathfrak{R}$. The basic assumption $char(\mathfrak{R}/\rho) \neq 2$ leads to $\xi\partial(\eta) \in \rho$ for every $\xi, \eta \in \mathfrak{R}$. That is, $\mathfrak{R}\partial(\eta) \subseteq \rho$. As $\rho \neq \mathfrak{R}$ and ρ is prime, we get $\partial(\eta) \in \rho$ for any $\eta \in \mathfrak{R}$. Thus, we deduce that $\partial(\mathfrak{R}) \subseteq \rho$. In the second case, we observe that $\partial(\tau)$ belongs to ρ for every $\tau \in \mathfrak{R}$, indicating that $\partial(\mathfrak{R}) \subseteq \rho$. So both cases lead to $\partial(\mathfrak{R}) \subseteq \rho$, which reduces (23) to $\vartheta(\xi)\vartheta(\eta) \in \rho$ for all $\xi, \eta \in \mathfrak{R}$. Replacing ξ by $\xi\tau$ in the last relation, we get $\vartheta(\tau)\mathfrak{R}\vartheta(\eta) \subseteq \rho$ for all $\tau, \eta \in \mathfrak{R}$. Therefore, we have $\vartheta(\mathfrak{R}) \subseteq \rho$ for both cases as required. □

As an immediate consequent of the above theorem, we have the following corollary when the imposed ring $\mathfrak{R}$ is prime.

Corollary 12. *Consider a prime ring $\mathfrak{R}$ with a characteristic that is not equal to 2. If $\mathfrak{R}$ admits a generalized reverse derivation ϑ associated with a reverse derivation ∂, satisfying the equation $\vartheta(\xi)\vartheta(\eta) + \partial(\xi)\partial(\eta) = 0$ for all ξ and η in $\mathfrak{R}$, then ϑ turns out to be zero.*

Next, we will explore some counterexamples that illustrate the necessity of assuming that ρ is prime in the hypotheses of our theorems.

Example 1. *Consider the ring of integers $\mathbb{Z}$ and let* $\Re = \{\begin{pmatrix} 0 & \alpha & \beta & \gamma \\ 0 & 0 & 0 & \beta \\ 0 & 0 & 0 & -\alpha \\ 0 & 0 & 0 & 0 \end{pmatrix} \mid \alpha, \beta, \gamma \in \mathbb{Z}\}$, $\rho = \{\begin{pmatrix} 0 & 0 & 0 & 2\gamma \\ 0 & 0 & 0 & 0 \\ 0 & 0 & 0 & 0 \\ 0 & 0 & 0 & 0 \end{pmatrix}\}$. *Define* $\vartheta, \partial : \Re \longrightarrow \Re$, *by* $\vartheta\begin{pmatrix} 0 & \alpha & \beta & \gamma \\ 0 & 0 & 0 & \beta \\ 0 & 0 & 0 & -\alpha \\ 0 & 0 & 0 & 0 \end{pmatrix} = \begin{pmatrix} 0 & 0 & 0 & -\gamma \\ 0 & 0 & 0 & 0 \\ 0 & 0 & 0 & 0 \\ 0 & 0 & 0 & 0 \end{pmatrix}$ *and* $\partial\begin{pmatrix} 0 & \alpha & \beta & \gamma \\ 0 & 0 & 0 & \beta \\ 0 & 0 & 0 & -\alpha \\ 0 & 0 & 0 & 0 \end{pmatrix} = \begin{pmatrix} 0 & 0 & 0 & -\gamma \\ 0 & 0 & 0 & \beta \\ 0 & 0 & 0 & -\alpha \\ 0 & 0 & 0 & 0 \end{pmatrix}$. *Thus, it is evident that $\Re$ is a ring, ρ is an ideal of $\Re$, and ϑ is a generalized reverse derivation associated with the reverse derivation ∂ that satisfies $\vartheta(\xi) \circ \eta \pm \vartheta(\xi \circ \eta) \in \rho$, $\vartheta(\xi)\vartheta(\eta) \pm [\xi, \eta] \in \rho$, and $\vartheta(\xi)\vartheta(\eta) + \partial(\xi)\partial(\eta) \in \rho$ for all $\xi, \eta \in \rho$. However, $\Re/\rho$ is non-commutative, $\partial(\Re) \nsubseteq \rho$, and $\vartheta(\Re) \nsubseteq \rho$. Moreover, ρ is not a prime ideal of $\Re$ since* $\begin{pmatrix} 0 & 0 & 0 & 0 \\ 0 & 0 & 0 & \beta \\ 0 & 0 & 0 & \alpha \\ 0 & 0 & 0 & 0 \end{pmatrix}\begin{pmatrix} 0 & 0 & \alpha & 0 \\ 0 & 0 & 0 & 0 \\ 0 & 0 & 0 & \alpha \\ 0 & 0 & 0 & 0 \end{pmatrix} \in \rho$, *but neither* $\begin{pmatrix} 0 & 0 & 0 & 0 \\ 0 & 0 & 0 & \beta \\ 0 & 0 & 0 & \alpha \\ 0 & 0 & 0 & 0 \end{pmatrix} \in \rho$ *nor* $\begin{pmatrix} 0 & 0 & \alpha & 0 \\ 0 & 0 & 0 & 0 \\ 0 & 0 & 0 & \alpha \\ 0 & 0 & 0 & 0 \end{pmatrix} \in \rho$; *hence, ρ is not prime ideal of $\Re$. Therefore, the assumption that ρ is prime in Theorems 1–3 and 6 cannot be omitted.*

Example 2. *Let $\Re = \{p\xi e_{12} + \eta e_{13} + \tau e_{23} \mid \xi, \eta, \tau \in \mathbb{C}, p$ is a prime number$\}$, where $\mathbb{C}$ is the complex number ring. Let $\rho = \{p\eta e_{13}\}$. Define $\vartheta, \partial : \Re \longrightarrow \Re$ as follows:*

$$\vartheta(p\xi e_{12} + \eta e_{13} + \tau e_{23}) = p\tau e_{23}, \qquad \text{with} \qquad \partial(p\xi e_{12} + \eta e_{13} + \tau e_{23}) = \xi e_{13}.$$

Thus, it is evident that $\Re$ is a ring, ρ is an ideal of $\Re$, and ϑ is a generalized reverse derivation associated with the reverse derivation ∂ that satisfies $\vartheta(\xi) \circ \eta \pm \vartheta(\xi \circ \eta) \in \rho$, $\vartheta(\xi)\vartheta(\eta) \pm [\xi, \eta] \in \rho$, $\vartheta(\xi\eta) \pm \partial(\xi)\partial(\eta) \in \rho$, $\vartheta(\xi\eta) \pm \partial(\eta)\partial(\xi) \in \rho$, and $\vartheta(\xi)\vartheta(\eta) + \partial(\xi)\partial(\eta) \in \rho$ for all $\xi, \eta \in \Re$. However, $\Re/\rho$ is non-commutative and $\partial(\Re) \nsubseteq \rho$. Moreover, ρ is not a prime ideal of $\Re$ since $\eta e_{31}\Re(\xi e_{31} + \eta e_{23}) \in \rho$, but $\eta e_{31} \notin \rho$ and $\xi e_{31} + \eta e_{23} \notin \rho$. Therefore, assumption that ρ is prime in Theorems 1–6 cannot be omitted.

Example 3. *Consider the ring of integers $\mathbb{Z}$ and let* $\Re = \{\begin{pmatrix} 0 & 0 & 0 \\ \alpha & 0 & 0 \\ \beta & 2\gamma & 0 \end{pmatrix} | \alpha, \beta, \gamma \in \mathbb{Z}\}$, $\rho = \{\begin{pmatrix} 0 & 0 & 0 \\ 0 & 0 & 0 \\ 2\beta & 0 & 0 \end{pmatrix} | \beta \in \mathbb{Z}\}$. *Define* $\vartheta, \partial : \Re \longrightarrow \Re$ *by* $\vartheta\begin{pmatrix} 0 & 0 & 0 \\ \alpha & 0 & 0 \\ \beta & 2\gamma & 0 \end{pmatrix} = \begin{pmatrix} 0 & 0 & 0 \\ 2\alpha & 0 & 0 \\ 0 & 0 & 0 \end{pmatrix}$, $\partial\begin{pmatrix} 0 & 0 & 0 \\ \alpha & 0 & 0 \\ \beta & 2\gamma & 0 \end{pmatrix} = \begin{pmatrix} 0 & 0 & 0 \\ 0 & 0 & 0 \\ \gamma & 0 & 0 \end{pmatrix}$. *Thus, it is evident that $\Re$ is a ring, ρ is an ideal of $\Re$, and ϑ is a generalized reverse derivation associated with the reverse derivation ∂ that satisfies the following identities for all $\xi, \eta, \tau \in \Re$: $\vartheta(\xi) \circ \eta - \vartheta(\xi \circ \eta) \in \rho$, $\vartheta(\xi) \circ \eta + \vartheta(\xi \circ \eta) \in \rho$, $\vartheta(\xi)\vartheta(\eta) \pm [\xi, \eta] \in \rho$, $\vartheta(\xi)\vartheta(\eta) + \partial(\xi)\partial(\eta) \in \rho$ for all* $\begin{pmatrix} 0 & 0 & 0 \\ \alpha & 0 & 0 \\ \beta & 2\gamma & 0 \end{pmatrix} \in \Re$. *However, $\Re/\rho$ is non-commutative and*

$\partial(\Re) \nsubseteq \rho$. *Moreover, ρ is not a prime ideal of $\Re$ since* $\begin{pmatrix} 0 & 0 & 0 \\ \alpha & 0 & 0 \\ 0 & 0 & 0 \end{pmatrix}\begin{pmatrix} 0 & 0 & 0 \\ 0 & 0 & 0 \\ 0 & 2\gamma & 0 \end{pmatrix} \in \rho$, *but* $\begin{pmatrix} 0 & 0 & 0 \\ \alpha & 0 & 0 \\ 0 & 0 & 0 \end{pmatrix} \notin \rho$ *and* $\begin{pmatrix} 0 & 0 & 0 \\ 0 & 0 & 0 \\ 0 & 2\gamma & 0 \end{pmatrix} \notin \rho$. *Therefore, the assumption that ρ is prime in Theorems 1–3 and 6 cannot be omitted.*

Example 4. *In Example 3, one can note that $\vartheta(\xi\eta) \pm \partial(\xi)\partial(\eta) \in \rho$ and $\vartheta(\xi\eta) \pm \partial(\eta)\partial(\xi) \in \rho$ hold for all $\xi, \iota \in \Re$ though $\vartheta(\Re) \nsubseteq \rho$. This emphasizes the necessity of primeness of ρ.*

4. Conclusions

In the current article, we continued the study of generalized reverse derivation associated with reverse derivation via a contemporary approach wherein we assume that ring $\Re$ has no restrictions and the studied identities are contained in prime ideal ρ. We have reached the following results: associated derivation maps a ring $\Re$ to ρ, or a quotient ring of $\Re$ by prime ideal ρ becomes a commutative integral domain, or the generalized reverse derivation mapping the ring to the chosen prime ideal ρ as proven in this article. We conclude with two examples clarifying the necessity of the considered assumption hypotheses.

In future studies of our current topic, the behavior of a quotient ring $\Re/\rho$ can be explored by replacing the generalized reverse derivation with any of the following mappings: a generalized (α, β)-derivation where α and β are automorphisms on $\Re$, or a multiplicative reverse derivation, or a generalized P-reverse derivation, or a generalized reverse homoderivation.

Author Contributions: This paper is the result of the joint effort of N.L.A., M.A.-S., R.M.A.-o. and Z.Z.A.-A. All authors have read and agreed to the published version of the manuscript.

Funding: The authors extend their appreciation to the Deanship of Scientific Research (DSR) at Northern Border University, Arar, KSA for funding this research work through the project number NBU-FPEJ-2025-2089-02.

Data Availability Statement: All of the data required for this article are included within this article.

Conflicts of Interest: The authors declare there are no conflicts of interest.

References

1. Al-omary, R.M.; Nauman, S.K. Generalized derivations on prime rings satisfying certain identities. *Commun. Korean Math. Soc.* **2021**, *36*, 229–238.
2. Herstein, I.N.N. Jordan derivations of prime rings. *Proc. Am. Math. Soc.* **1957**, *8*, 1104–1110. [CrossRef]
3. Filippov, V.T. On δ-derivations of Lie algebras. *Sib. Math. J.* **1998**, *39*, 1218–1230. [CrossRef]
4. Hopkins, N.C. Generalized derivations of nonassociative algebras. *Nova. J. Math. Game Theory Algebra.* **1996**, *5*, 215–224.
5. Kaygorodov, I. On (reverse) $(\alpha, \beta, \gamma)-$derivations of associative algebras. *Boll. dell'Unione Mat. Ital.* **2015**, *8*, 181–187. [CrossRef]
6. Samman, M.S.; Alyamani, N. Derivations and reverse derivations in semiprime rings. *Int. Math. Forum* **2007**, *2*, 1895–1902. [CrossRef]
7. Aboubakr, A.; Gonzalez, S. Generalized reverse derivations on semiprime rings. *Sib. Math. J.* **2015**, *56*, 199–205. [CrossRef]
8. Huang, S. Generalized reverse derivations and commutativity of prime rings. *Commun. Math.* **2019**, *27*, 43–50. [CrossRef]
9. Al-omary, R.M. Commutativity of prime ring with generalized $(\alpha, \beta)-$reverse derivations satisfing certain identities. *Bull. Transilv. Univ. Bras. III Math. Comput. Sci.* **2022**, *2*, 1–12.
10. Ibraheem, A.M. Right ideals and generalized reverse derivations on prime rings. *Am. J. Comput. Appl. Math.* **2016**, *6*, 162–164.
11. Bulak, T.; Ayran, A.; Aydın, N. Generalized reverse derivations on prime and semiprime rings. *Int. J. Open Probl. Compt. Math.* **2021**, *14*, 50–60.
12. Ayat, Ö.; Aydin, N.; AlBayrak, B. Generalized reverse derivation on closed Lie ideals. *J. Sci. Perspect.* **2018**, *2*, 61–74. [CrossRef]

13. Alsowait, N.; Al-omary, R.M.; Al-Amery, Z.; Al-Shomrani, M. Exploring commutativity via generalized (α, β)-derivations involving prime ideals. *Mathematics* **2024**, *12*, 2325. [CrossRef]
14. Bouchannafa, K.; Abdallah Idrissi, M.; Oukhtite, L. Relationship between the structure of a quotient ring and the behavior of certain additive mapping. *Commun. Korean Math. Soc.* **2022**, *37*, 359–370.
15. Mamouni, A.; Oukhtite, L.; Zerra, M. Some results on derivations and generalized derivations in rings. *Mathmatica* **2013**, *65*, 94–104. [CrossRef]
16. Mamouni, A.; Oukhtite, L.; Zerra, M. On derivations involving prime ideals and commutativity in rings. *São Paulo J. Math. Sci.* **2020**, *14*, 675–688. [CrossRef]
17. Mir, H.E.; Mamouni, A.; Oukhtite, L. Commutativity with algebraic identities involving prime ideals. *Commu. Korean Math. Soc.* **2020**, *35*, 723–731.
18. Rehman, N.; Alnoghashi, N.; Boua, A. Identities in a prime ideal of a ring involving generalized derivations. *Kyungpook Math. J.* **2021**, *61*, 727–735.
19. Rehman, N.; Alnoghashi, N.; Honagn, M. On generalized derivations involving prime ideals with involution. *Ukr. Math. J.* **2024**, *75*, 1219–1241. [CrossRef]
20. Rehman, N.; Al Noghashi, H. Action of prime ideals on generalized derivations-I. *arXiv* **2021**, arXiv:2107.06769.
21. Faraj, A.K.; Abduldaim, A.M. Commutativity and prime ideals with proposed algebraic identities. *Int. J. Math. Comput. Sci.* **2021**, *16*, 1607–1622.

Disclaimer/Publisher's Note: The statements, opinions and data contained in all publications are solely those of the individual author(s) and contributor(s) and not of MDPI and/or the editor(s). MDPI and/or the editor(s) disclaim responsibility for any injury to people or property resulting from any ideas, methods, instructions or products referred to in the content.

mathematics MDPI

Article

Lie Ideals and Homoderivations in Semiprime Rings

Ali Yahya Hummdi [1,†], Zeliha Bedir [2,†], Emine Koç Sögütcü [2,†], Öznur Gölbaşı [2,†] and Nadeem ur Rehman [3,*,†]

1 Department of Mathematics, College of Science, King Khalid University, Abha 61471, Saudi Arabia; ahmdy@kku.edu.sa
2 Department of Mathematics, Faculty of Science, Sivas Cumhuriyet University, Sivas 58140, Turkey; zelihabedir@cumhuriyet.edu.tr (Z.B.); eminekoc@cumhuriyet.edu.tr (E.K.S.); ogolbasi@cumhuriyet.edu.tr (Ö.G.)
3 Department of Mathematics, Aligarh Muslim University, Aligarh 202002, India
* Correspondence: nu.rehman.mm@amu.ac.in
† All authors contributed equally to this work.

Abstract: Let S be a 2-torsion free semiprime ring and U be a noncentral square-closed Lie ideal of S. An additive mapping $\hbar$ on S is defined as a homoderivation if $\hbar(ab) = \hbar(a)\hbar(b) + \hbar(a)b + a\hbar(a)$ for all $a, b \in S$. In the present paper, we shall prove that $\hbar$ is a commuting map on U if any one of the following holds: *(i)* $\hbar(\tilde{a}_1\tilde{a}_2) + \tilde{a}_1\tilde{a}_2 \in Z$, *(ii)* $\hbar(\tilde{a}_1\tilde{a}_2) - \tilde{a}_1\tilde{a}_2 \in Z$, *(iii)* $\hbar(\tilde{a}_1 \circ \tilde{a}_2) = 0$, *(iv)* $\hbar(\tilde{a}_1 \circ \tilde{a}_2) = [\tilde{a}_1, \tilde{a}_2]$, *(v)* $\hbar([\tilde{a}_1, \tilde{a}_2]) = 0$, *(vi)* $\hbar([\tilde{a}_1, \tilde{a}_2]) = (\tilde{a}_1 \circ \tilde{a}_2)$, *(vii)* $\tilde{a}_1\hbar(\tilde{a}_2) \pm \tilde{a}_1\tilde{a}_2 \in Z$, *(viii)* $\tilde{a}_1\hbar(\tilde{a}_2) \pm \tilde{a}_2\tilde{a}_1 = 0$, *(ix)* $\tilde{a}_1\hbar(\tilde{a}_2) \pm \tilde{a}_1 \circ \tilde{a}_2 = 0$, *(x)* $[\hbar(\tilde{a}_1), \tilde{a}_2] \pm \tilde{a}_1\tilde{a}_2 = 0$, *(xi)* $[\hbar(\tilde{a}_1), \tilde{a}_2] \pm \tilde{a}_2\tilde{a}_1 = 0$, for all $\tilde{a}_1, \tilde{a}_2 \in U$, where $\hbar$ is a homoderivation on S.

Keywords: semiprime ring; Lie ideal; derivation; homoderivation; commutativity

MSC: 16W25; 16N60; 16U80

1. Introduction

The symbol S used throughout this article denotes a ring with center Z. A ring S is called prime if $IJ \neq 0$ for any two nonzero ideals $I, J \subseteq S$, and semiprime if it contains no nonzero ideals whose square is zero. A proper ideal P of S is said to be prime if for any $\tilde{a}_1, \tilde{a}_2 \in S, \tilde{a}_1 S \tilde{a}_2 \subseteq P$ implies that $\tilde{a}_1 \in P$ or $\tilde{a}_2 \in P$. In other words, the ring S is prime ring if and only if (0) is a prime ideal of S, or equivalently, a ring S is prime if for $\tilde{a}_1, \tilde{a}_2 \in S$, $\tilde{a}_1 S \tilde{a}_2 = (0)$ implies either $\tilde{a}_1 = 0$ or $\tilde{a}_2 = 0$. Recall that a proper ideal P of S is said to be semiprime if for any $\tilde{a}_1 \in S, \tilde{a}_1 S \tilde{a}_1 \subseteq P$ implies that $\tilde{a}_1 \in P$ and the ring S is a semiprime ring if $P = (0)$ is a semiprime ideal of S. Every prime ideal is a semiprime ideal but the converse is not true in general. An additive subgroup U of S is called a Lie ideal of S if $[\tilde{a}_1, r] \in U$, for all $\tilde{a}_1 \in U, r \in S$. U is called a square-closed Lie ideal of S if U is a Lie ideal and $\tilde{a}_1^2 \in U$ for all $\tilde{a}_1 \in U$. If U is a square-closed Lie ideal of S, then we have $(\tilde{a}_1 + \tilde{a}_2)^2 \in U$ and so $(\tilde{a}_1 + \tilde{a}_2)^2 - \tilde{a}_1^2 - \tilde{a}_2^2 = \tilde{a}_1\tilde{a}_2 + \tilde{a}_2\tilde{a}_1 \in U$ for all $\tilde{a}_1, \tilde{a}_2 \in U$. Hence, we find $2\tilde{a}_1\tilde{a}_2 \in U$, for all $\tilde{a}_1, \tilde{a}_2 \in U$.

An additive mapping $d : S \to S$ is called a derivation if $d(\tilde{a}_1\tilde{a}_2) = d(\tilde{a}_1)\tilde{a}_2 + \tilde{a}_1 d(\tilde{a}_2)$ holds for all $\tilde{a}_1, \tilde{a}_2 \in S$. Research on the subject of derivations in prime rings was initiated by E. C. Posner [1]. Regarding commuting mappings, Posner's theorem, as discussed in this paper, is a crucial finding in the investigation of these mappings. It states that a prime ring possessing a nonzero commuting d mapping must be commutative. This theorem marks an important initial outcome in the study of commuting mappings. Afterwards, many researchers studied commutativity theorems for prime or semiprime rings admitting automorphisms or derivations on suitable subsets. A mapping $f : S \to S$ is called centralizing if $[f(\tilde{a}_1), \tilde{a}_1] \in Z(S)$ holds for all $\tilde{a}_1 \in S$; in the special case where $[f(\tilde{a}_1), \tilde{a}_1] = 0$ holds for all $\tilde{a}_1 \in S$, the mapping f is said to be commuting. In 2000, El Soufi [2] defined a homoderivation on S as an additive mapping $\hbar : S \to S$ satisfying $\hbar(\tilde{a}_1\tilde{a}_2) = \hbar(\tilde{a}_1)\hbar(\tilde{a}_2) + \hbar(\tilde{a}_1)\tilde{a}_2 + \tilde{a}_1\hbar(\tilde{a}_2)$ for all $\tilde{a}_1, \tilde{a}_2 \in S$. An example of such mapping is to let $\hbar(\tilde{a}_1) = f(\tilde{a}_1) - \tilde{a}_1$, for all $\tilde{a}_1, \tilde{a}_2 \in S$ where f is an endomorphism on S. It is clear that a homoderivation $\hbar$ is also a derivation if $\hbar(\tilde{a}_1)\hbar(\tilde{a}_2) = 0$ for all $\tilde{a}_1, \tilde{a}_2 \in S$. In this case, $\hbar(\tilde{a}_1)S\hbar(\tilde{a}_2) = 0$ for all $\tilde{a}_1, \tilde{a}_2 \in S$. Therefore, if S is a prime ring, then the only additive mapping which is both a derivation and a homoderivation is the zero mapping. Another example of homoderivations is when the additive mapping $\hbar : S \to S$ defined by $\hbar(x) = -x$ is a homoderivation of S.

In Daif and Bell, Let S be semiprime ring, d is nonzero derivation of S and I is nonzero ideal of S. S contains a nonzero central ideal if one of the following conditions is provide; (i) $d([\tilde{a}_1, \tilde{a}_2]) = [\tilde{a}_1, \tilde{a}_2]$ (ii) $d([\tilde{a}_1, \tilde{a}_2]) = -[\tilde{a}_1, \tilde{a}_2]$ for all $\tilde{a}_1, \tilde{a}_2 \in I$ has been proven in [3]. In [4], Quadri, Khan, and Rehman examined the following conditions for generalized derivation: (i) $f([\tilde{a}_1, \tilde{a}_2]) = [\tilde{a}_1, \tilde{a}_2]$, (ii) $f([\tilde{a}_1, \tilde{a}_2]) = -[\tilde{a}_1, \tilde{a}_2]$, (iii) $f(\tilde{a}_1 o \tilde{a}_2) = \tilde{a}_1 o \tilde{a}_2$, (iv) $f(\tilde{a}_1 o \tilde{a}_2) = -(\tilde{a}_1 o \tilde{a}_2)$. The conditions discussed above by various authors have been studied by many authors in recent years for different structures and derivation. For more details, see the references [5–9].

In [2], El Soufi also proved the commutativity of prime rings, admitting a homoderivation $\hbar$ that satisfies the condition $\hbar([\tilde{a}_1, \tilde{a}_2]) = \pm[\tilde{a}_1, \tilde{a}_2]$ for all $\tilde{a}_1, \tilde{a}_2 \in I$, with a nonzero two-sided ideal of S. Following this line of investigation, several authors studied homoderivations acting on appropriate subsets of the prime ring and semiprime rings. In [10], Asmaa Melaibari et al. studied the commutativity of rings admitting a homoderivation $\hbar$ such that $\hbar([\tilde{a}_1, \tilde{a}_2]) = 0$ for all $\tilde{a}_1, \tilde{a}_2 \in U$, where U is a nonzero ideal of S.

On the other hand, Ashraf and Rehman showed that if S is a prime ring with a nonzero ideal U of S and d is a derivation of S such that $d(\tilde{a}_1\tilde{a}_2) \pm \tilde{a}_1\tilde{a}_2 \in Z$, $d(\tilde{a}_1\tilde{a}_2) \pm \tilde{a}_2\tilde{a}_1 \in Z$, for all $\tilde{a}_1, \tilde{a}_2 \in U$, then R is commutative in [11]. Alharfie and Muthana proved similar results regarding homoderivations in [12].

In light of all these results, our aim in this article is to explore a more general context of differential identities involving a Lie ideal of the semiprime ring with homoderivation. Some conditions about commutativity on Lie ideals of prime rings with homoderivation were proved in [13]. Futhermore, in Section 4 of the paper [14], it was shown that the study of differential identities on algebras plays a crucial role. This approach provides us with the opportunity to generalize the results obtained earlier.

2. Results

The symbol S throughout this article will denote a $2-$torsion free semiprime ring. In addition, U will symbolize a noncentral square-closed Lie ideal of S and $\hbar$ will symbolize a homoderivation of S. In addition, for any $\tilde{a}_1, \tilde{a}_2 \in S$, $[\tilde{a}_1, \tilde{a}_2] = \tilde{a}_1\tilde{a}_2 - \tilde{a}_2\tilde{a}_1$ and $\tilde{a}_1 o \tilde{a}_2 = \tilde{a}_1\tilde{a}_2 + \tilde{a}_2\tilde{a}_1$ will denote the well-known Lie and Jordan product, respectively.

We will make use of the following fundamental identities that apply to every $\tilde{a}_1, \tilde{a}_2, \tilde{a}_3 \in S$ without explicitly mentioning them:

$$\begin{aligned}
[\tilde{a}_1, \tilde{a}_2\tilde{a}_3] &= \tilde{a}_2[\tilde{a}_1, \tilde{a}_3] + [\tilde{a}_1, \tilde{a}_2]\tilde{a}_3 \\
[\tilde{a}_1\tilde{a}_2, \tilde{a}_3] &= [\tilde{a}_1, \tilde{a}_3]\tilde{a}_2 + \tilde{a}_1[\tilde{a}_2, \tilde{a}_3] \\
\tilde{a}_1 o(\tilde{a}_2\tilde{a}_3) &= (\tilde{a}_1 o \tilde{a}_2)\tilde{a}_3 - \tilde{a}_2[\tilde{a}_1, \tilde{a}_3] = \tilde{a}_2(\tilde{a}_1 o \tilde{a}_3) + [\tilde{a}_1, \tilde{a}_2]\tilde{a}_3 \\
(\tilde{a}_1\tilde{a}_2) o \tilde{a}_3 &= \tilde{a}_1(\tilde{a}_2 o \tilde{a}_3) - [\tilde{a}_1, \tilde{a}_3]\tilde{a}_2 = (\tilde{a}_1 o \tilde{a}_3)\tilde{a}_2 + \tilde{a}_1[\tilde{a}_2, \tilde{a}_3].
\end{aligned}$$

Remark 1. *For all $\tilde{a}_1, \tilde{a}_2 \in S$, we obtain*

$$\begin{aligned} \hbar([\tilde{a}_1, \tilde{a}_2]) &= \hbar(\tilde{a}_1\tilde{a}_2 - \tilde{a}_2\tilde{a}_1) = \hbar(\tilde{a}_1\tilde{a}_2) - \hbar(\tilde{a}_2\tilde{a}_1) \\ &= \hbar(\tilde{a}_1)\hbar(\tilde{a}_2) + \hbar(\tilde{a}_1)\tilde{a}_2 + \tilde{a}_1\hbar(\tilde{a}_2) - \hbar(\tilde{a}_2)\hbar(\tilde{a}_1) - \hbar(\tilde{a}_2)\tilde{a}_1 - \tilde{a}_2\hbar(\tilde{a}_1) \\ &= [\hbar(\tilde{a}_1), \hbar(\tilde{a}_2)] + [\hbar(\tilde{a}_1), \tilde{a}_2] + [\tilde{a}_1, \hbar(\tilde{a}_2)]. \end{aligned}$$

Lemma 1 ([15], Corollary 2.1). *Let R be a $2-$torsion free semiprime ring, U a Lie ideal of R such that $U \nsubseteq Z(R)$ and $a, b \in U$.*

(i) *If $aUa = 0$, then $a = 0$.*
(ii) *If $aU = 0$ (or $Ua = 0$), then $a = 0$.*
(iii) *If U is square-closed and $aUb = 0$, then $ab = 0$ and $ba = 0$.*

Theorem 1. *Let S be a $2-$torsion free semiprime ring, U a noncentral square-closed Lie ideal of S, and $\hbar$ a homoderivation which is zero-power valued on U. If $\hbar$ is the centralizing map on U, then $\hbar$ is the commuting map on U.*

Proof. By the hypothesis, we have

$$[\tilde{a}_1, \hbar(\tilde{a}_1)] \in Z, \text{ for all } \tilde{a}_1 \in U. \quad (1)$$

Writing $\tilde{a}_1$ by $2\tilde{a}_1^2$ in the last equation, we have

$$\begin{aligned} Z \ni\ & 4[\tilde{a}_1^2, \hbar(\tilde{a}_1^2)] = 4[\tilde{a}_1^2, \hbar(\tilde{a}_1)\hbar(\tilde{a}_1) + \tilde{a}_1\hbar(\tilde{a}_1) + \hbar(\tilde{a}_1)\tilde{a}_1] \\ =\ & 4[\tilde{a}_1^2, \hbar(\tilde{a}_1)\hbar(\tilde{a}_1) + \tilde{a}_1\hbar(\tilde{a}_1) + \hbar(\tilde{a}_1)\tilde{a}_1 - \tilde{a}_1\hbar(\tilde{a}_1) + \tilde{a}_1\hbar(\tilde{a}_1)] \\ =\ & 4[\tilde{a}_1^2, \hbar(\tilde{a}_1)\hbar(\tilde{a}_1) + 2\tilde{a}_1\hbar(\tilde{a}_1) - [\tilde{a}_1, \hbar(\tilde{a}_1)]] \end{aligned}$$

Since S is 2-torsion free, we obtain

$$[\tilde{a}_1^2, \hbar(\tilde{a}_1)\hbar(\tilde{a}_1) + 2\tilde{a}_1\hbar(\tilde{a}_1) - [\tilde{a}_1, \hbar(\tilde{a}_1)]] \in Z.$$

By the hypothesis, we have

$$[\tilde{a}_1^2, \hbar(\tilde{a}_1^2)] \in Z.$$

Expanding this equation and using $[\tilde{a}_1, \hbar(\tilde{a}_1)] \in Z$, we obtain

$$\begin{aligned} [\tilde{a}_1^2, \hbar(\tilde{a}_1^2)] &= [\tilde{a}_1^2, \hbar(\tilde{a}_1)\hbar(\tilde{a}_1) + 2\tilde{a}_1\hbar(\tilde{a}_1)] = \tilde{a}_1[\tilde{a}_1, \hbar(\tilde{a}_1)\hbar(\tilde{a}_1)] + [\tilde{a}_1, \hbar(\tilde{a}_1)\hbar(\tilde{a}_1)]\tilde{a}_1 \\ &\quad + \tilde{a}_1[\tilde{a}_1, 2\tilde{a}_1\hbar(\tilde{a}_1)] + [\tilde{a}_1, 2\tilde{a}_1\hbar(\tilde{a}_1)]\tilde{a}_1 \\ &= \tilde{a}_1\hbar(\tilde{a}_1)[\tilde{a}_1, \hbar(\tilde{a}_1)] + \tilde{a}_1[\tilde{a}_1, \hbar(\tilde{a}_1)]\hbar(\tilde{a}_1) + \hbar(\tilde{a}_1)[\tilde{a}_1, \hbar(\tilde{a}_1)]\tilde{a}_1 \\ &\quad + [\tilde{a}_1, \hbar(\tilde{a}_1)]\hbar(\tilde{a}_1)\tilde{a}_1 + 2\tilde{a}_1^2[\tilde{a}_1, \hbar(\tilde{a}_1)] + 2\tilde{a}_1[\tilde{a}_1, \hbar(\tilde{a}_1)]\tilde{a}_1 \\ &= 2\tilde{a}_1\hbar(\tilde{a}_1)[\tilde{a}_1, \hbar(\tilde{a}_1)] + 2\hbar(\tilde{a}_1)\tilde{a}_1[\tilde{a}_1, \hbar(\tilde{a}_1)] + 4\tilde{a}_1^2[\tilde{a}_1, \hbar(\tilde{a}_1)] \\ &= 2\tilde{a}_1(\tilde{a}_1 + \hbar(\tilde{a}_1))[\tilde{a}_1, \hbar(\tilde{a}_1)] + 2(\hbar(\tilde{a}_1) + \tilde{a}_1)\tilde{a}_1[\tilde{a}_1, \hbar(\tilde{a}_1)] \\ &= (2\tilde{a}_1(\tilde{a}_1 + \hbar(\tilde{a}_1)) + 2(\hbar(\tilde{a}_1) + \tilde{a}_1)\tilde{a}_1)[\tilde{a}_1, \hbar(\tilde{a}_1)] \\ &= 2(2\tilde{a}_1^2 + \hbar(\tilde{a}_1)\tilde{a}_1 + \tilde{a}_1\hbar(\tilde{a}_1))[\tilde{a}_1, \hbar(\tilde{a}_1)] \end{aligned}$$

Since S is $2-$torsion free, we have

$$(2\tilde{a}_1^2 + \hbar(\tilde{a}_1)\tilde{a}_1 + \tilde{a}_1\hbar(\tilde{a}_1))[\tilde{a}_1, \hbar(\tilde{a}_1)] \in Z.$$

Commuting this term with $\tilde{a}_1$, we find that

$$[(2\tilde{a}_1^2 + \hbar(\tilde{a}_1)\tilde{a}_1 + \tilde{a}_1\hbar(\tilde{a}_1))[\tilde{a}_1, \hbar(\tilde{a}_1)], \tilde{a}_1] = 0.$$

Using the hypothesis, we obtain

$$[2\tilde{a}_1^2 + \hbar(\tilde{a}_1)\tilde{a}_1 + \tilde{a}_1\hbar(\tilde{a}_1), \tilde{a}_1][\tilde{a}_1, \hbar(\tilde{a}_1)] = 0$$

and so

$$([\hbar(\tilde{a}_1)\tilde{a}_1, \tilde{a}_1] + [\tilde{a}_1\hbar(\tilde{a}_1), \tilde{a}_1]) = 2\tilde{a}_1[\hbar(\tilde{a}_1), \tilde{a}_1][\tilde{a}_1, \hbar(\tilde{a}_1)] = 0.$$

Since S is $2-$torsion free, we have

$$\tilde{a}_1[\hbar(\tilde{a}_1), \tilde{a}_1]^2 = 0. \tag{2}$$

Multiplying Equation (2) from the left side by $\hbar(\tilde{a}_1)$, we find that

$$\hbar(\tilde{a}_1)\tilde{a}_1[\hbar(\tilde{a}_1), \tilde{a}_1]^2 = 0. \tag{3}$$

Multiplying (2) from the left side by $\hbar(\tilde{a}_1)$, we obtain

$$\tilde{a}_1[\hbar(\tilde{a}_1), \tilde{a}_1]^2\hbar(\tilde{a}_1) = 0.$$

Since $\hbar$ is centralizing map on U, we have

$$\tilde{a}_1\hbar(\tilde{a}_1)[\hbar(\tilde{a}_1), \tilde{a}_1]^2 = 0. \tag{4}$$

Comparing (3) and (4), we find that

$$[\tilde{a}_1, \hbar(\tilde{a}_1)]^3 = 0.$$

Since the center of a semiprime ring contains no nonzero nilpotent elements, we obtain $[\tilde{a}_1, \hbar(\tilde{a}_1)] = 0$ for all $\tilde{a}_1 \in U$. Hence, we conclude that $\hbar$ is a commuting map on U. □

Theorem 2. *Let S be a $2-$torsion free semiprime ring, U a noncentral square-closed Lie ideal of S, and $\hbar$ a homoderivation which is zero-power valued on U. If any of the following holds for all $\tilde{a}_1, \tilde{a}_2 \in U$,*

(i) $\hbar(\tilde{a}_1\tilde{a}_2) + \tilde{a}_1\tilde{a}_2 \in Z$, *or*

(ii) $\hbar(\tilde{a}_1\tilde{a}_2) - \tilde{a}_1\tilde{a}_2 \in Z$,

then $\hbar$ is a commuting map on U.

Proof. (i) By the hypothesis, we obtain

$$\hbar(\tilde{a}_1\tilde{a}_2) + \tilde{a}_1\tilde{a}_2 \in Z \text{ for all } \tilde{a}_1, \tilde{a}_2 \in U.$$

That is,

$$\hbar(\tilde{a}_1)\hbar(\tilde{a}_2) + \hbar(\tilde{a}_1)\tilde{a}_2 + \tilde{a}_1\hbar(\tilde{a}_2) + \tilde{a}_1\tilde{a}_2 \in Z.$$

Substituting $\tilde{a}_2$ by $2\tilde{a}_2\tilde{a}_3, \tilde{a}_3 \in U$ in the last equation, we obtain

$$2\hbar(\tilde{a}_1)\hbar(\tilde{a}_2)\hbar(\tilde{a}_3) + 2\hbar(\tilde{a}_1)\hbar(\tilde{a}_2)\tilde{a}_3 + 2\hbar(\tilde{a}_1)\tilde{a}_2\hbar(\tilde{a}_3) + 2\hbar(\tilde{a}_1)\tilde{a}_2\tilde{a}_3$$
$$+2\tilde{a}_1\hbar(\tilde{a}_2)\hbar(\tilde{a}_3) + 2\tilde{a}_1\hbar(\tilde{a}_2)\tilde{a}_3 + 2\tilde{a}_1\tilde{a}_2\hbar(\tilde{a}_3) + 2\tilde{a}_1\tilde{a}_2\tilde{a}_3 \in Z,$$

and so

$$2(\hbar(\tilde{a}_1)\hbar(\tilde{a}_2) + \hbar(\tilde{a}_1)\tilde{a}_2 + \tilde{a}_1\hbar(\tilde{a}_2) + \tilde{a}_1\tilde{a}_2)\hbar(\tilde{a}_3)$$
$$+2(\hbar(\tilde{a}_1)\hbar(\tilde{a}_2) + \hbar(\tilde{a}_1)\tilde{a}_2 + \tilde{a}_1\hbar(\tilde{a}_2) + \tilde{a}_1\tilde{a}_2)\tilde{a}_3 \in Z.$$

Substituting this term with $\tilde{a}_3$, we obtain

$$2[(\hbar(\tilde{a}_1)\hbar(\tilde{a}_2) + \hbar(\tilde{a}_1)\tilde{a}_2 + \tilde{a}_1\hbar(\tilde{a}_2) + \tilde{a}_1\tilde{a}_2)\hbar(\tilde{a}_3), \tilde{a}_3] = 0, \text{ for all } \tilde{a}_1, \tilde{a}_2, \tilde{a}_3 \in U.$$

That is

$$[(\hbar(2\tilde{a}_1\tilde{a}_2) + 2\tilde{a}_1\tilde{a}_2)\hbar(\tilde{a}_3), \tilde{a}_3] = 0, \text{ for all } \tilde{a}_1, \tilde{a}_2, \tilde{a}_3 \in U.$$

Since $\hbar$ is zero-power valued on U, there exists an integer $n > 1$ such that $\hbar^n(\tilde{a}_1) = 0$ for all $\tilde{a}_1 \in U$. Using $\tilde{a}_1, \tilde{a}_2 \in U$, we obtain that $2\tilde{a}_1\tilde{a}_2 \in U$. Replacing $2\tilde{a}_1\tilde{a}_2$ by $2\tilde{a}_1\tilde{a}_2 - 2\hbar(\tilde{a}_1\tilde{a}_2) + 2\hbar^2(\tilde{a}_1\tilde{a}_2) + \ldots + 2(-1)^{n-1}\hbar^{n-1}(\tilde{a}_1\tilde{a}_2)$ in this equation and using S is $2-$torsion free, we find that

$$[\tilde{a}_1\tilde{a}_2\hbar(\tilde{a}_3), \tilde{a}_3] = 0, \text{ for all } \tilde{a}_1, \tilde{a}_2, \tilde{a}_3 \in U.$$

That is

$$\tilde{a}_1\tilde{a}_2[\hbar(\tilde{a}_3), \tilde{a}_3] + \tilde{a}_1[\tilde{a}_2, \tilde{a}_3]\hbar(\tilde{a}_3) + [\tilde{a}_1, \tilde{a}_3]\tilde{a}_2\hbar(\tilde{a}_3) = 0. \quad (5)$$

Replacing $\tilde{a}_1$ by $2r\tilde{a}_1, r \in U$ in this equation, we obtain

$$2r\tilde{a}_1\tilde{a}_2[\hbar(\tilde{a}_3), \tilde{a}_3] + 2r\tilde{a}_1[\tilde{a}_2, \tilde{a}_3]\hbar(\tilde{a}_3) + 2r[\tilde{a}_1, \tilde{a}_3]\tilde{a}_2\hbar(\tilde{a}_3) + 2[r, \tilde{a}_3]\tilde{a}_1\tilde{a}_2\hbar(\tilde{a}_3) = 0.$$

Since S is $2-$torsion free, we see that

$$r\tilde{a}_1\tilde{a}_2[\hbar(\tilde{a}_3), \tilde{a}_3] + r\tilde{a}_1[\tilde{a}_2, \tilde{a}_3]\hbar(\tilde{a}_3) + r[\tilde{a}_1, \tilde{a}_3]\tilde{a}_2\hbar(\tilde{a}_3) + [r, \tilde{a}_3]\tilde{a}_1\tilde{a}_2\hbar(\tilde{a}_3) = 0.$$

Using Equation (5), we have

$$[r, \tilde{a}_3]\tilde{a}_1\tilde{a}_2\hbar(\tilde{a}_3) = 0, \text{ for all } \tilde{a}_1, \tilde{a}_2, \tilde{a}_3, r \in U.$$

Replacing $\tilde{a}_2$ by $4\tilde{a}_2[r, \tilde{a}_3]\tilde{a}_1$ and using S is $2-$torsion free, we obtain

$$[r, \tilde{a}_3]\tilde{a}_1\tilde{a}_2[r, \tilde{a}_3]\tilde{a}_1\hbar(\tilde{a}_3) = 0, \text{ for all } \tilde{a}_1, \tilde{a}_2, \tilde{a}_3, r \in U.$$

Writing $\tilde{a}_1$ by $2\tilde{a}_1\hbar(\tilde{a}_3)$ and again using S is $2-$torsion free, we have

$$[r, \tilde{a}_3]\tilde{a}_1\hbar(\tilde{a}_3)\tilde{a}_2[r, \tilde{a}_3]\tilde{a}_1\hbar(\tilde{a}_3) = 0, \text{ for all } \tilde{a}_1, \tilde{a}_2, \tilde{a}_3, r \in U.$$

By Lemma 1, we obtain that

$$[r, \tilde{a}_3]\tilde{a}_1\hbar(\tilde{a}_3) = 0, \text{ for all } \tilde{a}_1, \tilde{a}_3, r \in U. \quad (6)$$

Now, writing r by $\hbar(\tilde{a}_3)$ in (6) and multiplying this equation from the right by $\tilde{a}_3$, we have

$$[\hbar(\tilde{a}_3), \tilde{a}_3]\tilde{a}_1\hbar(\tilde{a}_3)\tilde{a}_3 = 0, \text{ for all } \tilde{a}_1, \tilde{a}_3 \in U. \quad (7)$$

Taking $\tilde{a}_1$ by $2\tilde{a}_1\tilde{a}_3$ in (7), we obtain that

$$2[\hbar(\tilde{a}_3), \tilde{a}_3]\tilde{a}_1\tilde{a}_3\hbar(\tilde{a}_3) = 0, \text{ for all } \tilde{a}_1, \tilde{a}_2, \tilde{a}_3 \in U.$$

Since S is $2-$torsion free,we obtain

$$[\hbar(\tilde{a}_3), \tilde{a}_3]\tilde{a}_1\tilde{a}_3\hbar(\tilde{a}_3) = 0, \text{ for all } \tilde{a}_1, \tilde{a}_2, \tilde{a}_3 \in U. \quad (8)$$

Combining (7) and (8), we find that

$$[\hbar(\tilde{a}_3), \tilde{a}_3]\tilde{a}_1[\hbar(\tilde{a}_3), \tilde{a}_3] = 0, \text{ for all } \tilde{a}_1, \tilde{a}_2, \tilde{a}_3 \in U. \quad (9)$$

Again by Lemma 1, we obtain that $\hbar$ is a commuting map on U.

(ii) If $\hbar$ is a homoderivation satisfying $\hbar(\tilde{a}_1\tilde{a}_2) - \tilde{a}_1\tilde{a}_2 \in Z$, for all $\tilde{a}_1, \tilde{a}_2 \in U$, then $(-\hbar)(\tilde{a}_1\tilde{a}_2) - \tilde{a}_1\tilde{a}_2 \in Z$. Since $(-\hbar)$ is a homoderivation on S, we obtain that $\hbar$ is a commuting map on U by Theorem 2 (i). □

Theorem 3. *Let S be a 2−torsion free semiprime ring, U a noncentral square-closed Lie ideal of S, and $\hbar$ a homoderivation on S. If any of the following holds for all $\tilde{a}_1, \tilde{a}_2 \in U$*

(i) $\hbar([\tilde{a}_1, \tilde{a}_2]) = \tilde{a}_1 \circ \tilde{a}_2$, *or*
(ii) $\hbar(\tilde{a}_1 \circ \tilde{a}_2) = [\tilde{a}_1, \tilde{a}_2]$, *or*
(iii) $\hbar(\tilde{a}_1 \circ \tilde{a}_2) = \tilde{a}_1 \circ \tilde{a}_2$, *or*
(iv) $\hbar([\tilde{a}_1, \tilde{a}_2]) = [\tilde{a}_1, \tilde{a}_2]$, *or*

then $U[S,S] = (0)$ and $[U,S] = (0)$. In particular, $[\hbar(\tilde{a}_1), \tilde{a}_1] = 0$ for all $\tilde{a}_1 \in U$.

Proof. (i) Assume that

$$\hbar([\tilde{a}_1, \tilde{a}_2]) = \tilde{a}_1 \circ \tilde{a}_2 \text{ for all } \tilde{a}_1, \tilde{a}_2 \in U \tag{10}$$

Putting $\tilde{a}_2 = \tilde{a}_1$ in (10), we have $0 = \tilde{a}_1 \circ \tilde{a}_1 \Rightarrow 2\tilde{a}_1^2 = 0$. Since S is 2-torsion free, we have $\tilde{a}_1^2 = 0$. By linearizing, we obtain

$$\tilde{a}_1 \circ \tilde{a}_2 = 0, \text{ for all } \tilde{a}_1, \tilde{a}_2 \in U. \tag{11}$$

Replacing $\tilde{a}_2$ by $2\tilde{a}_2 r$, where $r \in S$ in this equation, we have $(\tilde{a}_1 \circ \tilde{a}_2)r - \tilde{a}_2[\tilde{a}_1, r] = 0$, and by using (11), we obtain $[\tilde{a}_1, r]\tilde{a}_2[\tilde{a}_1, r] = 0$ for all $\tilde{a}_1, \tilde{a}_2 \in U$ and $r \in S$. Hence, $[\tilde{a}_1, r]U[\tilde{a}_1, r] = (0)$ for all $\tilde{a}_1, \tilde{a}_2 \in U$ and $r \in S$. Since $[\tilde{a}_1, r] \in U$ and by using Lemma 1, we obtain $[\tilde{a}_1, r] = 0$ for all $\tilde{a}_1 \in U$ and $r \in S$, that is, $[U,S] = (0)$, hence $U \subseteq Z(S)$, a contradiction with the fact that U is a noncentral. Therefore, we have to remove this condition.

Now, we will continue; we have $[\tilde{a}_1, r] = 0$ for all $\tilde{a}_1 \in U$ and $r \in S$. Replacing $\tilde{a}_1$ by $2\tilde{a}_1 s$, where $s \in S$, we obtain $\tilde{a}_1[s, r] = 0$ for all $\tilde{a}_1 \in U$ and $r, s \in S$. That is, $U[S,S] = (0)$ and $[U,S] = (0)$.

(ii) Assume that

$$\hbar(\tilde{a}_1 \circ \tilde{a}_2) = [\tilde{a}_1, \tilde{a}_2] \text{ for all } \tilde{a}_1, \tilde{a}_2 \in U. \tag{12}$$

Putting $\tilde{a}_2 = \tilde{a}_1$ in (12), we have $0 = \hbar(\tilde{a}_1 \circ \tilde{a}_1) \Rightarrow 2\hbar(\tilde{a}_1^2) = 0$. Since S is 2-torsion free, we obtain $\hbar(\tilde{a}_1^2) = 0$. By linearizing, we have

$$\hbar(\tilde{a}_1 \circ \tilde{a}_2) = 0, \text{ for all } \tilde{a}_1, \tilde{a}_2 \in U. \tag{13}$$

Using (13) in (12), we obtain

$$[\tilde{a}_1, \tilde{a}_2] = 0, \text{ for all } \tilde{a}_1, \tilde{a}_2 \in U. \tag{14}$$

Replacing $\tilde{a}_2$ by $2\tilde{a}_2 r$, where $r \in S$, we obtain $2[\tilde{a}_1, \tilde{a}_2]r + 2\tilde{a}_2[\tilde{a}_1, r] = 0$, hence $[\tilde{a}_1, \tilde{a}_2]r + \tilde{a}_2[\tilde{a}_1, r] = 0$, and by using (14), we obtain $\tilde{a}_2[\tilde{a}_1, r] = 0$. Hence, $[\tilde{a}_1, r]\tilde{a}_2[\tilde{a}_1, r] = 0$ for all $\tilde{a}_1, \tilde{a}_2 \in U$ and $r \in S$. Thus,

$$[\tilde{a}_1, r]U[\tilde{a}_1, r] = (0) \text{ for all } \tilde{a}_1 \in U \text{ and } r \in S.$$

Since$[\tilde{a}_1, r] \in U$ and by using Lemma 1, we obtain $[\tilde{a}_1, r] = 0$ for all $\tilde{a}_1 \in U$ and $r \in S$; that is, $[U,S] = (0)$, hence $U \subseteq Z(S)$, a contradiction with the fact that U is a noncentral. Therefore, we have to remove this condition. Now, we have $[\tilde{a}_1, r] = 0$ for all $\tilde{a}_1 \in U$ and

$r \in S$. Replacing $\tilde{a}_1$ by $2\tilde{a}_1 s$, where $s \in S$, we obtain $\tilde{a}_1[s,r] = 0$ for all $\tilde{a}_1 \in U$ and $r,s \in S$. That is, $U[S,S] = (0)$ and $[U,S] = (0)$.

(iii) Assume that

$$\hbar(\tilde{a}_1 \circ \tilde{a}_2) = \tilde{a}_1 \circ \tilde{a}_2 \text{ for all } \tilde{a}_1, \tilde{a}_2 \in U \tag{15}$$

Replacing $\tilde{a}_2$ by $2\tilde{a}_2\tilde{a}_1$ in (15), we have

$$\hbar((\tilde{a}_1 \circ \tilde{a}_2)\tilde{a}_1) = (\tilde{a}_1 \circ \tilde{a}_2)\tilde{a}_1$$

and so

$$\hbar(\tilde{a}_1 \circ \tilde{a}_2)\hbar(\tilde{a}_1) + \hbar(\tilde{a}_1 \circ \tilde{a}_2)\tilde{a}_1 + (\tilde{a}_1 \circ \tilde{a}_2)\hbar(\tilde{a}_1) = (\tilde{a}_1 \circ \tilde{a}_2)\tilde{a}_1.$$

Using (15),

$$(\tilde{a}_1 \circ \tilde{a}_2)\hbar(\tilde{a}_1) + (\tilde{a}_1 \circ \tilde{a}_2)\tilde{a}_1 + (\tilde{a}_1 \circ \tilde{a}_2)\hbar(\tilde{a}_1) = (\tilde{a}_1 \circ \tilde{a}_2)\tilde{a}_1$$

and so

$$\begin{aligned}(\tilde{a}_1 \circ \tilde{a}_2)\hbar(\tilde{a}_1) + (\tilde{a}_1 \circ \tilde{a}_2)\hbar(\tilde{a}_1) &= 0\\ 2(\tilde{a}_1 \circ \tilde{a}_2)\hbar(\tilde{a}_1) &= 0\\ (\tilde{a}_1 \circ \tilde{a}_2)\hbar(\tilde{a}_1) &= 0.\end{aligned}$$

Replacing $\tilde{a}_1$ by $\tilde{a}_1^2$ in the last relation, we obtain $(\tilde{a}_1^2 \circ \tilde{a}_2)\hbar(\tilde{a}_1^2) = 0$. Putting $\tilde{a}_2 = \tilde{a}_1$ in (15) and using this in last equation we obtain

$$(\tilde{a}_1^2 \circ \tilde{a}_2)\tilde{a}_1^2 = 0, \text{ for all } \tilde{a}_1, \tilde{a}_2 \in U. \tag{16}$$

Replacing $\tilde{a}_2$ by $2r\tilde{a}_2$, where $r \in S, 2r(\tilde{a}_1^2 \circ \tilde{a}_2)\tilde{a}_1^2 + 2[\tilde{a}_1^2, r]\tilde{a}_2\tilde{a}_1^2 = 0$. Using (16) in this relation, we obtain $2[\tilde{a}_1^2, r]\tilde{a}_2\tilde{a}_1^2 = 0$, and so $[\tilde{a}_1^2, r]\tilde{a}_2\tilde{a}_1^2 = 0 \Rightarrow [\tilde{a}_1^2, r]\tilde{a}_2[\tilde{a}_1^2, r] = 0$ for all $\tilde{a}_1 \in U$ and $r \in S$. By Lemma 1, we obtain $[\tilde{a}_1^2, r] = 0$ for all $\tilde{a}_1 \in U$ and $r \in S$. By linearizing, we obtain

$$[\tilde{a}_1 \circ \tilde{a}_2, r] = 0, \text{ for all } \tilde{a}_1, \tilde{a}_2 \in U, r \in S. \tag{17}$$

Replacing $\tilde{a}_2$ by $2\tilde{a}_2 r$, we obtain $[(\tilde{a}_1 \circ \tilde{a}_2)r - \tilde{a}_2[\tilde{a}_1, r], r] = 0$ for all $\tilde{a}_1 \in U$ and $r \in S$. Using (17), we obtain

$$\tilde{a}_2[[\tilde{a}_1, r], r] - [\tilde{a}_2, r][\tilde{a}_1, r] = 0, \text{ for all } \tilde{a}_1, \tilde{a}_2 \in U, r \in S \tag{18}$$

Replacing $\tilde{a}_2$ by $2\tilde{a}_1\tilde{a}_2$, in (18), we obtain

$$\tilde{a}_1\tilde{a}_2[[\tilde{a}_1, r], r] - \tilde{a}_1[\tilde{a}_2, r][\tilde{a}_1, r] - [\tilde{a}_1, r]\tilde{a}_2[\tilde{a}_1, r] = 0, \text{ for all } \tilde{a}_1, \tilde{a}_2 \in U, r \in S$$

and so

$$\tilde{a}_1(\tilde{a}_2[[\tilde{a}_1, r], r] - [\tilde{a}_2, r][\tilde{a}_1, r]) - [\tilde{a}_1, r]\tilde{a}_2[\tilde{a}_1, r] = 0, \text{ for all } \tilde{a}_1, \tilde{a}_2 \in U, r \in S.$$

Using (18) in the last relation, we obtain $[\tilde{a}_1, r]\tilde{a}_2[\tilde{a}_1, r] = 0$ for all $\tilde{a}_1, \tilde{a}_2 \in U$ and $r \in S$. By Lemma 1, we obtain $[\tilde{a}_1, r] = 0$ for all $\tilde{a}_1 \in U$ and $r \in S$. That is, $[U, S] = (0)$, hence $U \subseteq Z(S)$, a contradiction with the fact that U is a noncentral. Therefore, we have to remove this condition.

Now, we will continue; we have $[\tilde{a}_1, r] = 0$ for all $\tilde{a}_1 \in U$ and $r \in S$. Replacing $\tilde{a}_1$ by $2\tilde{a}_1 s$, where $s \in S$, we obtain $\tilde{a}_1[s, r] = 0$ for all $\tilde{a}_1 \in U$ and $r, s \in S$.That is, $U[S, S] = (0)$ and $[U, S] = (0)$.

(iv) Assume that

$$\hbar([\tilde{a}_1, \tilde{a}_2]) = [\tilde{a}_1, \tilde{a}_2] \text{ for all } \tilde{a}_1, \tilde{a}_2 \in U. \tag{19}$$

As in (iii), we obtain $[\tilde{a}_1, \tilde{a}_2]\hbar(\tilde{a}_1) = 0$ for all $\tilde{a}_1, \tilde{a}_2 \in U$. Replacing $\tilde{a}_1$ by $[\tilde{a}_1, r]$, where $z \in U$, we obtain $[[\tilde{a}_1, z], \tilde{a}_2]\hbar([\tilde{a}_1, z]) = 0$ for all $\tilde{a}_1, \tilde{a}_2, z \in U$. Using (19), we obtain $[[\tilde{a}_1, z], \tilde{a}_2][\tilde{a}_1, z] = 0$ for all $\tilde{a}_1, \tilde{a}_2, z \in U$. Replacing $\tilde{a}_2$ by $2r\tilde{a}_2$, where $r \in S$, we obtain $[[\tilde{a}_1, z], r]\tilde{a}_2[\tilde{a}_1, z] = 0$ for all $\tilde{a}_1, \tilde{a}_2, z \in U$ and $r \in S$. That is, $[[\tilde{a}_1, z], r]\tilde{a}_2[[\tilde{a}_1, z], r] = 0$ for all $\tilde{a}_1, \tilde{a}_2, z \in U$ and $r \in S$. By Lemma 1, we obtain $[[\tilde{a}_1, z], r] = 0$ for all $\tilde{a}_1, z \in U$ and $r \in S$. Replacing z by $z\tilde{a}_1$, we obtain $[\tilde{a}_1, z][\tilde{a}_1, r] = 0$ for all $\tilde{a}_1, z \in U$ and $r \in S$. Replacing z by rz, we obtain $[\tilde{a}_1, r]z[\tilde{a}_1, r] = 0$ for all $\tilde{a}_1, z \in U$ and $r \in S$. By Lemma 1, we obtain $[\tilde{a}_1, r] = 0$ for all $\tilde{a}_1 \in U$ and $r \in S$. That is, $[U, S] = (0)$, hence $U \subseteq Z(S)$, a contradiction with fact that U is a noncentral. So we have to remove this condition. Now we have $[\tilde{a}_1, r] = 0$ for all $\tilde{a}_1 \in U$ and $r \in S$. Replacing $\tilde{a}_1$ by $2\tilde{a}_1 s$, where $s \in S$, we obtain $\tilde{a}_1[s, r] = 0$ for all $\tilde{a}_1 \in U$ and $r, s \in S$. That is, $U[S, S] = (0)$ and $[U, S] = (0)$. □

Example 1. *Let* $S = \left\{ \begin{pmatrix} 0 & a & b & c \\ 0 & 0 & 0 & b \\ 0 & 0 & 0 & -a \\ 0 & 0 & 0 & 0 \end{pmatrix} : a, b, c \in \mathbb{Z} \right\}$ *be a 2-torsion free ring, and is not a semiprime ring* $U = \left\{ \begin{pmatrix} 0 & a & a & c \\ 0 & 0 & 0 & a \\ 0 & 0 & 0 & -a \\ 0 & 0 & 0 & 0 \end{pmatrix} : a, c \in \mathbb{Z} \right\}$ *be a noncentral square-closed Lie ideal of* S. $\hbar : S \to S$ $\hbar\left(\begin{pmatrix} 0 & a & b & c \\ 0 & 0 & 0 & b \\ 0 & 0 & 0 & -a \\ 0 & 0 & 0 & 0 \end{pmatrix}\right) = \begin{pmatrix} 0 & 0 & -b & c \\ 0 & 0 & 0 & -b \\ 0 & 0 & 0 & 0 \\ 0 & 0 & 0 & 0 \end{pmatrix}$. *Then, it easy to check that* $\hbar$ *is a homoderivation of* S. *The conditions* $(i) - (iv)$ *given in Theorem 3 are satisfied on* U. *However,* S *is not semiprime and* h *is not commuting in* U. *Thus, the conditions' semiprimeness is essential.*

Theorem 4. *Let* S *be a* $2-$*torsion semiprime ring,* U *a noncentral square-closed Lie ideal of* S, *and* $\hbar$ *a zero-power valued on* U. *Suppose that* S *admits a homoderivation* $\hbar$ *such that for all* $\tilde{a}_1, \tilde{a}_2 \in U$

(i) $\tilde{a}_1\hbar(\tilde{a}_2) \pm \tilde{a}_1\tilde{a}_2 \in Z$, *or*
(ii) $\tilde{a}_1\hbar(\tilde{a}_2) \pm \tilde{a}_2\tilde{a}_1 = 0$, *or*
(iii) $\tilde{a}_1\hbar(\tilde{a}_2) \pm \tilde{a}_1 \circ \tilde{a}_2 = 0$, *or*
(iv) $[\hbar(\tilde{a}_1), \tilde{a}_2] \pm \tilde{a}_1\tilde{a}_2 = 0$, *or*
(v) $[\hbar(\tilde{a}_1), \tilde{a}_2] \pm \tilde{a}_2\tilde{a}_1 = 0$.

Then $\hbar$ *is a commuting map on* U.

Proof. (i) By the hypothesis, we obtain

$$\tilde{a}_1\hbar(\tilde{a}_2) + \tilde{a}_1\tilde{a}_2 \in Z, \text{ for all } \tilde{a}_1, \tilde{a}_2 \in U.$$

That is

$$\tilde{a}_1(\hbar(\tilde{a}_2) + \tilde{a}_2) \in Z, \text{ for all } \tilde{a}_1, \tilde{a}_2 \in U.$$

Since $\hbar$ is zero-power valued on U, there exists an integer $n > 1$ such that $\hbar^n(\tilde{a}_1) = 0$ for all $\tilde{a}_1 \in U$. Replacing $\tilde{a}_2$ by $\tilde{a}_2 - \hbar(\tilde{a}_2) + \hbar^2(\tilde{a}_2) + ... + (-1)^{n-1}\hbar^{n-1}(\tilde{a}_2)$ in this equation, we obtain that

$$\tilde{a}_1\tilde{a}_2 \in Z, \text{ for all } \tilde{a}_1, \tilde{a}_2 \in U.$$

Commuting this term with $r \in S$, we obtain

$$0 = [\tilde{a}_1\tilde{a}_2, r] = [\tilde{a}_1, r]\tilde{a}_2 + \tilde{a}_1[\tilde{a}_2, r].$$

Replacing $\tilde{a}_1$ by $2\tilde{a}_3\tilde{a}_1$, $\tilde{a}_3 \in U$ in this equation and using this equation, we obtain

$$2[\tilde{a}_3, r]\tilde{a}_1\tilde{a}_2 = 0.$$

Since S is $2-$torsion free ring, we see that

$$[\tilde{a}_3, r]\tilde{a}_1\tilde{a}_2 = 0.$$

Taking $\tilde{a}_2$ by $[\tilde{a}_3, r]$ in this equation, we have

$$[\tilde{a}_3, r]\tilde{a}_1[\tilde{a}_3, r] = 0, \text{ for all } \tilde{a}_1, \tilde{a}_3 \in U,\ r \in S.$$

Replacig r by $\hbar(\tilde{a}_3)$ in this equation, we obtain

$$[\tilde{a}_3, \hbar(\tilde{a}_3)]\tilde{a}_1[\tilde{a}_3, \hbar(\tilde{a}_3)] = 0, \text{ for all } \tilde{a}_1, \tilde{a}_3 \in U.$$

By Lemma 1, we obtain that $\hbar$ is a commuting map on U.

$\tilde{a}_1\hbar(\tilde{a}_2) - \tilde{a}_1\tilde{a}_2 \in Z$ is proved similarly. We complete the proof.

(ii) We obtain

$$\tilde{a}_1\hbar(\tilde{a}_2) + \tilde{a}_2\tilde{a}_1 = 0, \text{ for all } \tilde{a}_1, \tilde{a}_2 \in U.$$

Replacing $\tilde{a}_2$ by $\tilde{a}_1\tilde{a}_2$, $\tilde{a}_2 \in U$ in this equation and using this, we have

$$\tilde{a}_1\hbar(\tilde{a}_1)(\hbar(\tilde{a}_2) + \tilde{a}_2) = 0.$$

Since $\hbar$ is zero-power valued on U, there exists an integer $n > 1$ such that $\hbar^n(\tilde{a}_1) = 0$ for all $\tilde{a}_1 \in U$. Replacing $\tilde{a}_2$ by $\tilde{a}_2 - \hbar(\tilde{a}_2) + \hbar^2(\tilde{a}_2) + \ldots + (-1)^{n-1}\hbar^{n-1}(\tilde{a}_2)$ in this equation, we obtain that

$$\tilde{a}_1\hbar(\tilde{a}_1)\tilde{a}_2 = 0, \text{ for all } \tilde{a}_1, \tilde{a}_2 \in U.$$

Writing $\tilde{a}_2$ by $4\tilde{a}_2\tilde{a}_1\hbar(\tilde{a}_1)$ in the last equation, we have

$$4\tilde{a}_1\hbar(\tilde{a}_1)\tilde{a}_2\tilde{a}_1\hbar(\tilde{a}_1) = 0, \text{ for all } \tilde{a}_1, \tilde{a}_2 \in U.$$

Since S is $2-$torsion free ring, we obtain that

$$\tilde{a}_1\hbar(\tilde{a}_1)\tilde{a}_2\tilde{a}_1\hbar(\tilde{a}_1) = 0, \text{ for all } \tilde{a}_1, \tilde{a}_2 \in U.$$

By Lemma 1, we obtain

$$\tilde{a}_1\hbar(\tilde{a}_1) = 0, \text{ for all } \tilde{a}_1, \tilde{a}_2 \in U. \tag{20}$$

By the hypothesis, we obtain

$$\tilde{a}_1\hbar(\tilde{a}_1) + \tilde{a}_1^2 = 0, \text{ for all } \tilde{a}_1 \in U.$$

Using Equation (20), we obtain that

$$\tilde{a}_1^2 = 0, \text{ for all } \tilde{a}_1 \in U. \tag{21}$$

Replacing $\tilde{a}_1$ by $\tilde{a}_1 + \tilde{a}_2$ in this equation, we have

$$\tilde{a}_1 \circ \tilde{a}_2 = 0, \text{ for all } \tilde{a}_1, \tilde{a}_2 \in U.$$

Replacing $\tilde{a}_2$ by $2\tilde{a}_2\tilde{a}_3, \tilde{a}_3 \in U$ in the above expression and using this, we obtain

$$2[\tilde{a}_1, \tilde{a}_2]\tilde{a}_3 = 0, \text{ for all } \tilde{a}_1, \tilde{a}_2, \tilde{a}_3 \in U.$$

Since S is 2−torsion free ring, we have

$$[\tilde{a}_1, \tilde{a}_2]\tilde{a}_3 = 0, \text{ for all } \tilde{a}_1, \tilde{a}_2, \tilde{a}_3 \in U.$$

Replacing $\tilde{a}_3$ by $2\tilde{a}_3[\tilde{a}_1, \tilde{a}_2]$ in this equation and using S is 2−torsion free ring, we have

$$[\tilde{a}_1, \tilde{a}_2]U[\tilde{a}_1, \tilde{a}_2] = (0), \text{ for all } \tilde{a}_1, \tilde{a}_2 \in U.$$

By Lemma 1, we find that

$$[\tilde{a}_1, \tilde{a}_2] = 0, \text{ for all } \tilde{a}_1, \tilde{a}_2 \in U.$$

Replacing $\tilde{a}_2$ by $\hbar(\tilde{a}_1)$ in this equation, we obtain $[\tilde{a}_1, \hbar(\tilde{a}_1)] = 0$. Hence, we conclude that $\hbar$ is a commuting map on U. This completes the proof.

$\tilde{a}_1\hbar(\tilde{a}_2) - \tilde{a}_2\tilde{a}_1 = 0$ is proved similarly.

(iii) By the hypothesis, we obtain

$$\tilde{a}_1\hbar(\tilde{a}_2) \pm \tilde{a}_1 \circ \tilde{a}_2 = 0.$$

Replacing $\tilde{a}_2$ by $2\tilde{a}_2\tilde{a}_1$ in this equation and using S is 2−torsion free ring, we get

$$\tilde{a}_1\hbar(\tilde{a}_2)\hbar(\tilde{a}_1) + \tilde{a}_1\hbar(\tilde{a}_2)\tilde{a}_1 + \tilde{a}_1\tilde{a}_2\hbar(\tilde{a}_1) \pm (\tilde{a}_1 \circ \tilde{a}_2)\tilde{a}_1 = 0.$$

Using the hypothesis, we get

$$\tilde{a}_1\hbar(\tilde{a}_2)\hbar(\tilde{a}_1) + \tilde{a}_1\tilde{a}_2\hbar(\tilde{a}_1) = 0.$$

That is

$$\tilde{a}_1(\hbar(\tilde{a}_2) + \tilde{a}_2)\hbar(\tilde{a}_1) = 0.$$

Since $\hbar$ is zero-power valued on U, there exists an integer $n > 1$ such that $\hbar^n(\tilde{a}_1) = 0$ for all $\tilde{a}_1 \in U$. Replacing $\tilde{a}_2$ by $\tilde{a}_2 - \hbar(\tilde{a}_2) + \hbar^2(\tilde{a}_2) + \cdots + (-1)^{n-1}\hbar^{n-1}(\tilde{a}_2)$ in this equation, we obtain that

$$\tilde{a}_1\tilde{a}_2\hbar(\tilde{a}_1) = 0, \text{ for all } \tilde{a}_1, \tilde{a}_2 \in U.$$

Taking $\tilde{a}_2$ by $4\hbar(\tilde{a}_1)\tilde{a}_2\tilde{a}_1$ in the above equation and using S is 2−torsion free ring, we see that

$$\tilde{a}_1\hbar(\tilde{a}_1)\tilde{a}_2\tilde{a}_1\hbar(\tilde{a}_1) = 0.$$

By Lemma 1, we have

$$\tilde{a}_1\hbar(\tilde{a}_1) = 0, \text{ for all } \tilde{a}_1, \tilde{a}_2 \in U.$$

By our hypothesis, we obtain

$$\tilde{a}_1\hbar(\tilde{a}_1) \pm \tilde{a}_1^2 = 0, \text{ for all } \tilde{a}_1 \in U$$

and so

$$\tilde{a}_1^2 = 0, \text{ for all } \tilde{a}_1 \in U.$$

The rest of the proof is the same as Equation (21).

(iv) We obtain

$$[\hbar(\tilde{a}_1), \tilde{a}_2] \pm \tilde{a}_1\tilde{a}_2 = 0, \text{ for all } \tilde{a}_1, \tilde{a}_2 \in U.$$

Taking $\tilde{a}_2$ by $2\tilde{a}_2\tilde{a}_1$ in this equation and using S is $2-$torsion free ring, we obtain

$$[\hbar(\tilde{a}_1), \tilde{a}_2]\tilde{a}_1 + \tilde{a}_2[\hbar(\tilde{a}_1), \tilde{a}_1] \pm \tilde{a}_1\tilde{a}_2\tilde{a}_1 = 0.$$

By the hypothesis, we find that

$$\tilde{a}_2[\hbar(\tilde{a}_1), \tilde{a}_1] = 0, \text{ for all } \tilde{a}_1, \tilde{a}_2 \in U. \tag{22}$$

Replacing $\tilde{a}_2$ by $2[\hbar(\tilde{a}_1), \tilde{a}_1]\tilde{a}_2$ in this equation and using S is $2-$torsion free ring, we obtain

$$[\hbar(\tilde{a}_1), \tilde{a}_1]r[\hbar(\tilde{a}_1), \tilde{a}_1] = 0.$$

By Lemma 1, we have

$$[\hbar(\tilde{a}_1), \tilde{a}_1] = 0, \text{ for all } \tilde{a}_1 \in U.$$

This completes the proof.

(v) By the hypothesis, we obtain

$$[\hbar(\tilde{a}_1), \tilde{a}_2] \pm \tilde{a}_2\tilde{a}_1 = 0, \text{ for all } \tilde{a}_1, \tilde{a}_2 \in U.$$

Replacing $\tilde{a}_2$ by $2\tilde{a}_1\tilde{a}_2$ in this equation, we have

$$2\tilde{a}_1[\hbar(\tilde{a}_1), \tilde{a}_2] + 2[\hbar(\tilde{a}_1), \tilde{a}_1]\tilde{a}_2 \pm 2\tilde{a}_1\tilde{a}_2\tilde{a}_1 = 0.$$

Since S is $2-$torsion free ring, we can write

$$\tilde{a}_1[\hbar(\tilde{a}_1), \tilde{a}_2] + [\hbar(\tilde{a}_1), \tilde{a}_1]\tilde{a}_2 \pm \tilde{a}_1\tilde{a}_2\tilde{a}_1 = 0.$$

By our hypothesis, we obtain

$$[\hbar(\tilde{a}_1), \tilde{a}_1]\tilde{a}_2 = 0, \text{ for all } \tilde{a}_1, \tilde{a}_2 \in U.$$

The rest of the proof is the same as Equation (22). Hence, we complete the proof. □

3. Open Problems

Our assumptions focus on a noncentral square-closed Lie ideal within a 2-torsion free semiprime ring. As a direction for future research, similar investigations can be conducted without imposing the square-closed condition on Lie ideals of rings. Additionally, this study extends to various algebraic structures, including alternative rings, algebras, and near-rings.

Ruth N. Ferreira and Bruno L. M. Ferreira established the following theorem in ([16], Theorem 1.1):

Theorem 5. *Let S be a $3-$torsion free alternative ring. S is a prime ring if and only if $aS{\cdot}b = 0$ (or $a{\cdot}Sb = 0$) implies $a = 0$ or $b = 0$ for $a, b \in S$.*

It is well known that the 3-torsion free condition is unnecessary in the case of associative rings. Therefore, the findings in this paper can also be explored within the framework of alternative rings. Several studies in the literature address related topics (see [16–18], etc.).

4. Conclusions

In this work, we examine the commutativity of semiprime rings influenced by the action of homoderivations. Our study generalizes prior results by identifying conditions under which a noncentral square-closed Lie ideal of a 2-torsion free semiprime ring admits a homoderivation. To demonstrate the necessity of these conditions, we present an illustrative example within the framework of our theorem. The findings contribute to the broader landscape of commutativity theorems, offering new insights into the structural properties of rings with derivations. Moreover, this research paves the way for further exploration of derivations in algebraic systems, with potential applications in operator algebras, noncommutative geometry, and other areas where ring theory plays a fundamental role.

Author Contributions: The material is the result of the joint efforts of A.Y.H., Z.B., E.K.S., Ö.G. and N.u.R. All authors have read and agreed to the published version of the manuscript.

Funding: The authors extend their appreciation to the Deanship of Research and Graduate Studies at King Khalid University for funding this work through the Large Research Project under grant number RGP2/293/45.

Institutional Review Board Statement: Not applicable.

Informed Consent Statement: Not applicable.

Data Availability Statement: All data required for this article are included within the article.

Acknowledgments: The authors are greatly indebted to the referee for their valuable suggestions and comments, which have immensely improved the article.

Conflicts of Interest: The authors declare no conflicts of interest.

References

1. Posner, E.C. Derivations in prime rings. *Proc. Am. Math. Soc.* **1957**, *8*, 1093–1100. [CrossRef]
2. El Sofy, M.M. Rings with some kinds of mappings. Master's Thesis, Cairo University, Branch of Fayoum, Fayoum, Egypt, 2000.
3. Daif, M.N.; Bell, H.E. Remarks on derivations on semiprime rings. *Int. J. Math. Math. Sci.* **1992**, *15*, 205–206. [CrossRef]
4. Quadri, M.A.; Khan, M.S.; Rehman, N. Generalized derivations and commutativity of prime rings. *Indian Pure Appl. Math.* **2003**, *34*, 1393–1396.
5. Koc, E.; Golbasi, Ö. Some results on ideals of semiprime rings with multiplicative generalized derivations. *Commun. Algebra* **2018**, *46*, 4905–4915. [CrossRef]
6. Bell, H.E.; Daif, M.N. On derivations and commutativity in prime rings. *Acta Math. Hung.* **1995**, *66*, 337–343. [CrossRef]
7. Nabiel, H. Semiderivations and commutativity in semiprime rings. *Gen. Math. Notes* **2013**, *19*, 71–82.
8. Hongan, M. A note on semiprime rings with derivation. *Internat. J. Math. Math. Sci.* **1997**, *20*, 413–415. [CrossRef]
9. De Filippis, V.; Mamouni, A.; Oukhtite, L. Semiderivations satisfying certain algebraic identities on Jordan ideals. *Int. Sch. Res. Not.* **2013**, *2013*, 738368. [CrossRef]
10. Melaibari, A.; Muthana, N.; Al-Kenani, A. On homoderivations in rings. *Gen. Math. Notes* **2016**, *35*, 1–8.
11. Ashraf, M.; Rehman, N. On derivations and commutativity in prime rings. *East-West J. Math.* **2001**, *3*, 87–91. [CrossRef]
12. Alharfie, E.F.; Muthana, N.M. The commutativity of prime ring with homoderivations. *Int. J. Adv. Appl. Sci.* **2018**, *5*, 79–81. [CrossRef]
13. Engin, A.; Aydın, N. Homoderivations in prime rings. *J. New Theory* **2023**, *43*, 23–34. [CrossRef]
14. Centrone, L.; Zargeh, C. Varieties of Null-Filiform Leibniz Algebras Under the Action of Hopf Algebras. *Algebr. Repr. Theory* **2023**, *26*, 631–648. [CrossRef]
15. Hongan, M.; Rehman, N.; Al-Omary, R.M. Lie ideals and Jordan triple derivations in rings. *Rend. Semin. Mat. Univ. Padova* **2011**, *125*, 147–156. [CrossRef]
16. Ferreira, R.N.; Ferreira, B.L.M. Jordan triple derivation on alternative rings. *Proyecciones* **2018**, *37*, 171–180. [CrossRef]

17. Ferreira, B.L.M.; Guzzo, H., Jr.; Ferreira, R.N.; Wei, F. Jordan derivations of alternative rings. *Commun. Algebra* **2020**, *48*, 717–723. [CrossRef]
18. Ferreira, B.L.M.; Kaygorodov, I. Commuting maps on alternative rings. *Ric. Mat.* **2022**, *71*, 67–78. [CrossRef]

Disclaimer/Publisher's Note: The statements, opinions and data contained in all publications are solely those of the individual author(s) and contributor(s) and not of MDPI and/or the editor(s). MDPI and/or the editor(s) disclaim responsibility for any injury to people or property resulting from any ideas, methods, instructions or products referred to in the content.

mathematics

MDPI

Article

The Equivalent Standard Forms of a Class of Tropical Matrices and Centralizer Groups

Yanliang Cheng

School of Mathematics, Northwest University, Xi'an 710127, China; 202110145@stumail.nwu.edu.cn

Abstract: In this paper, the equivalent standard forms of tropical idempotent strongly definite matrices are introduced. In particular, the observation of the equivalent standard forms of tropical idempotent normal matrices is given. An equivalence relation ρ on the set of all tropical idempotent normal matrices, which is relevant to their centralizer groups, is introduced and studied. It is proved that every ρ-class contains at least one strongly regular tropical idempotent normal matrix. Furthermore, a structural description of the centralizer groups of partial strongly regular tropical idempotent normal matrices is given.

Keywords: tropical semiring; tropical matrix; idempotent strongly definite matrix; idempotent normal matrix; centralizer group

MSC: 15A80; 20B99; 20H99

1. Introduction and Preliminaries

The *tropical semiring* $\overline{\mathbb{R}}$ is the set $\mathbb{R} \cup \{-\infty\}$ equipped with the operations of tropical addition $a \oplus b := max\{a, b\}$ and tropical multiplication $a \otimes b := a + b$, where 0 and $-\infty$ are the multiplicative neutral element and the additive neutral element, respectively. The completed tropical semiring $\overline{\overline{\mathbb{R}}}$ is the tropical semiring augmented with an extra element $+\infty$ (see [1]). Note that, by definition,

$$(-\infty) \otimes (+\infty) = (+\infty) \otimes (-\infty) = -\infty.$$

Let $M_n(\overline{\mathbb{R}})$ denote the set of $n \times n$ matrices with entries in $\overline{\mathbb{R}}$. As in conventional linear algebra, we can extend the operations $\oplus$ and $\otimes$ on the tropical semiring $\overline{\mathbb{R}}$ to $M_n(\overline{\mathbb{R}})$. Indeed, if $A = (a_{ij}), B = (b_{ij}) \in M_n(\overline{\mathbb{R}})$, then we have

$$(A \oplus B)_{ij} = a_{ij} \oplus b_{ij}, \ (A \otimes B)_{ij} = \bigoplus_{k=1}^{n} a_{ik} \otimes b_{kj},$$

for all $i, j \in [n](= \{1, 2, \ldots, n\})$, where $(A \oplus B)_{ij}$ and $(A \otimes B)_{ij}$ denote the (i, j)-th entries of the matrices $A \oplus B$ and $A \otimes B$, respectively. For brevity, we usually write AB in place of $A \otimes B$ for a product of matrices. It is easy to check that $(M_n(\overline{\mathbb{R}}), \oplus, \otimes)$ is an idempotent semiring. The additive neutral element of $M_n(\overline{\mathbb{R}})$ is the tropical $n \times n$ matrix whose entries are all $-\infty$, denoted by Z_n, and the multiplicative neutral element of $M_n(\overline{\mathbb{R}})$ is the tropical identity matrix whose diagonal entries are 0 and off-diagonal ones are $-\infty$, denoted by I_n. We are interested in studying the multiplicative structure of the tropical matrices. There is a series of papers in the literature studying the multiplicative structure of this semiring (see [2–5]).

Recall that a tropical matrix $E \in M_n(\overline{\mathbb{R}})$ is said to be *idempotent* if $E^2 = E$ and a tropical matrix $A = (a_{ij}) \in M_n(\overline{\mathbb{R}})$ is said to be *normal* if $-\infty \leq a_{ij} \leq 0$ and $a_{ii} = 0$ for all $i, j \in [n]$ (see [1,6]). Since we never refer to classical matrices in this paper, the following matrices refer to tropical matrices. A matrix $A \in M_n(\overline{\mathbb{R}})$ is said to be *strongly regular* if the system $Ax = b$ has a unique solution for some $b \in \mathbb{R}^n$. It is well known that an $n \times n$ matrix $A = (a_{ij})$ is strongly regular if and only if it has a strong permanent (see [1] [Proposition 6.2.2])—that is, there exists a unique $\sigma \in S_n$ such that

$$maper(A) = a_{1,1^\sigma} \otimes a_{2,2^\sigma} \otimes \cdots \otimes a_{n,n^\sigma},$$

where $maper(A) = \bigoplus_{\sigma \in S_n} a_{1,1^\sigma} \otimes a_{2,2^\sigma} \otimes \cdots \otimes a_{n,n^\sigma}$ is called the *permanent* of A. Throughout this paper, M_n^I and M_n^{IN} stand for the set of all idempotent $n \times n$ matrices and all idempotent normal $n \times n$ matrices, respectively. M_n^{SR} stands for the set of all strongly regular idempotent normal matrices and M_n^{NSR} stands for the set of all idempotent normal matrices that are not strongly regular (that is, $M_n^{NSR} = M_n^{IN} \setminus M_n^{SR}$). For more details about idempotent normal matrices, the reader is referred to [2,7–11].

An $n \times n$ matrix is called *diagonal*—notation $diag(\lambda_1, \lambda_2, \cdots, \lambda_n)$—if its diagonal entries are $\lambda_1, \lambda_2, \cdots, \lambda_n \in \mathbb{R}$ and the off-diagonal entries are $-\infty$. A matrix is said to be a *permutation matrix* (*generalized permutation matrix*, respectively) if it is formed from the identity matrix (the diagonal matrix, respectively) by reordering its columns and/or rows. Let $GL_n(\overline{\mathbb{R}})$ and $P_n(\overline{\mathbb{R}})$ denote the set of all generalized permutation matrices and the set of all permutation matrices in $M_n(\overline{\mathbb{R}})$, respectively. It is easy to see that $GL_n(\overline{\mathbb{R}})$ and $P_n(\overline{\mathbb{R}})$ are subgroups of the semigroup $(M_n(\overline{\mathbb{R}}), \otimes)$. In fact, the position of generalized permutation matrices in max-algebra is slightly more special than in conventional linear algebra as they are the only matrices having an inverse (see ([1], Theorem 1.1.3)). Let $A = (a_{ij}) \in M_n(\overline{\mathbb{R}})$. Define

$$U_n(A) := \{P \in GL_n(\overline{\mathbb{R}}) \mid PA = AP\}, \ P_n(A) := \{P_\sigma \in P_n(\overline{\mathbb{R}}) \mid P_\sigma A = AP_\sigma\},$$

where P_σ denotes an $n \times n$ permutation matrix whose i-th row is equal to the i^σ-th row of I_n for any $i \in [n]$. It is easy to check that $P_n(A) \leq U_n(A)$, $P_n(A) \cong G_A$, where

$$G_A := \{\sigma \in S_n \mid (\forall i, j \in [n]) \ a_{i^\sigma, j^\sigma} = a_{ij}\}.$$

$U_n(A)$ will be called the *generalized centralizer group* of A and $P_n(A)$(or G_A) will be called the *centralizer group* of A (see [11]).

There are a series of papers in the literature that study tropical matrix groups. In 2011, Johnson and Kambites [5] studied the algebraic structure of the multiplicative semigroup of all tropical 2×2 matrices. They described completely the structures of maximal subgroups of this semigroup. In 2012, Shitov [3] gave a complete description of the subgroups of the multiplicative semigroup of tropical $n \times n$ matrices up to isomorphism. They showed that every group of tropical matrices is isomorphic to a subgroup of $GL_n(\overline{\mathbb{R}})$ and therefore embeds into the permutation wreath product $\mathbb{R} \wr S_n$. In 2018, Izhakian et al. [12] studied the structure of the maximal subgroups of finitary tropical $n \times n$ matrices. They showed that the maximal subgroup containing a tropical idempotent matrix E is isomorphic to $U_n(E)$. Moreover, the maximal subgroup is, up to isomorphism, exactly the direct product of G_E and $\mathbb{R}$. In 2018, Yang [4,13] studied the generalized centralizer groups of nonsingular tropical idempotent matrices. In particular, a decomposition of the generalized centralizer groups of nonsingular symmetric tropical idempotent matrices was given. In 2022, Deng et al. [11] studied the generalized centralizer groups and centralizer groups of tropical $n \times n$ matrices. They proved that the centralizer group of a tropical matrix is isomorphic to the centralizer group of an idempotent normal matrix E. Moreover, the structure of the centralizer group of E is given when E is not strongly regular. In this paper, by means of the introduction of the equivalent standard form of idempotent strongly definite matrices, we obtain that the centralizer group of every not strongly regular idempotent normal matrix is equal to the centralizer group of some strongly regular idempotent normal matrix. Further, a structural description of the centralizer groups of partial strongly regular idempotent normal matrices is given. Our results generalize and enrich corresponding results about idempotent normal matrices and their centralizer groups (see [11]).

In the remainder of this section, we recall some notions and results related to the weighted digraph $D(A)$ of a matrix A (see [1]), which will be required later. Let $A = (a_{ij}) \in M_n(\overline{\mathbb{R}})$. The *weighted digraph associated with* A is $D(A) = (N(A), E(A), w)$, where the node set $N(A) = [n]$ and the edge set $E(A) = \{(i,j) \mid a_{ij} > -\infty\}$ with weights $w(i,j) = a_{ij}$ for all $(i,j) \in E(A)$. Suppose that $\pi = (i_1, i_2, \cdots, i_p)$ is a path in $D(A)$; then, the *weight* of π is defined to be $w(\pi, A) = a_{i_1,i_2} + a_{i_2,i_3} + \cdots + a_{i_{p-1},i_p}$ if $p > 1$ and $w(\pi, A) = -\infty$ if $p = 1$. The number $p - 1$ is called the *length* of π, denoted by $\ell(\pi)$. Recall that a path $(i_1, i_2, \cdots, i_p)$ is called a *cycle* if $p > 1$ and $i_1 = i_p$, and it is called an *elementary cycle* if, moreover, $i_k \neq i_\ell$ for any $k, \ell \in [p-1]$ and $k \neq \ell$. The *maximum cycle mean* of A, denoted by $\lambda(A)$, is defined by

$$\lambda(A) = max_\sigma \mu(\sigma, A),$$

where the maximization is taken over all elementary cycles in $D(A)$ and

$$\mu(\sigma, A) = \frac{w(\sigma, A)}{\ell(\sigma)}$$

denotes the mean of a cycle σ.

A cycle in $D(A)$ is called *critical* if its cycle mean is equal to $\lambda(A)$. The nodes and the edges of $D(A)$ that belong to some critical cycles are called *critical*. The *critical digraph of* A is the digraph $C(A) = (N_c(A), E_c(A))$, where $N_c(A)$ and $E_c(A)$ denote the set of critical nodes and critical edges of $D(A)$, respectively. If $i, j \in N_c(A)$ belong to the same critical cycle, then i and j are called *equivalent* in $D(A)$ and we write $i \sim_A j$. Clearly, $\sim_A$ is an equivalence relation on $N_c(A)$.

A matrix A is called *definite* if $\lambda(A) = 0$. Thus, a matrix is definite if and only if all cycles in $D(A)$ are non-positive (i.e., its cycle mean is non-positive) and at least one has weight zero. A matrix $A = (a_{ij}) \in M_n(\overline{\mathbb{R}})$ is called *increasing* if $a_{ii} \geq 0$ for all $i \in [n]$, and is called *strongly definite* if it is definite and increasing. Since the diagonal entries of A are the weights of cycles (loops), we have that $a_{ii} = 0$ for all $i \in [n]$ if A is strongly definite. In the following, M_n^{ISD} stands for the set of all idempotent strongly definite matrices. For more details about idempotent strongly definite matrices, the reader is referred to ([1], Section 6.2).

In addition to this introduction and preliminaries, this paper comprises two sections. In Section 2, we give some characterizations of $\sim_E$ and introduce the equivalent standard forms of E, where $E \in M_n^{ISD}$. In particular, we give the observation of the equivalent standard forms of $E \in M_n^{IN}$. In Section 3, by using the centralizer groups of idempotent normal matrices we introduce an equivalence relation ρ on M_n^{IN}. We prove that every ρ-class contains at least one strongly regular idempotent normal matrix. Let $E \in M_n^{SR}$. A new idempotent normal matrix $E^{(e_t)}$ is constructed from E, where e_t is an off-diagonal entry of E. We give the equivalent conditions for which $E^{(e_t)}$ is not strongly regular. Further, a structural description of G_E is given when $E^{(e_t)}$ is not strongly regular.

For other notations and terminologies not given in this article, the reader is referred to the books [1,14,15].

2. The Equivalent Standard Forms of Idempotent Strongly Definite Matrices

Let $\overline{\mathbb{R}}^n$ denote the set of all n-tuples x with entries in $\overline{\mathbb{R}}$. We write x_i for the i-th component of x. For any $x, y \in \overline{\mathbb{R}}^n$, we define

$$\langle x \mid y \rangle := max\{\lambda \in \overline{\overline{\mathbb{R}}} \mid \lambda \otimes x \leq y\} = min_{i \in [n]}\{y_i - x_i\},$$

where $\lambda \otimes x = (\lambda + x_1, \lambda + x_2, \ldots, \lambda + x_n)$. We set $(-\infty) - a = -\infty, a - (-\infty) = +\infty$ and $(-\infty) - (-\infty) = +\infty$ for any $a \in \mathbb{R}$. The map $(x, y) \mapsto \langle x \mid y \rangle$ is a residuation operator in the sense of residuation theory [16], and is ubiquitous in tropical algebra. Notice that $\langle x \mid y \rangle = +\infty$ if and only if $x = -\infty$. $\langle x \mid y \rangle = -\infty$ if and only if there exists $j \in [n]$ such that $y_j = -\infty$ and $x_j \neq -\infty$.

As a consequence of ([7], Lemma 5.3), we have the following:

Lemma 1. *Suppose that $E = (e_{ij}) \in M_n^I$. Let $r_1, r_2, \ldots, r_n$ denote the rows of E and $c_1, c_2, \ldots, c_n$ denote the columns of E. Then,*

(i) $e_{ij} \leq min\{\langle r_j \mid r_i \rangle, \langle c_i \mid c_j \rangle\}$ *for any* $i, j \in [n]$;

(ii) *If* $e_{ii} = 0$, *then* $e_{ij} = \langle c_i \mid c_j \rangle$ *and* $e_{ji} = \langle r_i \mid r_j \rangle$ *for all* $j \in [n]$.

Proof. Part (i) is a direct consequence of ([7], Lemma 5.3).

To prove part (ii), let $e_{ii} = 0$. Suppose that $e_{ij} < \langle c_i \mid c_j \rangle$ for some $j \in [n]$. Then, $e_{ij} < \langle c_i \mid c_j \rangle \otimes e_{ii}$. Since $\langle x \mid y \rangle \otimes x \leq y$ for any $x, y \in \overline{\mathbb{R}}^n$, it is implied that $\langle c_i \mid c_j \rangle \otimes c_i \leq c_j$. Hence, $\langle c_i \mid c_j \rangle \otimes e_{ki} \leq e_{kj}$ for all $k \in [n]$. This contradicts $e_{ij} < \langle c_i \mid c_j \rangle \otimes e_{ii}$. Thus, $e_{ij} = \langle c_i \mid c_j \rangle$ for all $j \in [n]$. Similarly, $e_{ji} = \langle r_i \mid r_j \rangle$ for all $j \in [n]$. □

Furthermore, we have the following lemma.

Lemma 2. *Let $E = (e_{ij}) \in M_n^{ISD}$ and $i, j \in [n]$. Then, the following are equivalent:*

(i) $e_{ij} = e_{ji} = 0$;

(ii) $e_{ik} = e_{jk}$ *for all* $k \in [n]$;

(iii) $e_{ki} = e_{kj}$ *for all* $k \in [n]$.

Proof. We need only to prove the equivalence of (i) and (ii), since the equivalence of (i) and (iii) may be showed dually.

$(i) \Rightarrow (ii)$. Suppose that $e_{ij} = e_{ji} = 0$. Then, by Lemma 1 and $E \in M_n^{ISD}$, $e_{ij} = \langle r_j \mid r_i \rangle$ and $e_{ji} = \langle r_i \mid r_j \rangle$, where r_i and r_j denote the i-th and j-th row of E, respectively. Moveover, $\langle r_j \mid r_i \rangle = \langle r_i \mid r_j \rangle = 0$, and so $r_i = r_j$. That is, $e_{ik} = e_{jk}$ for all $k \in [n]$.

$(ii) \Rightarrow (i)$. Suppose that $e_{ik} = e_{jk}$ for all $k \in [n]$. Setting $k = i$, we have $e_{ji} = e_{ii} = 0$. Setting $k = j$, we have $e_{ij} = e_{jj} = 0$. Thus, $e_{ij} = e_{ji} = 0$. □

Let $E = (e_{ij}) \in M_n^{ISD}$. It is easily seen that the maximum cycle mean $\lambda(E) = 0$ and that every node of $D(E)$ is critical, since all the diagonal entries of E are equal to 0. That is, $N_c(E) = [n]$. So, $\sim_E$ is an equivalence relation on $[n]$.

Note that $M_n^{IN} \subseteq M_n^{ISD}$. It is clear that Lemma 2 generalizes the part results of ([11], Lemma 3.2), which asserts that if $E = (e_{ij}) \in M_n^{IN}$ and $i, j \in [n]$, then $i \sim_E j$ if and only if $e_{ij} = e_{ji} = 0$. Now, let $E = (e_{ij}) \in M_n^{ISD}$. If $e_{ij} = e_{ji} = 0$, then $i \sim_E j$ by $\lambda(E) = 0$. However, the inverse of this result is not true. In fact, for idempotent strongly definite matrices, we have the following:

Proposition 1. *Let $E = (e_{ij}) \in M_n^{ISD}$ and $i, j \in [n]$. Then, the following are equivalent:*

(i) $i \sim_E j$;

(ii) $e_{ij} + e_{ji} = 0$;

(iii) $e_{ik} - e_{jk} = e_{ij}$ *for all* $k \in [n]$;

(iv) $e_{kj} - e_{ki} = e_{ij}$ *for all* $k \in [n]$.

Proof. We need only to prove the equivalence of (i), (ii), and (iii), since the equivalence of (i), (ii), and (iv) may be showed dually.

$(i) \Rightarrow (ii)$. Suppose that $i \sim_E j$. Then, there is a critical cycle π containing both i and j in $D(E)$. We shall write $\pi = (i_1 i_2 \ldots i_s \ldots i_p)$, where $i_1 = i$ and $i_s = j$. Moreover, $w(\pi, E) = e_{i_1,i_2} + \ldots + e_{i_{s-1},i_s} + e_{i_s,i_{s+1}} + \ldots + e_{i_p,i_1} = 0$. Since E is idempotent, it follows that $e_{i_1,i_2} + \ldots + e_{i_{s-1},i_s} \leq e_{ij}$ and $e_{i_s,i_{s+1}} + \ldots + e_{i_p,i_1} \leq e_{ji}$. Thus, $w(\pi, E) \leq e_{ij} + e_{ji} \leq 0$, and so $e_{ij} + e_{ji} = 0$.

$(ii) \Rightarrow (iii)$. Suppose that $e_{ij} + e_{ji} = 0$. Then, by Lemma 1, $\langle r_j \mid r_i \rangle + \langle r_i \mid r_j \rangle = 0$, and so $\langle r_j \mid r_i \rangle = -\langle r_i \mid r_j \rangle$—i.e.,

$$min_{k \in [n]} \{e_{ik} - e_{jk}\} = max_{k \in [n]} \{e_{ik} - e_{jk}\}.$$

This means that $e_{ik} - e_{jk} = e_{i\ell} - e_{j\ell}$ for any $k, \ell \in [n]$. Putting $\ell = j$, we deduce that $e_{ik} - e_{jk} = e_{ij}$ for all $k \in [n]$.

$(iii) \Rightarrow (i)$. Suppose that $e_{ik} - e_{jk} = e_{ij}$ for all $k \in [n]$. Putting $k = i$, we obtain that $e_{ij} + e_{ji} = 0$. Thus, $\tau = (ij)$ is a critical cycle with length two in $D(E)$. Consequently, $i \sim_E j$. □

It is clear that the above proposition is a generalization of ([11], Lemma 3.2). As usual, Δ (resp. ∇) stands for the equality relation (resp. universal relation).

Proposition 2. *Let $E = (e_{ij}) \in M_n^{ISD}$. Then, E is not strongly regular $\Longleftrightarrow \sim_E \neq \Delta$.*

Proof. Suppose that E is not strongly regular. Then, there exists $\tau \in S_n \setminus \{1\}$ such that $e_{1,\tau(1)} \otimes e_{2,\tau(2)} \otimes \cdots \otimes e_{n,\tau(n)} = 0$. Write τ as a product of non-trivial disjoint cycles, say, $\tau = \tau_1 \tau_2 \ldots \tau_\ell$ $(\ell < n)$. Then, any such cycle $\tau_i (i \in [\ell])$, say, $\tau_i = (j_1 j_2 \cdots j_k)$, satisfies $e_{j_1,j_2} \otimes e_{j_2,j_3} \otimes \cdots \otimes e_{j_k,j_1} = 0$. Since E is idempotent, it follows that $e_{j_1,j_k} \geq e_{j_1,j_2} \otimes \cdots \otimes e_{j_{k-1},j_k} = -e_{j_k,j_1}$. Moreover, $e_{j_1,j_k} + e_{j_k,j_1} \geq 0$. By $e_{j_1,j_k} \otimes e_{j_k,j_1} \leq e_{j_1,j_1} = 0$, which implies that $e_{j_1,j_k} + e_{j_k,j_1} = 0$. It follows from Proposition 1 that $j_1 \sim_E j_k$, and so $\sim_E \neq \Delta$.

Assume that $\sim_E \neq \Delta$. Then, by Proposition 1, $e_{ij} + e_{ji} = 0$ for some $i, j \in [n]$ and $i \neq j$. It follows from ([7], Lemma 3.3) that $mapor(E) = 0$. Hence, the transposition $(ij) \in S_n$ attains the permanent of E, as required. □

Let $G \leq S_n$. Recall that $\emptyset \neq \Gamma \subseteq [n]$ is called *a block* for G if for each $\sigma \in G$ either $\Gamma^\sigma = \Gamma$ or $\Gamma^\sigma \cap \Gamma = \emptyset$, where $\Gamma^\sigma = \{i^\sigma \mid i \in \Gamma\}$. Clearly, for each $\sigma \in G$, Γ^σ is also a block for G (see [14]). *A G-congruence* on $[n]$ is an equivalence relation $\sim$ on $[n]$ with the property that

$$i \sim j \Longleftrightarrow i^\sigma \sim j^\sigma \text{ for all } \sigma \in G.$$

Let G be transitive on $[n]$ and Γ a block for G. Then, $\{\Gamma^\sigma \mid \sigma \in G\}$ is a partition of $[n]$ and $|\Gamma^\sigma| = |\Gamma|$ for each $\sigma \in G$. $\{\Gamma^\sigma \mid \sigma \in G\}$ is called *a system of blocks* for G containing Γ. If $\sim$ is a G-congruence on $[n]$, then the equivalence classes of $\sim$ form a system of blocks for G (see ([14], Exercise 1.5.4)).

Proposition 3. *Let $E = (e_{ij}) \in M_n^{ISD}$ and $\{\Gamma_1, \Gamma_2, \ldots, \Gamma_m\}$ be the set of all classes of $\sim_E$. Then, $\sim_E$ is a G_E-congruence on $[n]$. Also, $\{\Gamma_1, \Gamma_2, \ldots, \Gamma_m\}$ is a system of blocks for G_E if G_E is transitive on $[n]$.*

Proof. Suppose that $\sigma \in G_E$. Then, for any $i, j \in [n]$,

$$\begin{aligned} i \sim_E j &\iff e_{ik} - e_{jk} = e_{ij} && \text{(by Proposition 1)} \\ &\iff e_{i^\sigma,k^\sigma} - e_{j^\sigma,k^\sigma} = e_{i^\sigma,j^\sigma} && \text{(since } \sigma \in G_E) \\ &\iff i^\sigma \sim_E j^\sigma. \end{aligned}$$

This shows that $\sim_E$ is a G_E-congruence on $[n]$, and so $\{\Gamma_1, \Gamma_2, \ldots, \Gamma_m\}$ is a system of blocks for G_E if G_E acts transitively on $[n]$. □

Now, suppose that $E \in M_n^{ISD}$ and $\{\Gamma_1, \Gamma_2, \ldots, \Gamma_m\}$ is the set of all classes of $\sim_E$, where $1 \leq m \leq n$. If E is not strongly regular, then $m \neq n$ by Proposition 2. Without loss of generality, let $1 \leq |\Gamma_1| \leq |\Gamma_2| \leq \cdots \leq |\Gamma_m| \leq n$ and $|\Gamma_k| = t_k$ for any $k \in [m]$. That is, $1 \leq t_1 \leq t_2 \leq \cdots \leq t_m \leq n$ and $t_1 + t_2 + \cdots + t_m = n$. It follows from Proposition 1 that for any $i, j \in \Gamma_k$ and $k \in [m]$, $c_j = e_{ij} \otimes c_i$ and $r_i = e_{ij} \otimes r_j$.

Next, for each $k \in [m]$, we shall write

$$\Omega_k = \{\sum_{i=1}^{k-1} t_i + 1, \sum_{i=1}^{k-1} t_i + 2, \ldots, \sum_{i=1}^{k} t_i\}.$$

Take $\tau \in S_n$ such that $\Omega_k^\tau = \Gamma_k$ for each $k \in [m]$. Further, by permuting simultaneously the rows and columns of E with τ, we obtain the following block matrix, $\overline{E} = P_\tau E P_\tau^{-1}$:

$$\overline{E} = (\overline{e}_{ij})_{n \times n} = \begin{pmatrix} \overline{E}_1 & \overline{E}_{12} & \cdots & \overline{E}_{1m} \\ \overline{E}_{21} & \overline{E}_2 & \cdots & \overline{E}_{2m} \\ \vdots & \vdots & \ddots & \vdots \\ \overline{E}_{m1} & \overline{E}_{m2} & \cdots & \overline{E}_m \end{pmatrix}, \quad (1)$$

where $1 \leq m \leq n$, for each $k \in [m]$, $\overline{E}_k$ is an antisymmetric $t_k \times t_k$ matrix, and for any $k, \ell \in [m]$ and $k \neq \ell$, $\overline{E}_{k\ell}$ is an $t_k \times t_\ell$ matrix with $c_j(\overline{E}_{k\ell}) = \overline{e}_{ij} \otimes c_i(\overline{E}_{k\ell})$ for any $i, j \in \Omega_\ell$ and $r_i(\overline{E}_{k\ell}) = \overline{e}_{ij} \otimes r_j(\overline{E}_{k\ell})$ for any $i, j \in \Omega_k$. In fact, since $\overline{E} = P_\tau E P_\tau^{-1}$, we have that $\overline{E} \in M_n^{ISD}$ and $\overline{e}_{ij} = e_{i^\tau,j^\tau}$ for any $i, j \in [n]$. Then, for each $k \in [m]$,

$$i, j \in \Omega_k \Leftrightarrow i^\tau, j^\tau \in \Gamma_k \Leftrightarrow i^\tau \sim_E j^\tau \Leftrightarrow e_{i^\tau,j^\tau} + e_{j^\tau,i^\tau} = 0 \Leftrightarrow \overline{e}_{ij} + \overline{e}_{ji} = 0 \Leftrightarrow i \sim_{\overline{E}} j.$$

This implies that $\{\Omega_1, \Omega_2, \ldots, \Omega_m\}$ is the set of all classes of $\sim_{\overline{E}}$ and $\overline{e}_{ij} = -\overline{e}_{ji}$ for any $i, j \in \Omega_k$. That is to say, $\overline{E}_k$ is an antisymmetric $t_k \times t_k$ matrix for each $k \in [m]$. Also, $c_j(\overline{E}) = \overline{e}_{ij} \otimes c_i(\overline{E})$ and $r_i(\overline{E}) = \overline{e}_{ij} \otimes r_j(\overline{E})$ for any $i, j \in \Omega_k$ and $k \in [m]$. Moreover, for any $k, \ell \in [m]$ with $k \neq \ell$, $\overline{E}_{k\ell}$ is an $t_k \times t_\ell$ matrix with $c_j(\overline{E}_{k\ell}) = \overline{e}_{ij} \otimes c_i(\overline{E}_{k\ell})$ for any $i, j \in \Omega_\ell$ and $r_i(\overline{E}_{k\ell}) = \overline{e}_{ij} \otimes r_j(\overline{E}_{k\ell})$ for any $i, j \in \Omega_k$.

Now, we shall call the block matrix $\overline{E}$ *the equivalent standard form* of $E \in M_n^{ISD}$. It is easy to see that every idempotent strongly definite $n \times n$ matrix E can be transformed in linear time by simultaneous permutations of the rows and columns to an equivalent standard form $\overline{E}$ as above.

In particular, let $E = (e_{ij}) \in M_n^{IN}$. Then, E is equivalent to the following equivalent standard form $\overline{E}$:

$$\overline{E} = (\overline{e}_{ij})_{n\times n} = \begin{pmatrix} 0 & \overline{E}_{12} & \cdots & \overline{E}_{1m} \\ \overline{E}_{21} & 0 & \cdots & \overline{E}_{2m} \\ \vdots & \vdots & \ddots & \vdots \\ \overline{E}_{m1} & \overline{E}_{m2} & \cdots & 0 \end{pmatrix}, \tag{2}$$

where $1 \leq m \leq n$ and $\overline{E}_{k\ell}$ is an $t_k \times t_\ell$ matrix with all entries $\widehat{e}_{k\ell} \leq 0$, for any $k, \ell \in [m]$ with $k \neq \ell$. In fact, since $\overline{e}_{ij} = -\overline{e}_{ji}$ for any $i, j \in \Omega_k$ and $k \in [m]$, it follows that $\overline{e}_{ij} = 0$ for any $i, j \in \Omega_k$ and $k \in [m]$ by $E \in M_n^{IN}$. Thus, all diagonal blocks of $\overline{E}$ are 0. Moreover, for any $k, \ell \in [m]$ with $k \neq \ell$, $c_j(\overline{E}_{k\ell}) = c_i(\overline{E}_{k\ell})$ for any $i, j \in \Omega_\ell$ and $r_j(\overline{E}_{k\ell}) = r_i(\overline{E}_{k\ell})$ for any $i, j \in \Omega_k$. Thus, all entries of $\overline{E}_{k\ell}$ are equal.

Notice that if $\widehat{e}_{k\ell} = 0$ for some $k, \ell \in [m]$ with $k \neq \ell$, then $\widehat{e}_{\ell k} < 0$. In fact, suppose that $\widehat{e}_{\ell k} = 0$. Then, $\overline{E}_{k\ell} = 0$ and $\overline{E}_{\ell k} = 0$. That is, $\overline{e}_{ij} = \overline{e}_{ji} = 0$ for any $i \in \Omega_k$ and $j \in \Omega_\ell$. This follows from ([11], Lemma 3.2) that $i \sim_{\overline{E}} j$ for any $i \in \Omega_k$ and $j \in \Omega_\ell$. This contradicts the fact that Ω_k and Ω_ℓ are two different $\sim_{\overline{E}}$-classes.

Remark 1. *In general, the equivalent standard forms of E are not unique. For instance, let*

$$E = \begin{pmatrix} 0 & -2 & -1 & -1 & -2 \\ -1 & 0 & -2 & -2 & 0 \\ -2 & -1 & 0 & 0 & -1 \\ -2 & -1 & 0 & 0 & -1 \\ -1 & 0 & -2 & -2 & 0 \end{pmatrix}. \tag{3}$$

It is easy to see that $E \in M_n^{IN} \subseteq M_n^{ISD}$. *If we take* $\tau_1 = (35) \in S_5$, *then* $\overline{E} = P_{\tau_1} E P_{\tau_1}^{-1}$ *is an equivalent standard form of E as follows:*

$$\overline{E} = \begin{pmatrix} 0 & -2 & -2 & -1 & -1 \\ -1 & 0 & 0 & -2 & -2 \\ -1 & 0 & 0 & -2 & -2 \\ -2 & -1 & -1 & 0 & 0 \\ -2 & -1 & -1 & 0 & 0 \end{pmatrix}. \tag{4}$$

If we take $\tau_2 = (24) \in S_5$, *then* $\overline{\overline{E}} = P_{\tau_2} E P_{\tau_2}^{-1}$ *is also an equivalent standard form of E as follows:*

$$\overline{\overline{E}} = \begin{pmatrix} 0 & -1 & -1 & -2 & -2 \\ -2 & 0 & 0 & -1 & -1 \\ -2 & 0 & 0 & -1 & -1 \\ -1 & -2 & -2 & 0 & 0 \\ -1 & -2 & -2 & 0 & 0 \end{pmatrix}. \tag{5}$$

In fact, for a general idempotent strongly definite matrix E, the diagonal blocks of the equivalent standard form of E are determined uniquely up to a simultaneous permutation of the rows and columns. Any such form is essentially determined by the critical components of $C(E)$. The form forms an interesting correspondence with the Frobenius normal form of E, which is essentially determined by the strongly connected components of $D(E)$ (see [1]).

3. The Centralizer Groups of Idempotent Normal Matrices

In this section, we shall study the centralizer groups of tropical matrices. By ([11], Proposition 3.1), we know that the centralizer group of every tropical matrix equals the centralizer group of some idempotent normal matrix. Based on this fact, we need only to consider the centralizer groups of idempotent normal matrices.

Define a binary relation ρ on M_n^{IN} by

$$A \,\rho\, B \Longleftrightarrow G_A \cong G_B.$$

Clearly, ρ is an equivalence relation on M_n^{IN}. It is easy to check that $G_{I_n} = S_n$, and $G_A = S_n$ if and only if all off-diagonal entries of A are $a \leq 0$, where $A \in M_n^{IN}$. Furthermore, we have immediately the following result.

Lemma 3. *$I_n\rho = \{A = (a_{ij}) \in M_n^{IN} \mid a_{ij} = a$ for any $i, j \in [n]$ with $i \neq j, a \leq 0\}$, where $I_n\rho$ denotes the ρ-class containing I_n.*

Let $[-\infty, 0]$ denote the set $\{a \in \overline{\mathbb{R}} \mid -\infty \leq a \leq 0\}$. Then, there exists a natural bijection between $I_n\rho$ and $[-\infty, 0]$. That is, A corresponds to a, where a is the off-diagonal entries of A.

Suppose that $E \in M_n^{IN}$ and $\overline{E}$ is the equivalent standard form of E related to $\tau \in S_n$, i.e., $\overline{E} = P_\tau E P_{\tau^{-1}}$. Then, $G_{\overline{E}} = G_{P_\tau E P_{\tau^{-1}}} = \tau G_E \tau^{-1}$. Further, $G_{\overline{E}} \cong G_E$. Therefore, in order to study the centralizer group G_E, we need only to consider $G_{\overline{E}}$ up to isomorphism.

Now, let $\overline{E} = (\overline{e}_{ij}) \in M_n^{NSR}$ be in the form (2). By replacing all diagonal blocks $t_k \times t_k$ matrix 0 of $\overline{E}$ with $t_k \times t_k$ matrix A, where $A \in I_{t_k}\rho$ and all off-diagonal entries are $a < 0$, we can obtain the following block matrix $\widetilde{E}$.

$$\widetilde{E} = (\widetilde{e}_{ij})_{n\times n} = \begin{pmatrix} A & \overline{E}_{12} & \cdots & \overline{E}_{1m} \\ \overline{E}_{21} & A & \cdots & \overline{E}_{2m} \\ \vdots & \vdots & \ddots & \vdots \\ \overline{E}_{m1} & \overline{E}_{m2} & \cdots & A \end{pmatrix}, \tag{6}$$

where $1 \leq m < n$, $\overline{E}_{k\ell}$ is an $t_k \times t_\ell$ matrix with all entries $\widehat{e}_{k\ell} \leq 0$, and $k, \ell \in [m]$ with $k \neq \ell$.

For each $k \in [m]$, we let

$$d_k = \bigoplus_{\ell \in [m]\setminus\{k\}} (\widehat{e}_{k\ell} \otimes \widehat{e}_{\ell k}).$$

Note that for any $k, \ell \in [m]$ and $k \neq \ell$, $\widehat{e}_{k\ell} = 0$ implies $\widehat{e}_{\ell k} < 0$. Thus, $d_k < 0$ for all $k \in [m]$. Suppose that $T = \{e_1, e_2, \ldots, e_h\}$ is the set of all entries in $\overline{E}$, where $1 \leq h \leq m^2 - m + 1$. We shall write

$$\Sigma := \{a \leq 0 \mid a \notin T \text{ and } a > d_k \text{ for all } k \in [m]\}.$$

Since T is finite and $d_k < 0$ for all $k \in [m]$, we have that $\Sigma \neq \emptyset$ by the denseness of the real numbers.

Lemma 4. *Let $\overline{E} \in M_n^{NSR}$ be in the form (2) and $\widetilde{E}$ be defined as above. If $a \in \Sigma$, then $\widetilde{E} \in M_n^{SR}$.*

Proof. It is clear that $\widetilde{E}$ is a normal matrix. Now, we shall show that $\widetilde{E}$ is idempotent. By $a \in \Sigma$, it is implied that $a > d_k$ for all $k \in [m]$. Hence, for any $k \in [m]$,

$$\overline{E}_{k1}\overline{E}_{1k} \oplus \overline{E}_{k2}\overline{E}_{2k} \oplus \cdots \oplus A^2 \oplus \cdots \oplus \overline{E}_{km}\overline{E}_{mk} = A^2 = A.$$

For any $k, \ell \in [m]$ and $k \neq \ell$, without loss the generality, let $k < \ell$. Since $\overline{E}$ is idempotent, it follows that

$$\overline{E}_{k1}\overline{E}_{1\ell} \oplus \overline{E}_{k2}\overline{E}_{2\ell} \oplus \cdots \oplus 0\overline{E}_{k\ell} \oplus \cdots \oplus \overline{E}_{k\ell}0 \oplus \cdots \oplus \overline{E}_{km}\overline{E}_{m\ell} = \overline{E}_{k\ell}.$$

It is easy to check that $A\overline{E}_{k\ell} = \overline{E}_{k\ell}A = 0\overline{E}_{k\ell} = \overline{E}_{k\ell}0 = \overline{E}_{k\ell}$. Moreover, we have

$$\overline{E}_{k1}\overline{E}_{1\ell} \oplus \overline{E}_{k2}\overline{E}_{2\ell} \oplus \cdots \oplus A\overline{E}_{k\ell} \oplus \cdots \oplus \overline{E}_{k\ell}A \oplus \cdots \oplus \overline{E}_{km}\overline{E}_{m\ell} = \overline{E}_{k\ell}.$$

This shows that $\widetilde{E}$ is idempotent. That is, $\widetilde{E} \in M_n^{IN}$. It follows from the construction of $\widetilde{E}$ that either $\widetilde{e}_{ij} = 0$ or $\widetilde{e}_{ji} = 0$ for any $i, j \in [n]$ with $i \neq j$. Thus, by ([11], Lemma 3.2), $\sim_{\widetilde{E}} = \Delta$, and so $\widetilde{E} \in M_n^{SR}$ by ([11], Lemma 3.3). □

Furthermore, we have the following theorem.

Theorem 1. *Let $\overline{E} = (\overline{e}_{ij}) \in M_n^{NSR}$ be in the form (2) and $\widetilde{E} = (\widetilde{e}_{ij}) \in M_n^{SR}$ as above. Then, $G_{\overline{E}} = G_{\widetilde{E}}$. Moreover, $\widetilde{E} \in \overline{E}\rho$.*

Proof. Suppose that $\sigma \in G_{\overline{E}}$ and $i, j \in [n]$. If $i, j \in \Omega_k$ for some $k \in [m]$, then by Proposition 3, $i^\sigma, j^\sigma \in \Omega_\ell$ for some $\ell \in [m]$. Thus, $\widetilde{e}_{ii} = \widetilde{e}_{i^\sigma,i^\sigma} = 0$ and $\widetilde{e}_{ij} = \widetilde{e}_{i^\sigma,j^\sigma} = a$ for any $i, j \in \Omega_k$ with $i \neq j$.

If $i \in \Omega_k$ and $j \in \Omega_\ell$ for some $k, \ell \in [m]$ with $k \neq \ell$, then $i^\sigma \in \Omega_u$ and $j^\sigma \in \Omega_v$ for some $u, v \in [m]$ and $u \neq v$. In fact, suppose that $u = v$. Then, $i^\sigma, j^\sigma \in \Omega_u$. That is, $i^\sigma \sim_{\overline{E}} j^\sigma$. Since $\sim_{\overline{E}}$ is a $G_{\overline{E}}$-congruence, it implies that $(i^\sigma)^{\sigma^{-1}} \sim_{\overline{E}} (j^\sigma)^{\sigma^{-1}}$ by $\sigma^{-1} \in G_{\overline{E}}$. That is, $i \sim_{\overline{E}} j$ and so $\Omega_k = \Omega_\ell$, yielding a contradiction. Clearly, $\widetilde{e}_{ij} = \overline{e}_{ij}$ and $\widetilde{e}_{i^\sigma,j^\sigma} = \overline{e}_{i^\sigma,j^\sigma}$. Notice that $\overline{e}_{ij} = \overline{e}_{i^\sigma,j^\sigma}$. This implies that $\widetilde{e}_{ij} = \widetilde{e}_{i^\sigma,j^\sigma}$. We conclude that $\widetilde{e}_{ij} = \widetilde{e}_{i^\sigma,j^\sigma}$ for any $i, j \in [n]$. Consequently, $\sigma \in G_{\widetilde{E}}$. Thus, $G_{\overline{E}} \leq G_{\widetilde{E}}$.

On the other hand, suppose that $\sigma \in G_{\widetilde{E}}$. Then, $\widetilde{e}_{ij} = \widetilde{e}_{i^\sigma,j^\sigma}$ for any $i, j \in [n]$. If $i, j \in \Omega_k$ for some $k \in [m]$, then $\widetilde{e}_{i^\sigma,i^\sigma} = \widetilde{e}_{ii} = 0$ and $\widetilde{e}_{i^\sigma,j^\sigma} = \widetilde{e}_{ij} = a$ for $i \neq j$. By $a \in \Sigma$, it is implied that $a \notin T$. Therefore, $i^\sigma, j^\sigma \in \Omega_\ell$ for some $\ell \in [m]$, and so $\overline{e}_{i^\sigma,j^\sigma} = \overline{e}_{ij} = 0$.

If $i \in \Omega_k$ and $j \in \Omega_\ell$ for some $k, \ell \in [m]$ with $k \neq \ell$, then $\widetilde{e}_{i^\sigma,j^\sigma} = \widetilde{e}_{ij} = \overline{e}_{ij}$. Since $a \notin T$, it implies that $\overline{e}_{ij} \neq a$ and so $\widetilde{e}_{i^\sigma,j^\sigma} \neq a$. By $i \neq j$, it follows that $i^\sigma \neq j^\sigma$. Thus, there exist $u, v \in [m]$ and $u \neq v$ such that $i^\sigma \in \Omega_u$ and $j^\sigma \in \Omega_v$. Moreover, $\widetilde{e}_{i^\sigma,j^\sigma} = \overline{e}_{i^\sigma,j^\sigma}$. Consequently, $\overline{e}_{i^\sigma,j^\sigma} = \overline{e}_{ij}$. This shows that $\overline{e}_{i^\sigma,j^\sigma} = \overline{e}_{ij}$ for any $i, j \in [n]$. Hence, $\sigma \in G_{\overline{E}}$, and so $G_{\widetilde{E}} \leq G_{\overline{E}}$. Thus, $G_{\overline{E}} = G_{\widetilde{E}}$. This completes the proof. □

From the above theorem, we know that every ρ-class contains at least one strongly regular idempotent normal matrix. Therefore, to study the centralizer groups of idempotent normal matrices, we need only to consider the centralizer groups of strongly regular idempotent normal matrices up to isomorphism.

Now, let $E = (e_{ij}) \in M_n^{SR}$ and $O(E) = \{e_1, e_2, \ldots, e_r\}$ be the set of all off-diagonal entries of E, where $1 \leq r \leq n^2 - n$. By replacing only all diagonal entries 0 of E with some $e_t \in O(E)$, we can obtain an $n \times n$ matrix E^{e_t} as follows:

$$E^{e_t} = (e_{ij}^{e_t})_{n\times n} = \begin{pmatrix} e_t & e_{12} & \cdots & e_{1n} \\ e_{21} & e_t & \cdots & e_{2n} \\ \vdots & \vdots & \ddots & \vdots \\ e_{n1} & e_{n2} & \cdots & e_t \end{pmatrix}. \quad (7)$$

It is easy to check that $G_E = G_{E^{e_t}}$. We define an equivalence relation $\sim^{E^{e_t}}$ on $[n]$ by

$$i \sim^{E^{e_t}} j \Longleftrightarrow e_{ik}^{e_t} = e_{jk}^{e_t} \text{ and } e_{ki}^{e_t} = e_{kj}^{e_t} \text{ for all } k \in [n].$$

That is, $i \sim^{E^{e_t}} j$ if and only if the i-th row and the j-th row of E^{e_t} are equal and so are the i-th column and the j-th column. In the following, we shall give the equivalent conditions of $\sim^{E^{e_t}} \neq \Delta$. Further, a structural description of the centralizer group G_E is obtained.

Suppose that $\{\Sigma_1, \Sigma_2, \dots, \Sigma_s\}$ is the set of all $\sim^{E^{e_t}}$-classes for some $e_t \in O(E)$, where $1 \leq s \leq n$. Let $E^{e_t}[\Sigma_k]$ denote the principal submatrix of E^{e_t} where the row indices and the column indices are taken from Σ_k for each $k \in [s]$. It is clear that all entries of $E^{e_t}[\Sigma_k]$ are e_t. In fact, for any $i, j \in \Sigma_k$, $e_{ij}^{e_t} = e_{ii}^{e_t} = e_t$ by $i \sim^{E^{e_t}} j$. By replacing $E^{e_t}[\Sigma_k]$ with 0 for all $k \in [s]$, we can obtain an $n \times n$ matrix $E^{(e_t)} = (e_{ij}^{(e_t)})$. That is to say, $e_{ij}^{(e_t)} = 0$ for any $i, j \in \Sigma_k$ and $k \in [s]$, and $e_{ij}^{(e_t)} = e_{ij}^{e_t} = e_{ij}$ for any $i \in \Sigma_k$ and $j \in \Sigma_\ell$, where $k, \ell \in [s]$ and $k \neq \ell$. Moreover, we obtain a preliminary lemma.

Lemma 5. *Suppose that $E = (e_{ij}) \in M_n^{SR}$ and $E^{(e_t)}$ is defined as above. Then, $E^{(e_t)} \in M_n^{IN}$.*

Proof. Clearly, $E^{(e_t)}$ is a normal matrix. Now, we shall show that $E^{(e_t)}$ is idempotent, i.e., $e_{ij}^{(e_t)} = max_{k \in [n]}\{e_{ik}^{(e_t)} + e_{kj}^{(e_t)}\}$ for any $i, j \in [n]$.

Suppose that $i, j \in \Sigma_\ell$ for some $\ell \in [s]$. Then, $e_{ij}^{(e_t)} = 0$. If $k \in \Sigma_\ell$, then $e_{ik}^{(e_t)} + e_{kj}^{(e_t)} = 0$. If $k \notin \Sigma_\ell$, then $e_{ik}^{(e_t)} + e_{kj}^{(e_t)} = e_{ik} + e_{kj}$. Since E is idempotent, it implies that $e_{ik} + e_{kj} \leq e_{ij}$ for any $k \in [n]$, and so $e_{ik}^{(e_t)} + e_{kj}^{(e_t)} \leq e_{ij} \leq 0$. Thus, $max_{k \in [n]}\{e_{ik}^{(e_t)} + e_{kj}^{(e_t)}\} = e_{ij}^{(e_t)} = 0$.

Assume that $i \in \Sigma_{\ell_1}$ and $j \in \Sigma_{\ell_2}$, where $\ell_1, \ell_2 \in [s]$ and $\ell_1 \neq \ell_2$. Then, $e_{ij}^{(e_t)} = e_{ij}$. If $k \in \Sigma_{\ell_1}$, then $e_{ik}^{(e_t)} + e_{kj}^{(e_t)} = e_{kj}^{(e_t)} = e_{kj}$. Since $i, k \in \Sigma_{\ell_1}$, i.e., $i \sim^{E^{e_t}} k$, we have that $e_{kj} = e_{ij}$. Thus, $e_{ik}^{(e_t)} + e_{kj}^{(e_t)} = e_{ij}$. If $k \in \Sigma_{\ell_2}$, then $e_{ik}^{(e_t)} + e_{kj}^{(e_t)} = e_{ik}^{(e_t)} = e_{ik}$. Since $j, k \in \Sigma_{\ell_2}$, i.e., $j \sim^{E^{e_t}} k$, we have that $e_{ik} = e_{ij}$. Thus, $e_{ik}^{(e_t)} + e_{kj}^{(e_t)} = e_{ij}$. If $k \notin \Sigma_{\ell_1} \cup \Sigma_{\ell_2}$, then $e_{ik}^{(e_t)} + e_{kj}^{(e_t)} = e_{ik} + e_{kj}$. Since E is idempotent, it implies that $e_{ik} + e_{kj} \leq e_{ij}$, and so $e_{ik}^{(e_t)} + e_{kj}^{(e_t)} \leq e_{ij}$. Consequently, $max_{k \in [n]}\{e_{ik}^{(e_t)} + e_{kj}^{(e_t)}\} = e_{ij}^{(e_t)} = e_{ij}$. This shows that $e_{ij}^{(e_t)} = max_{k \in [n]}\{e_{ik}^{(e_t)} + e_{kj}^{(e_t)}\}$ for any $i, j \in [n]$, as required. □

Now, we have the following:

Theorem 2. *Let $E = (e_{ij}) \in M_n^{SR}$ and $E^{(e_t)}$ be defined as above. Then, $\sim^{E^{e_t}} = \sim_{E^{(e_t)}}$.*

Proof. Suppose that $i \sim^{E^{e_t}} j$ for any $i, j \in [n]$. Then, $i, j \in \Sigma_\ell$ for some $\ell \in [s]$. Thus, $e_{ij}^{(e_t)} = e_{ji}^{(e_t)} = 0$. By $E^{(e_t)} \in M_n^{IN}$ and ([11], Lemma 3.2), it follows that $i \sim_{E^{(e_t)}} j$. Thus, $\sim^{E^{e_t}} \subseteq \sim_{E^{(e_t)}}$.

On the other hand, assume that $i \sim_{E^{(e_t)}} j$ for any $i, j \in [n]$. It follows from ([11], Lemma 3.2) that $e_{ik}^{(e_t)} = e_{jk}^{(e_t)}$ and $e_{ki}^{(e_t)} = e_{kj}^{(e_t)}$ for all $k \in [n]$. Now, we shall show that $i \sim^{E^{e_t}} j$, i.e., $\Sigma(i) = \Sigma(j)$, where $\Sigma(i)$ and $\Sigma(j)$ denote the $\sim^{E^{e_t}}$-classes containing i and j, respectively.

Suppose that $\Sigma(i) \neq \Sigma(j)$. For any $k \in \Sigma(i)$, i.e., $i \sim^{E^{e_t}} k$, we have $e_{ik}^{(e_t)} = e_{ki}^{(e_t)} = 0$. Moreover, by ([11], Lemma 3.2), $i \sim_{E^{(e_t)}} k$. Since $i \sim_{E^{(e_t)}} j$, it implies that $k \sim_{E^{(e_t)}} j$ and so $e_{jk}^{(e_t)} = e_{kj}^{(e_t)} = 0$. Note that $\Sigma(k) \neq \Sigma(j)$, which implies that $e_{jk}^{(e_t)} = e_{jk}^{e_t} = e_{jk}$ and $e_{kj}^{(e_t)} = e_{kj}^{e_t} = e_{kj}$. Moreover, $e_{jk} = e_{kj} = 0$. It follows from ([11], Lemma 3.2) that $j \sim_E k$. Therefore, $E \in M_n^{NSR}$—a contradiction. Consequently, $\Sigma(i) = \Sigma(j)$. That is, $i \sim^{E^{e_t}} j$. Thus, $\sim_{E^{(e_t)}} \subseteq \sim^{E^{e_t}}$, and so $\sim^{E^{e_t}} = \sim_{E^{(e_t)}}$. □

Corollary 1. *Suppose that $E \in M_n^{SR}$ and $e_t \in O(E)$. Then,*

$$\sim^{E^{e_t}} \neq \Delta \Longleftrightarrow \sim_{E^{(e_t)}} \neq \Delta \Longleftrightarrow E^{(e_t)} \in M_n^{NSR}.$$

By $G_E = G_{E^{e_t}}$, ([11], Theorem 3.7, Lemma 4.4) and Corollary 1, we have immediately the following theorem.

Theorem 3. *Let $E = (e_{ij}) \in M_n^{SR}$. If there exists $e_t \in O(E)$ such that $E^{(e_t)} \in M_n^{NSR}$, then G_E is a split extension of $\widetilde{G}_{E^{e_t}}$ by $H_{E^{e_t}}$, i.e., $G_E = \widetilde{G}_{E^{e_t}} \rtimes H_{E^{e_t}}$, where*

$$\widetilde{G}_{E^{e_t}} := \{\sigma \in S_n \mid P_\sigma E^{e_t} = E^{e_t} P_\sigma = E^{e_t}\}$$

and

$$H_{E^{e_t}} := \{\sigma \in G_{E^{e_t}} \mid (\forall k \in [s])\ (\forall i, j \in \Sigma_k)\ i \leq j \Leftrightarrow i^\sigma \leq j^\sigma\}.$$

Example 1. *Consider the centralizer group of the following strongly regular idempotent normal matrix:*

$$E = \begin{pmatrix} 0 & d & d & x & x \\ d & 0 & d & x & x \\ d & d & 0 & x & x \\ y & y & y & 0 & u \\ y & y & y & u & 0 \end{pmatrix}, \quad (8)$$

where $x, y, d, u \in [-1.1, -0.9]$ are distinct. By ([12], Theorem 5.10), it follows that $E \in M_n^{IN}$. It is easy to check that $\widetilde{G}_{E^d} \cong S_3$ and $H_{E^d} \cong S_2$. Thus, $G_E = S_3 \rtimes S_2$.

Remark 2. *According to Corollary 1 and Theorem 3, we give a structural description of the centralizer groups of partial idempotent normal matrices. The characterization of the centralizer groups of the remaining idempotent normal matrices, which are strongly regular idempotent normal matrices E satisfying $E^{(e_t)} \in M_n^{SR}$ for all $e_t \in O(E)$, is still an unsolved problem. It is well known that G is a finite two-closed permutation group if and only if G equals to G_E, where E is idempotent normal matrix. The polycirculant conjecture, which is important in graph theory, asserts that every non-trivial finite transitive two-closed permutation group contains a fixed-point-free element of prime order. By Theorem 3, it is clear that the centralizer groups of partial idempotent normal matrices contains a fixed-point-free element of prime order. Furthermore, the main results of this paper may be helpful for further research on the polycirculant conjecture.*

Funding: This paper was supported by the National Natural Science Foundation of China (11971383, 11571278) and Shaanxi Fundamental Science Research Project for Mathematics and Physics (Grant No. 22JSY023).

Data Availability Statement: All data generated or analyzed during this study are included in this published work.

Acknowledgments: The authors would like to express their gratitude to the academic editor and the anonymous reviewers for their valuable remarks and suggestions that helped to improve this work.

Conflicts of Interest: The author declares no conflicts of interest.

References

1. Butkovič, P. *Max-Linear Systems: Theory and Algorithms*; Springer: London, UK, 2010.
2. Johnson, M.; Kambites, M. Green's $\mathcal{J}$-order and the rank of tropical matrices. *J. Pure Appl. Algebra* **2013**, *217*, 280–292. [CrossRef]
3. Shitov, Y. Tropical matrices and group repersentations. *J. Algebra* **2012**, *370*, 1–4. [CrossRef]
4. Yang, L. Regular $\mathcal{D}$-classes of the semigroup of $n \times n$ tropical matrices. *Turk. J. Math.* **2018**, *42*, 2061–2070. [CrossRef]
5. Johnson, M.; Kambites, M. Multiplicative structrue of 2×2 tropical matrices. *Linear Algebra Appl.* **2011**, *435*, 1612–1625. [CrossRef]
6. Butkovič, P. Max-algebra: The linear algebra of combinatorics. *Linear Algebra Appl.* **2003**, *367*, 313–335. [CrossRef]
7. Johnson, M.; Kambites, M. Idempotent tropical matrices and finite metric spaces. *Adv. Geom.* **2014**, *14*, 253–276.

8. Izhakian, Z.; Johnson, M.; Kambites, M. Pure dimension and projectivity of tropical polytopes. *Adv. Math.* **2016**, *303*, 1236–1263. [CrossRef]
9. Linde, J.; Puente, M.J.d. Matrices commuting with a given normal tropical matrix. *Linear Algebra Appl.* **2015**, *482*, 101–121. [CrossRef]
10. Yu, B.M.; Zhao, X.Z.; Zeng, L.L. A congruence on the semiring of normal tropical matrices. *Linear Algebra Appl.* **2018**, *555*, 321–335. [CrossRef]
11. Deng, W.N.; Zhao, X.Z.; Cheng, Y.L.; Yu, B.M. On the groups associated with a tropical $n \times n$ matrix. *Linear Algebra Appl.* **2022**, *639*, 1–17. [CrossRef]
12. Izhakian, Z.; Johnson, M.; Kambites, M. Tropical matrix groups. *Semigroup Forum.* **2018**, *96*, 178–196. [CrossRef]
13. Yang, L. The tropical matrix groups with symmetric idempotents. *Discret. Dyn. Nat. Soc.* **2018**, *2018*, 1–9. [CrossRef]
14. Dixon, J.D.; Mortimer, B. *Permutation Groups*; Springer: New York, NY, USA, 1996.
15. Cameron, P.J. *Permutation Groups (London Mathematical Society Student Texts Vol 45)*; Cambridge University Press: Cambridge, UK, 1999.
16. Blyth, T.S.; Janowitz, M.F. *Residuation Theory*; Pergamon Press: Oxford, UK, 1972.

Disclaimer/Publisher's Note: The statements, opinions and data contained in all publications are solely those of the individual author(s) and contributor(s) and not of MDPI and/or the editor(s). MDPI and/or the editor(s) disclaim responsibility for any injury to people or property resulting from any ideas, methods, instructions or products referred to in the content.

mathematics

MDPI

Article

An Introduction to i-Commutative Rings

Muhammad Saad *, Usama A. Aburawash, Ahmed M. A. El-Sayed and Nour Nabil

Department of Mathematics and Computer Science, Faculty of Science, Alexandria University, Alexandria 21511, Egypt; aburawash@alexu.edu.eg (U.A.A.); amasayed@alexu.edu.eg (A.M.A.E.-S.); noureldine.nabil@alexu.edu.eg (N.N.)
* Correspondence: m.saad@alexu.edu.eg

Abstract: In this paper, we introduce a new class of rings, called i-commutative rings, by extending the concept of commutative-like rings using idempotent elements. In particular, we study rings with the property that, whenever $ab + cd$ is a nontrivial idempotent, then $ba + dc$ is idempotent. We explore the basic properties of these rings and their relations with other rings. Moreover, we provide some examples using matrices and describe the structure of the idempotent elements in these rings.

Keywords: i-commutative; i-reversible; idempotent; triangular matrix rings; Morita context

MSC: Primary 16U80; Secondary 16U40; 16U99

1. Introduction

In this paper, all rings are assumed to be nonzero associative with an identity, unless otherwise stated. For a given ring R, the set of idempotents of R, the set of all *square-zero* elements of R (i.e., the nilpotent elements of index 2 or 1), the set of all *involutory* elements of R (i.e., the invertible elements that are own inverse), the Jacobson radical of R, the n-by-n full matrix ring over R, and the n-by-n upper triangular matrix ring over R are denoted by $\mathcal{I}(R)$, $\mathcal{N}_2(R)$, $\mathcal{I}_2(R)$, $\mathcal{J}(R)$, $\mathbb{M}_n(R)$, and $\mathbb{T}_n(R)$, respectively.

Recall that two idempotents e and f of a ring R are said to be *commutating* if $ef = fe$ and *orthogonal* if the additionally satisfy $ef = 0$. Furthermore, e and f are said to be *isomorphic*, denoted by $e \cong f$, if $eR = fR$ as right R-modules. It is well known that idempotents e and f of R are isomorphic if and only if there exist elements $a, b \in R$, such that $e = ab$ and $f = ba$ (see [1], (21.20)). Notice that the isomorphism of idempotents is an equivalence relation. Idempotents e and f are said to be *isomorphic complements* if $1 - e$ and $1 - f$ are isomorphic. We say that the idempotents e and f are *conjugate* if they are both isomorphic and isomorphic complements, denoted by $e \overset{c}{\cong} f$. Recall that two elements a and b of a ring R are called *equivalent* if there exist invertible elements u and v of R, such that $b = vau$. According to [2] (Theorem 2), two idempotents in a ring are equivalent if and only if they are conjugate. In commutative rings, an idempotent is isomorphic only to itself. Therefore, the isomorphism of idempotents is considered only in non-commutative rings.

A ring is termed *reduced* if it contains no nonzero nilpotent elements, and it is referred to as *directly finite* if $ba = 1$ whenever $ab = 1$ for all $a, b \in R$. An idempotent e of a ring R is considered *left* (resp. *right*) *semicentral* if $ae = eae$ (resp., $ea = eae$) for all $a \in R$. The sets of left and right semicentral idempotents of R are denoted by $\mathcal{S}_l(R)$ and $\mathcal{S}_r(R)$, respectively. An idempotent is *central* if it is both left and right semicentral. A ring R is deemed *abelian* if every idempotent element is central.

Cohn [3] presented the concept of *reversible* rings as a generalization of commutative rings and defined it as a ring R for which $ab = 0$ if and only if $ba = 0$ for $a, b \in R$. In [4], (Proposition 1.4), an equivalent definition for reversible rings using idempotents is given. A ring R is reversible if and only if ba is an idempotent whenever ab is an idempotent for every $a, b \in R$. In [5], Khurana showed that the condition ba is a nonzero idempotent if and only if ab is also, so this is not sufficient to make R reversible.

For this reason, i-reversible rings, which are a generalization of reversible rings, are defined to contain the property that if ab is a nonzero idempotent, then so is ba. I-reversible rings are also referred to as *quasi-reversible* rings (see [6]). All of the above inspired us to find an equivalent definition of commutative rings using idempotents in the next theorem. Let us recall the celebrated commutativity result of Herstein (see [7]).

Theorem 1 (Herstein's Identity). *A ring R is commutative if and only if for each $x, y \in R$ there exists an integer $n(x,y) > 1$, such that $(xy - yx)^{n(x,y)} = (xy - yx)$.*

Theorem 2. *A ring R is commutative if and only if $ab + cd$ is idempotent, for some $a, b, c, d \in R$, which implies $ba + dc$ is also idempotent.*

Proof. The sufficiency is obvious. For necessity, for $a, b \in R$, we have $0 = ab - ab = ab + (-1)(ab)$ as an idempotent. Hence, $ba - ab$ is an idempotent and R is commutative, according to Herstein's identity. □

Observe that changing the condition in the previous theorem from "$ab + cd$ is an idempotent" to "$ab + cd$ is a nontrivial idempotent" does not suffice to make R commutative, as the following examples illustrate.

Example 1. *Let R be the ring of 2-by-2 upper triangular matrices over a field F. The nontrivial idempotents of R have the two forms $\begin{bmatrix} 1 & \alpha \\ 0 & 0 \end{bmatrix}$ and $\begin{bmatrix} 0 & \alpha \\ 0 & 1 \end{bmatrix}$, where α is arbitrary in F. For all elements a, b, c, d of R, we have $[ab + cd]_{11} = [ba + dc]_{11}$ and $[ab + cd]_{22} = [ba + dc]_{22}$. Therefore, $ab + cd$ can only be considered a nontrivial idempotent if $ba + dc$ also is. However, R is not commutative.*

Motivated by the previous example and Theorem 2, we delve into introducing a concept that pertains to a ring R satisfying that $ba + dc$ is idempotent whenever $ab + cd$ is a nontrivial idempotent for $a, b, c, d \in R$, and calling it *i-commutative*. This work primarily aims to introduce i-commutative rings, a new class of rings that extends commutative-like structures through idempotent elements. This paper sets up the basic properties of this structure and shows that it is not the same as other generalizations of commutative rings, like reversible and abelian rings, by using carefully thought-out examples that demonstrate independence.

2. Definitions and Basic Properties

We initiate this section by introducing the following definition.

Definition 1. *A ring R is said to be* i-commutative *if either R has only trivial idempotents or $ab + cd$ is a nontrivial idempotent for some $a, b, c, d \in R$, which implies $ba + dc$ is idempotent.*

From Theorem 2, every commutative ring is i-commutative, while the converse is not necessarily true, as shown in Example 1. Moreover, the next proposition gives an equivalent definition for i-reversible rings, showing that every i-commutative ring is i-reversible.

Proposition 1. *A ring R is i-reversible if and only if R has only trivial idempotents or ab is a nontrivial idempotent implies ba is idempotent, where $a, b \in R$.*

Proof. If R is i-reversible, then it is satisfying the condition. Conversely, let R satisfy the assumption, such that ab is a nonzero idempotent for some $a, b \in R$. If R has only trivial idempotent, then $ab = 1$ and $(ba)^2 = baba = ba$ and ba is an idempotent. If not, then ba is an idempotent from the assumption. □

Corollary 1. *Every i-commutative ring is i-reversible.*

The next example illustrates that the converse of the previous result is not necessary, as there exists an i-reversible ring that is not i-commutative.

Example 2. *Let $\mathbb{H}$ be the Hamilton quaternions over the real number field and $R = \mathbb{T}_2(H)$. Indeed, $\mathbb{H}$ is reduced (consequentially reversible) and has no nontrivial idempotents. Therefore, R is i-reversible by [5] (Corollary 3.2). However, S is not i-commutative since the elements* $\alpha = \begin{bmatrix} i & i+j \\ 0 & j \end{bmatrix}$, $\beta = \begin{bmatrix} 1 & k \\ 0 & 1 \end{bmatrix}$, $\gamma = \begin{bmatrix} 1-i & -j \\ 0 & i \end{bmatrix}$, *and* $\delta = \begin{bmatrix} 1 & -k \\ 0 & k \end{bmatrix}$ *satisfy that* $\alpha\beta + \gamma\delta = \begin{bmatrix} 1 & -j-k \\ 0 & 0 \end{bmatrix}$ *is idempotent while* $\beta\alpha + \delta\gamma = \begin{bmatrix} 1 & -j \\ 0 & 2j \end{bmatrix}$ *is not an idempotent.*

From the last proposition and [5] (Proposition 2.1 (6)), we obtain the following corollary.

Corollary 2. *Every i-commutative ring is directly finite.*

It is widely recognized that every abelian ring is directly finite. However, the abelian and i-commutative properties are independent. The ring R in Example 1 is i-commutative but not abelian. The next proposition provides a sufficient condition to make an i-commutative ring abelian.

Proposition 2. *A semiprime i-commutative ring is abelian.*

Proof. Let R be a semiprime i-commutative ring, and let e be a nontrivial idempotent of R. So, the element $e(1 + r - er) - es(1 - e)$ is a nontrivial idempotent for every $r, s \in R$. Applying the i-commutativity condition, we get $(1 + r - er)e - es(1 - e) = e + (1 - e)re - es(1 - e)$ is idempotent and $e + (1 - e)re - es(1 - e) = e + (1 - e)re - es(1 - e) - (1 - e)res(1 - e) - es(1 - e)re$ implies $(1 - e)res(1 - e) + es(1 - e)re = 0$. Multiplying the last equation by e from the left, we get $es(1 - e)re = 0$, for every $r, s \in R$ and $eR(1 - e)Re = 0$. For every $x \in R$, we have $((1 - e)xe)R((1 - e)Re) \subseteq R(1 - e)R(eR(1 - e)Re) = 0$ and $(1 - e)xe = 0$ using the semiprimeness of R. So, $e \in \mathcal{S}_l(R)$ and, similarly, we obtain $e \in \mathcal{S}_r(R)$. Thus, R is abelian. □

Moreover, there is an abelian ring that is not i-commutative. For example, the ring $D \oplus D$, where D is a non-reversible local ring, is abelian but not i-reversible, as shown in [5] (Proposition 2.1), and, therefore, R is not i-commutative from Corollary 1.

The classes of reversible rings and i-commutative rings do not contain each other. Indeed, the ring R in Example 1 is i-commutative but not reversible, since the elements $a = \begin{bmatrix} 0 & 1 \\ 0 & 1 \end{bmatrix}$ and $b = \begin{bmatrix} 1 & 1 \\ 0 & 0 \end{bmatrix}$ satisfy $ab = 0$ while $ba \neq 0$. Moreover, the next example demonstrates a reversible ring that is not i-commutative.

Example 3. *Let D be a non-commutative reversible ring. Hence, the ring $R = D \oplus D$ is reversible. From the assumed non-commutativity of R and Herstein's identity, we can find elements $\alpha, \beta \in D$, such that $\alpha\beta - \beta\alpha$ is not idempotent. Define the elements $a = (1, \alpha)$, $b = (1, \beta)$, $c = (0, 1)$, and $d = (1, \alpha\beta)$ of R. We have $ab + cd = (1, 0)$ is a nontrivial idempotent of R, but $ba + cd = (1, \alpha\beta - \beta\alpha)$ is not idempotent. Therefore, R is not i-commutative.*

Below are shown some interesting nontrivial implications in the class of rings presented in this article.

$$\begin{array}{ccccccc} & & \text{commutative} & \Longrightarrow & \text{reversible} & \Longrightarrow & \text{abelian} \\ & & \Downarrow & & \Downarrow & & \Downarrow \\ \mathcal{I}(R) = \{0,1\} & \Longrightarrow & \text{i-commutative} & \Longrightarrow & \text{i-reversible} & \Longrightarrow & \text{directly finite} \end{array}$$

Proposition 3. *Every subring (not necessarily with identity) of an i-commutative ring is i-commutative.*

Proof. Straightforward. □

Note that the class of i-commutative rings is not closed under direct sums, as in the next example.

Example 4. *Let R be the i-commutative ring in Example 1 and $S = R \oplus R$. The elements $\alpha = \left(\begin{bmatrix} 1 & 2 \\ 0 & 1 \end{bmatrix}, \begin{bmatrix} 0 & 1 \\ 0 & 1 \end{bmatrix} \right)$ and $\beta = \left(\begin{bmatrix} 1 & -2 \\ 0 & 1 \end{bmatrix}, \begin{bmatrix} 1 & 1 \\ 0 & 0 \end{bmatrix} \right)$ of S satisfy $\alpha\beta = (1, 0)$, which is a nontrivial idempotent of S, but $\beta\alpha$ is not idempotent. Therefore, S is not i-reversible, and, consequently, it is not i-commutative.*

Proposition 4. *If an i-commutative ring R has nonorthogonal commutating nontrivial idempotents e and f, then the subring $(1-e)R(1-f)$ (as a ring without identity) is commutative.*

Proof. Let a and b be arbitrary elements in $(1-e)R(1-f)$. Define the elements $\alpha = a + e$ and $\beta = b + f$ in R. So, $\alpha\beta = ab + ef$ and $1(\alpha\beta) + (-a)b = ef$. However, $ef \neq 0$ and $ef \neq 1$, since both e and f are nontrivial idempotents. Hence, ef is a nontrivial idempotent. So, $\alpha\beta - ba$ is an idempotent, and $ab - ba + ef = \alpha\beta - ba = (\alpha\beta - ba)^2 = (ab - ba + ef)^2 = (ab - ba)^2 + ef$. Therefore, $(ab - ba)^2 = ab - ba$ and eRf is commutative from Herstein's identity. □

Corollary 3. *If an i-commutative ring R has a nontrivial idempotent e, then the corner eRe is commutative.*

In [8], a ring whose central idempotents are only 0 and 1 is called *central reduced*. The next proposition gives a sufficient condition for an i-commutative ring to be commutative.

Proposition 5. *A ring R is commutative if it is i-commutative and not central reduced.*

Proof. If R is not central reduced, then it has a nontrivial central idempotent e. From Corollary 3, eR and $(1-e)R$ are commutative, since R is i-commutative. Therefore, $R = eR \oplus (1-e)R$ is also commutative, following Proposition 3. □

3. i-Commutativity of Matrix Rings

In this section, we study the i-commutativity condition for matrix rings and their subrings. First, we show that the matrix ring $\mathbb{M}_n(R)$ over a ring R is not i-commutative for any ring R and $n \geq 2$.

Proposition 6. *For any ring R and integer $n \geq 2$, $\mathbb{M}_n(R)$ is not i-commutative.*

Proof. For a ring R, consider the elements $\alpha = \begin{bmatrix} 0 & 0 \\ 1 & 1 \end{bmatrix}$, $\beta = \begin{bmatrix} 1 & 0 \\ 1 & 1 \end{bmatrix}$, $\gamma = \begin{bmatrix} 0 & 1 \\ 0 & 0 \end{bmatrix}$, and $\delta = \begin{bmatrix} 1 & 0 \\ 0 & 0 \end{bmatrix}$ in $\mathbb{M}_2(R)$. We have $\alpha\beta + \gamma\delta = \begin{bmatrix} 0 & 0 \\ 0 & 1 \end{bmatrix}$ as a nontrivial idempotent, while $\beta\alpha + \delta\gamma = \begin{bmatrix} 0 & 1 \\ 1 & 1 \end{bmatrix}$ is not idempotent. Thus, $\mathbb{M}_2(R)$ is not i-commutative and, therefore, $\mathbb{M}_n(R)$ is not i-commutative, for every $n \geq 2$, according to Proposition 3. □

The next corollary gives another counterexample of an i-reversible ring that is not i-commutative.

Corollary 4. *For any commutative ring S with only trivial idempotents, $\mathbb{M}_2(S)$ is i-reversible but not i-commutative.*

Proof. It is taken directly from of the previous proposition and [5] (Theorem 4.3). □

While it is impossible to obtain a matrix ring satisfying the i-commutativity condition, we will explore the extent to which this property holds in some of its subrings or certain matrix contexts.

For rings R and S, let M and N be (R,S)-bimodule and (S,R)-bimodule, respectively. The set of all matrices of the form $\begin{bmatrix} r & m \\ n & s \end{bmatrix}$, where $r \in R$, $s \in S$, $m \in M$, and $n \in N$. With the standard matrix addition, this is an abelian group. To define a matrix multiplication for these elements, we need to define the products of mn and nm in R and S, respectively, for every $m \in M$ and $n \in N$. We assume that there are two bimodule homomorphisms, as follows: $\phi : (M,N) \to R$ and $\psi : (N,M) \to S$. Simply, $mn = \phi(m,n)$ and $nm = \psi(n,m)$ for all $m \in M$ and $n \in N$. These maps satisfy the associativity conditions that are required to make the set with usual matrix addition and context multiplication an associative ring with identity, notated by $\begin{bmatrix} R & M \\ N & S \end{bmatrix}$. This ring is called the *Morita context* (R, M, N, S, ϕ, ψ), or a *formal matrix* ring (of order 2), or a *ring of generalized matrices*. The readers are referred to [9–12], as well as the references therein, for detailed information on studies on Morita contexts.

Theorem 3. *Let R and S be commutative rings with only trivial idempotents and let $T = \begin{bmatrix} R & M \\ N & S \end{bmatrix}$ be a Morita context, such that $MN \subseteq \mathcal{N}_2(R)$ and $NM \subseteq \mathcal{N}_2(S)$. An element e of T is a nontrivial idempotent if and only if it takes one of the following forms:*

$$\begin{bmatrix} 1-mn & m \\ n & nm \end{bmatrix} \quad \text{and} \quad \begin{bmatrix} mn & m \\ n & 1-nm \end{bmatrix}$$

for some $m \in M$ and $n \in N$.

Proof. Let $e = \begin{bmatrix} r & m \\ n & s \end{bmatrix}$ be an idempotent in T. So, we have $r = r^2 + mn$, $s = s^2 + nm$, $m = rm + ms$, and $n = nr + sn$. Indeed, $1 - 2e$ is invertible in T and, therefore, both $1 - 2r$ and $1 - 2s$ are invertible in R and S, respectively, from [13] (Lemma 3.1 (2)), since $\mathcal{N}_2(R) \subseteq \mathcal{J}(R)$ and $\mathcal{N}_2(S) \subseteq \mathcal{J}(S)$. Now, $(r-1)^4 = (1 - 2r + r^2)(r-1)^2 = (1-2r)(r-1)^2 + r^2(r-1)^2 = (1-2r)(r-1)^2 + (mn)^2 = (1-2r)(r-1)^2$ and $(1-2r)^{-2}(r-1)^4 = (1-2r)^{-1}(r-1)^2$. Hence, $(1-2r)^{-1}(r-1)^2$ is an idempotent in R. From the assumption, either $(1-2r)^{-1}(r-1)^2 = 0$ or $(1-2r)^{-1}(r-1)^2 = 1$. For the first case, we have $(r-1)^2 = 0$ and $r = r^2 + mn = 2r - 1 + mn$; that is, $r = 1 - mn$. For the second case, $1 - 2r = (r-1)^2 = r^2 - 2r + 1$ and $r^2 = 0$; that is, $r = mn$. Similarly, we find out that $s = 1 - nm$ or $s = nm$. If $r = mn$ and $s = nm$, we obtain $m = rm + ms = (mn)m + m(nm) = 2mnm$. So, $r = mn = 2(mn)^2 = 0$ and $s = nm = 2(nm)^2 = 0$. Therefore, $m = 0$ and $n = 0$; that is, $e = 0$. If $r = 1 - mn$ and $s = 1 - nm$, we obtain $m = (1-mn)m + m(1-nm) = 2m - 2mnm$ and $m = 2mnm$. Again, $mn = 0$ and $nm = 0$; here, $e = 1$. Therefore, the nontrivial idempotents of T take one of the following forms, $e = \begin{bmatrix} 1-mn & m \\ n & nm \end{bmatrix}$ or $e = \begin{bmatrix} mn & m \\ n & 1-nm \end{bmatrix}$, for some $m \in M$ and $n \in N$.

Conversely, the given forms of matrices in the statement can be proved to be idempotents via the direct calculations and by using the assumptions. □

Recall from [14] that a Morita context, $T = \begin{bmatrix} R & M \\ N & S \end{bmatrix}$, is called *trivial* if $MN = 0$ and $NM = 0$.

Corollary 5. *Let R and S be commutative rings with only trivial idempotents, and $T = \begin{bmatrix} R & M \\ N & S \end{bmatrix}$ be a trivial Morita context. An element e of T is a nontrivial idempotent if and only if it takes one of the following forms:*

$$\begin{bmatrix} 1 & m \\ n & 0 \end{bmatrix} \quad or \quad \begin{bmatrix} 0 & m \\ n & 1 \end{bmatrix}$$

for some $m \in M$ and $n \in N$.

Theorem 4. *Let $T = \begin{bmatrix} R & M \\ N & S \end{bmatrix}$ be a trivial Morita context, such that M and N cannot be zero simultaneously. Then, T is i-commutative if and only if R and S are commutative rings with only trivial idempotents.*

Proof. For sufficiency, assume that T is i-commutative. Therefore, both R and S are commutative from Corollary 3 and T is i-reversible from Corollary 1. Now, let e be a nontrivial idempotent of R and consider the elements $\alpha = \begin{bmatrix} e & m \\ 0 & 0 \end{bmatrix}$ and $\beta = \begin{bmatrix} 1 & 0 \\ 0 & 0 \end{bmatrix}$ of T for an arbitrary element m of M. So, $\alpha\beta = \begin{bmatrix} e & 0 \\ 0 & 0 \end{bmatrix}$ is a nontrivial idempotent. Hence $\beta\alpha = \begin{bmatrix} e & m \\ 0 & 0 \end{bmatrix}$ is idempotent, from the i-reversibility of T, and $em = m$ for every $m \in M$; that is, $(1-e)M = 0$. Furthermore, $1 - e$ is a nontrivial idempotent and, similarly, we have $eM = 0$ and therefore $M = 0$. By applying the previous steps using $\gamma = \begin{bmatrix} e & 0 \\ n & 0 \end{bmatrix}$, where n is an arbitrary element of N, instead of α, we obtain $N = 0$. So R has only trivial idempotents, and, similarly, we can show that S also does not have nontrivial idempotents.

For necessity, let R and S be commutative rings with only trivial idempotents. Now, the elements $a_i = \begin{bmatrix} r_i & m_i \\ n_i & s_i \end{bmatrix}$ of T, where $i = 1, 2, 3, 4$, satisfy the following:

$$a_1a_2 + a_3a_4 = \begin{bmatrix} r_1r_2 + r_3r_4 & r_1m_2 + m_1s_2 + r_3m_4 + m_3s_4 \\ n_1r_2 + s_1n_2 + n_3r_4 + s_3n_4 & s_1s_2 + s_3s_4 \end{bmatrix}$$

which is a nontrivial idempotent. From Corollary 5, we obtain $r_1r_2 + r_3r_4$ and $s_1s_2 + s_3s_4$, which are distinct trivial idempotents. So, $a_2a_1 + a_4a_3$ is a nontrivial idempotent. Thus, T is i-commutative. □

Notice that formal triangular matrix rings are obvious examples of trivial Morita contexts. Therefore, we have the following corollaries.

Corollary 6. *Let M be a nonzero (R, S)-bimodule for some rings R and S. Then, $T = \begin{bmatrix} R & M \\ 0 & S \end{bmatrix}$ is i-commutative if and only if both R and S are commutative and have only trivial idempotents.*

Corollary 7. *For any ring R and any integer $n > 1$, the ring $\mathbb{T}_n(R)$ is i-commutative if and only if $n = 2$, R is commutative, and R has only trivial idempotents.*

Corollary 8. *If R is a non-commutative i-commutative ring of minimal order, then R is of order 8 and is isomorphic to $\mathbb{T}_2(\mathbb{Z}_2)$.*

Proof. It is taken directly from Corollary 6 and the results in [15]. □

The next proposition provides a sufficient condition for a commutative ring R with trivial idempotents to make $\mathbb{M}_2(R)$, which has maximal i-commutative subrings.

Proposition 7. *Let R be a commutative reduced ring with only trivial idempotents. Then, $\mathbb{T}_2(R)$ is a maximal i-commutative subring of $\mathbb{M}_2(R)$.*

Proof. Let $S = \begin{bmatrix} R & R \\ V & R \end{bmatrix}$, where V is a nontrivial subring of R, be i-commutative. So, T is a subring of $\mathbb{M}_2(R)$ that contains $\mathbb{T}_2(R)$, and V is an ideal of R. For arbitrary $v \in V$, consider the elements $\alpha = \begin{bmatrix} 0 & 0 \\ v & 0 \end{bmatrix}$, $\beta = \begin{bmatrix} 1 & 1 \\ 0 & 0 \end{bmatrix}$, $\gamma = \begin{bmatrix} 1 & 0 \\ 0 & -1 \end{bmatrix}$, and $\delta = \begin{bmatrix} 1 & -1 \\ v & v \end{bmatrix}$ of S. We have $\alpha\beta + \gamma\delta = \begin{bmatrix} 1 & 1 \\ 0 & 0 \end{bmatrix}$ is a nontrivial idempotent of S. Due to the i-commutativity of S, we obtain $\beta\alpha + \delta\gamma = \begin{bmatrix} v+1 & -1 \\ v & -v \end{bmatrix}$, which is an idempotent. So, $v^2 = 0$ and $v = 0$ form the reducedness of R. Thus, $V = 0$, and $\mathbb{T}_2(R)$ is a maximal i-commutative subring of R. □

4. i-Commutativity and Commutative-like Rings

In this section, we explore the connection between i-commutativity and various commutative-like ring structures. We highlight how i-commutativity helps to reveal nontrivial properties of these generalized classes of rings.

Recalling [16], an element x of a ring R is called *exchange* if there exists $e \in I(R)$, such that $e \in aR$ and $1 - e \in (1 - a)R$. Furthermore, a is called *clean* if $a = e + u$ for some idempotent e and unit u in R. A ring is said to be *exchange* (resp. *clean*) if all its elements are *exchange* (resp. *clean*). In [16] (Proposition 1.8), Nicholson showed that clean elements of a ring R are exchange and the converse holds when R is abelian. However, as we demonstrated in the previous section, the independence between abelian and i-commutative properties indicates that Nicholson's result also applies to i-commutative rings.

Proposition 8. *Let R be an i-commutative ring. If a is an exchange element of R, then a is a clean element.*

Proof. Since a is an exchange element, there is therefore an idempotent e of R, such that $e \in aR$ and $1-e \in (1-a)R$. If $e=1$, a is invertible and consequently clean. If $e=0$, then $1-a$ is invertible, and, again, a is clean. Now, assume that e is a nontrivial idempotent, such that $e = ax$ and $1-e = (1-a)y$ for some $x, y \in R$. Therefore, $(a-1+e)(x-y) = ax + (1-a)y - x + ex - ey = e + 1 - e - x + ex - ey = 1 - (1-e)x - ey$. For every $r \in R$, the element $e(1+r-er) - ey(1-e)$ is a nontrivial idempotent. Applying the i-commutativity condition implies that $(1+r-er)e - ey(1-e) = e + (1-e)re - ey(1-e)$ is idempotent. Therefore, $e + (1-e)re - ey(1-e) = e + (1-e)re - ey(1-e) - (1-e)rey(1-e) - ey(1-e)re$ gives $(1-e)rey(1-e) + ey(1-e)re = 0$. Multiplying the last equation by e from the left, we obtain $ey(1-e)re = 0$. Notice that choosing $y = y(1-e)$ and $x = xe$ does not lose the generality of proof. Hence, $(eyr)^2 = eyreyr = ey(1-e)reyr = 0$, for every $r \in R$, which means that $ey \in \mathcal{J}(R)$. Similarly, we can obtain $(1-e)x \in \mathcal{J}(R)$ and, hence, $(a-1+e)(x-y) = 1-(1-e)x - ey$ is a unit. According to Corollary 2, R is directly finite, and, therefore, $(a-1+e)$ is a unit in R, which implies that a is clean. □

Corollary 9. *An i-commutative exchange ring is clean.*

Recall from [17] that a ring R is said to be *semiabelian* if every idempotent of R is left or right semicentral. The ring $\mathbb{T}_2(F)$, for some field F, is i-commutative, as is shown in Example 2. Furthermore, $\mathcal{I}(R) = \mathcal{S}_l(R) \cup \mathcal{S}_r(R)$, and R is semiabelian. However, the semiabelianity and i-commutativity are independent. The ring R defined in Example 1 is semiabelian but not i-commutative. Furthermore, Example 5 gives an i-commutative ring that is not semiabelian.

Example 5. *Let $S = \mathbb{Z}_2[x]/\langle x^2 \rangle$ and $M = xS$. Then, the trivial Morita context $T = \begin{bmatrix} S & M \\ M & S \end{bmatrix}$ is i-commutative, according to Theorem 4. Furthermore, the idempotent $e = \begin{bmatrix} 1 & x \\ x & 0 \end{bmatrix}$ is neither left nor right semicentral, since the elements $\alpha = \begin{bmatrix} 0 & x \\ 0 & 0 \end{bmatrix}$ and $\beta = \begin{bmatrix} 0 & 0 \\ x & 0 \end{bmatrix}$ satisfy $e\alpha e \neq e\alpha$ and $e\beta e \neq \beta e$. Therefore, T is not semiabelian.*

A ring R is called *regular* (in the sense of von Neumann) if, for each $a \in R$, there exists $b \in R$, such that $a = aba$. A ring R is called *strongly regular* if, for every element $a \in R$, $a \in a^2R \cap Ra^2$. It is well known that a ring is strongly regular if and only if it is abelian and regular.

Although the abelianity and i-commutativity properties are independent, as we have previously shown, we prove that the i-commutativity of a ring is sufficient to make it strongly regular.

Proposition 9. *An i-commutative regular ring is either a division ring or commutative ring.*

Proof. Let R be an i-commutative regular ring. If R has only trivial idempotents, then R is a division ring. If R has a nontrivial idempotent e, define the nilpotent element $a = er(1-e)$, where r is an arbitrary element of R. Since R is regular, there exists $b \in R$, such that $a = aba$. However, $a = ea(1-e)$, and, therefore, we can choose $b = (1-e)be$. Now, $(e+a)(e+b) - ab = e$ and, hence, $(e+b)(e+a) - ab$ is idempotent. Therefore, $(e+b)(e+a) - ab = e + a + b + ba - ab = e + baba + abab + a + b + ba - ab + bab - bab = e + 2ba + a + b$ and $ba = -ab$. Hence, $a = aba = -a^2b = 0$ and $e \in \mathcal{S}_r(R)$. Similarly, $e \in \mathcal{S}_l(R)$ and e is central. Thus, R is commutative from Proposition 5. □

Corollary 10. *An i-commutative regular ring is strongly regular.*

Recall that a ring R is called *π-regular* (resp. strongly π-regular) if, for every $a \in R$, there is a positive integer n, such that $a^n \in a^n R a^n$ (resp. $a^n \in a^{n+1}R \cap Ra^{n+1}$). Chen, in [17], showed that the semiabelian condition is sufficient to make a π-regular ring strongly π-regular. By applying the same techniques as used to prove Proposition 9, we can obtain the i-commutative property, which is independent of the semiabelian property and is sufficient to make π-regular ring strongly π-regular.

Proposition 10. *An i-commutative π-regular ring is strongly π-regular.*

5. Idempotents in i-Commutative Rings

In this section, we study the properties of idempotents in i-commutative rings and construct the idempotents in some extensions of i-commutative rings.

The next theorem generalizes the result of Proposition 5.

Theorem 5. *If R is an i-commutative ring and has a pair of nonorthogonal commutating distinct nontrivial idempotents, then R is commutative.*

Proof. Let e and f be nontrivial idempotents of R, such that $ef = fe \neq 0$ and $e \neq f$. Notice that $ef = efe \in eRe$ and that eRe is a commutative ring from Corollary 3. So, $(ef)(ere) = (ere)(ef)$, and, consequently, $efre = eref$, for every $r \in R$. Similarly, if fRf is commutative and $ef \in fRf$, then $efrf = fref$ for every $r \in R$. Furthermore, $efref = e(fref) = e(efrf) = efrf$ and $efref = ferfe = f(eref) = f(efre) = efre$. From all the previous steps, we obtain the following:

$$efref = efre = efrf = eref = fref.$$

Additionally, $(1-e)$ and $(1-f)$ represent distinct nontrivial idempotents, which are nonorthogonal idempotents of R. Swapping e and f by $1-e$ and $1-f$, we obtain the following:

$$efr - ref = fr(1-e) - (1-e)rf = er(1-e) - (1-f)rf = fr(1-f) - (1-e)re = er(1-f) - (1-f)re,$$

for every $r \in R$. Multiplying the previous augmented equation by e and f from left and right independently, we obtain the below equations:

$$ref = (1-e-f+2ef)re; \quad (1)$$
$$ref = (1-e-f+2ef)rf; \quad (2)$$
$$efr = er(1-e-f+2ef); \quad (3)$$
$$efr = fr(1-e-f+2ef). \quad (4)$$

Notice that $1-e-f+2ef$ is a nontrivial idempotent, since $1-e-f+2ef=0$ if $ef=0$ and $1-e-f+2ef=1$ if $e=f$. Furthermore, $(1-e-f+2ef)e=(1-e-f+2ef)f=ef$. Using Equations (1) and (2), we obtain the following:

$$\begin{aligned}(1-e-f+2ef)r(1-e-f+2ef) &= (1-e-f+2ef)r-(1-e-f+2ef)re\\ &\quad -(1-e-f+2ef)rf+2(1-e-f+2ef)ref\\ &= (1-e-f+2ef)r-ref-ref+ref\\ &= (1-e-f+2ef)r,\end{aligned}$$

for every $r\in R$. Therefore, $(1-e-f+2ef)\in\mathcal{S}_l(R)$. Similarly, we obtain $(1-e-f+2ef)\in\mathcal{S}_r(R)$, using Equations (3) and (4). Therefore, $(1-e-f+2ef)$ is a nontrivial central idempotent, and R is not central reduced. Thus, R is commutative, according to Proposition 5. □

In [2], sufficient conditions for two idempotents to be conjugate are given. The next proposition shows that this condition is necessary for isomorphic idempotents in i-commutative rings.

Proposition 11. *For a ring R and its idempotents e and f, the following two statements are valid:*

(i) *If $e-f\in\mathcal{N}_2(R)$, then e and f are conjugate.*
(ii) *If $e-f\in\mathcal{I}_2(R)$, then e and $1-f$ are conjugate.*

If, additionally, R is i-commutative, then the following two statements are valid:

(iii) *If e and f are conjugate, then $e-f\in\mathcal{N}_2(R)$ or $Char(R)=2$.*
(iv) *If e and $1-f$ are conjugate, then $e-f\in\mathcal{I}_2(R)$ or $Char(R)=2$.*

Proof.

(i) It is part of [2] (Proposition 3).
(ii) In the case of $e-f\in\mathcal{I}_2(R)$, we have $((1-e)-f)^2=((1-2e)+(e-f))^2=1+1+(1-2e)(e-f)+(e-f)(1-2e)=2+e-f-2e+2ef+e-f-2e+2fe=2-2f-2e+2ef+2fe=2-2(e-f)^2=0$ and $((1-e)-f)\in\mathcal{N}_2(R)$. So, $(1-e)\overset{c}{\cong}f$ and, consequently, $(1-f)\overset{c}{\cong}e$ from (i).

For the last two implications, consider that R is i-commutative.

(iii) Assume that e and f are conjugate. If e and f are trivial and isomorphic, then $e-f=0$, and the condition holds. If e and f are nontrivial isomorphic, then $e=xy$ and $f=yx$ for some $x,y\in R$. So, $xy+1(yx-xy)$ is a nontrivial idempotent. Also, $2f-e$ is an idempotent, and, therefore, $2(e-f)^2=0$. Moreover, $(ef)f+1(e-ef)$ is a nontrivial idempotent. So, $fef-ef+e$ is idempotent and $fef-efef+efe-fefe=0$. Furthermore, $(e-f)^4=(e+f-ef-fe)^2=((1-f)e+(1-e)f)^2=(1-f)e(1-f)e+(1-e)f(1-e)f=((1-f)e+(1-e)f)-(efe-fefe+fef-efef)=(e-f)^2$. Therefore, $(e-f)^2$ is an idempotent. In summary, we obtain the following cases:
Case 1. If $(e-f)^2=0$, then $e-f\in\mathcal{N}_2(R)$ follows.
Case 2. If $(e-f)^2=1$, then $Char(R)=2$, since $2(e-f)^2=0$.
Case 3. Finally, we have $(e-f)^2$, which is a nontrivial idempotent that commutes with both e and f.
Subcase 3.1. If $(e-f)^2e=0$ or $(e-f)^2f=0$, then $e=efe$ and $f=fef$, which implies $(e-f)^2=(efe-fef)^2=efefe+fefef-efefef-fefefe=ef(efe-efef)+fe(fef-fefe)=ef(fef-fefe)+fe(efe-efef)=e(fef-fefe)+$

$f(efe-efef) = e(efe-efef)+f(fef-fefe) = efe-efef+fef-fefe = 0$ and $e-f \in \mathcal{N}_2(R)$.

Subcase 3.2. If $(e-f)^2 = e$ and $(e-f)^2 = f$, then $0 = e-f \in \mathcal{N}_2(R)$.

Subcase 3.3. Finally, at least one of e and f forms, with $(e-f)^2$, nonorthogonal commutating distinct nontrivial idempotents. According to Theorem 5, R is commutative and $f = e$; that is, $e-f \in \mathcal{N}_2(R)$.

(iv) If e and $1-f$ are conjugate, then $Char(R) = 2$ or $0 = (e-(1-f))^2 = ((e-f)+(2f-1))^2 = (e-f)^2+(2f-1)^2+(e-f)(2f-1)+(2f-1)(e-f) = (e-f)^2+1-2(e-f)^2$ and $(e-f)^2 = 1$, using the result in (iii).

□

Proposition 12. *For a non-commutative i-commutative ring R with $\mathcal{I}(R) \neq \{0,1\}$, nontrivial idempotents e and f satisfy $e \overset{c}{\cong} f$ or $e \overset{c}{\cong} (1-f)$.*

Proof. Obviously, if e and f are equal, then they are conjugate. So, we assume, without loss of generality, that $e \neq f$ through the proof. For every nontrivial idempotent e of a ring R, we have $1(ef)+e(1-f)$, which is a nontrivial idempotent. So, $(ef)1+(1-f)e = e+ef-fe$ is idempotent, and $efe+fef = efef+fefe$. Multiplying the obtained equation by e, we obtain $efe = efefe$ and, hence, efe is idempotent. Therefore, we have the following cases:

Case 1. If $efe = 1$, then e is invertible and $e = 1$ is a contradiction.

Case 2. If $efe = 0$, then $efe+f$ is a nontrivial idempotent, and $ef+f$ is idempotent from the i-commutative condition. So, $ef+f = efef+f+ef+fef$ and $fef = 0$. Then, $(e-f)^2 = e+f-ef-fe$ and $(e-f)^4 = (e+f-ef-fe)^2 = e+f+efef+fefe+ef+fe-ef-efe-efe-fe-fef-ef-fe-fef+efe+fef = e+f-ef-fe$. So, $(e-f)^2$ is idempotent, and we have the following subcases:

Subcase 2.1. If $(e-f)^2 = 1$, then $e \overset{c}{\cong} (1-f)$, according to Proposition 11.

Subcase 2.2. If $(e-f)^2 = 0$, then $e-f \in \mathcal{N}_2(R)$ and $e \overset{c}{\cong} f$, according to Proposition 11.

Subcase 2.3. If $(e-f)^2 = e+f-ef-fe$ is a nontrivial idempotent, then $e+f-2ef$ by applying the i-commutativity of R. So, $ef = fe$ and $fe = ef = e(ef) = efe = 0$. If $(1-e)(1-f) = 0$, then $f = 1-e$ and $e \overset{c}{\cong} (1-f)$. If this is not the case, then $1-e$ and $1-f$ are nonorthogonal and nontrivial commutating idempotents. Hence, R is commutative, according to Theorem 5, which contradicts the assumption.

Case 3. If efe is a nontrivial idempotent, then ef and fe also qualify as nontrivial idempotents, due to the i-commutativity of R. If $efe = e$ and $f = fef$, then $e = (ef)(fe)$ and $f = (fe)(ef)$; that is, $e \overset{c}{\cong} f$. If $efe \neq e$ or $fef \neq f$, then at least one of $e-efe$ and $f-efe$ is a nontrivial idempotent. In case $e-efe$ is a trivial idempotent, then $e-ef$ and $e-fe$ are idempotent. If so, we obtain the result that $fe = ef$, and, consequently, R is commutative, according to Theorem 5; this is a contradiction. In the case of $f-efe$, we obtain the same result. □

For a ring R, the trivial extension of R by R, denoted by $T(R,R)$, is *Morita context* $(R,R,0,R,\phi,\psi)$, where ϕ and ψ are trivial homomorphisms. Therefore, $T(R,R) = R \oplus R$ with the componentwise addition and multiplication defined as $(r_1,r_2)(r_3,r_4) = (r_1r_2, r_1r_4+r_2r_3)$, for every $r_i \in R$ with $i = 1,2,3,4$. The idempotents of trivial extension over an i-commutative ring are constructed in the next proposition.

Proposition 13. *If R is an i-commutative ring with $Char(R) \neq 2$, then the following is true:*

$$\mathcal{I}(T(R,R)) = \left\{ (e, e-f) \mid e \in \mathcal{I}(R) \text{ and } e \overset{c}{\cong} f \right\}.$$

Proof. If R has only trivial idempotents, then $T(R,R)$ does not have nontrivial idempotents, and, therefore, $\mathcal{I}(T(R,R)) = \{(0,0),(1,0)\}$. Furthermore, R is commutative if and only if $T(R,R)$ is also. Here, each idempotent is isomorphic to itself only and $\mathcal{I}(T(R,R)) = \{(e,0) \mid e \in \mathcal{I}(R)\}$. In the remainder of the proof, we consider that R is a non-commutative i-commutative ring with nontrivial idempotents. Let (a,b) be a nontrivial idempotent of $T(R,R)$, then $a^2 = a = e$ is a nontrivial idempotent in R and $eb + be = b$. Notice that $ebe = 0$ and $eb^2 = b^2e$. By applying the i-commutativity of R to the nontrivial idempotent $e(b+1) + b(e-1)$, we derive $e(b+1) + (e-1)b = e - (1-2e)b$, which is an idempotent, and $e - (1-2e)b = (e-(1-2e)b)^2$. Simplifying this, we obtain $2beb = (1-2e)b^2$. Multiplying both sides of the obtained equation by $(1-2e)$ from the left, we obtain $b^2 = 2beb$. Now, $b^2 = (eb+be)^2 = ebeb + bebe + eb^2e + beb = beb$, and, therefore, $b^2 = beb = 0$. Hence, $(e-b)^2 = e - eb - be + b^2 = e - b$, and $e - b$ is an idempotent, say f. So, $b = e - f$ and $(e-f)^2 = b^2 = 0$. Thus, $e - f \in \mathcal{N}_2(R)$ and $e \overset{c}{\cong} f$, according to Proposition 11. Conversely, let $\epsilon = (e', e' - f')$ for some isomorphic nontrivial idempotents e' and f' of R. If $Char(R) \neq 2$, then $\epsilon^2 = (e', e' - e'f' + e' - f'e') = (e', e' - f(e'-f')^2) = (e', e' - f')$, according to Proposition 11, and ϵ is an idempotent in $T(R,R)$. □

Finally, we describe the idempotents of the polynomial ring $R[x]$ with an indeterminate x and the power series ring $R[[x]]$ with an indeterminate x over R, respectively.

Proposition 14. *Let R be an i-commutative ring with $Char(R) \neq 2$; then, teh following is true:*

$$\mathcal{I}(R[[x]])) = \left\{ e + \sum_{i=1}^{\infty}(e - f_i)x^i \mid e \in \mathcal{I}(R) \text{ and } f_i \overset{c}{\cong} e, \text{for all } i \right\}$$

Proof. If $e(x)$ is an idempotent of $R[[x]]$, then $e_0 = e$ is also an idempotent of R. Indeed, $R[x]$ does not have nontrivial idempotents if and only if R does not. So, we assume that R has nontrivial idempotents, and we obtain the following equations:

$$ee_1 + e_1e = e_1; \tag{5}$$

$$e_2e + e_1^2 + ee_2 = e_2; \tag{6}$$

$$e_3e + e_2e_1 + e_1e_2 + ee_3 = e_3; \tag{7}$$

$$\vdots \quad .$$

Applying the same technique used to prove Proposition 13 on Equation (5), we obtain $e_1 = e - f_1$ for some idempotent f_1 conjugate to e, and $e_1^2 = 0$. Equation (6) becomes $e_2e + ee_2 = e_2$ and, again, $e_2 = e - f_2$ where $f_2 \overset{c}{\cong} e$. Therefore, f_1 and f_2 are also dual isomeric, since $\overset{c}{\cong}$ is a transitive relation. Now, $e_2e_1 + e_1e_2 = (e-f_2)(e-f_1) + (e-f_1)(e-f_2) = e - ef_1 - f_2e + f_2f_1 + e - ef_2 - f_1e + f_1f_2 = e - f_1 - e + f_1 + e - f_2 - e + f_1 = 0$. Therefore, Equation (7) becomes $e_3e + ee_3 = e_3$ and again $e_3 = e - f_3$, where f_3 is a conjugate idempotent of e. Continuing, we obtain $e(x) = e + \sum_{i=1}^{\infty}(e-f_i)x^i$, where f_i's are idempotents conjugate to e. Conversely, let $e(x) = e + \sum_{i=1}^{\infty}(e-f_i)x^i$, where $\{e, f_1, f_2, f_3, \cdots\}$ are conjugate idempotents of R. Therefore, the coefficient of x^i in $e^2(x)$ is given by the following:

$$e(e-f_i) + (e-f_i)e + \sum_{k=1}^{i}(e-f_k)(e-f_{i-k}).$$

If i is even, then the coefficient of x^i in $e^2(x)$ can be written as follows:

$$e(e-f_i)+(e-f_i)e+\sum_{k=1}^{\frac{i}{2}}(e-f_k)(e-f_{i-k})+(e-f_{i-k})(e-f_k).$$

However,

$$\begin{aligned}(e-f_k)(e-f_{i-k})+(e-f_{i-k})(e-f_k) &= e-ef_{i-k}-f_ke+f_kf_{i-k}+e-ef_k-f_{i-k}e+f_{i-k}f_k \\ &= (e-f_k)^2+(e-f_{i-k})^2-(f_k-f_{i-k})^2=0.\end{aligned}$$

Furthermore, $e(e-f_i)+(e-f_i)e=(e-f_i)^2+(e-f_i)=e-f_i$. Similarly, $e^2(x)=e(x)$. In a case where n is odd, the coefficient of x^i is $e^2(x)$ and can be written as follows:

$$e(e-f_i)+(e-f_i)e+\left(e-e_{\frac{i-1}{2}}\right)^2+\sum_{k=1}^{\frac{i-1}{2}}(e-f_k)(e-f_{i-k})+(e-f_{i-k})(e-f_k).$$

Again, $e^2(x)=e(x)$. □

We can prove the next proposition using the same technique we used to prove the last one.

Proposition 15. *Let R be an i-commutative ring with Char(R) $\neq 2$; then, the following is true:*

$$\mathcal{I}(R[x]))=\left\{e+\sum_{i=1}^{n}(e-f_i)x^i \mid e\in\mathcal{I}(R) \text{ and } f_i\overset{c}{\cong}e, \text{for all } i,n\in\mathbb{Z}^+\right\}.$$

6. Conclusions

This paper introduced a new class of rings, termed i-commutative rings, characterized by the condition that $ba+dc$ is idempotent whenever $ab+c$ is a nontrivial idempotent. We proved that every i-commutative ring is i-reversible, although the converse is not true. Furthermore, we showed that nontrivial corner subrings of an i-commutative ring are commutative, and i-commutative rings with nontrivial central idempotents are necessarily commutative. In the context of matrix rings, we demonstrated that $\mathbb{M}_n(R)$ over any ring R does not satisfy the i-commutativity condition. We looked at how this property works in some structures related to matrices, like upper triangular rings and Morita contexts. We also introduced maximal i-commutative subrings of matrix rings. We also looked at the connections between i-commutative rings and other types of commutative rings, like abelian and semi-abelian rings, using counterexamples to show that they are independent. Additionally, we investigated the behavior of i-commutative rings under regularity conditions and studied the properties of idempotents in such rings. Finally, we discussed the construction of idempotents in polynomial extensions of i-commutative rings, offering insights into their structural behavior.

Author Contributions: Conceptualization, M.S.; methodology, M.S., U.A.A. and N.N.; validation, M.S., U.A.A. and A.M.A.E.-S.; formal analysis, M.S. and U.A.A.; investigation, M.S., U.A.A. and A.M.A.E.-S.; writing—original draft preparation, M.S. and N.N.; writing—review and editing, M.S. and U.A.A.; visualization, M.S.; supervision, U.A.A.; project administration, A.M.A.E.-S. All authors have read and agreed to the published version of the manuscript.

Funding: This research received no external funding

Data Availability Statement: No new data were created or analyzed in this study.

Conflicts of Interest: The authors declare no conflicts of interest.

References

1. Lam, T.Y. *A First Course in Noncommutative Rings*; Springer Science & Business Media: New York, NY, USA; Heidelberg, Germany; Dordrecht, The Netherlands; London, UK, 2013; Volume 131. [CrossRef]
2. Song, G.; Guo, X. Diagonability of idempotent matrices over noncommutative rings. *Linear Algebra Its Appl.* **1999**, *297*, 1–7. [CrossRef]
3. Cohn, P.M. Reversible rings. *Lond. Math. Soc.* **1999**, *31*, 641–648. [CrossRef]
4. Jung, D.W.; Kim, N.K.; Lee, Y.; Ryu, S.J. On properties related to reversible rings. *Bull. Korean Math. Soc.* **2015**, *52*, 247–261. [CrossRef]
5. Khurana, A.; Khurana, D. I-reversible rings. *J. Algebra Its Appl.* **2020**, *19*, 2050076. [CrossRef]
6. Jung, D.W.; Lee, C.I.; Lee, Y.; Park, S.; Ryu, S.J.; Sung, H.J.; Yun, S.J. On reversibility related to idempotents. *Bull. Korean Math. Soc.* **2019**, *56*, 993–1006. [CrossRef]
7. Herstein, I.N. A condition for the commutativity of rings. *Can. J. Math.* **1957**, *9*, 583–586. [CrossRef]
8. Saad, M. Rings in which every semicentral idempotent is central. *Korean J. Math.* **2023**, *31*, 405–417. [CrossRef]
9. Loustaunau, P.; Shapiro, J. Morita contexts. In *Non-Commutative Ring Theory: Proceedings of a Conference, Athens, OH, 29–30 September 1989*; Springer: Berlin/Heidelberg, Germany, 2006; pp. 80–92. [CrossRef]
10. Morita, K. Duality for modules and its applications to the theory of rings with minimum condition. *Sci. Rep. Tokyo Kyoiku Daigaku Sect. A* **1958**, *6*, 83–142.
11. Amitsur, S.A. Rings of quotients and Morita contexts. *J. Algebra* **1971**, *17*, 273–298. [CrossRef]
12. Krylov, P.; Tuganbaev, A. *Formal Matrices*; Springer: Cham, Switzerland, 2017; Volume 23. [CrossRef]
13. Tang, G.; Li, C.; Zhou, Y. Study of Morita contexts. *Commun. Algebra* **2014**, *42*, 1668–1681. [CrossRef]
14. Marianne, M. Rings of quotients of generalized matrix rings. *Commun. Algebra* **1987**, *15*, 1991–2015. [CrossRef]
15. Eldridge, K.E. Orders for finite noncommutative rings with unity. *Am. Math. Mon.* **1968**, *75*, 512–514. [CrossRef]
16. Nicholson, W.K. Lifting idempotents and exchange rings. *Trans. Am. Math. Soc.* **1977**, *229*, 269–278. [CrossRef]
17. Chen, W. On semiabelian π-regular rings. *Int. J. Math. Math. Sci.* **2007**, *2007*, 63171. [CrossRef]

Disclaimer/Publisher's Note: The statements, opinions and data contained in all publications are solely those of the individual author(s) and contributor(s) and not of MDPI and/or the editor(s). MDPI and/or the editor(s) disclaim responsibility for any injury to people or property resulting from any ideas, methods, instructions or products referred to in the content.

mathematics

MDPI

Article

The Category $\mathfrak{G}$-*GrR-Mod* and Group Factorization

Rahmah Al-Omari and Mohammed Al-Shomrani *

Department of Mathematics, Faculty of Science, King Abdulaziz University, Jeddah 21589, Saudi Arabia; ralomari0054@stu.kau.edu.sa
* Correspondence: malshamrani@kau.edu.sa

Abstract: In this work, we use the concept of $\mathfrak{G}$-weak graded rings and $\mathfrak{G}$-weak graded modules, which are based on grading by a set $\mathfrak{G}$ of left coset representatives for the left action of a subgroup $\mathfrak{H}$ of a finite $\mathfrak{X}$ on $\mathfrak{X}$, to define the conjugation action of the set $\mathfrak{G}$ and to generalize and prove some results from the literature. In particular, we prove that a $\mathfrak{G}$-weak graded ring R is strongly graded if and only if each $\mathfrak{G}$-weak graded R-module V is induced by an $R_{\mathfrak{e}_{\mathfrak{G}}}$-module. Moreover, we prove that the additive induction functor $(-)^R$ and the restriction functor $(-)_{\mathfrak{e}_{\mathfrak{G}}}$ form an equivalence between the categories $\mathfrak{G}$-*GrR-Mod* and $R_{\mathfrak{e}_{\mathfrak{G}}}$-*Mod* when R is strongly $\mathfrak{G}$-weak graded. Furthermore, some related results and illustrative examples of $\mathfrak{G}$-weak graded R-modules and their morphisms are provided.

Keywords: left coset representatives; weak graded rings; weak graded module; weak graded homomorphisms; equivalence between categories

MSC: 16W50; 16W20; 16W22; 13A02

1. Introduction

Recall that, for a group $\mathfrak{X}$ and an $\mathfrak{X}$-graded ring R, a left R-module M is called an $\mathfrak{X}$-graded module if it can be written as a direct sum decomposition $M = \bigoplus_{\mathfrak{x}\in\mathfrak{X}} M_{\mathfrak{x}}$ such that, for all $\mathfrak{x}, \mathfrak{y} \in \mathfrak{X}$, we have $R_{\mathfrak{x}}M_{\mathfrak{y}} \subseteq M_{\mathfrak{x}\mathfrak{y}}$, where $M_{\mathfrak{y}}$ is an $R_{\mathfrak{e}}$-submodule for each $\mathfrak{y} \in \mathfrak{X}$ and $\mathfrak{e}$ is the identity element of $\mathfrak{X}$. If the condition $R_{\mathfrak{x}}M_{\mathfrak{y}} \subseteq M_{\mathfrak{x}\mathfrak{y}}$ is replaced by $R_{\mathfrak{x}}M_{\mathfrak{y}} = M_{\mathfrak{x}\mathfrak{y}}$ for all $\mathfrak{x}, \mathfrak{y} \in \mathfrak{X}$, then M is called a strongly $\mathfrak{X}$-graded module. Group-graded rings and modules have been extensively studied, either alone or in connection with different areas of mathematics; see ref. [1]. Many mathematicians have generalized the concept of group-graded rings and modules by using monoids or semigroups for grading; see, for example, refs. [2,3]. The concept of semi-graded rings and modules was introduced as a different means to generalize group-graded rings and modules; see ref. [4].

The properties of graded rings and modules have been investigated using various methods, such as duality theorems [5] and categorical methods, which are used to study separable functors; see refs. [6,7].

In ref. [8], an algebraic structure consisting of a set $\mathfrak{G}$ of left coset representatives and a binary operation "$*$" was constructed. This structure led to interesting categories; see refs. [8,9]. Additionally, it was used to introduce the new concept of $\mathfrak{G}$-weak graded rings and modules, which generalizes the concept of group-graded rings and modules; see ref. [10].

This work is a continuation of [11], which generalized the concepts of group-graded rings and group-graded modules by associating the grading with the factorization of a given finite group and using a set of left coset representatives for grading, rather than groups. In this work, we generalize and prove some important results given in the literature concerning the category $\mathfrak{G}$-*GrR-Mod* and its objects of $\mathfrak{G}$-weak graded left R-modules. Specifically, we prove that a $\mathfrak{G}$-weak graded ring R is strongly graded if and only if each $\mathfrak{G}$-weak graded R-module V is induced from an $R_{\mathfrak{e}_{\mathfrak{G}}}$-module. We also prove that the additive induction functor $(-)^R$, which takes any left $R_{\mathfrak{e}_{\mathfrak{G}}}$-module K to the tensor product

$R \otimes_{R_{\mathfrak{e}_{\mathfrak{G}}}} K$, and the restriction functor $(-)_{\mathfrak{e}_{\mathfrak{G}}}$ form an equivalence between the categories $\mathfrak{G}$-*GrR-Mod* and $R_{\mathfrak{e}_{\mathfrak{G}}}$-*Mod* if R is a strongly $\mathfrak{G}$-weak graded ring. Some other important related results are also proven. Finally, some illustrative examples of $\mathfrak{G}$-weak graded R-modules are provided.

The significance of this work lies in the fact that it presents a generalization of the important concepts of group-graded rings and group-graded modules, which play a vital rule in abstract algebra. Consequently, the exploration of $\mathfrak{G}$-weak graded rings and modules and their properties remains an active field for interested researchers. Furthermore, this work may lead to further generalization to the quantum case, particularly to the bicrossproduct Hopf algebras associated with the factorization of a finite group $\mathfrak{X} = \mathfrak{H}\mathfrak{G}$; see refs. [12,13].

Throughout this research, we assume, unless otherwise stated, that all groups are finite, all rings are associative with unity, and all modules are unital.

2. Preliminaries

In this section, we include fundamental definitions and results that are essential to prove our results.

Recall that the category of $\mathfrak{G}$-weak graded left R-modules is denoted by $\mathfrak{G}$-*GrR-Mod* [11]. If a morphism $\varphi : V \longrightarrow W$ in $\mathfrak{G}$-*GrR-Mod*, then $\varphi(v) \in W_{\mathfrak{p}}$ for all $v \in V_{\mathfrak{p}}$ and $\mathfrak{p} \in \mathfrak{G}$, where V and W are $\mathfrak{G}$-weak graded left R-modules. We denote the class of these morphisms by $\mathfrak{G}$-$GrHom_R(V, W)$ [11]. Based on this, we denote the category of strongly $\mathfrak{G}$-weak graded R-modules by $\mathfrak{G}$-*StGrR-Mod*, with $\mathfrak{G}$-*Gr-R* as the category of $\mathfrak{G}$-weak graded rings and $\mathfrak{G}$-*StGr-R* as the category of strongly $\mathfrak{G}$-weak graded rings.

Definition 1 ([8]). *Consider a group $\mathfrak{X}$ and a subgroup $\mathfrak{H}$. The set $\mathfrak{G} \subset \mathfrak{X}$ is called a set of left coset representatives if there exists a unique $\mathfrak{p} \in \mathfrak{G}$ for each $\mathfrak{x} \in \mathfrak{X}$ such that $\mathfrak{x} \in \mathfrak{H}\mathfrak{p}$. We define a binary operation $*$ on $\mathfrak{G}$ that satisfies the right division property with a unique left identity $\mathfrak{e}_{\mathfrak{G}} \in \mathfrak{G}$.*

Definition 2 ([8]). *For $\mathfrak{p}, \mathfrak{q} \in \mathfrak{G}$, $f(\mathfrak{p}, \mathfrak{q}) \in \mathfrak{H}$ and $\mathfrak{p} * \mathfrak{q} \in \mathfrak{G}$ are defined by the unique factorization $\mathfrak{p}\mathfrak{q} = g(\mathfrak{p}, \mathfrak{q})(\mathfrak{p} * \mathfrak{q})$ in $\mathfrak{X}$, where g is the cocycle map satisfying $\mathfrak{o} \triangleleft g(\mathfrak{p}, \mathfrak{q}) * (\mathfrak{p} * \mathfrak{q}) = (\mathfrak{o} * \mathfrak{p}) * \mathfrak{q}$, provided that $\triangleright : \mathfrak{G} \times \mathfrak{H} \to \mathfrak{H}$ and $\triangleleft : \mathfrak{G} \times \mathfrak{H} \to \mathfrak{G}$ are defined by $\mathfrak{p}\mathfrak{h} = (\mathfrak{p} \triangleright \mathfrak{h})(\mathfrak{p} \triangleleft \mathfrak{h})$, for $\mathfrak{h} \in \mathfrak{H}$, which is also unique.*

Definition 3 ([10]). *A $\mathfrak{G}$-weak graded ring R is a ring that satisfies*

$$R = \bigoplus_{\mathfrak{p} \in \mathfrak{G}} R_{\mathfrak{p}}, \tag{1}$$

and

$$R_{\mathfrak{p}} R_{\mathfrak{q}} \subseteq R_{\mathfrak{p} * \mathfrak{q}} \quad \textit{for all} \quad \mathfrak{p}, \mathfrak{q} \in \mathfrak{G}, \tag{2}$$

where $R_{\mathfrak{p}}$ is an additive subgroup for each $\mathfrak{p} \in \mathfrak{G}$. If, instead of (2), we have

$$R_{\mathfrak{p}} R_{\mathfrak{q}} = R_{\mathfrak{p} * \mathfrak{q}}, \tag{3}$$

for all $\mathfrak{p}, \mathfrak{q} \in \mathfrak{G}$, then R is called a strongly $\mathfrak{G}$-weak graded ring.

Definition 4 ([10]). *A $\mathfrak{G}$-weak graded R-module V is a left R-module that satisfies*

$$V = \bigoplus_{\mathfrak{p} \in \mathfrak{G}} V_{\mathfrak{p}} \qquad (\textit{in } R_{\mathfrak{e}_{\mathfrak{G}}}\textit{-Mod}) \tag{4}$$

and

$$R_{\mathfrak{p}} V_{\mathfrak{q}} \subseteq V_{\mathfrak{p} * \mathfrak{q}} \quad \textit{for all} \quad \mathfrak{p}, \mathfrak{q} \in \mathfrak{G}, \tag{5}$$

where $R \in \mathfrak{G}$-Gr-R. If, instead of (5), we have

$$R_{\mathfrak{p}} V_{\mathfrak{q}} = V_{\mathfrak{p}*\mathfrak{q}}, \tag{6}$$

for all $\mathfrak{p}, \mathfrak{q} \in \mathfrak{G}$, then V is called a strongly $\mathfrak{G}$-weak graded R-module.

Definition 5 ([11]). *For $V, W \in \mathfrak{G}$-GrR-Mod, the additive subgroup $\mathfrak{G}$-$GrHom_R(V, W)_{\mathfrak{q}}$ of $\mathfrak{G}$-$GrHom_R(V, W)$ for $\mathfrak{q} \in \mathfrak{G}$ is defined by*

$$\mathfrak{G}\text{-}GrHom_R(V, W)_{\mathfrak{q}} = \{\varphi \in \mathfrak{G}\text{-}GrHom_R(V, W) \ : \ \varphi(V_{\mathfrak{p}}) \subseteq W_{\mathfrak{p}*\mathfrak{q}}, \text{ for all } \mathfrak{p} \in \mathfrak{G}\}.$$

Definition 6 ([10]). *Let K be a left $R_{\mathfrak{e}_{\mathfrak{G}}}$-module. The tensor product $R \otimes_{R_{\mathfrak{e}_{\mathfrak{G}}}} K$ is a left R-module with*

$$(r_1(r_2 \otimes k) = (r_1 r_2) \otimes k, \ \text{for all } r_1, r_2 \in R \text{ and } k \in K. \tag{7}$$

Theorem 1 ([10]). *For $R \in \mathfrak{G}$-Gr-R, the composite functor*

$$\beta_{R_{\mathfrak{e}_{\mathfrak{G}}},-} = (R \otimes_{R_{\mathfrak{e}_{\mathfrak{G}}}} -)_{\mathfrak{e}_{\mathfrak{G}}} = (R_{\mathfrak{e}_{\mathfrak{G}}} \otimes_{R_{\mathfrak{e}_{\mathfrak{G}}}} -) : R_{\mathfrak{e}_{\mathfrak{G}}}\text{-}Mod \to \mathfrak{G}\text{-}GrR\text{-}Mod,$$

which is defined by

$$\beta_{R_{\mathfrak{e}_{\mathfrak{G}}},K} = (R \otimes_{R_{\mathfrak{e}_{\mathfrak{G}}}} K)_{\mathfrak{e}_{\mathfrak{G}}} = R_{\mathfrak{e}_{\mathfrak{G}}} \otimes_{R_{\mathfrak{e}_{\mathfrak{G}}}} K \cong K,$$

for any left $R_{\mathfrak{e}_{\mathfrak{G}}}$-module K, forms the following natural isomorphisms:

$$((-)^R)_{\mathfrak{e}_{\mathfrak{G}}} \approx I_{R_{\mathfrak{e}_{\mathfrak{G}}}\text{-}Mod}, \tag{8}$$

where $(-)^R = (R \otimes_{R_{\mathfrak{e}_{\mathfrak{G}}}} -)$ and $I_{R_{\mathfrak{e}_{\mathfrak{G}}}\text{-}Mod}$ is the identity functor on the category $R_{\mathfrak{e}_{\mathfrak{G}}}$-Mod.

Proposition 1 ([10]). *If a right inverse $\mathfrak{p}^R$ exists for any $\mathfrak{p} \in \mathfrak{G}$, and if the ring R is strongly $\mathfrak{G}$-weak graded, then every $\mathfrak{G}$-weak graded R-module V is strongly graded.*

3. The Category of $\mathfrak{G}$-Weak Graded Modules

Definition 7. *For all $\mathfrak{p}, \mathfrak{q} \in \mathfrak{G}$, and all modules V, W and morphisms $\varphi : V \to W$ in $\mathfrak{G}$-GrR-Mod, a conjugation action of the set $\mathfrak{G}$ as automorphisms of $\mathfrak{G}$-GrR-Mod is defined by $V^{\mathfrak{p}} = V$ in R-Mod, $(V^{\mathfrak{p}})_{\mathfrak{q}} = V_{\mathfrak{q}*\mathfrak{p}}$ in $R_{\mathfrak{e}_{\mathfrak{G}}}$-Mod, and $\varphi^{\mathfrak{p}} = \varphi$ in $Hom_R(V, W) = Hom_R(V^{\mathfrak{p}}, W^{\mathfrak{p}})$, where $\mathfrak{e}_{\mathfrak{G}}$ is a two-sided identity.*

It can be noted that the $\mathfrak{G}$-weak grading is the only effect of this action for each module.

Theorem 2. *For any strongly $\mathfrak{G}$-weak graded R-module V, the natural map*

$$\beta_{R,V_{\mathfrak{e}_{\mathfrak{G}}}} : R \otimes_{R_{\mathfrak{e}_{\mathfrak{G}}}} V_{\mathfrak{e}_{\mathfrak{G}}} \to V,$$

which sends $r \otimes v_{\mathfrak{e}_{\mathfrak{G}}}$ into $r v_{\mathfrak{e}_{\mathfrak{G}}} \in V$ for all $r \in R$ and $v_{\mathfrak{e}_{\mathfrak{G}}} \in V_{\mathfrak{e}_{\mathfrak{G}}}$, is an isomorphism in $\mathfrak{G}$-GrR-Mod.

Proof. Let $V \in \mathfrak{G}$-*StGrR-Mod*; then, $V = \bigoplus_{\mathfrak{p} \in \mathfrak{G}} V_{\mathfrak{p}}$ in $R_{\mathfrak{e}_{\mathfrak{G}}}$-*Mod* and $V_{\mathfrak{p}} R_{\mathfrak{q}} = V_{\mathfrak{p}*\mathfrak{q}}$ for all $\mathfrak{p}, \mathfrak{q} \in \mathfrak{G}$. Since $V = \bigoplus_{\mathfrak{p} \in \mathfrak{G}} V_{\mathfrak{p}}$, we have

$$\beta_{R,V_{\mathfrak{e}_{\mathfrak{G}}}} : R \otimes_{R_{\mathfrak{e}_{\mathfrak{G}}}} V_{\mathfrak{e}_{\mathfrak{G}}} \to V,$$

which is an epimorphism in $\mathfrak{G}$-*GrR-Mod* for any $V \in \mathfrak{G}$-*StGrR-Mod*.

The kernel W of $\beta_{R,V_{\mathfrak{e}_{\mathfrak{G}}}}$ is a $\mathfrak{G}$-weak graded R-submodule of $R \otimes_{R_{\mathfrak{e}_{\mathfrak{G}}}} V_{\mathfrak{e}_{\mathfrak{G}}}$. Since, for any left $R_{\mathfrak{e}_{\mathfrak{G}}}$-module K, we have

$$(K^R)_{\mathfrak{p}} = R_{\mathfrak{p}} \otimes_{R_{\mathfrak{e}_{\mathfrak{G}}}} K, \quad (\text{ in } R_{\mathfrak{e}_{\mathfrak{G}}}\text{-}Mod) \text{ for all } \mathfrak{p} \in \mathfrak{G},$$

and

$$R_{\mathfrak{e}_{\mathfrak{G}}} \otimes_{\mathfrak{e}_{\mathfrak{G}}} V_{\mathfrak{e}_{\mathfrak{G}}} \cong V_{\mathfrak{e}_{\mathfrak{G}}}.$$

Then, the kernel of

$$\beta_{R_{\mathfrak{e}_{\mathfrak{G}}},V_{\mathfrak{e}_{\mathfrak{G}}}} : R_{\mathfrak{e}_{\mathfrak{G}}} \otimes_{R_{\mathfrak{e}_{\mathfrak{G}}}} V_{\mathfrak{e}_{\mathfrak{G}}} \xrightarrow{onto} V_{\mathfrak{e}_{\mathfrak{G}}}$$

is the $\mathfrak{e}_{\mathfrak{G}}$-component of W

$$W_{\mathfrak{e}_{\mathfrak{G}}} = W \cap (R_{\mathfrak{e}_{\mathfrak{G}}} \otimes_{R_{\mathfrak{e}_{\mathfrak{G}}}} V_{\mathfrak{e}_{\mathfrak{G}}}).$$

Hence, $W_{\mathfrak{e}_{\mathfrak{G}}} = 0$. Moreover, as $W \in \mathfrak{G}$-*StGrR-Mod*, we have, for all $\mathfrak{p}$ in $\mathfrak{G}$,

$$W_{\mathfrak{p}} = R_{\mathfrak{p}} W_{\mathfrak{e}_{\mathfrak{G}}} = 0.$$

Hence,

$$W = \bigoplus_{\mathfrak{p} \in \mathfrak{G}} W_{\mathfrak{p}} = 0.$$

Thus, $\beta_{R,V_{\mathfrak{e}_{\mathfrak{G}}}}$ is also a monomorphism and therefore is an isomorphism map as required. □

Theorem 3. *Let $R \in \mathfrak{G}$-StGr-R. Then, $\beta_{R,V_{\mathfrak{e}_{\mathfrak{G}}}}$ forms a natural isomorphism of the composite functor $((-)_{\mathfrak{e}_{\mathfrak{G}}})^R$ with the identity functor of $\mathfrak{G}$-GrR-Mod, i.e.,*

$$((-)_{\mathfrak{e}_{\mathfrak{G}}})^R \approx I_{\mathfrak{G}\text{-}GrR\text{-}Mod} \tag{9}$$

for all $\mathfrak{G}$-weak graded R-modules V in $\mathfrak{G}$-GrR-Mod.

Proof. The additive induction functor

$$(-)^R = R \otimes_{R_{\mathfrak{e}_{\mathfrak{G}}}} - : R_{\mathfrak{e}_{\mathfrak{G}}}\text{-}Mod \to \mathfrak{G}\text{-}GrR\text{-}Mod \tag{10}$$

is given, for any left $R_{\mathfrak{e}_{\mathfrak{G}}}$-module K, by

$$(K)^R = R \otimes_{R_{\mathfrak{e}_{\mathfrak{G}}}} K. \tag{11}$$

The $\mathfrak{p}$-component of K^R in $R_{\mathfrak{e}_{\mathfrak{G}}}$-*Mod* is given by

$$(K^R)_{\mathfrak{p}} = R_{\mathfrak{p}} \otimes_{R_{\mathfrak{e}_{\mathfrak{G}}}} K, \tag{12}$$

for all $\mathfrak{p} \in \mathfrak{G}$. For any map $\varphi : K \to L$ in $R_{\mathfrak{e}_{\mathfrak{G}}}$-*Mod*, we have

$$\varphi^R = I_R \otimes_{R_{\mathfrak{e}_{\mathfrak{G}}}} \varphi : R \otimes_{R_{\mathfrak{e}_{\mathfrak{G}}}} K \to R \otimes_{R_{\mathfrak{e}_{\mathfrak{G}}}} L, \tag{13}$$

where I_R is the identity map of R onto itself. In addition, the restriction functor

$$(-)_{\mathfrak{e}_{\mathfrak{G}}} : \mathfrak{G}\text{-}GrR\text{-}Mod \to R_{\mathfrak{e}_{\mathfrak{G}}}\text{-}Mod \tag{14}$$

sends any $V \in \mathfrak{G}$-*GrR-Mod* into its $R_{\mathfrak{e}_{\mathfrak{G}}}$-component $V_{\mathfrak{e}_{\mathfrak{G}}}$ and any morphism

$$\varphi : V \to W \quad \text{in } \mathfrak{G}\text{-}GrR\text{-}Mod$$

into its restriction

$$\varphi_{\mathfrak{e}_{\mathfrak{G}}} : V_{\mathfrak{e}_{\mathfrak{G}}} \to W_{\mathfrak{e}_{\mathfrak{G}}} \quad \text{in } R_{\mathfrak{e}_{\mathfrak{G}}}\text{-}Mod.$$

Combining the additive induction functor (10) and the restriction functor (14) gives the following composite functor:

$$((-)_{\mathfrak{e}_{\mathfrak{G}}})^R : \mathfrak{G}\text{-}GrR\text{-}Mod \to R_{\mathfrak{e}_{\mathfrak{G}}}\text{-}Mod \to \mathfrak{G}\text{-}GrR\text{-}Mod,$$

which is defined by

$$R \otimes_{R_{\mathfrak{e}_\mathfrak{G}}} V_{\mathfrak{e}_\mathfrak{G}} \to R_{\mathfrak{e}_\mathfrak{G}} \otimes_{R_{\mathfrak{e}_\mathfrak{G}}} V_{\mathfrak{e}_\mathfrak{G}} \to R \otimes_{R_{\mathfrak{e}_\mathfrak{G}}} V_{\mathfrak{e}_\mathfrak{G}},$$

for any $V_{\mathfrak{e}_\mathfrak{G}} \in R_{\mathfrak{e}_\mathfrak{G}}$*-Mod*. Since $R_{\mathfrak{e}_\mathfrak{G}} \otimes_{R_{\mathfrak{e}_\mathfrak{G}}} V_{\mathfrak{e}_\mathfrak{G}} \cong V_{\mathfrak{e}_\mathfrak{G}}$, we have

$$R \otimes_{R_{\mathfrak{e}_\mathfrak{G}}} V_{\mathfrak{e}_\mathfrak{G}} \to V_{\mathfrak{e}_\mathfrak{G}} \to R \otimes_{R_{\mathfrak{e}_\mathfrak{G}}} V_{\mathfrak{e}_\mathfrak{G}}.$$

□

Note that, for any $V \in \mathfrak{G}$*-GrR-Mod*, the map $\beta_{R,V_{\mathfrak{e}_\mathfrak{G}}}$ always forms a natural transformation of $((-)_{\mathfrak{e}_\mathfrak{G}})^R$ into the identity functor on $\mathfrak{G}$*-GrR-Mod*.

Corollary 1. *Let $R \in \mathfrak{G}$-StGr-R. Then, the additive induction functor $(-)^R$ and the restriction functor $(-)_{\mathfrak{e}_\mathfrak{G}}$ form an equivalence between the categories $\mathfrak{G}$-GrR-Mod and $R_{\mathfrak{e}_\mathfrak{G}}$-Mod.*

Proof. The proof is derived directly from Theorems 1 and 3. □

Theorem 4. *Let $\mathfrak{e}_\mathfrak{G}$ be a two-sided identity in $\mathfrak{G}$ and $R \in \mathfrak{G}$-Gr-R. Then, $R \in \mathfrak{G}$-StGr-R if and only if each $\mathfrak{G}$-weak graded R-module V in $\mathfrak{G}$-GrR-Mod is isomorphic in $\mathfrak{G}$-GrR-Mod to a module K^R induced from some $R_{\mathfrak{e}_\mathfrak{G}}$-module K.*

Proof. ($\Longrightarrow$) Assume that $R \in \mathfrak{G}$*-StGr-R*. Then, each $V \in \mathfrak{G}$*-GrR-Mod* is strongly graded according to Proposition 1. Thus, V is isomorpmic in $\mathfrak{G}$*-GrR-Mod* to a module K^R induced from some $R_{\mathfrak{e}_\mathfrak{G}}$-module K via Theorem 2 and Corollary 1.

($\Longleftarrow$) Here, assume that each $V \in \mathfrak{G}$*-GrR-Mod* is isomorphic in $\mathfrak{G}$*-GrR-Mod* to a module K^R induced from some $R_{\mathfrak{e}_\mathfrak{G}}$-module K. Then, according to Corollary 3.3 and Proposition 3.5 in [10], we have

$$R_\mathfrak{q} R_{\mathfrak{e}_\mathfrak{G}} = R_\mathfrak{q},$$

for any $q \in \mathfrak{G}$. Thus, from the tensor product's definition, and since $(K^R)_\mathfrak{p} = R_\mathfrak{p} \otimes_{R_{\mathfrak{e}_\mathfrak{G}}} K$, for all $\mathfrak{p} \in \mathfrak{G}$, we have

$$R_\mathfrak{q}(K^R)_{\mathfrak{e}_\mathfrak{G}} = R_\mathfrak{q}(R_{\mathfrak{e}_\mathfrak{G}} \otimes_{R_{\mathfrak{e}_\mathfrak{G}}} K) = (R_\mathfrak{q} R_{\mathfrak{e}_\mathfrak{G}}) \otimes_{R_{\mathfrak{e}_\mathfrak{G}}} K = R_\mathfrak{q} \otimes_{R_{\mathfrak{e}_\mathfrak{G}}} K = (K^R)_\mathfrak{q} \tag{15}$$

for any $R_{\mathfrak{e}_\mathfrak{G}}$-module K. Since each $V \in \mathfrak{G}$*-GrR-Mod* is isomorphic in $\mathfrak{G}$*-GrR-Mod* to a module K^R, we conclude that

$$R_\mathfrak{q} V_{\mathfrak{e}_\mathfrak{G}} = V_{\mathfrak{q} * \mathfrak{e}_\mathfrak{G}} = V_\mathfrak{q},$$

for any $V \in \mathfrak{G}$*-GrR-Mod*. The regular R-module R with its $\mathfrak{G}$-weak grading $R = \bigoplus_{\mathfrak{p} \in \mathfrak{G}} R_\mathfrak{p}$ is in $\mathfrak{G}$*-GrR-Mod* by $R_\mathfrak{q} R_\mathfrak{p} \subseteq R_{\mathfrak{q} * \mathfrak{p}}$. Let V be the conjugate module $R^\mathfrak{p}$ for some $\mathfrak{p} \in \mathfrak{G}$, and we conclude that

$$R_\mathfrak{q} R_\mathfrak{p} = R_\mathfrak{q}(R_{\mathfrak{e}_\mathfrak{G} * \mathfrak{p}}) = R_\mathfrak{q}(R^\mathfrak{p})_{\mathfrak{e}_\mathfrak{G}} = (R^\mathfrak{p})_\mathfrak{q} = R_{\mathfrak{q} * \mathfrak{p}}$$

according to Definition 7 and relation (15). Therefore, $R \in \mathfrak{G}$*-StGr-R*. □

Corollary 2. *Let $\mathfrak{e}_\mathfrak{G}$ be a two-sided identity in $\mathfrak{G}$ and R be a strongly $\mathfrak{G}$-graded ring; let $\varphi : V \to W$ be a morphism in $\mathfrak{G}$-GrR-Mod; and let $\mathfrak{p}$ be an element of $\mathfrak{G}$. Then, φ is a monomorphism in $\mathfrak{G}$-GrR-Mod if and only if its restriction $\varphi_\mathfrak{p} : V_\mathfrak{p} \to W_\mathfrak{p}$ is a monomorphism in $R_{\mathfrak{e}_\mathfrak{G}}$-Mod.*

Proof. From Definition 7, we have $\varphi^\mathfrak{p} = \varphi$ in $Hom_R(V, W)$, which is equal to $Hom_R(V^\mathfrak{p}, W^\mathfrak{p})$. The map φ is also a morphism $\varphi^\mathfrak{p}$ from $V^\mathfrak{p}$ to $W^\mathfrak{p}$ in $\mathfrak{G}$*-GrR-Mod*. From Corollary 1, $\varphi^\mathfrak{p}$ is a monomorphism if and only if its restriction $(\varphi^\mathfrak{p})_{\mathfrak{e}_\mathfrak{G}}$ is a monomorphism. Definition 7 implies that $(\varphi^{\mathfrak{p}})_{\mathfrak{e}_{\mathfrak{G}}}$ is precisely the map $\varphi_{\mathfrak{p}}$ of $(V^{\mathfrak{p}})_{\mathfrak{e}_{\mathfrak{G}}} = V_{\mathfrak{e}_{\mathfrak{G}}*\mathfrak{p}} = V_{\mathfrak{p}}$ into $(W^{\mathfrak{p}})_{\mathfrak{e}_{\mathfrak{G}}} = W_{\mathfrak{e}_{\mathfrak{G}}*\mathfrak{p}} = W_{\mathfrak{p}}$. Hence, the corollary holds. □

Corollary 3. *Let $\mathfrak{e}_{\mathfrak{G}}$ be a two-sided identity in $\mathfrak{G}$ and R be a strongly $\mathfrak{G}$-graded ring; let $\varphi : V \to W$ be a morphism in $\mathfrak{G}$-GrR-Mod; and let $\mathfrak{p}$ be an element of $\mathfrak{G}$. Then, φ is an epimorphism in $\mathfrak{G}$-GrR-Mod if and only if its restriction $\varphi_{\mathfrak{p}} : V_{\mathfrak{p}} \to W_{\mathfrak{p}}$ is an epimorphism in $R_{\mathfrak{e}_{\mathfrak{G}}}$-Mod.*

Proof. Similarly to the proof of Corollary 2, the map φ is also a morphism $\varphi^{\mathfrak{p}} : V^{\mathfrak{p}} \to W^{\mathfrak{p}}$ in $\mathfrak{G}$-*GrR-Mod*. From Corollary 1, the map $\varphi^{\mathfrak{p}}$ is an epimorphism if and only if its restriction $(\varphi^{\mathfrak{p}})_{\mathfrak{e}_{\mathfrak{G}}}$ is an epimorphism. Moreover, we find that $(\varphi^{\mathfrak{p}})_{\mathfrak{e}_{\mathfrak{G}}}$ is precisely the map $\varphi_{\mathfrak{p}}$ of $(V^{\mathfrak{p}})_{\mathfrak{e}_{\mathfrak{G}}} = V_{\mathfrak{e}_{\mathfrak{G}}*\mathfrak{p}} = V_{\mathfrak{p}}$ into $(W^{\mathfrak{p}})_{\mathfrak{e}_{\mathfrak{G}}} = W_{\mathfrak{e}_{\mathfrak{G}}*\mathfrak{p}} = W_{\mathfrak{p}}$ via Definition 7. □

Corollary 4. *Let $\mathfrak{e}_{\mathfrak{G}}$ be a two-sided identity in $\mathfrak{G}$ and R be a strongly $\mathfrak{G}$-graded ring; let $\varphi : V \to W$ be a morphism in $\mathfrak{G}$-GrR-Mod; and let $\mathfrak{p}$ be an element of $\mathfrak{G}$. Then, φ is an isomorphism in $\mathfrak{G}$-GrR-Mod if and only if its restriction $\varphi_{\mathfrak{p}} : V_{\mathfrak{p}} \to W_{\mathfrak{p}}$ is an isomorphism in $R_{\mathfrak{e}_{\mathfrak{G}}}$-Mod.*

Proof. The proof follows via Corollaries 2 and 3. □

Next, we use Definition 7 and relations (11)–(13) to obtain the following definition.

Definition 8. *For a two-sided identity $\mathfrak{e}_{\mathfrak{G}}$ in $\mathfrak{G}$, $R \in \mathfrak{G}$-Gr-R and $\mathfrak{p}$ in $\mathfrak{G}$, we define an additive functor $(-)^{\mathfrak{p}} : \mathfrak{G}$-GrR-Mod $\to \mathfrak{G}$-GrR-Mod as*

$$K^{\mathfrak{p}} = (K^R)_{\mathfrak{p}} = R_{\mathfrak{p}} \otimes_{R_{\mathfrak{e}_{\mathfrak{G}}}} K. \tag{16}$$

Equivalently, we write the composite additive functor $(-)^{\mathfrak{p}}$ as follows:

$$(-)^{\mathfrak{p}} = (((-)^R)^{\mathfrak{p}})_{\mathfrak{e}_{\mathfrak{G}}} : R_{\mathfrak{e}_{\mathfrak{G}}}\text{-}Mod \to R_{\mathfrak{e}_{\mathfrak{G}}}\text{-}Mod. \tag{17}$$

Moreover, we define $\varphi^{\mathfrak{p}} : R_{\mathfrak{p}} \otimes_{R_{\mathfrak{e}_{\mathfrak{G}}}} K \to R_{\mathfrak{p}} \otimes_{R_{\mathfrak{e}_{\mathfrak{G}}}} L$ as

$$\varphi^{\mathfrak{p}} = I_{\mathfrak{p}} \otimes_{R_{\mathfrak{e}_{\mathfrak{G}}}} \varphi, \tag{18}$$

for any $R_{\mathfrak{e}_{\mathfrak{G}}}$-modules K and L and any $R_{\mathfrak{e}_{\mathfrak{G}}}$-homomorphism $\varphi : K \to L$, where $I_{\mathfrak{p}}$ is the identity map of $R_{\mathfrak{p}}$ onto itself.

Theorem 5. *Let $\mathfrak{e}_{\mathfrak{G}}$ be a two-sided identity in $\mathfrak{G}$ and $R \in \mathfrak{G}$-Gr-R. Then, for any $\mathfrak{p}$, $\mathfrak{q}$ in $\mathfrak{G}$ and for any left $R_{\mathfrak{e}_{\mathfrak{G}}}$-module K, the map*

$$\beta_{R_{\mathfrak{q}},K^{\mathfrak{p}}} = R_{\mathfrak{q}} \otimes_{R_{\mathfrak{e}_{\mathfrak{G}}}} (R_{\mathfrak{p}} \otimes_{R_{\mathfrak{e}_{\mathfrak{G}}}} K) \to R_{\mathfrak{q}*\mathfrak{p}} \otimes_{R_{\mathfrak{e}_{\mathfrak{G}}}} K, \tag{19}$$

which sends $r_{\mathfrak{q}} \otimes (r_{\mathfrak{p}} \otimes k)$ into $(r_{\mathfrak{q}} r_{\mathfrak{p}}) \otimes k$ for any $k \in K, r_{\mathfrak{p}} \in R_{\mathfrak{p}}$, and $r_{\mathfrak{q}} \in R_{\mathfrak{q}}$, forms the following natural transformation:

$$((-)^{\mathfrak{p}})^{\mathfrak{q}} \text{ into } (-)^{\mathfrak{q}*\mathfrak{p}} : R_{\mathfrak{e}_{\mathfrak{G}}}\text{-}Mod \to R_{\mathfrak{e}_{\mathfrak{G}}}\text{-}Mod.$$

Proof. From Definition 8, we have the composite additive functor

$$(-)^{\mathfrak{p}} = (((-)^R)^{\mathfrak{p}})_{\mathfrak{e}_{\mathfrak{G}}} : R_{\mathfrak{e}_{\mathfrak{G}}}\text{-}Mod \to \mathfrak{G}\text{-}GrR\text{-}Mod \to \mathfrak{G}\text{-}GrR\text{-}Mod \to R_{\mathfrak{e}_{\mathfrak{G}}}\text{-}Mod.$$

From Theorem 1, we have

$$(-)^{\mathfrak{e}_{\mathfrak{G}}} = (((-)^R)^{\mathfrak{e}_{\mathfrak{G}}})_{\mathfrak{e}_{\mathfrak{G}}} = ((-)^R)_{\mathfrak{e}_{\mathfrak{G}}} \approx I_{R_{\mathfrak{e}_{\mathfrak{G}}}\text{-}Mod}.$$

Thus, in light of the relation (16) of Definition 8, we conclude that

$$\beta_{R_{\mathfrak{q}},K^{\mathfrak{p}}} = R_{\mathfrak{q}} \otimes_{R_{\mathfrak{e}_{\mathfrak{G}}}} K^{\mathfrak{p}} = R_{\mathfrak{q}} \otimes_{R_{\mathfrak{e}_{\mathfrak{G}}}} (R_{\mathfrak{p}} \otimes_{R_{\mathfrak{e}_{\mathfrak{G}}}} K) \to R_{\mathfrak{q}*\mathfrak{p}} \otimes_{R_{\mathfrak{e}_{\mathfrak{G}}}} K,$$

which sends $r_{\mathfrak{q}} \otimes (r_{\mathfrak{p}} \otimes k)$ into $(r_{\mathfrak{q}} r_{\mathfrak{p}}) \otimes k$ for any $k \in K, r_{\mathfrak{p}} \in R_{\mathfrak{p}}$, and $r_{\mathfrak{q}} \in R_{\mathfrak{q}}$ forms a natural transformation of $((-)^{\mathfrak{p}})^{\mathfrak{q}}$ into $(-)^{\mathfrak{q}*\mathfrak{p}} : R_{\mathfrak{e}_{\mathfrak{G}}}\text{-}Mod \to R_{\mathfrak{e}_{\mathfrak{G}}}\text{-}Mod$. □

Corollary 5. *Let $\mathfrak{e}_{\mathfrak{G}}$ be a two-sided identity in $\mathfrak{G}$ and $R \in \mathfrak{G}$-StGr-R. Then, the map $\beta_{R_{\mathfrak{q}},K^{\mathfrak{p}}}$ is an $R_{\mathfrak{e}_{\mathfrak{G}}}$-isomorphism of $(K^{\mathfrak{p}})^{\mathfrak{q}}$ onto $K^{\mathfrak{q}*\mathfrak{p}}$ for any $R_{\mathfrak{e}_{\mathfrak{G}}}$-module K.*

Proof. From Theorem 5, there is a natural transformation between $((-)^{\mathfrak{p}})^{\mathfrak{q}}$ and $(-)^{\mathfrak{q}*\mathfrak{p}}$: $\mathfrak{G}$-*GrR-Mod* $\to$ $\mathfrak{G}$-*GrR-Mod*, for any $\mathfrak{p}, \mathfrak{q} \in \mathfrak{G}$. Thus, Theorem 3 and relation (17) of Definition 8 yield that $\beta_{R_{\mathfrak{q}},K^{\mathfrak{p}}}$ is a natural isomorphism of $((-)^{\mathfrak{p}})^{\mathfrak{q}}$ onto $(-)^{\mathfrak{q}*\mathfrak{p}}$: $R_{\mathfrak{e}_{\mathfrak{G}}}$-*Mod* $\to R_{\mathfrak{e}_{\mathfrak{G}}}$-*Mod*. □

Example 1. *Consider the Morita ring*

$$T = \left\{ \begin{pmatrix} r & v \\ w & s \end{pmatrix} : r \in R, v \in V, w \in W \text{ and } s \in S \right\},$$

with a Morita contex $(R, S, {}_R V_S, {}_S W_R, \varphi, \psi)$ such that the bimodule homomorphisms

$$\varphi : V \otimes_S W \to R \quad \text{and} \quad \psi : W \otimes_R V \to S$$

satisfy $(vw)v' = v(wv')$ as $\varphi(v,w) = vw$ and $\psi(w,v) = wv$, i.e., $\varphi(v \otimes w)v' = v\psi(w \otimes v')$ and $\psi(w \otimes v)w' = w\varphi(v \otimes w')$ for all $v, v' \in V$ and $w, w' \in W$. It is well known that T with the usual matrix addition and multiplication forms a ring. Here, let $\mathfrak{X}$ be the permutation group S_3 and $\mathfrak{H}$ be the non-normal subgroup $\{\mathfrak{e}, (23)\}$. We choose $\mathfrak{G} = \{(\mathfrak{e}, (132), (13)\}$ to be the set of left coset representatives. Then, the operation $*$ is as given in the following table (Table 1).

Table 1. The binary operation $*$.

$*$	$\mathfrak{e}$	(132)	(13)
$\mathfrak{e}$	$\mathfrak{e}$	(132)	(13)
(132)	(132)	(13)	$\mathfrak{e}$
(13)	(13)	$\mathfrak{e}$	(132)

Thus, $T = T_{\mathfrak{e}} \oplus T_{(132)} \oplus T_{(13)}$, where

$$T_{\mathfrak{e}} = \begin{pmatrix} R & 0 \\ 0 & S \end{pmatrix} = \left\{ \begin{pmatrix} r & 0 \\ 0 & s \end{pmatrix} : r \in R \text{ and } s \in S \right\},$$

$$T_{(132)} = \begin{pmatrix} 0 & V \\ 0 & 0 \end{pmatrix} = \left\{ \begin{pmatrix} 0 & v \\ 0 & 0 \end{pmatrix} : v \in V \right\} \text{ and}$$

$$T_{(13)} = \begin{pmatrix} 0 & 0 \\ W & 0 \end{pmatrix} = \left\{ \begin{pmatrix} 0 & 0 \\ w & 0 \end{pmatrix} : w \in W \right\}.$$

Next, we check the property $R_{\mathfrak{p}} R_{\mathfrak{q}} \subseteq R_{\mathfrak{p}*\mathfrak{q}}$ for all $\mathfrak{p}, \mathfrak{q} \in \mathfrak{G}$ as follows:

1. $T_{\mathfrak{e}} T_{\mathfrak{e}} \subseteq T_{\mathfrak{e}*\mathfrak{e}}$, *as, for all* $\begin{pmatrix} r_1 & 0 \\ 0 & s_1 \end{pmatrix}, \begin{pmatrix} r_2 & 0 \\ 0 & s_2 \end{pmatrix} \in T_e$, *we have*
$\begin{pmatrix} r_1 & 0 \\ 0 & s_1 \end{pmatrix} \begin{pmatrix} r_2 & 0 \\ 0 & s_2 \end{pmatrix} = \begin{pmatrix} r_1 r_2 & 0 \\ 0 & s_1 s_2 \end{pmatrix} \in T_e = T_{e*e}$.
2. $T_{\mathfrak{e}} T_{(132)} \subseteq T_{\mathfrak{e}*(132)}$, *as, for all* $\begin{pmatrix} r & 0 \\ 0 & s \end{pmatrix} \in T_{\mathfrak{e}}, \begin{pmatrix} 0 & v \\ 0 & 0 \end{pmatrix} \in T_{(132)}$, *we have*
$\begin{pmatrix} r & 0 \\ 0 & s \end{pmatrix} \begin{pmatrix} 0 & v \\ 0 & 0 \end{pmatrix} = \begin{pmatrix} 0 & rv \\ 0 & 0 \end{pmatrix} \in T_{(132)} = T_{e*(132)}$, *since $rv \in V$ as V is a left R-module.*

3. $T_{\mathfrak{e}}T_{(13)} \subseteq T_{\mathfrak{e}*(13)}$, as, for all $\begin{pmatrix} r & 0 \\ 0 & s \end{pmatrix} \in T_{\mathfrak{e}}$, $\begin{pmatrix} 0 & 0 \\ w & 0 \end{pmatrix} \in T_{(13)}$, we have $\begin{pmatrix} r & 0 \\ 0 & s \end{pmatrix}\begin{pmatrix} 0 & 0 \\ w & 0 \end{pmatrix} = \begin{pmatrix} 0 & 0 \\ sw & 0 \end{pmatrix} \in T_{(13)} = T_{2*(13)}$, since $sw \in W$ as W is a left S-module.
4. $T_{(132)}T_{\mathfrak{e}} \subseteq T_{(132)*\mathfrak{e}}$, as, for all $\begin{pmatrix} 0 & v \\ 0 & 0 \end{pmatrix} \in T_{(132)}$, $\begin{pmatrix} r & 0 \\ 0 & s \end{pmatrix} \in T_{\mathfrak{e}}$, we have $\begin{pmatrix} 0 & v \\ 0 & 0 \end{pmatrix}\begin{pmatrix} r & 0 \\ 0 & s \end{pmatrix} = \begin{pmatrix} 0 & vs \\ 0 & 0 \end{pmatrix} \in T_{(132)} = T_{(132)*\mathfrak{e}}$.
5. $T_{(132)}T_{(132)} \subseteq T_{(132)*(132)}$, as, for all $\begin{pmatrix} 0 & v_1 \\ 0 & 0 \end{pmatrix}, \begin{pmatrix} 0 & v_2 \\ 0 & 0 \end{pmatrix} \in T_{(132)}$, we have $\begin{pmatrix} 0 & v_1 \\ 0 & 0 \end{pmatrix}\begin{pmatrix} 0 & v_2 \\ 0 & 0 \end{pmatrix} = \begin{pmatrix} 0 & 0 \\ 0 & 0 \end{pmatrix} \in T_{(13)} = T_{(132)*(132)}$.
6. $T_{(132)}T_{(13)} \subseteq T_{(132)*(13)}$, as, for all $\begin{pmatrix} 0 & v \\ 0 & 0 \end{pmatrix} in T_{(132)}$, $\begin{pmatrix} 0 & 0 \\ w & 0 \end{pmatrix} \in T_{(13)}$, we have $\begin{pmatrix} 0 & v \\ 0 & 0 \end{pmatrix}\begin{pmatrix} 0 & 0 \\ w & 0 \end{pmatrix} = \begin{pmatrix} vw & 0 \\ 0 & 0 \end{pmatrix} \in T_{\mathfrak{e}} = T_{(132)*(13)}$.
7. $T_{(13)}T_{\mathfrak{e}} \subseteq T_{(13)*\mathfrak{e}}$, as, for all $\begin{pmatrix} 0 & 0 \\ w & 0 \end{pmatrix} \in T_{(13)}$, $\begin{pmatrix} r & 0 \\ 0 & s \end{pmatrix} \in T_{\mathfrak{e}}$, we have $\begin{pmatrix} 0 & 0 \\ w & 0 \end{pmatrix}\begin{pmatrix} r & 0 \\ 0 & s \end{pmatrix} = \begin{pmatrix} 0 & 0 \\ wr & 0 \end{pmatrix} \in T_{(13)} = T_{(13)*\mathfrak{e}}$.
8. $T_{(13)}T_{(132)} \subseteq T_{(13)*(132)}$, as, for all $\begin{pmatrix} 0 & 0 \\ w & 0 \end{pmatrix} \in T_{(13)}$, $\begin{pmatrix} 0 & v \\ 0 & 0 \end{pmatrix} \in T_{(132)}$, we have $\begin{pmatrix} 0 & 0 \\ w & 0 \end{pmatrix}\begin{pmatrix} 0 & v \\ 0 & 0 \end{pmatrix} = \begin{pmatrix} 0 & 0 \\ 0 & wv \end{pmatrix} \in T_{\mathfrak{e}} = T_{(13)*(132)}$.
9. $T_{(13)}T_{(13)} \subseteq T_{(13)*(13)}$, as, for all $\begin{pmatrix} 0 & 0 \\ w_1 & 0 \end{pmatrix}, \begin{pmatrix} 0 & 0 \\ w_2 & 0 \end{pmatrix} \in T_{(13)}$, we have $\begin{pmatrix} 0 & 0 \\ w_1 & 0 \end{pmatrix}\begin{pmatrix} 0 & 0 \\ w_2 & 0 \end{pmatrix} = \begin{pmatrix} 0 & 0 \\ 0 & 0 \end{pmatrix} \in T_{(132)} = T_{(13)*(13)}$.

Therefore, T is a $\mathfrak{G}$-weak graded ring. However, T is not strongly graded. For example, $T_{(13)}T_{(13)} \neq T_{(13)*(13)}$ as $T_{(132)} = T_{(13)*(13)} \nsubseteq T_{(13)}T_{(13)}$.

Example 2. *Let $R = M_2(\mathbb{R}) = \left\{\begin{pmatrix} a & b \\ c & d \end{pmatrix} : a,b,c,d \in \mathbb{R}\right\}$ and let $\mathfrak{X} = \mathbb{Z}_2 \times \mathbb{Z}_3 = \{(0,0),$
$(0,1),(0,2),(1,0),(1,1),(1,2)\}$ under addition with a subgroup $\mathfrak{H} = \{(0,0),(1,0)\}$. Choose $\mathfrak{G} = \{(1,0),(0,1),(1,2)\}$. Then, the $*$ operation is as given in the following table (Table 2).*

Table 2. The binary operation $*$.

$*$	(1,0)	(0,1)	(1,2)
(1,0)	(1,0)	(0,1)	(1,2)
(0,1)	(0,1)	(1,2)	(1,0)
(1,2)	(1,2)	(1,0)	(0,1)

Hence, we have $R = R_{(1,0)} \oplus R_{(0,1)} \oplus R_{(1,2)}$, where $R_{(1,0)} = \left\{\begin{pmatrix} a & 0 \\ 0 & d \end{pmatrix} : a,d \in \mathbb{R}\right\}$, $R_{(0,1)} = \left\{\begin{pmatrix} 0 & b \\ 0 & 0 \end{pmatrix} : b \in \mathbb{R}\right\}$, and $R_{(1,2)} = \left\{\begin{pmatrix} 0 & 0 \\ c & 0 \end{pmatrix} : c \in \mathbb{R}\right\}$. Here, we check the property $R_{\mathfrak{p}}R_{\mathfrak{q}} \subseteq R_{\mathfrak{p}*\mathfrak{q}}$ for all $\mathfrak{p},\mathfrak{q} \in \mathfrak{G}$ as follows:

1. $R_{(1,0)}R_{(1,0)} \subseteq R_{(1,0)*(1,0)} = R_{(1,0)}$, *as, for all* $\begin{pmatrix} a_1 & 0 \\ 0 & d_1 \end{pmatrix}$ *and* $\begin{pmatrix} a_2 & 0 \\ 0 & d_2 \end{pmatrix} \in R_{(1,0)}$, *we have*
$$\begin{pmatrix} a_1 & 0 \\ 0 & d_1 \end{pmatrix}\begin{pmatrix} a_2 & 0 \\ 0 & d_2 \end{pmatrix} = \begin{pmatrix} a_1a_2 & 0 \\ 0 & d_1d_2 \end{pmatrix} \in R_{(1,0)} = R_{(1,0)*(1,0)}.$$
2. $R_{(1,0)}R_{(0,1)} \subseteq R_{(1,0)*(0,1)} = R_{(0,1)}$, *as, for all* $\begin{pmatrix} a & 0 \\ 0 & d \end{pmatrix} \in R_{(1,0)}$ *and* $\begin{pmatrix} 0 & b \\ 0 & 0 \end{pmatrix} \in R_{(0,1)}$, *we have*
$$\begin{pmatrix} a & 0 \\ 0 & d \end{pmatrix}\begin{pmatrix} 0 & b \\ 0 & 0 \end{pmatrix} = \begin{pmatrix} 0 & ab \\ 0 & 0 \end{pmatrix} \in R_{(0,1)} = R_{(1,0)*(0,1)}.$$
3. $R_{(1,0)}R_{(1,2)} \subseteq R_{(1,0)*(1,2)} = R_{(1,2)}$, *as, for all* $\begin{pmatrix} a & 0 \\ 0 & d \end{pmatrix} \in R_{(1,0)}$ *and* $\begin{pmatrix} 0 & 0 \\ c & 0 \end{pmatrix} \in R_{(1,2)}$, *we have*
$$\begin{pmatrix} a & 0 \\ 0 & d \end{pmatrix}\begin{pmatrix} 0 & 0 \\ c & 0 \end{pmatrix} = \begin{pmatrix} 0 & 0 \\ dc & 0 \end{pmatrix} \in R_{(1,2)} = R_{(1,0)*(1,2)}.$$
4. $R_{(0,1)}R_{(1,0)} \subseteq R_{(0,1)*(1,0)} = R_{(0,1)}$, *as, for all* $\begin{pmatrix} 0 & b \\ 0 & 0 \end{pmatrix} \in R_{(0,1)}$ *and* $\begin{pmatrix} a & 0 \\ 0 & d \end{pmatrix} \in R_{(1,0)}$, *we have*
$$\begin{pmatrix} 0 & b \\ 0 & 0 \end{pmatrix}\begin{pmatrix} a & 0 \\ 0 & d \end{pmatrix} = \begin{pmatrix} 0 & ab \\ 0 & 0 \end{pmatrix} \in R_{(0,1)} = R_{(0,1)*(1,0)}.$$
5. $R_{(0,1)}R_{(0,1)} \subseteq R_{(0,1)*(0,1)} = R_{(1,2)}$, *as, for all* $\begin{pmatrix} 0 & b_1 \\ 0 & 0 \end{pmatrix}$ *and* $\begin{pmatrix} 0 & b_2 \\ 0 & 0 \end{pmatrix} \in R_{(0,1)}$, *we have*
$$\begin{pmatrix} 0 & b_1 \\ 0 & 0 \end{pmatrix}\begin{pmatrix} 0 & b_2 \\ 0 & 0 \end{pmatrix} = \begin{pmatrix} 0 & 0 \\ 0 & 0 \end{pmatrix} \in R_{(1,2)} = R_{(0,1)*(0,1)}.$$
6. $R_{(0,1)}R_{(1,2)} \subseteq R_{(0,1)*(1,2)} = R_{(1,0)}$, *as, for all* $\begin{pmatrix} 0 & b \\ 0 & 0 \end{pmatrix} \in R_{(0,1)}$ *and* $\begin{pmatrix} 0 & 0 \\ c & 0 \end{pmatrix} \in R_{(1,2)}$, *we have*
$$\begin{pmatrix} 0 & b \\ 0 & 0 \end{pmatrix}\begin{pmatrix} 0 & 0 \\ c & 0 \end{pmatrix} = \begin{pmatrix} bc & 0 \\ 0 & 0 \end{pmatrix} \in R_{(1,0)} = R_{(0,1)*(1,2)}.$$
7. $R_{(1,2)}R_{(1,0)} \subseteq R_{(1,2)*(1,0)} = R_{(1,2)}$, *as, for all* $\begin{pmatrix} 0 & 0 \\ c & 0 \end{pmatrix} \in R_{(1,2)}$ *and* $\begin{pmatrix} a & 0 \\ 0 & d \end{pmatrix} \in R_{(1,0)}$, *we have*
$$\begin{pmatrix} 0 & 0 \\ c & 0 \end{pmatrix}\begin{pmatrix} a & 0 \\ 0 & d \end{pmatrix} = \begin{pmatrix} 0 & 0 \\ ac & 0 \end{pmatrix} \in R_{(1,2)} = R_{(1,2)*(1,0)}.$$
8. $R_{(1,2)}R_{(0,1)} \subseteq R_{(1,2)*(0,1)} = R_{(1,0)}$, *as, for all* $\begin{pmatrix} 0 & 0 \\ c & 0 \end{pmatrix} \in R_{(1,2)}$ *and* $\begin{pmatrix} 0 & b \\ 0 & 0 \end{pmatrix} \in R_{(1,0)}$, *we have*
$$\begin{pmatrix} 0 & 0 \\ c & 0 \end{pmatrix}\begin{pmatrix} 0 & b \\ 0 & 0 \end{pmatrix} = \begin{pmatrix} 0 & 0 \\ 0 & bc \end{pmatrix} \in R_{(1,0)} = R_{(1,2)*(0,1)}.$$
9. $R_{(1,2)}R_{(1,2)} \subseteq R_{(1,2)*(1,2)} = R_{(0,1)}$, *as, for all* $\begin{pmatrix} 0 & 0 \\ c_1 & 0 \end{pmatrix}$ *and* $\begin{pmatrix} 0 & 0 \\ c_2 & 0 \end{pmatrix} \in R_{(1,2)}$, *we have*
$$\begin{pmatrix} 0 & 0 \\ c_1 & 0 \end{pmatrix}\begin{pmatrix} 0 & 0 \\ c_2 & 0 \end{pmatrix} = \begin{pmatrix} 0 & 0 \\ 0 & 0 \end{pmatrix} \in R_{(0,1)} = R_{(1,2)*(1,2)}.$$

Thus, R is a $\mathfrak{G}$*-weak graded ring. However, it is not strongly graded—for instance,* $R_{(1,2)*(1,2)} \neq R_{(1,2)}R_{(1,2)}$ *as* $R_{(0,1)} = R_{(1,2)*(1,2)} \nsubseteq R_{(1,2)}R_{(1,2)}$.

Next, if we define $V = M_{2\times 3}(\mathbb{R})$, then V is a $\mathfrak{G}$-graded R-module with $V = V_{(1,0)} \oplus V_{(0,1)} \oplus V_{(1,2)}$, where $V_{(0,1)} = \begin{pmatrix} \mathbb{R} & 0 & 0 \\ 0 & \mathbb{R} & 0 \end{pmatrix}$, $V_{(1,0)} = \begin{pmatrix} 0 & 0 & \mathbb{R} \\ \mathbb{R} & 0 & 0 \end{pmatrix}$ *and* $V_{(1,2)} = \begin{pmatrix} 0 & \mathbb{R} & 0 \\ 0 & 0 & \mathbb{R} \end{pmatrix}$.

Here, we show that the inclusion property $R_{\mathfrak{p}} V_{\mathfrak{q}} \subseteq V_{\mathfrak{p}*\mathfrak{q}}$ is satisfied for all $\mathfrak{p}, \mathfrak{q} \in \mathfrak{G}$ as follows:

1. $R_{(1,0)} V_{(0,1)} \subseteq V_{(0,1)*(0,1)}$, *as, for all* $\begin{pmatrix} a & 0 \\ 0 & d \end{pmatrix} \in R_{(1,0)}$ *and* $\begin{pmatrix} r_1 & 0 & 0 \\ 0 & r_5 & 0 \end{pmatrix} \in V_{(0,1)}$, *we have* $\begin{pmatrix} a & 0 \\ 0 & d \end{pmatrix}\begin{pmatrix} r_1 & 0 & 0 \\ 0 & r_5 & 0 \end{pmatrix} = \begin{pmatrix} ar_1 & 0 & 0 \\ 0 & dr_5 & 0 \end{pmatrix} \in V_{(0,1)} = V_{(1,0)*(0,1)}$.
2. $R_{(1,0)} V_{(1,0)} \subseteq V_{(1,0)*(1,0)}$, *as, for all* $\begin{pmatrix} a & 0 \\ 0 & d \end{pmatrix} \in R_{(1,0)}$ *and* $\begin{pmatrix} 0 & 0 & r_3 \\ r_4 & 0 & 0 \end{pmatrix} \in V_{(1,0)}$, *we have* $\begin{pmatrix} a & 0 \\ 0 & d \end{pmatrix}\begin{pmatrix} 0 & 0 & r_3 \\ r_4 & 0 & 0 \end{pmatrix} = \begin{pmatrix} 0 & 0 & ar_3 \\ r_4 & 0 & 0 \end{pmatrix} \in V_{(1,0)} = V_{(1,0)*(1,0)}$.
3. $R_{(1,0)} V_{(1,2)} \subseteq V_{(1,0)*(1,2)}$, *as, for all* $\begin{pmatrix} a & 0 \\ 0 & d \end{pmatrix} \in R_{(1,0)}$ *and* $\begin{pmatrix} 0 & r_2 & 0 \\ 0 & 0 & r_6 \end{pmatrix} \in V_{(1,2)}$, *we have* $\begin{pmatrix} a & 0 \\ 0 & d \end{pmatrix}\begin{pmatrix} 0 & r_2 & 0 \\ 0 & 0 & r_6 \end{pmatrix} = \begin{pmatrix} 0 & ar_2 & 0 \\ 0 & 0 & dr_6 \end{pmatrix} \in V_{(1,2)} = V_{(1,0)*(1,2)}$.
4. $R_{(0,1)} V_{(0,1)} \subseteq V_{(0,1)*(0,1)}$, *as, for all* $\begin{pmatrix} 0 & b \\ 0 & 0 \end{pmatrix} \in R_{(0,1)}$ *and* $\begin{pmatrix} r_1 & 0 & 0 \\ 0 & r_5 & 0 \end{pmatrix} \in V_{(0,1)}$, *we have* $\begin{pmatrix} 0 & b \\ 0 & 0 \end{pmatrix}\begin{pmatrix} r_1 & 0 & 0 \\ 0 & r_5 & 0 \end{pmatrix} = \begin{pmatrix} 0 & br_5 & 0 \\ 0 & 0 & 0 \end{pmatrix} \in V_{(1,2)} = V_{(0,1)*(0,1)}$.
5. $R_{(0,1)} V_{(1,0)} \subseteq V_{(0,1)*(1,0)}$, *as, for all* $\begin{pmatrix} 0 & b \\ 0 & 0 \end{pmatrix} \in R_{(0,1)}$ *and* $\begin{pmatrix} 0 & 0 & r_3 \\ r_4 & 0 & 0 \end{pmatrix} \in V_{(1,0)}$, *we have* $\begin{pmatrix} 0 & b \\ 0 & 0 \end{pmatrix}\begin{pmatrix} 0 & 0 & r_3 \\ r_4 & 0 & 0 \end{pmatrix} = \begin{pmatrix} br_4 & 0 & 0 \\ 0 & 0 & 0 \end{pmatrix} \in V_{(0,1)} = V_{(0,1)*(1,0)}$.
6. $R_{(0,1)} V_{(1,2)} \subseteq V_{(0,1)*(1,2)}$, *as, for all* $\begin{pmatrix} 0 & b \\ 0 & 0 \end{pmatrix} \in R_{(0,1)}$ *and* $\begin{pmatrix} 0 & r_2 & 0 \\ 0 & 0 & r_6 \end{pmatrix} \in V_{(1,0)}$, *we have* $\begin{pmatrix} 0 & b \\ 0 & 0 \end{pmatrix}\begin{pmatrix} 0 & r_2 & 0 \\ 0 & 0 & r_6 \end{pmatrix} = \begin{pmatrix} 0 & 0 & br_6 \\ 0 & 0 & 0 \end{pmatrix} \in V_{(1,0)} = V_{(0,1)*(1,2)}$.
7. $R_{(1,2)} V_{(0,1)} \subseteq V_{(1,2)*(0,1)}$, *as, for all* $\begin{pmatrix} 0 & 0 \\ c & 0 \end{pmatrix} \in R_{(1,2)}$ *and* $\begin{pmatrix} r_1 & 0 & 0 \\ 0 & r_5 & 0 \end{pmatrix} \in V_{(0,1)}$, *we have* $\begin{pmatrix} 0 & 0 \\ c & 0 \end{pmatrix}\begin{pmatrix} r_1 & 0 & 0 \\ 0 & r_5 & 0 \end{pmatrix} = \begin{pmatrix} 0 & 0 & 0 \\ cr_1 & 0 & 0 \end{pmatrix} \in V_{(1,0)} = V_{(1,2)*(0,1)}$.
8. $R_{(1,2)} V_{(1,0)} \subseteq V_{(1,2)*(1,0)}$, *as, for all* $\begin{pmatrix} 0 & 0 \\ c & 0 \end{pmatrix} \in R_{(1,2)}$ *and* $\begin{pmatrix} 0 & 0 & r_3 \\ r_4 & 0 & 0 \end{pmatrix} \in V_{(1,0)}$, *we have* $\begin{pmatrix} 0 & 0 \\ c & 0 \end{pmatrix}\begin{pmatrix} 0 & 0 & r_3 \\ r_4 & 0 & 0 \end{pmatrix} = \begin{pmatrix} 0 & 0 & 0 \\ 0 & 0 & cr_3 \end{pmatrix} \in V_{(1,2)} = V_{(1,2)*(1,0)}$.
9. $R_{(1,2)} V_{(1,2)} \subseteq V_{(1,2)*(1,2)}$, *as, for all* $\begin{pmatrix} 0 & 0 \\ c & 0 \end{pmatrix} \in R_{(1,2)}$ *and* $\begin{pmatrix} 0 & r_2 & 0 \\ 0 & 0 & r_6 \end{pmatrix} \in V_{(1,2)}$, *we have* $\begin{pmatrix} 0 & 0 \\ c & 0 \end{pmatrix}\begin{pmatrix} 0 & r_2 & 0 \\ 0 & 0 & r_6 \end{pmatrix} = \begin{pmatrix} 0 & 0 & 0 \\ 0 & cr_2 & 0 \end{pmatrix} \in V_{(0,1)} = V_{(1,2)*(1,2)}$. *Therefore, V is a $\mathfrak{G}$-weak graded R-module. It can be noted that V is not strongly graded as $R_{(0,1)} V_{(0,1)} \subseteq V_{(1,2)}$ but $V_{(1,2)} = V_{(0,1)*(0,1)} \nsubseteq R_{(0,1)} V_{(0,1)}$.*

4. $\mathfrak{G}$-Weak Homomorphism Groups

In ref. [11], it was proven that $\mathfrak{G}$-$GrHom_R(V, W)$ is an additive subgroup of $Hom_R(V, W)$ and that $\mathfrak{G}$-$GrHom_R(V, W) = \bigoplus_{\mathfrak{p}\in\mathfrak{G}} \mathfrak{G}$-$GrHom_R(V, W)_{\mathfrak{p}}$ as an additive subgroup. We can now prove the following.

Proposition 2. *Let $\mathfrak{e}_{\mathfrak{G}}$ be a two-sided identity in $\mathfrak{G}$ and $V, W \in \mathfrak{G}$-GrR-Mod. Then, for any $\mathfrak{p}$, $\mathfrak{q}$ in $\mathfrak{G}$, $\mathfrak{G}$-$GrHom_R(V, W)_{\mathfrak{q}}$ is the additive subgroup $\mathfrak{G}$-$GrHom_R(V^{\mathfrak{p}}, W^{\mathfrak{p}*\mathfrak{q}})$ of $Hom_R(V, W)$.*

Proof. Since $\mathfrak{G}$-$GrHom_R(V, W)_{\mathfrak{q}}$ is an additive subgroup of $\mathfrak{G}$-$GrHom_R(V, W)$ of $Hom_R(V, W)$, then Definition 7 yields the required result for the conjugation action. □

Proposition 3. *For the $\mathfrak{G}$-weak graded R-modules L, V, and W in $\mathfrak{G}$-GrR-Mod, we have*

$$\mathfrak{G}\text{-}GrHom_R(V,W)_{\mathfrak{p}}\mathfrak{G}\text{-}GrHom_R(L,V)_{\mathfrak{q}} \subseteq \mathfrak{G}\text{-}GrHom_R(L,W)_{\mathfrak{p}*\mathfrak{q}}, \forall \mathfrak{p}, \mathfrak{q} \in \mathfrak{G}. \tag{20}$$

Proof. Let φ in $\mathfrak{G}$-$GrHom_R(V,W)_{\mathfrak{p}}$ and ψ in $\mathfrak{G}$-$GrHom_R(L,V)_{\mathfrak{q}}$; then, for all $\mathfrak{p}, \mathfrak{q} \in \mathfrak{G}$, we have

$$\varphi(V_{\mathfrak{p}}) \subseteq W_{\mathfrak{p}*\mathfrak{q}},$$

and

$$\psi(L_{\mathfrak{q}}) \subseteq V_{\mathfrak{q}*\mathfrak{p}}.$$

From [8], Proposition 2.4, we have

$$\varphi(\psi(L_{\mathfrak{q}})) \subseteq \varphi(V_{\mathfrak{q}*\mathfrak{p}}) \subseteq W_{(\mathfrak{q}*\mathfrak{p})*\mathfrak{q}} = W_{\left(\mathfrak{q}\triangleleft g(\mathfrak{p},\mathfrak{q})\right)*(\mathfrak{p}*\mathfrak{q})}.$$

As $\mathfrak{q} \triangleleft g(\mathfrak{p},\mathfrak{q})$ is also in $\mathfrak{G}$, we have

$$(\psi \circ \varphi) \in \mathfrak{G}\text{-}GrHom_R(L,W)_{\mathfrak{p}*\mathfrak{q}}.$$

□

Lemma 1. *Let V and W be $\mathfrak{G}$-weak graded R-modules. Then, for any φ in $\mathfrak{G}$-$GrHom_R(V,W)$ and for all $\mathfrak{p}$ in $\mathfrak{G}$, we have*

$$\varphi(V_{\mathfrak{p}}) \subseteq \sum_{\mathfrak{q}\in\mathfrak{G}} W_{\mathfrak{p}*\mathfrak{q}}. \tag{21}$$

Proof. The proof follows directly via Definition 5 and [11], Theorem 1. □

Theorem 6. *For any $\mathfrak{G}$-weak graded R-modules V and W in $\mathfrak{G}$-GrR-Mod, the equality*

$$\mathfrak{G}\text{-}GrHom_R(V,W) = Hom_R(V,W)$$

is satisfied.

Proof. Since $\mathfrak{G}$-$GrHom_R(V,W)$ is an additive subgroup of $Hom_R(V,W)$, we have

$$\mathfrak{G}\text{-}GrHom_R(V,W) \subseteq Hom_R(V,W).$$

Here, let φ in $Hom_R(V,W)$, $\mathfrak{p} \in \mathfrak{G}$ and $v \in V$. Since $\mathfrak{G}$ is a finite set, we can write $v_{\mathfrak{p}}$ as the finite sum of its homogeneous components as follows: $v = \sum_{\mathfrak{p}\in\mathfrak{G}} v_{\mathfrak{p}}$, for all $\mathfrak{p} \in \mathfrak{G}$ and $v_{\mathfrak{p}} \in V_{\mathfrak{p}}$. Since $\mathfrak{G}$ is closed under the $*$ operation and W is a $\mathfrak{G}$-weak graded R-module, the direct sum $W = \bigoplus_{\mathfrak{p}\in\mathfrak{G}} W_{\mathfrak{p}}$ is equivalent to

$$W = \bigoplus_{\mathfrak{q}\in\mathfrak{G}} W_{\mathfrak{p}*\mathfrak{q}},$$

for any $\mathfrak{p} \in \mathfrak{G}$. Thus, there exists $\varphi_{\mathfrak{p}*\mathfrak{q}} \in Hom_{R_e}(V_{\mathfrak{p}}, W_{\mathfrak{p}*\mathfrak{q}})$ for $\mathfrak{p}, \mathfrak{q} \in \mathfrak{G}$, such that

$$\varphi(v_{\mathfrak{p}}) = \sum_{\mathfrak{q}\in\mathfrak{G}} \varphi_{\mathfrak{p}*\mathfrak{q}}(v_{\mathfrak{p}}) \text{ for all } \mathfrak{p} \in \mathfrak{G} \text{ and } v_{\mathfrak{p}} \in V_{\mathfrak{p}},$$

where $\varphi_{\mathfrak{p}*\mathfrak{q}}(v_{\mathfrak{p}})$ is the homogeneous component of $\varphi(v_{\mathfrak{p}})$ that lies in $W_{\mathfrak{p}*\mathfrak{q}}$. Here, for any $\mathfrak{q} \in \mathfrak{G}$, we define a map $\varphi_{\mathfrak{q}} \in \mathfrak{G}$-$GrHom_R(V,W)$ as

$$\varphi_{\mathfrak{q}}(\sum_{\mathfrak{p}\in\mathfrak{G}} v_{\mathfrak{p}}) = \sum_{\mathfrak{p}\in\mathfrak{G}} \varphi_{\mathfrak{p}*\mathfrak{q}}(v_{\mathfrak{p}}) = \varphi_{\mathfrak{p}*\mathfrak{q}}(\sum_{\mathfrak{p}\in\mathfrak{G}} v_{p}). \tag{22}$$

Since $\mathfrak{G}$ is a finite set, this sum is finite and well defined. Moreover, for all $\mathfrak{p} \in \mathfrak{G}$ and all $v_{\mathfrak{p}} \in V_{\mathfrak{p}}$, we know that $\varphi(v_{\mathfrak{p}}) \in W$ because φ is an R-homomorphism. Hence,

$\varphi_{\mathfrak{q}}(V_{\mathfrak{p}}) = \sum_{\mathfrak{q}\in\mathfrak{G}} \varphi_{\mathfrak{p}*\mathfrak{q}}(V_{\mathfrak{p}}) = \varphi_{\mathfrak{p}*\mathfrak{q}}(\sum_{\mathfrak{q}\in\mathfrak{G}} V_{\mathfrak{p}}) \subseteq W_{\mathfrak{p}*\mathfrak{q}}$. Thus, from Definition 5, each $\varphi_{\mathfrak{q}} \in \mathfrak{G}\text{-}GrHom_R(V,W)_{\mathfrak{q}}$. From (22), we have

$$\varphi(v_{\mathfrak{p}}) = \sum_{\mathfrak{q}\in\mathfrak{G}} \varphi_{\mathfrak{p}*\mathfrak{q}}(v_{\mathfrak{p}}) = \sum_{\mathfrak{q}\in\mathfrak{G}} \varphi_{\mathfrak{q}}(v_{\mathfrak{p}}),$$

which implies that $\varphi = \sum_{\mathfrak{q}\in\mathfrak{G}} \varphi_{\mathfrak{q}}$. This sum is finite and well defined since $\mathfrak{G}$ is a finite set. Therefore, $\varphi \in \mathfrak{G}\text{-}GrHom_R(V,W)$. □

Proposition 4. *If $\mathfrak{e}_{\mathfrak{G}}$ is a two-sided identity in $\mathfrak{G}$, R is a strongly $\mathfrak{G}$-graded ring, and K and L are $R_{\mathfrak{e}_{\mathfrak{G}}}$-modules. Then, the restriction to $K^{\mathfrak{p}} = (K^R)_{\mathfrak{p}}$ induces*

$$Hom_R(K^R, L^R)_{\mathfrak{q}} \cong Hom_{R_{\mathfrak{e}_{\mathfrak{G}}}}(K^{\mathfrak{p}}, L^{\mathfrak{p}*\mathfrak{q}}) \quad \textit{for all } \mathfrak{p},\mathfrak{q} \textit{ in } \mathfrak{G}.$$

Proof. From Definition 8, the functor $(-)_{\mathfrak{e}_{\mathfrak{G}}}$ sends $((K)^R)^{\mathfrak{p}}$ into $K^{\mathfrak{p}}$, for any $R_{\mathfrak{e}_{\mathfrak{G}}}$-module K. We know from Proposition 2 that $Hom_R(V,W)_{\mathfrak{q}}$ is the additive subgroup $\mathfrak{G}\text{-}GrR\text{-}Hom_R(V^{\mathfrak{p}}, W^{\mathfrak{p}*\mathfrak{q}})$ of $Hom_R(V,W)$, for any $\mathfrak{p},\mathfrak{q}$ in $\mathfrak{G}$. Moreover, we know from Corollary 1 that the functors $(-)_{\mathfrak{e}_{\mathfrak{G}}}$ and $(-)^R$ form $\mathfrak{G}\text{-}GrR\text{-}Mod \approx R_{\mathfrak{e}_{\mathfrak{G}}}\text{-}Mod$. Thus, we conclude that the restriction to $K^{\mathfrak{p}} = (K^R)_{\mathfrak{p}}$ is an isomorphism of the additive group $Hom_R(K^R, L^R)_{\mathfrak{q}}$ onto $Hom_{R_{\mathfrak{e}_{\mathfrak{G}}}}(K^{\mathfrak{p}}, L^{\mathfrak{p}*\mathfrak{q}})$ for all $\mathfrak{p},\mathfrak{q}$ in $\mathfrak{G}$. □

Example 3. *Let $\mathfrak{X} = D_6 = \{1, a, a^2, a^3, a^4, a^5, b, ab, a^2b, a^3b, a^4b, a^5b\}$ and*

$$\mathfrak{H} = \{1, a^2, a^4, b, a^2b, a^4b\}$$

be a subgroup of $\mathfrak{X}$. Choose the set of left coset representatives to be $\mathfrak{G} = \{1, a\}$. Then, the $*$ is as given in the following table (Table 3).

Table 3. The binary operation $*$.

$*$	1	a
1	1	a
a	a	1

Consider the ring of polynomials with integer coefficients $R = \mathbb{Z}[x]$ to be graded by $\mathfrak{G} = \{1, a\}$. In this case, the grading is determined by the degree of the polynomial. The subgroups R_1 and R_a correspond to polynomials with even and odd degrees, respectively:

$$R_1 = \{c_0 + c_2x^2 + c_4x^4 + \dots | c_i \in \mathbb{Z} \textit{ for all even } i\},$$
$$R_a = \{c_1x + c_3x^3 + c_5x^5 + \dots | c_i \in \mathbb{Z} \textit{ for all odd } i\}.$$

Hence, R is a $\mathfrak{G}$-weak graded ring. Here, let V be defined as the module of polynomials; thus, $V = V_1 \oplus V_a$, where V_1 is defined as the module of polynomials with even degrees:

$$V_1 = \{c_0 + c_2x^2 + c_4x^4 + \dots | c_i \in \mathbb{Z} \textit{ for all even } i\}$$

and V_a is defined as the module of polynomials with odd degrees:

$$V_a = \{c_1x + c_3x^3 + c_5x^5 + \dots | c_i \in \mathbb{Z} \textit{ for all odd } i\}.$$

Hence, $V \in \mathfrak{G}$-GrR-Mod. Similarly, let W be the module of polynomials; thus, $W = W_1 \oplus W_a$, where W_1 is defined as the module of polynomials with even degrees:

$$W_1 = \{d_0 + d_2x^2 + d_4x^4 + \dots | d_i \in \mathbb{Z} \textit{ for all even } i\}$$

and W_a is defined as the module of polynomials with odd degrees:

$$W_a = \{d_1 x + d_3 x^3 + d_5 x^5 + \ldots | d_i \in \mathbb{Z} \text{ for all odd } i\}.$$

Then, $W \in \mathfrak{G}$-GrR-Mod. Here, we can define a morphism $\varphi : V \rightarrow W$ as follows:

$$\varphi(c_0 + c_2 x^2 + c_4 x^4 + \ldots) = d_2 x^2 + d_4 x^4 + \cdots \subseteq W_1,$$

and

$$\varphi(c_1 x + c_3 x^3 + c_5 x^4 + \ldots) = d_3 x^3 + d_5 x^5 + \cdots \subseteq W_a,$$

where $c_i = d_{i+2}$ for all i. Hence, $\varphi \in \mathfrak{G}$-GrHom$_R(V, W)$ since $\varphi(V_1) \subseteq W_1$ and $\varphi(V_a) \subseteq W_a$. Thus, $\varphi(V_\mathfrak{g}) \subseteq W_\mathfrak{g}$ for all $v \in V_\mathfrak{g}$ and $\mathfrak{g} \in \mathfrak{G}$. Note that, since $\mathfrak{G}$ is a finite set, according to Theorem 6, we have $\mathfrak{G}$-GrHom$_R(V, W) =$ Hom$_R(V, W)$.

5. Conclusions

In this work, it was shown that many results in the literature concerning group-graded rings and group-graded modules can be generalized and proven using the new concepts of $\mathfrak{G}$-weak graded rings and $\mathfrak{G}$-weak graded modules. Moreover, this generalization may form a bridge between the classical group theory and the theory of quantum groups. Using these new concepts, interested readers can study several properties of group- or semigroup-graded rings and modules in the literature, such as simplicity and semi-simplicity.

Author Contributions: Conceptualization, M.A.-S.; Software, R.A.-O.; Validation, M.A.-S.; Formal analysis, R.A.-O.; Investigation, R.A.-O.; Resources, R.A.-O.; Data curation, R.A.-O.; Writing—original draft, R.A.-O.; Writing—review & editing, M.A.-S.; Visualization, M.A.-S.; Supervision, M.A.-S.; Funding acquisition, R.A.-O. All authors have read and agreed to the published version of the manuscript.

Funding: This research received no external funding.

Data Availability Statement: The original contributions presented in the study are included in the article, further inquiries can be directed to the corresponding author.

Acknowledgments: The authors would like to express their gratitude to the academic editor and the anonymous reviewers for their valuable remarks and suggestions that helped to improve this work.

Conflicts of Interest: The authors declare no conflicts of interest.

References

1. Dade, E.C. Group graded rings and modules. *Math. Z.* **1980**, *174*, 241–262. [CrossRef]
2. Dascalescu, S.; Kelarev, A.V.; Van Wyk, L. Semigroup gradings of full matrix rings. *Comm. Algebra* **2001**, *29*, 5023–5031. [CrossRef]
3. Nystedt, P.; Oinert, J. Simple semigroup graded rings. *J. Algebra Appl.* **2015**, *14*, 1–10. [CrossRef]
4. Lezama, O.; Latorre, E. Non-commutative algebraic geometry of semigraded rings. *Int. J. Algebra Comput.* **2017**, *27*, 361–389. [CrossRef]
5. Cohen, M.; Montgomery, S. Group-graded rings, smash product and group actions. *Trans. Amer. Math. Soc.* **1984**, *282*, 237–258. [CrossRef]
6. Năstăsescu, C.; Bergh, M.; Oystaeyen, F. Separable functor, applications to graded rings and modules. *J. Algebra* **1989**, *123*, 397–413. [CrossRef]
7. Rafael, M.; Oinert, J. Separable functors revisited. *Comm. Algebra* **1990**, *18*, 144–1459. [CrossRef]
8. Beggs, E.J. Making non-trivially associated tensor categories from left coset representatives. *J. Pure Appl. Algebra* **2003**, *177*, 5–41. [CrossRef]
9. Al-Shomrani, M.M.; Beggs, E.J. Making nontrivially associated modular categories from finite groups. *Int. J. Math. Math. Sci.* **2004**, *2004*, 2231–2264. [CrossRef]
10. Al-Shomrani, M.M. A construction of graded rings using a set of left coset representatives. *JP J. Algebra Number T.* **2012**, *25*, 105–112.
11. Al-Shomrani, M.M.; Al-Subaie, N. A Generalization of Group-Graded Modules. *Symmetry* **2022**, *14*, 835. [CrossRef]

12. Cohen, M.; Westreich, S. Solvability for semisimple Hopf algebras via integrals. *J. Algebra* **2017**, *472*, 67–94. [CrossRef]
13. Alyoubi, B.M.; Al-Shomrani, M.M. The groups of prime power order and the structure of hopf algebras. *JP J. Algebra Number T.* **2021**, *51*, 145–182. [CrossRef]

Disclaimer/Publisher's Note: The statements, opinions and data contained in all publications are solely those of the individual author(s) and contributor(s) and not of MDPI and/or the editor(s). MDPI and/or the editor(s) disclaim responsibility for any injury to people or property resulting from any ideas, methods, instructions or products referred to in the content.

mathematics

Article

The Connection between $\mathrm{Der}(U_q^+(\mathfrak{g}))$ and $\mathrm{Der}(U_{r,s}^+(\mathfrak{g}))$

Yongyue Zhong [1] and Xiaomin Tang [2,*]

[1] School of Mathematical Sciences, Harbin Engineering University, Harbin 150001, China; yyzhong@hrbeu.edu.cn
[2] School of Mathematical Sciences, Heilongjiang University, Harbin 150080, China
* Correspondence: tangxm@hlju.edu.cn

Abstract: To facilitate the parallel development of the structures and properties of two-parameter quantum groups with those of one-parameter quantum groups, this paper primarily elucidates the interrelations and distinctions between the derivation algebras of these two types of quantum groups. Additionally, we also proposed a method for deriving the derivation algebra of one-parameter quantum groups from known two-parameter quantum group derivations, and vice versa.

Keywords: two-parameter quantum groups; one-parameter quantum groups; iterated Ore extension; derivations

MSC: 17B3; 81R50

1. Introduction

In 1985, Drinfel'd introduced the concept of quantum groups while investigating the quantum Yang–Baxter equation [1]. Over the past three decades, scholars have extensively explored and demonstrated the significant influence of quantum group theory across diverse domains of mathematics and physics. In 1990, Kulish introduced a two-parameter quantum group utilizing the constant solution of the Yang–Baxter equation.

Benkart and Witherspoon studied the two-parameter quantum groups $U_{r,s}(gl_n)$ and $U_{r,s}(sl_n)$ through down–up algebra [2,3]. Bergeron, Gao and Hu extended this analysis to two-parameter quantum orthogonal and symplectic groups [4,5]. Subsequently, Hu and Shi investigated the two-parameter quantum group for exceptional types G_2 [6]; Hu and Wang further developed the B_n-type [7].

In particular, Hu and Pei presented a simplified definition for a class of two-parameter quantum groups $U_{r,s}$, demonstrating that the two-parameter quantum groups $U_{r,s}(\mathfrak{g})$ can be obtained from the one-parameter quantum group $U_{q,q^{-1}}(\mathfrak{g})$ by twisting the multiplication via an explicit Hopf 2-cocycle σ [8,9].

In 2015, building on Lusztig's work, Fan and Li constructed another version of the two-parameter quantum group using simple perverse sheaves [10]. This geometric construction provides a new representation of the generators and generation relationships of two-parameter quantum group $U_{v,t}$.

In the study of quantum groups, derivations may be used to describe some deformation or evolution of quantum groups, or to reveal relationships between quantum groups and other algebraic structures. In this paper, our main focus is to explore the connection between derivative algebras of one-parameter quantum groups and derivation algebras of two-parameter quantum groups, where one-parameter and two-parameter quantum groups correspond to simple Lie algebras of the same finite type. Unlike previous studies of derivation algebra of a quantum group, a key contribution of this study is the establishment of the structure of derivation algebra of an iterated Ore extension, so that through this structure, we can obtain the derivation algebra of any quantum group, thus building a bridge for understanding the relationship between the derivative algebras of single-parameter quantum groups and two-parameter quantum groups.

In Section 4, we initially derive the corresponding one-parameter quantum group derivation algebra from the derivation algebra of the two-parameter quantum group. This process is relatively straight forward. Conversely, constructing a two-parameter quantum group from a one-parameter quantum group is complex, thus making it challenging to construct the derivation algebra of a two-parameter quantum group from that of a one-parameter quantum group. Finally, we employ the method proposed by Fan and Li to construct two-parameter quantum groups from one-parameter quantum groups. Building upon this approach, we derive the derivation algebra of a two-parameter quantum group from that of a one-parameter quantum group.

2. Preliminaries

Before delving into the main topic of this article, we will first review some pertinent preparatory knowledge to ensure that readers are equipped for subsequent discussions. In this section, we fix the notations that will be used throughout this paper. For any $n, k, v > 0$, let

$$(n)_v = \frac{v^n - 1}{v - 1}, \qquad [n]_v = \frac{v^n - v^{-n}}{v - v^{-1}}$$
$$(n)_v! = (1)_v \cdots (n)_v, \qquad [n]_v! = [1]_v \cdots [n]_v$$
$$\binom{n}{k}_v = \frac{(n)_v!}{(k)_v!(n-k)_v!}, \qquad \begin{bmatrix} n \\ k \end{bmatrix}_v = \frac{[n]_v!}{[k]_v![n-k]_v!}$$

and $[0]_v! = 1$, $(0)_v! = 1$.

2.1. The Algebras $U_q(\mathfrak{g})$ and $U_{r,s}(\mathfrak{g})$

This subsection introduces the definitions of one-parameter quantum groups and two-parameter quantum groups, which will serve as the foundation for our subsequent research and analysis.

Let $\mathfrak{g}$ be a finite-dimensional simple Lie algebra over a field $\mathbb{C}$ and $A = (a_{ij})_{n\times n}$ be an associated Cartan matrix, there exists a diagonal matrix $D = \mathrm{diag}(d_1, \cdots, d_n)$ such that $d_i \in \mathbb{Z}\backslash\{0\}$ and $DA = (DA)^T$. Let $q \in \mathbb{C}^*$ be such that q is not a unit root.

Definition 1. *The one-parameter quantum group $U_q(\mathfrak{g})$ is a unital associative algebra over $\mathbb{C}$ by generators E_i, F_i, $K_i^{\pm 1}$ $(1 \le i \le n)$, and relations*

$$\text{(A1)} \quad K_iK_i^{-1} = K_i^{-1}K_i = 1, \qquad K_iK_j = K_jK_i$$
$$\text{(A2)} \quad K_iE_iK_i^{-1} = q^{d_ia_{ij}}E_j, \qquad K_iF_iK_i^{-1} = q^{d_ia_{ij}}F_j$$
$$\text{(A3)} \quad E_iF_j - F_jE_i = \delta\frac{K_i^2 - K_i^{-2}}{q^{2d_i} - q^{-2d_i}}$$
$$\text{(A4)} \quad \sum_{v=0}^{1-a_{ij}} (-1)^v \begin{bmatrix} 1-a_{ij} \\ v \end{bmatrix}_{q^{2d_i}} E_i^{1-a_{ij}-v}E_jE_i^v = 0 \qquad (i \neq j)$$
$$\text{(A5)} \quad \sum_{v=0}^{1-a_{ij}} (-1)^v \begin{bmatrix} 1-a_{ij} \\ v \end{bmatrix}_{q^{2d_i}} F_i^{1-a_{ij}-v}F_jF_i^v = 0 \qquad (i \neq j)$$

The above content described the generators and generating relations for one-parameter quantum groups. Next, let us review the generators and generating relations for two-parameter quantum groups.

Let $\Pi = \{\alpha_i | i \in I\}$ be the set of simple roots, Φ be the set of roots and Φ^+ positive roots. Let $\mathbb{Q}(r,s)$ be the rational functions field in two variables r, s over $\mathbb{Q}$. Let $r_i = r^{d_i}$, $s_i = s^{d_i}$ for $i \in I$ and $\langle -, - \rangle$ be the Euler bilinear form on $\mathbb{Z}$ defined by

$$\langle i,j \rangle := \langle \alpha_i, \alpha_j \rangle = \begin{cases} d_i a_{ij} & i < j \\ d_i & i = j \\ 0 & i > j \end{cases} \tag{1}$$

Definition 2. *The two-parameter quantum group $U_{r,s}(\mathfrak{g})$ is a unital associative algebra over $\mathbb{Q}(r,s)$ generated by e_i, f_i, $\omega_i^{\pm 1}$, $\omega_i'^{\pm 1}$ $(1 \le i \le n)$, subject to the relations:*

$$\begin{aligned}
&(\mathrm{B1}) \quad && \omega_i^{\pm 1}\omega_j^{\pm 1} = \omega_j^{\pm 1}\omega_i^{\pm 1}, && \omega_i'^{\pm 1}\omega_j'^{\pm 1} = \omega_j'^{\pm 1}\omega_i'^{\pm 1} \\
& && \omega_i^{\pm 1}\omega_j'^{\pm 1} = \omega_j'^{\pm 1}\omega_i^{\pm 1}, && \omega_i^{\pm 1}\omega_i^{\mp 1} = \omega_i'^{\pm 1}\omega_i'^{\mp 1} \\
&(\mathrm{B2}) && \omega_i e_j \omega_i^{-1} = r^{\langle j,i \rangle} s^{-\langle i,j \rangle} e_j, && \omega_i' e_j \omega_i'^{-1} = r^{-\langle i,j \rangle} s^{\langle j,i \rangle} e_j \\
& && \omega_i f_j \omega_i^{-1} = r^{-\langle j,i \rangle} s^{\langle i,j \rangle} f_j, && \omega_i' f_j \omega_i'^{-1} = r^{\langle i,j \rangle} s^{-\langle j,i \rangle} f_j \\
&(\mathrm{B3}) && e_i f_j - f_j e_i = \delta_{i,j} \frac{\omega_i - \omega_i'}{v_i - v_i^{-1}} && \\
&(\mathrm{B4}) && \sum_{k=0}^{1-a_{ij}} (-1)^k \binom{1-a_{ij}}{k}_{r_i s_i^{-1}} c_{ij}^{(k)} e_i^{1-a_{ij}-k} e_j e_i^k = 0 && i \ne j \\
&(\mathrm{B5}) && \sum_{k=0}^{1-a_{ij}} (-1)^k \binom{1-a_{ij}}{k}_{r_i s_i^{-1}} c_{ij}^{(k)} f_i^k f_j f_i^{1-a_{ij}-k} = 0 && i \ne j
\end{aligned}$$

Let $U_q^+(\mathfrak{g})$ (resp., $U_q^-(\mathfrak{g})$) be the subalgebra of $U_q(\mathfrak{g})$ generated by the elements E_i (resp., F_i) for $1 \le i \le n$, and $U_q^0(\mathfrak{g})$ is subalgebra of $U_q(\mathfrak{g})$ generated by $K_i^{\pm 1}$ for $1 \le i \le n$. Moreover, we know

$$U_q(\mathfrak{g}) \cong U_q^+(\mathfrak{g}) \otimes U_q^0(\mathfrak{g}) \otimes U_q^-(\mathfrak{g})$$

Similary, Let $U_{r,s}^+(\mathfrak{g})$ (resp., $U_{r,s}^-(\mathfrak{g})$) be the subalgebra of $U_{r,s}(\mathfrak{g})$ generated by the elements e_i (resp., f_i) for $1 \le i \le n$, and $U_{r,s}^0$ the subalgebra of $U_{r,s}(\mathfrak{g})$ generated by $\omega_i^{\pm 1}$, $\omega_i'^{\pm 1}$ for $1 \le i \le n$, we have

$$U_{r,s}(\mathfrak{g}) \cong U_{r,s}^+(\mathfrak{g}) \otimes U_{r,s}^0(\mathfrak{g}) \otimes U_{r,s}^-(\mathfrak{g})$$

In this paper, our primary focus is on the derivation algebras of the positive parts of both one-parameter and two-parameter quantum groups.

2.2. Iterated Ore Extension

This subsection will furnish the definitions and properties of iterative Ore extensions, crucial for the subsequent discussion regarding the derivation algebra of quantum groups.

Let R be a ring. An Ore extension $R[x, \sigma, \delta]$ is a ring with elements of the form $f(x) = \sum_{i=0}^n a_i x^i$, $a_i \in R$ and multiplication satisfying $xr = \sigma(r)x + \delta(r)$ for all $r \in R$, where σ is an endomorphism of R and δ is a σ-derivation of R, i.e.,

$$\delta(r_1 r_2) = \sigma(r_1)\delta(r_2) + \delta(r_1) r_2, \qquad \textit{for all } r_1, r_2 \in R$$

Definition 3. *An iterated Ore extension $R[x_1, \sigma_1, \delta_1] \cdots [x_n, \sigma_n, \delta_n]$ is an Ore extension where for all $j \ge 1$, σ_j and δ_j are a ring endomorphism and a σ_j-derivation of $R_{(j-1)} := R[x_1, \sigma_1, \delta_1] \cdots [x_{j-1}, \sigma_{j-1}, \delta_{j-1}]$. Elements in this extension have the form $\sum_{i=0}^n a_i x_1^{i_1} \cdots x_n^{i_n}$, $a_i \in R$.*

Let us review the concept of quantum root vectors in quantum groups and the exchange relationship.

Let $\mathfrak{g}$ be a finite dimensional simple Lie algebra, Φ^+ be a positive root system of the complex simple Lie algebra of $\mathfrak{g}$ and $|\Phi^+| = n$. The following lemma holds.

Lemma 1 ([11]). *For each of the trees in Figure 1, the set of words determined by the Lyndon paths in the tree is the complete set of standard Lyndon words for the corresponding finite-dimensional simple Lie algebra.*

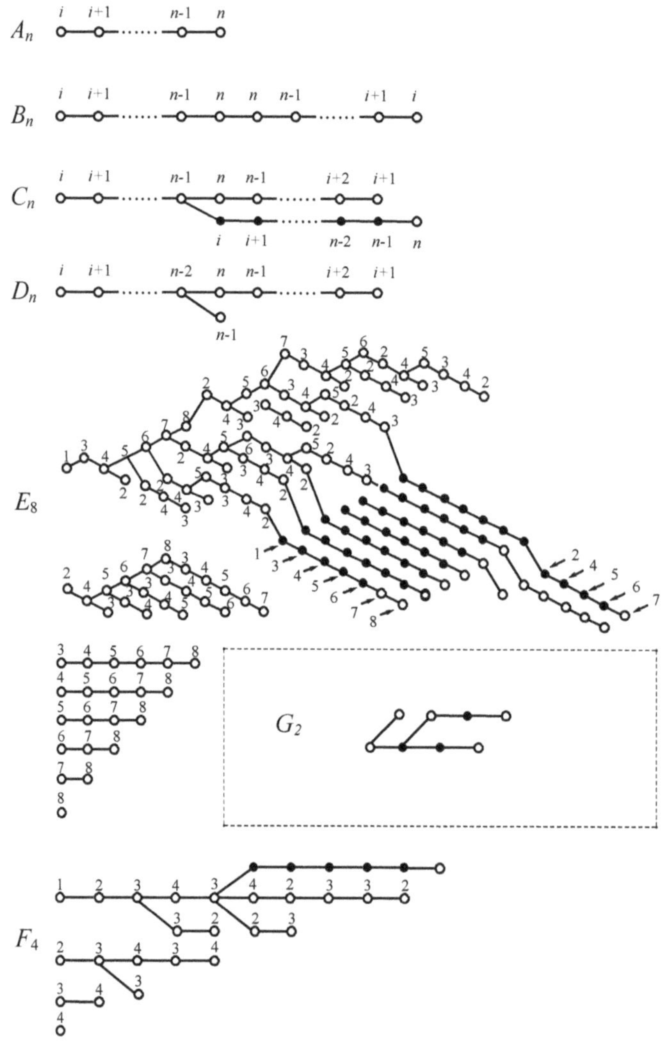

Figure 1. The tree given standard Lyndon paths. The root of each tree is the leftmost vertex.

Assuming that $\beta_i, \beta_j \in \Phi^+$, $\mathcal{X}_i$ and $\mathcal{X}_j$ are the quantum root vectors corresponding to β_i and β_j, respectively. We have that $U_q^+(\mathfrak{g})$ consists of quantum root vectors $\mathcal{X}_1, \cdots, \mathcal{X}_n$

and the set of products $\{\mathcal{X}_1^{a_1}\cdots\mathcal{X}_n^{a_n}|a_i\in\mathbb{Z}\}$ forms a basis for $U_q^+(\mathfrak{g})$. If i and j are two integers such that $1\le i<j\le n$, then we can obtain

$$\mathcal{X}_i\mathcal{X}_j-q^{(i,j)}\mathcal{X}_j\mathcal{X}_i=\sum_{k=(k_{i+1},\cdots,k_{j-1})}c_k\mathcal{X}_{i+1}^{k_{i+1}}\cdots\mathcal{X}_{j-1}^{k_{j-1}} \tag{2}$$

where $c_k\in\mathbb{C}$, $q^{(i,j)}:=q^{(\beta_i,\beta_j)}$, and (β_i,β_j) is the inner product of β_i and β_j. Similarly, X_i and X_j are the quantum root vectors corresponding to β_i and β_j, respectively. The two-parameter quantum group $U_{r,s}^+(\mathfrak{g})$ contains a set of quantum root vector and the products $\{X_1^{a_1}\cdots X_n^{a_n}|a_i\in\mathbb{Z}\}$ form a basis of $U_{r,s}^+(\mathfrak{g})$. If i and j are two integers such that $1\le i<j\le l$, then we can obtain

$$X_iX_j-(\omega_i',\omega_j)X_jX_i=\sum_{k=(k_{i+1},\cdots,k_{j-1})}e_kX_{i+1}^{k_{i+1}}\cdots X_{j-1}^{k_{j-1}} \tag{3}$$

where $e_k\in\mathbb{C}$, $(\omega_i',\omega_j)=r^{\langle\beta_i,\beta_j\rangle}s^{-\langle\beta_j,\beta_i\rangle}$.

Based on the Definition 3, in conjunction with Equations (2) and (3), it is evident that the following lemma is valid.

Lemma 2. *$U_q^+(\mathfrak{g})$ and $U_{r,s}^+(\mathfrak{g})$ are two skew polynomial rings, which can be expressed as*

$$U_q^+(\mathfrak{g})=\mathbb{C}[\mathcal{X}_1][\mathcal{X}_2;\sigma_2,\delta_2]\cdots[\mathcal{X}_l;\sigma_l,\delta_l]$$
$$U_{r,s}^+(\mathfrak{g})=\mathbb{C}[X_1][X_2;\sigma_2',\delta_2']\cdots[X_l;\sigma_l',\delta_l']$$

where the σ_j's are $\mathbb{C}$-linear automorphisms and the δ_j's are $\mathbb{C}$-linear σ_j-derivations such that for $1\le i<j\le l$, $\sigma_j(\mathcal{X}_i)=q^{(i,j)}\mathcal{X}_i$ and $\delta_j(\mathcal{X}_i)=\sum_{k=(k_{i+1},\cdots,k_{j-1})}c_k\mathcal{X}_{i+1}^{k_{i+1}}\cdots\mathcal{X}_{j-1}^{k_{j-1}}$; for $1\le i<j\le l$, $\sigma_j'(X_i)=\langle\omega_i',\omega_j\rangle X_i$ and $\delta_j'(X_i)=\sum_{k=(k_{i+1},\cdots,k_{j-1})}e_kX_{i+1}^{k_{i+1}}\cdots X_{j-1}^{k_{j-1}}$.

In [9], Hu and Pei offer a more straightforward definition for a class of two-parameter quantum groups, denoted as $U_{r,s}(\mathfrak{g})$, associated with semisimple Lie algebras. They do so by employing the Euler form and further elucidate the connection between two-parameter quantum groups and the one-parameter Drinfel'd–Jimbo quantum group. More specifically, In the subsequent lemma, they detail the method of deriving a one-parameter quantum group from a two-parameter one by adjusting the parameters.

Lemma 3. *Let $r=q$, $s=q^{-1}$. Then, $U_{q,q^{-1}}(\mathfrak{g})$ modulo is the Hopf ideal generated by $\omega_i'-\omega_i^{-1}$ ($i\in[1,n]$) is isomorphic to the standard one-parameter quantum group $U_q(\mathfrak{g})$.*

3. Derivations of Iterated Ore Extension

Drawing on the foundational principles outlined in Section 2, it is clear that both one-parameter quantum groups and two-parameter quantum groups can be characterized as iterated Ore extensions. As a result, the central objective of this section is to clarify the structural underpinnings of the derivative algebra associated with iterative Ore extensions. This elucidation forms a crucial basis for delving deeper into the relationships between the derivation algebra of one-parameter quantum groups and two-parameter quantum groups.

Definition 4 ([12]). *Let R be an algebra over the field $\mathbb{F}$, and δ be a linear transformation over R. If δ satisfies the following conditions:*

$$\delta(r+s)=\delta(r)+\delta(s),\ \forall r,s\in R,$$
$$\delta(rs)=\delta(r)s+r\delta(s).\ \forall r,s\in R,$$

then δ is called a derivation of R.

Example 1. *Let R be a polynomial ring over the complex field $\mathbb{C}$, δ be a mapping over R, and satisfying the following:*

$$\delta(\sum_i a_i X^i) = \sum_i i a_i X^{i-1},$$

so δ is a derivative on R.

Let $R_n := \mathbb{C}[X_1][X_2;\sigma_2,\delta_2]\cdots[X_n;\sigma_n,\delta_n]$ be a special type of iterated Ore extension, for $1 \leq j < i \leq n$,

$$X_j X_i - \lambda(X_j, X_i) X_i X_j = P(X_j, X_i), \tag{4}$$

where $P(X_j, X_i) = \sum_{\bar{k}=k_{i+1},\cdots,k_{j-1}} c_{\bar{k}} X_{i+1}^{k_{i+1}} \cdots X_{j-1}^{k_{j-1}}$. It is worth noting that $U_{r,s}^+(\mathfrak{g})$ and $U_q^+(\mathfrak{g})$ are all iterated Ore extensions of this type.

We give a mapping a_r, which is mapped from R_n to $\mathbb{C}$ and satisfies $a_{X_i^k+X_j^l}(X_i^k + X_j^l) = 2^{k-1}a_{X_i}(X_i) + 2^{l-1}a_{X_j}(X_j)$

Theorem 1. *If R_n is a special type of iterated Ore extension, then the derivation of R_n can be uniquely written in the following form:*

$$D(X_i) = a_{X_i}(X_i)X_i,$$

for some $r \in R_n$, and where $a_{X_i}(X_i) \in \mathbb{C}$ and

$$a_{X_i}(X_i) + a_{X_j}(X_j) = a_{P(X_j,X_i)}(P(X_j, X_i)). \tag{5}$$

Proof. Let D be the derivation of R_n; we have

$$D(y) = \sum_r a_r(y) r, \tag{6}$$

where a_r is the mapping from R_n to $\mathbb{C}$. In fact, we know $X_j X_i - \lambda(X_j, X_i) X_i X_j = P(X_j, X_i)$ for $P(X_j, X_i) = \sum_{\bar{k}=k_{i+1},\cdots,k_{j-1}} c_{\bar{k}} X_{i+1}^{k_{i+1}} \cdots X_{j-1}^{k_{j-1}}$. Based on the definition of derivations, there is

$$\begin{aligned} D(X_j X_i) &= D(X_j)X_i + X_j D(X_i) \\ &= \sum_r a_r(X_j) r X_i + \sum_r a_r(X_i)\lambda(X_j, r) r X_j + \sum_r a_r(X_i) P(X_j, r). \end{aligned} \tag{7}$$

Since D is a bilinear mapping; thus, we have

$$\begin{aligned} D(X_j X_i) =& \lambda(X_j, X_i) D(X_i X_j) + D(P(X_j, X_i)) \\ =& \lambda(X_j, X_i)(\sum_r a_r(X_i) r X_j + \sum_r a_r(X_j)\lambda(X_i, r) r X_i + \sum_r a_r(X_j) P(X_i, r)) \\ &+ \sum_r a_r(P(X_j, X_i)) r, \end{aligned} \tag{8}$$

then $P(X_j, X_i)$ does not include $X_j X_i$, so that

$$\sum_r a_r(X_i)\lambda(X_j, r) r X_j = \sum_r a_r(X_i)\lambda(X_j, X_i) r X_j, \tag{9}$$

$$\sum_r a_r(X_j) r X_i = \sum_r a_r(X_j)\lambda(X_j, X_i)\lambda(X_i, r) r X_i, \tag{10}$$

$$\sum_r a_r(X_i) P(X_j, r) = \sum_r a_r(X_j)\lambda(X_j, X_i) P(X_i, r)) + \sum_r a_r(P(X_j, X_i)) r. \tag{11}$$

From this, by comparing coefficients of (9), when $r = X_i$, there is $a_{X_i}(X_i)\lambda(X_j, X_i)X_iX_j = a_{X_i}(X_i)\lambda(X_j, X_i)X_iX_j$, and when $r \neq X_i$, there is $a_r(X_i) = 0$. Similarly, in Equation (10), when $r = X_j$, $a_{X_j}(X_j)X_jX_i = a_{X_j}(X_j)\lambda(X_j, X_i)\lambda(X_i, X_j)X_jX_i$ holds, and when $r \neq X_j$, $a_r(X_j) = 0$.

In Equation (11), there is $a_{X_i}(X_i)P(X_j, X_i) = a_{X_j}(X_j)\lambda(X_j, X_i)P(X_i, X_j) + a_{P(X_j,X_i)}P(X_j, X_i)$. Since $P(X_i, X_j) = -\lambda(X_j, X_i)^{-1}P(X_j, X_i)$, we obtain

$$a_{X_i}(X_i) = -a_{X_j}(X_j) + a_{P(X_i,X_j)}(P(X_i, X_j)).$$

Under the above results, we further discuss the action of mapping $a_{P(X_i,X_j)}(P(X_i, X_j))$. We can characterize $a_{P(X_i,X_j)}(P(X_i, X_j))$ in two situations.

We first suppose that $a_{P(X_i,X_j)}(P(X_i, X_j))$ contains only one generator and its exponent is 1, i.e., $X_jX_i = \lambda(X_j, X_i)X_iX_j + c_kX_k$ for $1 \leq i < k < j \leq n$. Therefore, we would have

$$a_{X_i}(X_i) = -a_{X_j}(X_j) + a_{X_k}(X_k).$$

Next, we will prove by using mathematical induction that $D(X_i^k) = 2^{k-1}a_{X_i}(X_i)X_i^k$.

$$\begin{aligned} D(X_i^2) &= D(X_i)X_i + X_iD(X_i) \\ &= 2a_{X_i}(X_i)X_i^2. \end{aligned}$$

Suppose that $D(X_i^{k-1}) = 2^{k-2}a_{X_i}(X_i)X_i^{k-1}$ for $k \in [\![1, n]\!]$, then

$$\begin{aligned} D(X_i^k) &= D(X_i^{k-1})X_i + X_iD(X_i^{k-1}) \\ &= 2^{k-2}a_{X_i}(X_i)X_i^{k-1}X_i + X_i2a_{X_i}(X_i)X_i^{k-2} \\ &= 2^{k-1}a_{X_i}(X_i)X_i^k, \end{aligned}$$

it can be concluded that $a_{X_i^k}(X_i^k) = 2^{k-1}a_{X_i}(X_i)$. We thus obtain

$$D(\sum_{\bar{k}} c_{\bar{k}}X_{i+1}^{k_{i+1}} \cdots X_{j-1}^{k_{j-1}}) = \sum_{\bar{k}} c_{\bar{k}}(2^{k_{i+1}-1}a_{X_{i+1}}(X_{i+1}) + \cdots + 2^{k_{j-1}-1}a_{X_{j-1}}(X_{j-1}))X_{i+1}^{k_{i+1}} \cdots X_{j-1}^{k_{j-1}},$$

where $\bar{k} = k_{i+1}, \cdots, k_{j-1}$. The proof is complete. □

4. The Relationship between $\mathrm{Der}(U_q^+(\mathfrak{g}))$ and $\mathrm{Der}(U_{r,s}^+(\mathfrak{g}))$

In this section, we delve into the structure of the derivative algebra of one-parameter quantum groups and two-parameter quantum groups. This exploration is aimed at inspiring further research on the relationship between the derivations of these two types of quantum groups.

4.1. Derivations of Quantum Groups

As $U_q^+(\mathfrak{g})$ and $U_{r,s}^+(\mathfrak{g})$ are iterated Ore extensions, this means that the derivations of $U_q^+(\mathfrak{g})$ or $U_{r,s}^+(\mathfrak{g})$ have the following structure: $D(x_i) = a_ix_i$, where x_i is the quantum root vector of $U_q^+(\mathfrak{g})$ or $U_{r,s}^+(\mathfrak{g})$.

For the convenience of subsequent operations, we first provide a proposition.

Proposition 1. *Let $Z(U_{r,s}^+(\mathfrak{g}))$ be the center of $U_{r,s}^+(\mathfrak{g})$ and D be a derivation of $U_{r,s}^+(\mathfrak{g})$; then, for all $\mu \in Z(U_{r,s}^+(\mathfrak{g}))$, μD is a derivation of $U_{r,s}^+(\mathfrak{g})$.*

Proof. Since $\mu \in Z(U_{r,s}^{+}(\mathfrak{g}))$, we have

$$\begin{aligned}\mu D(X_j X_i) &= \mu D(X_j)X_i + X_j \mu D(X_i)\\ &= \mu a_j X_j X_i + X_j \mu a_i^{(k)} X_i\\ &= \mu(a_j + a_i)X_j X_i.\end{aligned}$$

This is precisely the assertion of the proposition. □

Theorem 2. *Let $U_{r,s}^{+}(\mathfrak{g})$ be the positive part of the two-parameter quantum group $U_{r,s}(\mathfrak{g})$ corresponding to $\mathfrak{g}$; then, each derivation D of $U_{r,s}^{+}(\mathfrak{g})$ must be written in the following form:*

$$D(X_i) = ad_{\xi}(X_i) + \sum_k \mu_k a_{X_i}^{(k)}(X_i)X_i, \tag{12}$$

where $\xi \in U_{r,s}^{+}(\mathfrak{g})$, $\mu_k \in Z(U_{r,s}^{+}(\mathfrak{g}))$, $a_{X_i}^{(k)}(X_i) \in \mathbb{C}$, $k = 1, \cdots, p(p \leq n)$ and the following equation holds:

$$a_{X_i}^{(k)}(X_i) + a_{X_j}^{(k)}(X_j) = a_{P(X_j,X_i)}^{(k)}(P(X_j, X_i))$$

Proof. Based on Lemma 2, the positive part $U_{r,s}^{+}(\mathfrak{g})$ of the two-parameter quantum group $U_{r,s}(\mathfrak{g})$ constitutes an iterated Ore extension. Let $X_1, \cdots, X_n$ be the quantum root vectors of $U_{r,s}^{+}(\mathfrak{g})$ and $D_k, k = 1, \cdots, p(p \leq n)$ represent the derivation of $U_{r,s}^{+}(\mathfrak{g})$; we have

$$D_k(X_i) = a_{X_i}^{(k)}(X_i)X_i$$

and

$$a_{X_i}^{(k)}(X_i) + a_{X_j}^{(k)}(X_j) = a_{P(X_j,X_i)}^{(k)}(P(X_j, X_i)).$$

By consolidating Proposition 1, we can conclude that

$$\begin{aligned}\mu D_k(X_i X_j) &= \mu D_k(X_i)X_j + \mu X_i D_k(X_j)\\ &= \mu D_k(X_i)X_j + X_i \mu D_k(X_j)\end{aligned}$$

Therefore, we can conclude that any outer derivation of $U_{r,s}^{+}(\mathfrak{g})$ can be expressed in the form of $\sum_k \mu_k a_{X_i}^{(k)}(X_i)X_i$. It can be seen from this that the theorem proof is completed. □

For convenience, in subsequent studies, we will denote $a_{X_i}^{(k)}(X_i)$ by the symbol a_{ki}.

Theorem 3. *Let D be the derivation of a two-parameter quantum group $U_{r,s}^{+}(\mathfrak{g})$ as shown in Equation (21); then, the derivation of the one-parameter quantum group $U_q^{+}(\mathfrak{g})$ corresponding to $U_{r,s}^{+}(\mathfrak{g})$ can be uniquely written in the following form:*

$$D'(\mathcal{X}_i) = ad_{\xi'}(\mathcal{X}_i) + \sum_i c'_k a_{kj} \mathcal{X}_j \tag{13}$$

where $\xi' \in U_q^{+}(\mathfrak{g})$, $c_k s' \in Z(U_q^{+}(\mathfrak{g}))$.

Proof. Let $D_k(k = 1, \cdots, p)$ be the derivations of $U_{r,s}^{+}(\mathfrak{g})$ and

$$D_k(X_j) = a_{kj}X_j.$$

According to Lemma 3, when $r = q$ and $s = q^{-1}$, there is $U_{q,q^{-1}}^{+}(\mathfrak{g}) \cong U_q^{+}(\mathfrak{g})$. Let

$$\psi : U_{q,q^{-1}}^{+}(\mathfrak{g}) \to U_q^{+}(\mathfrak{g})$$

be a mapping from $U^+_{q,q^{-1}}(\mathfrak{g})$ to $U_q^+(\mathfrak{g})$; so, we have

$$\psi D_k(X_j) = a_{kj}\mathcal{X}_j.$$

Let D'_k be a map on $U_q^+(\mathfrak{g})$ and $D'_k(\mathcal{X}_j) = a_{kj}\mathcal{X}_j = \psi D_k(X_j)$; then, we prove that D'_k $(k = 1, \cdots, p)$ are derivations of $U_q^+(\mathfrak{g})$. According to the definition of D'_k, we can obtain

$$\begin{aligned} D'_k(\mathcal{X}_j\mathcal{X}_i) &= \psi(D_k(X_jX_i)) = a_{kj}\mathcal{X}_j\mathcal{X}_i + a_{ki}\mathcal{X}_j\mathcal{X}_i \\ &= D'_k(\mathcal{X}_j)\mathcal{X}_i + \mathcal{X}_jD'_k(\mathcal{X}_i) \end{aligned}$$

From the above results, we can know that D'_i $(i = 1, \cdots, p)$ are the derivations of $U_q^+(\mathfrak{g})$. According to Proposition 1, if $\mu \in Z(U_q^+(\mathfrak{g}))$, then $\mu D'_k$ is also a derivation of $U_q^+(\mathfrak{g})$. Therefore, we obtain that all outer derivations of $U_q^+(\mathfrak{g})$ have the form of $\sum\limits_i c'_i a_{ij}\mathcal{X}_j$, where $c'_i \in Z(U_q^+(\mathfrak{g}))$. Therefore, all derivations of $U_q^+(\mathfrak{g})$ can be uniquely written in the form of Equation (22). □

Example 2. *Suppose $\mathfrak{g}$ is a finite-dimensional complex simple Lie algebra of B_2-type, the Cartan matrix for the B_2-type Lie algebra is*

$$B := \begin{bmatrix} 2 & -1 \\ -2 & 2 \end{bmatrix}$$

Moreover, it can be deduced that $U^+_{r,s}(B_2)$ is a $\mathbb{C}$-algebra generated by generators e_1 and e_2, satisfying the following relationship:

$$\begin{aligned} &e_1^2e_2 - (r^2+s^2)e_1e_2e_2 + r^2s^2e_2e_1 = 0, \\ &e_1e_2^3 - (r^2+rs+s^2)e_2e_1e_2^2 + rs(r^2+rs+s^2)e_2^2e_1e_2 - r^3s^3e_2^3e_1 = 0. \end{aligned}$$

Based on the standard Lyndon basis presented in Figure 1, we can obtain an ordering of the positive roots of B_2: $\alpha_1, \alpha_1+\alpha_2, \alpha_1+2\alpha_2, \alpha_2$, which corresponds to the quantum root vectors in $U^+_{r,s}(B_2)$:

$$X_1 = e_1, \qquad X_2 = e_1e_2 - r^2e_2e_1, \qquad X_3 = e_2X_2 - s^{-2}X_2e_2, \qquad X_4 = e_2,$$

and there is an exchange relationship:

$$\begin{aligned} X_1X_2 &= s^2X_2X_1, \\ X_1X_3 &= r^2s^2X_3X_1, \\ X_2X_3 &= rsX_3X_2, \\ X_1X_4 &= r^2X_4X_1 + X_2, \\ X_2X_4 &= s^2X_4X_2 - s^2X_3, \\ X_4X_3 &= r^{-1}s^{-1}X_3X_4. \end{aligned}$$

In the above exchange relationship, when $i = 1, j = 4$, we have $P(X_i, X_j)$ is X_2 and $i = 2, j = 4$, we have $P(X_i, X_j)$ is X_3; in other cases, $P(X_i, X_j) = 0$. Therefore, assuming that D is a derivation of $U^+_{r,s}(B_2)$, there is $D(X_i) = a_{X_i}(X_i)X_i$, $a_{X_i}(X_i) \in \mathbb{C}$, $i \in [\![1,4]\!]$ and

$$a_{X_1}(X_1) + a_{X_4}(X_4) = a_{X_2}(X_2) \tag{14}$$

$$a_{X_2}(X_2) + a_{X_4}(X_4) = a_{X_3}(X_3) \tag{15}$$

The fundamental solution system can be derived by solving Equations (14) and (15): $\xi_1 = (1,1,1,0)^T$ and $\xi_2 = (0,1,2,1)^T$. We introduce the following notations: ai, ai', with $1 \le i \le 4$:

$$a_1 = 1, \qquad a_2 = 1, \qquad a_3 = 1, \qquad a_4 = 0,$$

$$a'_1 = 0, \qquad a'_2 = 1, \qquad a'_3 = 2, \qquad a'_4 = 1.$$

Let D_1 and D_2 be derivations corresponding to two fundamental solution systems; therefore, there are

$$\begin{aligned} &D_1(X_1) = X_1, && D_1(X_2) = X_2, && D_1(X_3) = X_3, && D_1(X_4) = 0, \\ &D_2(X_1) = 0, && D_2(X_2) = X_2, && D_2(X_3) = 2X_3, && D_2(X_4) = X_4. \end{aligned}$$

Then, each derivation Dof $U^+_{r,s}(B_2)$ can be written in the following form:

$$D = ad_x + \mu_1 D_1 + \mu_2 D_2 \tag{16}$$

where $\mu_1, \mu_2 \in Z(U^+_{r,s}(B_2))$.

According to Theorem 3, there exist two mappings D'_1 and D'_2 on $U^+_q(B_2)$, such that

$$\begin{aligned} &D'_1(\mathcal{X}_1) = \mathcal{X}_1, && D'_1(\mathcal{X}_2) = \mathcal{X}_2, && D'_1(\mathcal{X}_3) = \mathcal{X}_3, && D'_1(\mathcal{X}_4) = 0, \\ &D'_2(\mathcal{X}_1) = 0, && D'_2(\mathcal{X}_2) = \mathcal{X}_2, && D'_2(\mathcal{X}_3) = 2\mathcal{X}_3, && D'_2(\mathcal{X}_4) = \mathcal{X}_4. \end{aligned}$$

Therefore, the derivation D' of $U^+_q(B_2)$ can be written as

$$D'(\mathcal{X}_i) = ad_g(\mathcal{X}_i) + a_i\zeta_1\mathcal{X}_i + a'_i\zeta_2\mathcal{X}_i \tag{17}$$

where $g \in U^+_q(B_2)$ and $\zeta_i \in Z(U^+_v(B_2))$.

Next, we need to verify that every derivation of $U^+_q(B_2)$ can be expressed as shown in Equation (17). Suppose D'' is any derivation of $U^+_q(B_2)$.

By combining Theorem 1 and applying D'' on $\mathcal{X}_1\mathcal{X}_4$ and $\mathcal{X}_2\mathcal{X}_4$, respectively, it can be determined that

$$D''(\mathcal{X}_4\mathcal{X}_1) = D''(q^{-2}\mathcal{X}_1\mathcal{X}_4) - D''(q^{-2}\mathcal{X}_2) \tag{18}$$

$$D''(\mathcal{X}_4\mathcal{X}_2) = D''(q^2\mathcal{X}_2\mathcal{X}_4) + D''(\mathcal{X}_3) \tag{19}$$

We can obtain the fundamental solution system by solving Equations (18) *and* (19)*: $\xi_1 = (1,1,1,0)^T$ and $\xi_2 = (0,1,2,1)^T$.*

Let D''_1 and D''_2 be the derivatives corresponding to the fundamental solution system; therefore,

$$\begin{aligned} &D''_1(\mathcal{X}_1) = \mathcal{X}_1, && D''_1(\mathcal{X}_2) = \mathcal{X}_2, && D''_1(\mathcal{X}_3) = \mathcal{X}_3, && D''_1(\mathcal{X}_4) = 0, \\ &D''_2(\mathcal{X}_1) = 0, && D''_2(\mathcal{X}_2) = \mathcal{X}_2, && D''_2(\mathcal{X}_3) = 2\mathcal{X}_3, && D''_2(\mathcal{X}_4) = \mathcal{X}_4. \end{aligned}$$

Clearly, $D''_1 = D'_1$ and $D''_2 = D'_2$, so it can be concluded that the derivations of $U^+_q(B_2)$ can be expressed as

$$D'' = ad_g + \zeta_1 D''_1 + \zeta_2 D''_2 = D'$$

where $g \in U^+_q(B_2)$ and $\zeta_q, \zeta_2 \in Z(U^+_q(B2))$.

4.2. Obtain $Der(U^+_{v,t}(\mathfrak{g}))$ from $Der(U^+_v(\mathfrak{g}))$

It is worth noting that while it is relatively easy to derive a one-parameter quantum group from a two-parameter quantum group, the reverse process of obtaining a two-parameter quantum group from a one-parameter quantum group is usually more challenging. Therefore, in order to facilitate future research, this section begins with a review of the definition and key properties of the two-parameter quantum group introduced by Fan and Li.

Let I be a finite set, and fix a matrix $\Omega = (\Omega_{ij})_{i,j\in I}$ satisfying the following conditions:

(i) $\Omega_{ii} \in \mathbb{Z}_{>0}, \Omega_{ij} \in \mathbb{Z}_{\leq 0}$ for all $i \neq j \in I$;

(ii) $\frac{\Omega_{ij}+\Omega_{ji}}{\Omega_{ii}} \in \mathbb{Z}_{\leq 0}$ for all $i \neq j \in I$;

(iii) The greatest common divisor of all Ω_{ii} is equal to 1.

Connect matrix Ω with three bilinear forms on $\mathbb{Z}^I$:

$$\begin{aligned} &\langle i,j\rangle = \Omega_{ij}, \qquad \forall i,j \in I. \\ &[i,j] = 2\delta_{ij}\Omega_{ii} - \Omega_{ij}, \qquad \forall i,j \in I. \\ &i\cdot j = \langle i,j\rangle + \langle j,i\rangle, \qquad \forall i,j \in I. \end{aligned} \tag{20}$$

Definition 5. *Let $\Omega = (\Omega_{ij})_{i,j\in I}$ be the matrix as described above. The two-parameter quantum group $U_{v,t}$ associated to Ω is an associative $Q(v,t)$-algebra with 1 generated by symbols E_i, F_i, $K_i^{\pm 1}$, $K_i'^{\pm 1}$, $\forall \in I$ and subject to the following relations:*

$$\begin{aligned}
&(\mathrm{R1}) \quad K_i^{\pm 1}K_j^{\pm 1} = K_j^{\pm 1}K_i^{\pm 1}, \qquad K_i'^{\pm 1}K_j'^{\pm 1} = K_j'^{\pm 1}K_i'^{\pm 1}, \\
&\qquad\quad K_i^{\pm 1}K_j'^{\pm 1} = K_j'^{\pm 1}K_i^{\pm 1}, \qquad K_i^{\pm 1}K_i^{\mp 1} = 1 = K_i'^{\pm 1}K_i'^{\mp 1}, \\
&(\mathrm{R2}) \quad K_iE_jK_i^{-1} = v^{i\cdot j}t^{\langle i,j\rangle - \langle j,i\rangle}E_j, \qquad K_i'E_jK_i'^{-1} = v^{-i\cdot j}t^{\langle i,j\rangle - \langle j,i\rangle}E_j, \\
&\qquad\quad K_iF_jK_i^{-1} = v^{-i\cdot j}t^{\langle j,i\rangle - \langle i,j\rangle}F_j, \qquad K_i'F_jK_i'^{-1} = v^{i\cdot j}t^{\langle j,i\rangle - \langle i,j\rangle}F_j, \\
&(\mathrm{R3}) \quad E_iF_j - F_jE_i = \delta_{ij}\frac{K_i - K_i'}{v_i - v_i^{-1}}, \\
&(\mathrm{R4}) \quad \sum_{p+p'=1-2\frac{i\cdot j}{i\cdot i}} (-1)^p t_i^{-p\left(p'-2\frac{\langle i,j\rangle}{i\cdot i}+2\frac{\langle j,i\rangle}{i\cdot i}\right)} E_i^{(p')}E_jE_i^{(p)} = 0, \qquad if\ i \neq j, \\
&\qquad\quad \sum_{p+p'=1-2\frac{i\cdot j}{i\cdot i}} (-1)^p t_i^{-p\left(p'-2\frac{\langle i,j\rangle}{i\cdot i}+2\frac{\langle j,i\rangle}{i\cdot i}\right)} F_i^{(p)}F_jF_i^{(p')} = 0, \qquad if\ i \neq j,
\end{aligned}$$

where $E_i^{(p)} = \frac{E_i^p}{[p]!_{v_i,t_i}}$.

In reference [10], the author compared the algebraic structure $U_{v,t}$ with the two-parameter quantum group defined in Definition 2 and concluded that when $v = (rs^{-1})^{\frac{1}{2}}$ and $t = (rs)^{-\frac{1}{2}}$, the Serre relations of the algebraic $U_{v,t}$ are entirely consistent with those given in Definition 2. Therefore, our primary focus will be on studying how to derive the derivation algebra of $U_{v,t}^+(\mathfrak{g})$ from that of $U_v^+(\mathfrak{g})$.

We denote by $U_v^+(\mathfrak{g})$ the positive part of the quantum group $U = U_v(\mathfrak{g})$ over $\mathbb{Q}(v)$; it is the free $\mathbb{Q}(v)$ - algebra. Let Φ^+ be a positive root system of the complex simple Lie algebra of $\mathfrak{g}$, and $|\Phi^+| = n$. Let $\mathcal{X}_1, \cdots, \mathcal{X}_n$ be the quantum root vector of $U_v^+(\mathfrak{g})$ and satisfy the exchange relation (2).

Theorem 4. *Let $U_v^+(\mathfrak{g})$ be the positive part of the one-parameter quantum group $U_v(\mathfrak{g})$ corresponding to $\mathfrak{g}$; then, each derivation D of $U_v^+(\mathfrak{g})$ must be written in the following form:*

$$D(X_i) = ad_{\xi}(X_i) + \sum_k \mu_k a_{X_i}^{(k)}(X_i)X_i, \tag{21}$$

where $\xi \in U_v^+(\mathfrak{g})$, $\mu_k \in Z(U_v^+(\mathfrak{g}))$, $a_{X_i}^{(k)}(X_i) \in \mathbb{C}$, and $k = 1, \cdots, p(p \leq n)$, and the following equation holds:

$$a_{X_i}^{(k)}(X_i) + a_{X_j}^{(k)}(X_j) = a_{P(X_j,X_i)}^{(k)}(P(X_j,X_i)).$$

Proof. The proof for Theorem 4 mirrors that of Theorem 2; thus, we will not present a detailed proof. □

Theorem 5. *If $D_i(i = 1, \cdots, n)$ are the derivations of $U_v^+(\mathfrak{g})$ and $D_i(\mathcal{X}_j) = a_{ij}\mathcal{X}_j$, then there exists a mapping $D_i'(i = 1, \cdots, n)$, where $D_i'(X_j) = a_{ij}X_j$ are the derivations of $U_{v,t}^+(\mathfrak{g})$, and each derivation of $U_{v,t}^+(\mathfrak{g})$ can be uniquely written in the following form:*

$$D'(X_i) = ad_{\xi'}(X_i) + \sum_i c_i' a_{ij} X_j, \tag{22}$$

where $\xi' \in U_{v,t}^+(\mathfrak{g})$, $c_i' \in Z(U_{v,t}^+(\mathfrak{g}))$.

Proof. Let $U_{v,t} = U_v \otimes_{\mathbb{Q}(v)} \mathbb{Q}(v,t)$; according to Theorem 4 in reference [10], the bialgebra structure of U_v can be naturally extended to $U_{v,t}$. We define a new multiplication "$\circ$" on $U_{v,t}$ by

$$x \circ y = t^{[|x|,|y|]} xy,$$

for any homogeneous elements $x, y \in U_{v,t}$, where $[,]$ is defined in (20).

Since $\mathcal{X}_1, \cdots, \mathcal{X}_n$ are quantum root vectors of $U_v^+(\mathfrak{g})$ and satisfy Equation (2), the following formula holds for the algebra $U_{v,t}^+(\mathfrak{g})$:

$$\begin{aligned} & t^{-[|\mathcal{X}_i|,|\mathcal{X}_j|]}\mathcal{X}_i \circ \mathcal{X}_j - v^{(i,j)} t^{-[|\mathcal{X}_j|,|\mathcal{X}_i|]}\mathcal{X}_j \circ \mathcal{X}_i \\ = & \sum_{k=(k_{i+1},\cdots,k_{j-1})} c_k t^{-\left[\overbrace{|\mathcal{X}_{i+1}|,\cdots,|\mathcal{X}_{i+1}|}^{k_{i+1}},\cdots,\overbrace{|\mathcal{X}_{j-1}|,\cdots,|\mathcal{X}_{j-1}|}^{k_{j-1}}\right]} \mathcal{X}_{i+1}^{k_{i+1}} \circ \cdots \circ \mathcal{X}_{j-1}^{k_{j-1}}. \end{aligned} \tag{23}$$

If D' is the derivation of $U_{v,t}^+(\mathfrak{g})$, then we have

$$\begin{aligned} D'(\mathcal{X}_i \circ \mathcal{X}_j) &= D'(t^{[|\mathcal{X}_i|,|\mathcal{X}_j|]}\mathcal{X}_i\mathcal{X}_j) \\ &= t^{[|X_i|,|X_j|]} D'(\mathcal{X}_i\mathcal{X}_j). \end{aligned}$$

Therefore, we can conclude that if D' is a derivation of $U_{v,t}^+(\mathfrak{g})$, then D' acting on $U_v^+(\mathfrak{g})$ must be a derivation of $U_v^+(\mathfrak{g})$.

According to the given assumption, $D_i, i = 1, \cdots, n$ represents the derivation of $U_v^+(\mathfrak{g})$, with $D_i(\mathcal{X}_j) = a_{ij}\mathcal{X}_j$. Referring to Proposition 4, we can determine that $\mu D_i'$ are the derivation of $U_{v,t}^+(\mathfrak{g})$, where $\mu \in Z(U_{v,t}^+(\mathfrak{g}))$, $D_i'(\mathcal{X}_j) = a_{ij}\mathcal{X}_j$, Based on this, we can conclude that the theorem is valid. □

Example 3. *Suppose $\mathfrak{g}$ is a finite-dimensional complex simple Lie algebra of B_2-type. Moreover, it can be deduced that $U_v^+(B_2)$ is a $\mathbb{C}$-algebra generated by generators E_1 and E_2, and satisfies the following relationship:*

$$\begin{aligned} & E_1^2E_2 - (v^2 + v^{-2})E_1E_2E_1 + E_2E_1^2 = 0, \\ & E_1E_2^3 - (v^2 + 1 + v^{-2})E_2E_1E_2^2 + (v^2 + 1 + v^{-2})E_2^2E_1E_2 - E_2^3E_1 = 0. \end{aligned}$$

On the other hand, $\alpha_1, \alpha_1 + \alpha_2, \alpha_1 + 2\alpha_2, \alpha_2$ correspond to the quantum root vectors $\mathcal{X}_1$, $\mathcal{X}_2$, $\mathcal{X}_3$, $\mathcal{X}_4$ in $U_v^+(B_2)$:

$$\mathcal{X}_1 = E_1, \qquad \mathcal{X}_2 = E_1E_2 - v^2E_2E_2, \qquad \mathcal{X}_3 = E_2\mathcal{X}_2 - v^2\mathcal{X}_2E_2, \qquad \mathcal{X}_4 = E_2.$$

And there is an exchange relationship:

$$\begin{aligned} &\mathcal{X}_2\mathcal{X}_3 = \mathcal{X}_3\mathcal{X}_1, && \mathcal{X}_1\mathcal{X}_3 = \mathcal{X}_3\mathcal{X}_1, && \mathcal{X}_1\mathcal{X}_2 = v^{-2}\mathcal{X}_2\mathcal{X}_1, \\ &\mathcal{X}_4\mathcal{X}_3 = \mathcal{X}_3\mathcal{X}_4, && \mathcal{X}_4\mathcal{X}_2 = v^2\mathcal{X}_2\mathcal{X}_4 + \mathcal{X}_3, && \mathcal{X}_4\mathcal{X}_1 = v^{-2}\mathcal{X}_1\mathcal{X}_4 - v^{-2}\mathcal{X}_2. \end{aligned}$$

Suppose D is a derivation of $U_v^+(B_2)$. Since $U_v^+(B_2)$ is an iterated Ore extension, there is $D(\mathcal{X}_i) = a_{\mathcal{X}_i}(\mathcal{X}_i)\mathcal{X}_i$, $a_{\mathcal{X}_i}(\mathcal{X}_i) \in \mathbb{C}$. Therefore, we have

$$a_{\mathcal{X}_1}(\mathcal{X}_1) + a_{\mathcal{X}_4}(\mathcal{X}_4) = a_{\mathcal{X}_2}(\mathcal{X}_2), \tag{24}$$
$$a_{\mathcal{X}_2}(\mathcal{X}_2) + a_{\mathcal{X}_4}(\mathcal{X}_4) = a_{\mathcal{X}_3}(\mathcal{X}_3). \tag{25}$$

The fundamental solution system can be derived by solving Equations (24) and (27): $\xi_1 = (1,1,1,0)^T$ and $\xi_2 = (0,1,2,1)^T$. Let D_1 and D_2 be derivations corresponding to two fundamental solution systems; therefore, there are

$$\begin{array}{llll} D_1(\mathcal{X}_1) = \mathcal{X}_1, & D_1(\mathcal{X}_2) = \mathcal{X}_2, & D_1(\mathcal{X}_3) = \mathcal{X}_3, & D_1(\mathcal{X}_4) = 0, \\ D_2(\mathcal{X}_1) = 0, & D_2(\mathcal{X}_2) = \mathcal{X}_2, & D_2(\mathcal{X}_3) = 2\mathcal{X}_3, & D_2(\mathcal{X}_4) = \mathcal{X}_4. \end{array}$$

Then, each derivation D of $U_v^+(B_2)$ can be written in the following form:

$$D = ad_x + \mu_1 D_1 + \mu_2 D_2 \tag{26}$$

where $\mu_1, \mu_2 \in Z(U_v^+(B_2))$. Let $U_{v,t}(B_2) = U_v(B_2) \otimes_{\mathbb{Q}(v)} \mathbb{Q}(v,t)$; the bialgebra structure of $U_v(B_2)$ can be naturally extended to $U_{v,t}(B_2)$. According to Theorem 5, there exist two mappings D_1' and D_2' on $U_{v,t}^+(B_2)$, such that

$$\begin{array}{llll} D_1'(\mathcal{X}_1) = \mathcal{X}_1, & D_1'(\mathcal{X}_2) = \mathcal{X}_2, & D_1'(\mathcal{X}_3) = \mathcal{X}_3, & D_1'(\mathcal{X}_4) = 0, \\ D_2'(\mathcal{X}_1) = 0, & D_2'(\mathcal{X}_2) = \mathcal{X}_2, & D_2'(\mathcal{X}_3) = 2\mathcal{X}_3, & D_2'(\mathcal{X}_4) = \mathcal{X}_4. \end{array}$$

Therefore, the derivation D' of $U_{v,t}^+(B_2)$ can be written as

$$D'(\mathcal{X}_i) = ad_g(\mathcal{X}_i) + \zeta_1 D_1'(\mathcal{X}_i) + \zeta_2 D_2'(\mathcal{X}_i) \tag{27}$$

where $g \in U_{v,t}^+(B_2)$ and $\zeta_i \in Z(U_{v,t}^+(B_2))$.

Similar to the conclusion in Example 2, we can verify that each derivation of $U_{v,t}^+(B_2)$ can be represented as Equation (27).

5. Conclusions

In conclusion, this paper gives the derivation algebraic structure of a special class of iterated Ore extension, and discusses the relationship between derivation of one-parameter quantum groups and derivation of two-parameter quantum groups. Our results provide a new perspective for understanding the derivation algebra of quantum groups. Despite the important progress made in this paper, the application of derivation algebras to broader quantum groups needs to be further explored. For example, the derivation has a close relationship with the automorphism group of quantum groups; this relationship will help us gain a deeper understanding of quantum groups and their intrinsic properties of algebraic structures.

Author Contributions: Methodology, Y.Z.; validation, Y.Z. and X.T.; writing—original draft, Y.Z.; writing—review and editing, X.T. All authors have read and agreed to the published version of the manuscript.

Funding: This work has received funding from the National Natural Science Foundation of China (No. 12271085), the Heilongjiang Provincial Natural Science Foundation (No. LH2020 A020), and the Central University Basic Research Business Fund-Doctoral Research Innovation Fund Project (No. 3072022GIP2404).

Data Availability Statement: The original contributions presented in the study are included in the article, further inquiries can be directed to the corresponding author.

Conflicts of Interest: The authors declare no conflict of interest.

References

1. Drinfel'D, V. Hopf algebras and quantum Yang-Baxter equation. *Dokl. Akad.* **1985**, *32*, 254–258.
2. Benkart, G.; Witherspoon, S. A Hopf structure for down-up algebras. *Math. Z.* **2001**, *238*, 523–553. [CrossRef]
3. Benkart, G.; Witherspoon, S. Quantum group actions, twisting elements, and deformations of algebras. *J. Pure Appl. Algebra* **2007**, *208*, 371–389. [CrossRef]
4. Bergeron, N.; Yun, G.; Hu, N. Drinfel'd doubles and Lusztig's symmetries of two-parameter quantum groups. *J. Algebra* **2006**, *301*, 378–405. [CrossRef]
5. Bergeron, N.; Yun, G.; Hu, N. Representations of two-parameter quantum orthogonal groups and symplectic groups. *AMS/IP Stud. Adv. Math.* **2007**, *39*, 1–21.
6. Hu, N.; Shi, Q. The two-parameter quantum group of exceptional type G2 and Lusztig's symmetries. *Pac. J. Math.* **2007**, *230*, 327–345. [CrossRef]
7. Hu, N.; Wang, X. Convex PBW-type Lyndon bases and restricted two-parameter quantum groups of type B. *J. Geom. Phys.* **2010**, *6*, 430–453. [CrossRef]
8. Hu, N.; Pei, Y. Notes on two-parameter quantum groups (II). *Commun. Algebra* **2012**, *40*, 3202–3220. [CrossRef]
9. Hu, N.; Pei, Y. Notes on two-parameter quantum groups, (I). *Sci. China Ser. Math.* **2008**, *51* 1101–1110. [CrossRef]
10. Fan, Z.; Li, Y. Two-Parameter quantum algebras, canonical bases, and categorifications. *Int. Math. Res. Not.* **2015**, *16*, 7016–7062. [CrossRef]
11. Lalonde, P.; Arun, R. Standard Lyndon bases of Lie algebras and enveloping algebras. *Trans. Am. Math. Soc.* **1995**, *347*, 1821–1830. [CrossRef]
12. Elle, S. Classification of relation types of Ore extensions of dimension 5. *Commun. Ina.* **2017**, *45*, 1323–1346. [CrossRef]

Disclaimer/Publisher's Note: The statements, opinions and data contained in all publications are solely those of the individual author(s) and contributor(s) and not of MDPI and/or the editor(s). MDPI and/or the editor(s) disclaim responsibility for any injury to people or property resulting from any ideas, methods, instructions or products referred to in the content.

mathematics MDPI

Article

Exploring Commutativity via Generalized (α, β)-Derivations Involving Prime Ideals

Nawaf Alsowait [1], Radwan M. Al-omary [2,*], Zakia Al-Amery [3] and Mohammed Al-Shomrani [4]

[1] Department of Mathematics, College of Science, Northern Border University, Arar 73213, Saudi Arabia; Nawaf.Lazzam@nbu.edu.sa
[2] Department of Mathematics, Ibb University, Ibb, Yemen
[3] Department of Mathematics, Aden University, Aden, Yemen; alameryzakia@gmail.com
[4] Department of Mathematics, Faculty of Science, King Abdulaziz University, Jeddah 21589, Saudi Arabia; Malshamrani@kau.edu.sa
* Correspondence: raradwan959@gmail.com

Abstract: The purpose of this article is to enhance the previous studies regarding the behavior of a quotient ring $\Im/\wp$, where $\wp$ is a prime ideal in a ring $\Im$. In particular, we are going to explore more general scenarios whenever a ring $\Im$ admits a generalized (α,β)-derivation associated with an (α,β)-derivation ∂ that satisfies certain criteria involving $\wp$, where α and β are automorphisms on $\Im$. Moreover, we provide some examples to demonstrate the importance of the assumptions made in our results.

Keywords: prime ideal; integral domain; (α,β)-derivation; generalized (α,β)-derivations; quotient ring

MSC: 16W25; 16N60; 16U80

1. Introduction

Throughout this paper $\Im$ stands for an associative ring and its center is $Z(\Im)$. It is appropriate to start by recalling some well-known concepts about rings. A ring $\Im$ is called a prime ring if $\varsigma\Im\iota = 0$ for each $\varsigma,\iota \in \Im$, then either $\varsigma = 0$ or $\iota = 0$. An ideal $\wp$ of a ring $\Im$ with $\wp \neq \Im$ is called prime if $\varsigma\Im\iota \subseteq \wp$ ($\varsigma\iota \in \wp$) for $\varsigma,\iota \in \Im$, which implies that either $\varsigma \in \wp$ or $\iota \in \wp$. Consequently, $\Im$ is a prime ring if and only if $\{0\}$ is a prime ideal of $\Im$. We recall that a ring without non-zero divisors is a domain, and the integral domain is a commutative domain with identity. It is known that every integral domain is a prime ring and the converse needs not to be true in general. It is also known that $\wp$ is a prime ideal if and only if $\Im/\wp$ is an integral domain. Additionally, if $\wp$ is an ideal in a commutative ring $\Im$, then $\Im/\wp$ is commutative. It is worth mentioning prime ideal would make an interesting fertile topic to research, not only in rings, but also in algebras such as $BCI-$algebras, $C*$-algebra and Lie algebra (for more details, see refs. [1–4]). An additive map $\partial : \Im \longrightarrow \Im$ that satisfies $\partial(\varsigma\iota) = \partial(\varsigma)\iota + \varsigma\partial(\iota)$ for all $\varsigma,\iota \in \Im$ is called an ordinary derivation, while an additive map $\vartheta : \Im \longrightarrow \Im$ which satisfies $\vartheta(\varsigma\iota) = \vartheta(\varsigma)\iota + \varsigma\partial(\iota)$ for every $\varsigma,\iota \in \Im$ is called a generalized derivation, where ∂ is just an associated derivation map.

Suppose that $\alpha,\beta : \Im \longrightarrow \Im$ are automorphisms on $\Im$, then an additive map $\partial : \Im \longrightarrow \Im$ is called an (α,β)-derivation if it satisfies $\partial(\varsigma\iota) = \partial(\varsigma)\alpha(\iota) + \beta(\varsigma)\partial(\iota)$ for any two elements $\varsigma,\iota \in \Im$. Afterwards, this concept was expanded to a generalized $(\alpha,\beta)-$derivation as follows: $\vartheta(\varsigma\iota) = \vartheta(\varsigma)\alpha(\iota) + \beta(\varsigma)\partial(\iota)$ for any two elements $\varsigma,\iota \in \Im$. Without any controversy, this concept covers the generalized derivation when $\alpha = \beta = I$ as well as the ordinary derivation when $\vartheta = \partial$ and $\alpha = \beta = I$, where I the identity map on $\Im$. One of the basic problems in ring theory is to investigate the various conditions under which a ring $\Im$ becomes commutative. For this purpose, there has been a great deal of effort to link the commutativity of a prime or a semiprime ring $\Im$ with the existence of additive maps defined on it, such as a generalized (α,β)-derivation and an (α,β)-derivation that satisfy differential identities over the entire ring or any appropriate subset of it. For more details, the reader can refer—for example—to refs. [5–8]. As an extension of these studies, instead of proving commutativity on a prime or a semiprime ring, Almahdi et al. [9] strengthened it without imposing any restrictions on the ring $\Im$. They proved that either $\Im/\wp$ is a commutative integral domain or $\partial(\Im) \subseteq \wp$, if $\Im$ admits a derivation ∂ that satisfies $[[\partial(\varsigma),\varsigma],\iota] \in \wp$ for any $\varsigma,\iota \in \Im$, where $\wp$ is a prime ideal on $\Im$, which is generalized by the second Posner's Theorem. Before these authors, in ref. [10], Creedon generalized the first Posner's Theorem in prime ideal with two iterates of derivations when a ring is restricted by a characteristic two. In this direction, studies and interests have been continued by many researchers; see for example refs. [11–14]. In this article, instead of considering a generalized derivation, we examine differential identities involving a generalized (α,β)-derivation ϑ associated with an (α,β)-derivation ∂. Consequently, we prove that either $\Im/\wp$ is a commutative integral domain or $\partial(\Im) \subseteq \wp$, where $\wp$ is a prime ideal of an arbitrary ring $\Im$. Furthermore, we explore several sequels and special cases as corollaries of our results. Finally, we devote several examples to emphasize the necessity of the various hypotheses imposed in our theorems.

2. Preliminaries

For any pair of elements $\varsigma,\iota \in \Im$, the symbol $[\varsigma,\iota]$ indicates the commutator $\varsigma\iota - \iota\varsigma$ while $\varsigma \circ \iota$ indicates the anticommutator $\varsigma\iota + \iota\varsigma$. The following identities will be used vastly throughout this paper to make access easier to the proofs of our theorems that hold for all $\varsigma,\iota,\kappa \in \Im$:

$$
\begin{aligned}
[\varsigma\iota,\kappa] &= \varsigma[\iota,\kappa] + [\varsigma,\kappa]\iota \\
[\varsigma,\iota\kappa] &= \iota[\varsigma,\kappa] + [\varsigma,\iota]\kappa \\
\varsigma \circ (\iota\kappa) &= (\varsigma \circ \iota)\kappa - \iota[\varsigma,\kappa] = \iota(\varsigma \circ \kappa) + [\varsigma,\iota]\kappa \\
(\varsigma\iota) \circ \kappa &= \varsigma(\iota \circ \kappa) - [\varsigma,\kappa]\iota = (\varsigma \circ \kappa)\iota + \varsigma[\iota,\kappa].
\end{aligned}
$$

To develop our results, we exhibit the following important lemma:

Lemma 1 ([14], Lemma 1). *Let $\Im$ be a ring. If $\wp$ is a prime ideal of $\Im$, then $\Im/\wp$ is a commutative integral domain if any of the following holds, for every $\varsigma,\iota \in \Im$:*

(i) $[\varsigma,\iota] \in \wp$,
(ii) $\varsigma \circ \iota \in \wp$.

3. Main Results

In the context of this paper, the pair (ϑ,∂) stands for a generalized (α,β)-derivation associated with an (α,β)-derivation ∂, where the two maps $\alpha,\beta : \Im \longrightarrow \Im$ are automorphisms on $\Im$, unless we mention otherwise. Moreover, the map $I : \Im \longrightarrow \Im$, defined by $I(\varsigma) = \varsigma$ for any $\varsigma \in \Im$, expresses the identity map on $\Im$.

In ref. [15] (Lemma 2.1), Bera et al. showed that ∂ maps $\Im$ to $Z(\Im)$, if a semiprime ring $\Im$ admits a generalized (α,β)-derivation ϑ associated with an (α,β)-derivation ∂ such that $[\partial(\varsigma),\beta(\varsigma)] \in Z(\Im)$ for every $\varsigma \in \Im$. Here, we will verify a similar result without imposing any restrictions on $\Im$, as shown below:

Theorem 1. *Assume that ∂ is an (α,β)-derivation on an arbitrary ring $\Im$ such that $[\partial(\varsigma),\beta(\varsigma)] \in \wp$ for every $\varsigma \in \Im$, where $\wp$ is a prime ideal of $\Im$. Then $\Im/\wp$ is a commutative integral domain or the associated (α,β)-derivation ∂ maps $\Im$ to $\wp$.*

Proof. The given hypothesis states

$$[\partial(\varsigma),\beta(\varsigma)] \in \wp, \quad \text{for all } \varsigma \in \Im, \tag{1}$$

applying the linearity in the previous equation, we obtain

$$[\partial(\varsigma), \beta(\iota)] + [\partial(\iota), \beta(\varsigma)] \in \wp, \quad \text{for all } \varsigma, \iota \in \Im, \tag{2}$$

if we set $\varsigma\iota$ instead of ι in Equation (2) and use it in Equation (1), we have

$$\partial(\varsigma)[\alpha(\iota), \beta(\varsigma)] \in \wp, \quad \text{for all } \varsigma, \iota \in \Im,$$

again, we set $\iota\kappa$ instead of ι in the above relation to obtain

$$\partial(\varsigma)\alpha(\iota)[\alpha(\kappa), \beta(\varsigma)] \in \wp, \quad \text{for all } \varsigma, \iota, \kappa \in \Im, \tag{3}$$

according to the assumption that $\wp$ is prime and α is an automorphism on $\Im$, we deduce either $\partial(\varsigma) \in \wp$ or $[\alpha(\kappa), \beta(\varsigma)] \in \wp, \quad \text{for all } \varsigma, \kappa \in \Im$. Let $\Gamma = \{\varsigma \in \Im : \partial(\varsigma) \in \wp\}$ and $\Lambda = \{\varsigma \in \Im : [\alpha(\kappa), \beta(\varsigma)] \in \wp, \quad \text{for all } \kappa \in \Im\}$. Then, it can be easily verified that both Γ and Λ are additive subgroups of $\Im$ and their union equals $\Im$. Applying Brauer's trick, we obtain either $\Gamma = \Im$ or $\Lambda = \Im$. If $\Gamma = \Im$, then $\partial(\varsigma) \in \wp$, for all $\varsigma \in \Im$ and hence $\partial(\Im) \subseteq \wp$. On the other hand, if $\Lambda = \Im$, then $[\alpha(\kappa), \beta(\varsigma)] \in \wp, \quad \text{for all } \varsigma, \kappa \in \Im$. In the previous relation, as α, β are automorphisms on $\Im$, it is possible to set $\kappa = \alpha^{-1}(\nu)$ and $\varsigma = \beta^{-1}(\mu)$ to obtain $[\nu, \mu] \in \wp, \quad \text{for all } \nu, \mu \in \Im$. Thus, $\Im/\wp$ is a commutative integral domain, according to Lemma 1. □

Remark 1. *Lemma 2.1 of ref.* [9] *will be a special case of Theorem 1 by putting* $\alpha = \beta = I$.

The conclusion of ref. [14], Proposition 1.3, is that either $\Im/\wp$ or $\partial(\Im) \subseteq \wp$, when $\Im$ admits a generalized derivation that satisfies $[\vartheta(\varsigma), \varsigma] \in \wp$, for every $\varsigma \in \Im$, where $\wp$ is a prime ideal of $\Im$. Also, in ref. [11], Theorem 3.1, the same conclusion is obtained, when $\Im$ admits a multiplicative left-generalized (α, β)-derivation associated with an (α, β)-derivation ∂ that satisfies $[\alpha(\varsigma), \vartheta(\iota)] \in \wp$ for each $\varsigma, \iota \in \Im$, where α and β are automorphisms of $\Im$. The following theorem aims to discuss the effect of the identity $[\vartheta(\varsigma), \alpha(\varsigma)] \in \wp$ for any $\varsigma \in \Im$ on the behavior of the ring $\Im$.

Theorem 2. *Assume that* (ϑ, ∂) *is a generalized* (α, β)*-derivation on an arbitrary ring* $\Im$ *such that* $[\vartheta(\varsigma), \alpha(\varsigma)] \in \wp$ *for every* $\varsigma \in \Im$, *where* $\wp$ *is a prime ideal of* $\Im$. *Then,* $\Im/\wp$ *is a commutative integral domain or the associated* (α, β)*-derivation* ∂ *maps* $\Im$ *to* $\wp$.

Proof. For each $\varsigma \in \Im$, we have the following assumption:

$$[\vartheta(\varsigma), \alpha(\varsigma)] \in \wp. \tag{4}$$

Using the linearity in the previous equation, we obtain

$$[\vartheta(\varsigma), \alpha(\iota)] + [\vartheta(\iota), \alpha(\varsigma)] \in \wp, \quad \text{for all } \varsigma, \iota \in \Im.$$

Replacing ι with $\iota\varsigma$ in the last expression and using it in Equation (4) gives

$$\beta(\iota)[\partial(\varsigma), \alpha(\varsigma)] + [\beta(\iota), \alpha(\varsigma)]\partial(\varsigma) \in \wp, \quad \text{for all } \varsigma, \iota \in \Im. \tag{5}$$

For each $\kappa \in \Im$, we put $\kappa\iota$ in the place of ι in Equation (5) to obtain

$$\beta(\kappa)\beta(\iota)[\partial(\varsigma), \alpha(\varsigma)] + \beta(\kappa)[\beta(\iota), \alpha(\varsigma)]\partial(\varsigma) + [\beta(\kappa), \alpha(\varsigma)]\beta(\iota)\partial(\varsigma) \in \wp.$$

Multiplying Equation (5) from the left by $\beta(\kappa)$ and subtracting it from the previous equation, we obtain

$$[\beta(\kappa), \alpha(\varsigma)]\beta(\iota)\partial(\varsigma) \in \wp, \quad \text{for all } \varsigma, \iota, \kappa \in \Im. \tag{6}$$

Now, applying a similar argument as that after Equation (3), we obtain the desired conclusion. □

In ref. [8], Rehman et al. showed that L is contained in the center of a prime ring $(\Im, *)$ admitting a generalized (α, β)-derivation ϑ associated with an (α, β)-derivation ∂, that satisfies $\vartheta[\varsigma, \iota] - \alpha(\varsigma \circ \iota) = 0$ for all $\varsigma, \iota \in L$, where L is a Lie ideal and $*$ is an involution on $\Im$. In the following theorem, we will see what happens when the prior identity involves a prime ideal $\wp$ of a ring $\Im$ that is neither prime nor equipped with $*$.

Theorem 3. *Assume that (ϑ, ∂) is a generalized (α, β)-derivation on an arbitrary ring $\Im$ such that $\vartheta([\varsigma, \iota]) \pm \alpha(\varsigma \circ \iota) \in \wp$ for every $\varsigma, \iota \in \Im$, where $\wp$ is a prime ideal of $\Im$. Then, $\Im/\wp$ is a commutative integral domain or the associated (α, β)-derivation ∂ maps $\Im$ to $\wp$.*

Proof. From the given assumption, we have

$$\vartheta([\varsigma, \iota]) \pm \alpha(\varsigma \circ \iota) \in \wp, \quad \text{for all } \varsigma, \iota \in \Im, \tag{7}$$

if $\vartheta = 0$, then $\alpha(\varsigma \circ \iota) \in \wp$, for all $\varsigma, \iota \in \Im$. The automorphism property of α implies that $\alpha(\varsigma) \circ \alpha(\iota) \in \wp$, for all $\varsigma, \iota \in \Im$. We set $\varsigma = \alpha^{-1}(\nu)$ and $\iota = \alpha^{-1}(\mu)$ to obtain $\nu \circ \mu \in \wp$, for all $\nu, \mu \in \Im$. Hence, using Lemma 1, $\Im/\wp$ is a commutative integral domain.

From now on, let $\vartheta \neq 0$. Then, for all $\varsigma, \iota \in \Im$, we have

$$\vartheta([\varsigma, \iota]) \pm \alpha(\varsigma \circ \iota) \in \wp, \tag{8}$$

setting $\iota\varsigma$ instead of ι in Equation (8) gives

$$\vartheta[\varsigma, \iota]\alpha(\varsigma) + \beta[\varsigma, \iota]\partial(\varsigma) \pm \alpha(\varsigma \circ \iota)\alpha(\varsigma) \in \wp, \quad \text{for all } \varsigma, \iota \in \Im,$$

if we multiply Equation (8) by $\alpha(\varsigma)$ from the right and comparing it with the previous equation, we obtain

$$\beta[\varsigma, \iota]\partial(\varsigma) \in \wp, \quad \text{for all } \varsigma, \iota \in \Im,$$

but β is an automorphism on $\Im$, so the previous equation can be rewritten as $[\beta(\varsigma), \beta(\iota)]\partial(\varsigma) \in \wp$ for all $\varsigma, \iota \in \Im$. If we change ι by $\kappa\iota$ in the last relation and apply it, we find $[\beta(\varsigma), \beta(\kappa)]\beta(\iota)\partial(\varsigma) \in \wp$ for all $\varsigma, \iota, \kappa \in \Im$. By repeating the similar arguments and techniques after Equation (3), we obtain the desired result. □

Remark 2. *Corollary 11(1) of ref.* [13], *will be an immediate consequence of Theorem 3 by putting $\alpha = \beta = I$.*

As an application of the previous theorem, if $\Im$ is a prime ring, then we have the following corollary:

Corollary 1. *Assume that (ϑ, ∂) is a generalized (α, β)-derivation on a prime ring $\Im$ such that $\vartheta([\varsigma, \iota]) \pm \alpha(\varsigma \circ \iota) = 0$ for every $\varsigma, \iota \in \Im$. Then, $\Im$ is either commutative or the (α, β)-associated derivation ∂ is zero (in this case, ϑ outputs a left centralizer).*

The following theorem is an extension of ref. [7], Theorem 3.5.

Theorem 4. *Assume that (ϑ, ∂) is a generalized (α, β)-derivation on an arbitrary ring $\Im$ such that $\vartheta(\varsigma \circ \iota) \in \wp$, for every $\varsigma, \iota \in \Im$, where $\wp$ is a prime ideal of $\Im$. Then, $\Im/\wp$ is a commutative integral domain or the associated (α, β)-derivation ∂ maps $\Im$ to $\wp$.*

Proof. We start with the given assumption

$$\vartheta(\varsigma \circ \iota) \in \wp, \quad \text{for all } \varsigma, \iota \in \Im, \tag{9}$$

and set $\iota\varsigma$ instead of ι to have

$$\vartheta(\varsigma \circ \iota)\alpha(\varsigma) + \beta(\varsigma \circ \iota)\partial(\varsigma) \in \wp, \quad \text{for all } \varsigma, \iota \in \Im.$$

We multiply Equation (9) by $\alpha(\varsigma)$ from the right and subtract it from the previous equation to obtain

$$\beta(\varsigma \circ \iota)\partial(\varsigma) \in \wp, \quad \text{for all } \varsigma, \iota \in \Im.$$

Putting $\kappa\iota$ instead of ι in the previous equation and using it give $\beta([\varsigma, \kappa])\beta(\iota)\partial(\varsigma) \in \wp$ for each $\varsigma, \iota, \kappa \in \Im$, this equation is similar to Equation (3); so, following similar arguments and techniques with some necessary modifications leads to the desired result. □

Theorem 5. *Assume that (ϑ, ∂) is a generalized (α, β)-derivation on an arbitrary ring $\Im$ such that $\vartheta(\varsigma^2) \in \wp$ for every $\varsigma \in \Im$, where $\wp$ is a prime ideal of $\Im$. Then, $\Im/\wp$ is a commutative integral domain or otherwise the associated (α, β)-derivation ∂ maps $\Im$ to $\wp$.*

Proof. The given assumption states that

$$\vartheta(\varsigma^2) \in \wp, \quad \text{for all } \varsigma \in \Im,$$

Linearizing the previous equation and then applying it give $\vartheta(\varsigma\iota + \iota\varsigma) \in \wp$ for all $\varsigma, \iota \in \Im$, that is, $\vartheta(\varsigma \circ \iota) \in \wp$ for all $\varsigma, \iota \in \Im$ which is the same as the identity in Theorem 4. Therefore, following it induces the desired conclusion. □

Remark 3. *It is easy to verify that, if ϑ is a generalized (α, β)-derivation associated with an (α, β)-derivation ∂, then $\vartheta \pm \alpha$ is also a generalized (α, β)-derivation associated with an (α, β)-derivation ∂.*

Applying the previous remark in Theorem 4 leads to the following result:

Theorem 6. *Assume that (ϑ, ∂) is a generalized (α, β)-derivation on an arbitrary ring $\Im$ such that $\vartheta(\varsigma \circ \iota) \pm \alpha(\varsigma \circ \iota) \in \wp$ for every $\varsigma, \iota \in \Im$, where $\wp$ is a prime ideal of $\Im$. Then, $\Im/\wp$ is a commutative integral domain or ∂ maps $\Im$ to $\wp$.*

Proof. Given that ϑ is a generalized (α, β)-derivation with an (α, β)-derivation ∂, hence, according to Remark 3, $\vartheta \pm \alpha$ is also a generalized (α, β)-derivation that satisfies Identity 9. Thus, $(\vartheta \pm \alpha)(\varsigma \circ \iota) = \vartheta(\varsigma \circ \iota) \pm \alpha(\varsigma \circ \iota) \in \wp$ for each $\varsigma, \iota \in \Im$. Therefore, by employing similar arguments as those mentioned above, we can achieve the desired outcome. □

The question which arises here is whether Theorem 6 is still valid in the case of a commutator. The following theorem provides the answer:

Theorem 7. *Assume that (ϑ, ∂) is a generalized (α, β)-derivation on an arbitrary ring $\Im$ such that $\vartheta([\varsigma, \iota]) \pm \alpha[\varsigma, \iota] \in \wp$ for every $\varsigma, \iota \in \Im$, where $\wp$ is a prime ideal of $\Im$. Then, $\Im/\wp$ is a commutative integral domain or ∂ maps $\Im$ to $\wp$.*

Proof. Applying arguments and techniques similar to those used to prove Theorem 3 with a few necessary modifications yields the required proof. □

As an application of the previous theorem, we present the following corollary, which is a generalization of ref. [13], Theorem 6:

Corollary 2. *Assume that (ϑ, ∂) is a generalized (α, β)-derivation on an arbitrary ring $\Im$ such that $\vartheta([\varsigma, \iota]) \in \wp$ for every $\varsigma, \iota \in \Im$, where $\wp$ is a prime ideal of $\Im$. Then, $\Im/\wp$ is a commutative integral domain or ∂ maps $\Im$ to $\wp$.*

Proof. Note that Remark 3 states that $\vartheta \pm \alpha$ is a generalized (α, β)-derivation associated with an (α, β)-derivation ∂. Hence, we can immediately derive the proof by applying the identity $\vartheta([\varsigma, \iota]) \pm \alpha[\varsigma, \iota] \in \wp$ for every $\varsigma, \iota \in \Im$ in Theorem 7. □

Remark 4. *In the previous corollary, if we choose both α and β to be equal to the identity map, then ref.* [13], *Corollary 11(2), is directly taken as a special case.*

In ref. [15], Theorem 3.1, Bera et al. discuss the identities $\varrho(\varsigma\iota)+\partial(\varsigma)\vartheta(\iota)+\alpha(\varsigma\iota)=0$, $\varrho(\varsigma\iota)+\partial(\iota)\vartheta(\varsigma)+\alpha(\iota\varsigma)=0$ and $\varrho(\varsigma\iota)+\partial(\varsigma)\vartheta(\iota)+\alpha(\iota\varsigma)=0$ for all $\varsigma,\iota\in\aleph$, where $\aleph$ is a left ideal of a semiprime ring $\Im$ and ϱ,ϑ are two generalized (α,β)-derivations associated with (α,β)-derivations ζ,∂, respectively. In the following theorem, without imposing any restrictions on the ring $\Im$, we will discuss analog identities in a prime ideal for one generalized (α,β)-derivation ϑ associated with an (α,β)-derivation ∂.

Theorem 8. *Assume that (ϑ,∂) is a generalized (α,β)-derivation on an arbitrary ring $\Im$ such that $\vartheta(\varsigma\iota)+\partial(\varsigma)\vartheta(\iota)+\alpha(\varsigma\iota)\in\wp$ for every $\varsigma,\iota\in\Im$, where $\wp$ is a prime ideal of $\Im$. Then, the associated (α,β)-derivation ∂ maps $\Im$ to $\wp$ and $(\vartheta+\alpha)(\Im)\subseteq\wp$.*

Proof. We have

$$\vartheta(\varsigma\iota)+\partial(\varsigma)\vartheta(\iota)+\alpha(\varsigma\iota)\in\wp,\quad \text{for all } \varsigma,\iota\in\Im. \tag{10}$$

For each $\kappa\in\Im$, we put $\iota\kappa$ instead of ι in Equation (10) to obtain

$$\vartheta(\varsigma\iota)\alpha(\kappa)+\beta(\varsigma\iota)\partial(\kappa)+\partial(\varsigma)(\vartheta(\iota)\alpha(\kappa)+\beta(\iota)\partial(\kappa))+\alpha(\varsigma\iota)\alpha(\kappa)\in\wp. \tag{11}$$

Multiplying Equation (10) from the right by $\alpha(\kappa)$ and then comparing with Equation (11) yields

$$\beta(\varsigma\iota)\partial(\kappa)+\partial(\varsigma)\beta(\iota)\partial(\kappa)\in\wp,\quad \text{for all } \varsigma,\iota,\kappa\in\Im. \tag{12}$$

Once again, if we put $\varsigma\iota$ instead of ι in Equation (12), we obtain

$$\beta(\varsigma)\beta(\varsigma\iota)\partial(\kappa)+\partial(\varsigma)\beta(\varsigma)\beta(\iota)\partial(\kappa)\in\wp,\quad \text{for all } \varsigma,\iota,\kappa\in\Im. \tag{13}$$

Multiplying Equation (12) from the left by $\beta(\varsigma)$ and then comparing with Equation (13) yields

$$[\beta(\varsigma),\partial(\varsigma)]\beta(\iota)\partial(\kappa)\in\wp,\quad \text{for all } \varsigma,\iota,\kappa\in\Im,$$

that is

$$[\beta(\varsigma),\partial(\varsigma)]\Im\partial(\kappa)\subseteq\wp,\quad \text{for all } \varsigma,\kappa\in\Im.$$

Applying the hypothesis that $\wp$ is prime together with Brauer's trick, we obtain either $[\beta(\varsigma),\partial(\varsigma)]\in\wp$ for all $\varsigma\in\Im$, or $\partial(\kappa)\in\wp$ for all $\kappa\in\Im$.

We begin by assuming that for each $\kappa\in\Im$, $\partial(\kappa)\in\wp$. Hence, Equation (10) is reduced to $\vartheta(\varsigma)\alpha(\iota)+\alpha(\varsigma\iota)\in\wp$ for every $\varsigma,\iota\in\Im$. Thus, $(\vartheta(\varsigma)+\alpha(\varsigma))\alpha(\iota)\in\wp$ for every $\varsigma,\iota\in\Im$. Since $\wp$ is a prime ideal and α is an automorphism, then $\vartheta(\varsigma)+\alpha(\varsigma)\in\wp$ for every $\varsigma\in\Im$. Therefore, $(\vartheta+\alpha)(\Im)\subseteq\wp$.

On the other hand, if $[\beta(\varsigma),\partial(\varsigma)]\in\wp$, for all $\varsigma\in\Im$, then by Theorem 1, either $\Im/\wp$ is a commutative integral domain or ∂ maps $\Im$ to $\wp$. The second case was discussed above, so we consider the case that $\Im/\wp$ is a commutative integral domain. Hence, Equation (12): $\beta(\varsigma\iota)\partial(\kappa)+\partial(\varsigma)\beta(\iota)\partial(\kappa)\in\wp$, for all $\varsigma,\iota,\kappa\in\Im$ can be rewritten as $\beta(\iota)(\beta(\varsigma)+\partial(\varsigma))\partial(\kappa)\in\wp$, for all $\varsigma,\iota,\kappa\in\Im$. Using the two assumptions that β is an automorphism and $\wp\neq\Im$ is a prime ideal gives $(\beta(\varsigma)+\partial(\varsigma))\partial(\kappa)\in\wp$, for all $\varsigma,\kappa\in\Im$. Now, we put $\ell\varsigma$ instead of ς in the last equation and use it to have $\partial(\ell)\alpha(\varsigma)\partial(\kappa)\in\wp$ for all $\varsigma,\ell,\kappa\in\Im$. Since α is an automorphism, the previous equation becomes $\partial(\ell)\Im\partial(\kappa)\in\wp$ for all $\ell,\kappa\in\Im$. Thus, either $\partial(\ell)\in\wp$ or $\partial(\kappa)\in\wp$. Both cases yield $\partial(\Im)\subseteq\wp$. Therefore, as above, we conclude that $(\vartheta+\alpha)(\Im)\subseteq\wp$ as required. □

In the case that either $\alpha=\beta=I$ or $\Im$ is prime, we derive the following two corollaries, respectively:

Corollary 3. *Assume that* (ϑ, ∂) *is a generalized derivation on an arbitrary ring* $\Im$ *such that* $\vartheta(\varsigma\iota) + \partial(\varsigma)\vartheta(\iota) + \varsigma\iota \in \wp$ *for every* $\varsigma, \iota \in \Im$*, where* $\wp$ *is a prime ideal of* $\Im$*. Then,* ∂ *maps* $\Im$ *to* $\wp$ *and* $(\vartheta + I)(\Im) \subseteq \wp$*.*

Corollary 4. *Assume that* (ϑ, ∂) *is a generalized* (α, β)*-derivation on a prime ring* $\Im$ *such that* $\vartheta(\varsigma\iota) + \partial(\varsigma)\vartheta(\iota) + \alpha(\varsigma\iota) = 0$ *for every* $\varsigma, \iota \in \Im$*. Then, the associated* (α, β)*-derivation* ∂ *is zero and* $\vartheta = -\alpha$*.*

Theorem 9. *Assume that* (ϑ, ∂) *is a generalized* (α, β)*-derivation on an arbitrary ring* $\Im$ *such that* $\vartheta(\varsigma\iota) + \partial(\iota)\vartheta(\varsigma) + \alpha(\iota\varsigma) \in \wp$ *for every* $\varsigma, \iota \in \wp$*, where* $\wp$ *is a prime ideal of* $\Im$*. Then,* $\Im/\wp$ *is a commutative integral domain.*

Proof. According to the given hypothesis, we have

$$\vartheta(\varsigma\iota) + \partial(\iota)\vartheta(\varsigma) + \alpha(\iota\varsigma) \in \wp, \quad \text{for all } \varsigma, \iota \in \Im. \tag{14}$$

Setting $\varsigma\iota$ instead of ς in Equation (14) gives

$$\vartheta(\varsigma\iota)\alpha(\iota) + \beta(\varsigma\iota)\partial(\iota) + \partial(\iota)(\vartheta(\varsigma)\alpha(\iota) + \beta(\varsigma)\partial(\iota)) + \alpha(\iota\varsigma)\alpha(\iota) \in \wp. \tag{15}$$

Multiplying Equation (14) from the right by $\alpha(\iota)$ and then comparing with Equation (15) yields

$$\beta(\varsigma\iota)\partial(\iota) + \partial(\iota)\beta(\varsigma)\partial(\iota) \in \wp, \quad \text{for all } \varsigma, \iota \in \Im. \tag{16}$$

If we set $\iota\varsigma$ instead of ς in Equation (16), we obtain

$$\beta(\iota)\beta(\varsigma\iota)\partial(\iota) + \partial(\iota)\beta(\iota)\beta(\varsigma)\partial(\iota) \in \wp, \quad \text{for all } \varsigma, \iota \in \Im. \tag{17}$$

Now, multiplying Equation (16) from the left by $\beta(\iota)$ and comparing with Equation (17) yields

$$[\beta(\iota), \partial(\iota)]\beta(\varsigma)\partial(\iota) \in \wp, \quad \text{for all } \varsigma, \iota \in \Im.$$

The automorphism property of β gives

$$[\beta(\iota), \partial(\iota)]\Im\partial(\iota) \subseteq \wp, \quad \text{for all } \iota \in \Im.$$

where $\wp$ is prime, and applying Brauer's trick implies either $[\beta(\iota), \partial(\iota)] \in \wp$ for all $\iota \in \Im$, or $\partial(\iota) \in \wp$ for all $\iota \in \Im$. We start with the first case when $[\beta(\iota), \partial(\iota)] \in \wp$ for all $\iota \in \Im$ and apply Theorem 1, which implies that either $\Im/\wp$ is a commutative integral domain or ∂ maps $\Im$ to $\wp$. When ∂ maps $\Im$ to $\wp$, then Equation (14) can be reduced to $\vartheta(\varsigma)\alpha(\iota) + \alpha(\iota\varsigma) \in \wp$ for every $\varsigma, \iota \in \Im$. We set $\iota\kappa$ instead of ι in the previous equation and apply some calculations to obtain $\alpha(\iota)\alpha(\kappa)\alpha(\varsigma) - \alpha(\iota)\alpha(\varsigma)\alpha(\kappa) \in \wp$ for all $\varsigma, \iota, \kappa \in \Im$, which is equivalent to $\alpha(\iota)[\alpha(\kappa), \alpha(\varsigma)] \in \wp$ for any $\varsigma, \iota, \kappa \in \Im$. Since α is an automorphism on $\Im$, the previous expression becomes $\iota[\kappa, \varsigma] \in \wp$ for any $\varsigma, \iota, \kappa \in \Im$, which means that $\Im[\kappa, \varsigma] \subseteq \wp$. As $\wp$ is prime and does not equal to $\Im$, then the last relation becomes $[\kappa, \varsigma] \in \wp$ for any $\varsigma, \kappa \in \Im$. Then, applying Lemma 1 implies that $\Im/\wp$ is a commutative integral domain which completes the proof. □

Corollary 5. *Assume that* (ϑ, ∂) *is a generalized derivation on an arbitrary ring* $\Im$ *such that* $\vartheta(\varsigma\iota) + \partial(\iota)\vartheta(\varsigma) + \iota\varsigma \in \wp$ *for every* $\varsigma, \iota \in \Im$*, where* $\wp$ *is a prime ideal of* $\Im$*. Then,* $\Im/\wp$ *is a commutative integral domain.*

Corollary 6. *Assume that* (ϑ, ∂) *is a generalized derivation on a prime ring* $\Im$ *such that* $\vartheta(\varsigma\iota) + \partial(\iota)\vartheta(\varsigma) + \iota\varsigma = 0$ *for every* $\varsigma, \iota \in \Im$*. Then,* $\Im$ *is commutative.*

Theorem 10. *Assume that (ϑ, ∂) is a generalized (α, β)-derivation on an arbitrary ring $\Im$ such that $\vartheta(\varsigma\iota) + \partial(\varsigma)\vartheta(\iota) + \alpha(\iota\varsigma) \in \wp$ for every $\varsigma, \iota \in \Im$, where $\wp$ is a prime ideal of $\Im$. Then, $\Im/\wp$ is a commutative integral domain.*

Proof. By this hypothesis, we have

$$\vartheta(\varsigma\iota) + \partial(\varsigma)\vartheta(\iota) + \alpha(\iota\varsigma) \in \wp, \quad \text{for all } \varsigma, \iota \in \Im, \tag{18}$$

for any $\kappa \in \Im$, set $\iota\kappa$ instead of ι in Equation (18) to have

$$\vartheta(\varsigma\iota)\alpha(\kappa) + \beta(\varsigma\iota)\partial(\kappa) + \partial(\varsigma)\vartheta(\iota)\alpha(\kappa) + \partial(\varsigma)\beta(\iota)\partial(\kappa) + \alpha(\iota\kappa\varsigma) \in \wp. \tag{19}$$

Then, multiplying Equation (18) from the right by $\alpha(\kappa)$ and then comparing with Equation (19) yields

$$\beta(\varsigma\iota)\partial(\kappa) + \partial(\varsigma)\beta(\iota)\partial(\kappa) + \alpha(\iota\kappa\varsigma) - \alpha(\iota\varsigma\kappa) \in \wp, \quad \text{for all } \varsigma, \iota, \kappa \in \Im. \tag{20}$$

Choose $\varsigma = \kappa$ in Equation (20) to obtain

$$\beta(\varsigma\iota)\partial(\varsigma) + \partial(\varsigma)\beta(\iota)\partial(\varsigma) \in \wp, \quad \text{for all } \varsigma, \iota \in \Im.$$

The previous equation is similar to Equation (16), so we repeat similar arguments and techniques to obtain the desired goal. □

We can derive the following two corollaries:

Corollary 7. *Assume that (ϑ, ∂) is a generalized derivation on an arbitrary ring $\Im$ such that $\vartheta(\varsigma\iota) + \partial(\varsigma)\vartheta(\iota) + \iota\varsigma \in \wp$ for every $\varsigma, \iota \in \Im$, where $\wp$ is a prime ideal of $\Im$. Then, $\Im/\wp$ is a commutative integral domain.*

Corollary 8. *Assume that (ϑ, ∂) is a generalized derivation on a prime ring $\Im$ such that $\vartheta(\varsigma\iota) + \partial(\varsigma)\vartheta(\iota) + \iota\varsigma = 0$ for every $\varsigma, \iota \in \Im$. Then, $\Im$ is a commutative.*

Finally, we devoted the following examples to emphasize the necessity of the various hypotheses imposed in our theorems:

Example 1. *Let $\Im$ be the quaternions ring $\mathbb{H}$, that is*

$$\Im = \mathbb{H} = \{\mu = \alpha + \beta i + \gamma j + \delta k \quad | \quad \alpha, \beta, \gamma, \delta \in \mathbb{R}\}.$$

and let $\wp = \{0\}$ be a prime ideal of the quaternions ring $\mathbb{H}$. Define $(\vartheta, \partial), \alpha, \beta : \Im \longrightarrow \Im$ by

$$\vartheta(\mu) = \quad \partial(\mu) = n\mu, \quad \alpha(\mu) = 2n\mu, \quad \text{and} \quad \beta(\mu) = -2(n-1)\mu$$

where $n \in \mathbb{Z}$. It is easy to see that (ϑ, ∂) is a generalized (α, β)-derivation associated with ∂ where α and β are automorphisms on $\Im$. Furthermore, we can see that $[\partial(\varsigma), \beta(\varsigma)] \in \wp$ and $[\vartheta(\varsigma), \alpha(\varsigma)] \in \wp$ for every $\varsigma, \iota \in \Im$, although $\Im/\wp$ is not commutative and $\partial(\Im) \nsubseteq \wp$.

Example 2. *Let Λ be a ring with property $\rho^2 = 0$ and let $\Im = \{\begin{pmatrix} \varsigma & \iota \\ 0 & \varsigma \end{pmatrix} | \varsigma, \iota \in \Lambda\}$. Since $(\rho + \varrho)^2 = 0$ and $(\rho - \varrho)^2 = 0$, then $\rho \circ \varrho = 0$ and $[\rho, \varrho] = 0$ for any $\rho, \varrho \in \Lambda$. Let $\wp = \{\begin{pmatrix} 0 & \iota \\ 0 & 0 \end{pmatrix}\}$. Define $(\vartheta, \partial), \alpha, \beta : \Im \longrightarrow \Im$ by $\vartheta(\begin{pmatrix} \varsigma & \iota \\ 0 & \varsigma \end{pmatrix}) = \partial(\begin{pmatrix} \varsigma & \iota \\ 0 & \varsigma \end{pmatrix}) = \begin{pmatrix} 0 & \iota \\ 0 & 0 \end{pmatrix}$, $\alpha(\begin{pmatrix} \varsigma & \iota \\ 0 & \varsigma \end{pmatrix}) = \begin{pmatrix} 0 & 0 \\ 0 & \varsigma \end{pmatrix}$ and $\beta(\begin{pmatrix} \varsigma & \iota \\ 0 & \varsigma \end{pmatrix}) = \begin{pmatrix} \varsigma & 0 \\ 0 & 0 \end{pmatrix}$. It is easy to check that (ϑ, ∂) is a generalized (α, β)-derivation of $\Im$. Furthermore, (i) $[\partial(\varsigma), \beta(\varsigma)] \in \wp$, (ii) $[\vartheta(\varsigma), \alpha(\varsigma)] \in \wp$, (iii) $\vartheta([\varsigma, \iota]) \pm \alpha(\varsigma \circ \iota) \in \wp$, (iv) $\vartheta(\varsigma \circ \iota) \in \wp$, (v) $\vartheta(\varsigma^2) \in \wp$, (vi) $\vartheta(\varsigma \circ \iota) \pm \alpha(\varsigma \circ \iota) \in \wp$,* *(vii)* $\vartheta([\varsigma,\iota]) \in \wp$ *for every* $\varsigma,\iota \in \Im$. *Also, we note that* $\Im/\wp$ *is not an integral domain and* $\wp$ *is not a prime ideal as* $\begin{pmatrix} 0 & \iota \\ 0 & 0 \end{pmatrix}\begin{pmatrix} 0 & \varsigma \\ 0 & 0 \end{pmatrix} \in \wp$, *but neither* $\begin{pmatrix} 0 & \varsigma \\ 0 & 0 \end{pmatrix} \in \wp$ *nor* $\begin{pmatrix} 0 & \iota \\ 0 & 0 \end{pmatrix} \in \wp$. *Also,* α *and* β *are not automorphisms whenever* $\partial(\Im) \subseteq \wp$.

Example 3. *Let* $\Im = \mathbb{Z}[\varsigma]$ *be the ring of polynomial with integers coefficient, and let* $\wp =< \varsigma^2 >$. *Define* $(\vartheta,\partial),\alpha,\beta : \mathbb{Z}[\varsigma] \longrightarrow \mathbb{Z}[\varsigma]$ *by* $\vartheta(f(\varsigma)) = \partial(f(\varsigma)) = \varsigma f'(\varsigma)$, $\alpha(f(\varsigma)) = -f'(\varsigma)$, *and* $\beta(f(\varsigma)) = 2f'(\varsigma)$. *It is easy to verify that* (ϑ,∂) *is a generalized* (α,β)*-derivation associated with* ∂. *One can check that (i)* $[\partial(\varsigma),\beta(\varsigma)] \in \wp$, *(ii)* $[\vartheta(\varsigma),\alpha(\varsigma)] \in \wp$, *(iii)* $\vartheta([\varsigma,\iota]) \pm \alpha[\varsigma,\iota] \in \wp$, *(iv)* $\vartheta([\varsigma,\iota]) \in \wp$ *for every* $\varsigma,\iota \in \Im$, *although neither* $\mathbb{Z}[\varsigma]/ < \varsigma^2 >$ *is an integral domain nor* $\partial(\Im) \subseteq \wp$. *Also,* $\wp$ *is not a prime ideal in* $\mathbb{Z}[\varsigma]$, *since* $\varsigma(\varsigma+\varsigma^3) \in \wp$, *but* $\varsigma, \varsigma+\varsigma^3 \notin \wp$ *as well as* α *and* β *are not automorphisms. So, the primeness of* $\wp$ *and the automorphism property of* α *and* β *are necessary conditions.*

Example 4. *Let* $\Im = \{\begin{pmatrix} 0 & 0 & 0 \\ \varsigma & 0 & 0 \\ \iota & \kappa & 0 \end{pmatrix} | \varsigma,\iota,\kappa \in \mathbb{H}\}$, *where* $\mathbb{H}$ *is the Hamilton ring as in Example 1 and let* $\wp = \{\begin{pmatrix} 0 & 0 & 0 \\ 0 & 0 & 0 \\ 0 & 0 & 0 \end{pmatrix}\}$. *Define* $(\vartheta,\partial),\alpha,\beta : \Im \longrightarrow \Im$ *by* $\vartheta\begin{pmatrix} 0 & 0 & 0 \\ \varsigma & 0 & 0 \\ \iota & \kappa & 0 \end{pmatrix} = \begin{pmatrix} 0 & 0 & 0 \\ 0 & 0 & 0 \\ 0 & \kappa & 0 \end{pmatrix}$, $\partial\begin{pmatrix} 0 & 0 & 0 \\ \varsigma & 0 & 0 \\ \iota & \kappa & 0 \end{pmatrix} = \begin{pmatrix} 0 & 0 & 0 \\ \varsigma & 0 & 0 \\ 0 & 0 & 0 \end{pmatrix}$, $\alpha\begin{pmatrix} 0 & 0 & 0 \\ \varsigma & 0 & 0 \\ \iota & \kappa & 0 \end{pmatrix} = \begin{pmatrix} 0 & 0 & 0 \\ 0 & 0 & 0 \\ 2\kappa & 0 & 0 \end{pmatrix}$, *and* $\beta\begin{pmatrix} 0 & 0 & 0 \\ \varsigma & 0 & 0 \\ \iota & \kappa & 0 \end{pmatrix} = \begin{pmatrix} 0 & 0 & 0 \\ 2\kappa & 0 & 0 \\ 0 & 0 & 0 \end{pmatrix}$. *It is easy to verify that* (ϑ,∂) *is a generalized* $(\alpha,\ \beta)$*-derivation associated with an* $(\alpha,\ \beta)$*-derivation* ∂. *Also, one can check that (i)* $[\partial(\varsigma),\beta(\varsigma)] \in \wp$, *(ii)* $\vartheta([\varsigma,\iota]) \pm \alpha(\varsigma \circ \iota) \in \wp$, *(iii)* $\vartheta(\varsigma \circ \iota) \in \wp$, *(iv)* $\vartheta(\varsigma^2) \in \wp$, *(v)* $\vartheta(\varsigma \circ \iota) \pm \alpha(\varsigma \circ \iota) \in \wp$, *(vi)* $\vartheta[\varsigma,\iota] \pm [\varsigma,\iota] \in \wp$, *(vii)* $\vartheta([\varsigma,\iota]) \in \wp$, *(viii)* $\vartheta(\varsigma\iota) + \partial(\varsigma)\vartheta(\iota) + \alpha(\varsigma\iota) \in \wp$, *(ix)* $\vartheta(\varsigma\iota) + \partial(\iota)\vartheta(\varsigma) + \alpha(\iota\varsigma) \in \wp$, *for all* $\varsigma,\iota \in \Im$. *However, neither* $\Im/\wp$ *commutative nor* ∂ *maps the ring* $\Im$ *to a prime ideal* $\wp$. *Note that* $\wp$ *is not a prime ideal of* $\Im$ *since* $\begin{pmatrix} 0 & 0 & 0 \\ \varsigma & 0 & 0 \\ 0 & 0 & 0 \end{pmatrix}^2 \in \wp$ *but* $\begin{pmatrix} 0 & 0 & 0 \\ \varsigma & 0 & 0 \\ 0 & 0 & 0 \end{pmatrix} \notin \wp$.

4. Conclusions

In the current article, we continued the study of generalized (α,β)-derivation associated with (α,β)-derivation via a contemporary approach wherein we assume the ring $\Im$ is without restriction and the studied identities involved in prime ideal $\wp$. We have reached the following results: associated derivation maps a ring $\Im$ to $\wp$, or a quotient ring of $\Im$ by prime ideal $\wp$ becomes a commutative integral domain, or a combination of generalized (α,β)-derivation with automorphism α maps a ring $\Im$ to $\wp$, where one or more holds, as proven in this article. We conclude with four examples clarifying the necessity of the considered assumption herein.

Author Contributions: This paper is the result of the joint effort of N.A., R.M.A.-o., Z.A.-A. and M.A.-S. All authors have read and agreed to the published version of the manuscript.

Funding: The authors extend their appreciation to the Deanship of Scientific Research (DSR) at Northern Border University, Arar, KSA, for funding this research work "through the project number" NBU-FPEJ-2024-2089-01.

Data Availability Statement: All data required of this article be included within this article.

Conflicts of Interest: The authors declare no conflicts of interest.

References

1. Acar, U.; Öztürk, Y. Maximal, irreducible, and prime soft ideals of $BCK/BCI-$algebras. *Hacettepe J. Math. Stats.* **2015**, *44*, 1–13. [CrossRef]
2. Kawamoto, N. On prime ideals of Lie algebra. *Hiroshima Math. J.* **1974**, *4*, 679–684. [CrossRef]
3. Gardella, E.; Thiel, H. Prime ideal in C^*-algebra and application to Lie Theory. *arXiv* **2023**, arXiv:2306.16510v2[math.0A].
4. Fitira, E.; Gemawati, S.; Kartini. Prime ideal in $B-$algebras. *Int. J. Algeb.* **2017**, *11*, 301–309. [CrossRef]
5. Ali, F.; Chaudhry, M.A. On generalized (α, β)-derivations of semiprime rings. *Turk. J. Math.* **2011**, *35*, 399–404. [CrossRef]
6. Garg, C.; Sharma, R.K. On generalized (α, β)-derivations in prime rings. *Rend. Circ. Math. Palermo Ser. 2* **2016**, *65*, 175–184. [CrossRef]
7. Marubayashi, H.; Ashraf, M.; Rehman, N.; Ali, S. On generalized (α, β)-derivations in prime rings. *Algeb. Colloq.* **2010**, *17*, 865–874. [CrossRef]
8. Rehman, N.; Al-Omary, R.M.; Shuliang, H. Lie ideals and generalized (α, β)-derivations of $*$-prime Rings. *Afr. Math.* **2013**, *24*, 503–510. [CrossRef]
9. Almahdi, F.; Mamouni, A.; Tamekkante, M. A generalization of Posner's theorem on derivations in ring. *Indian J. Pure Appl. Math.* **2020**, *51*, 187–194. [CrossRef]
10. Creedon, T. Derivations and prime ideals. *Math. Proc. R. Irish Acad.* **1998**, *A*, 223–225.
11. Boua, A.; Sandhu, G.S. Results on Various Derivations and Posner's Theorem in Prime Ideals of Rings. *Bol. Soc. Paran. Mat.* **2023**, *3*, 1–13. [CrossRef]
12. Rehman, N.; Alnoghashi, N.; Honagn, M. On generalized derivations involving prime ideals with involution. *Ukr. Math. J.* **2024**, *75*, 1219–1241. [CrossRef]
13. Rehman, N.; Alnoghashi, H.M. $\mathcal{T}$-commuting generalized derivations on ideals and semiprime ideal-*II*. *Math. Stud.* **2022**, *57*, 98–110. [CrossRef]
14. Rehman, N.; Al Noghashi, H. Action of prime ideals on generalized derivations-I. *arXiv* **2021**, arXiv:2107.06769.
15. Bera, M.; Dhara, B.; Kar, S. Some identities involving generalized (α, β)-derivations in prime and semiprime rings. *Asian-Eur. J. Math.* **2023**, *16*, 1–14. [CrossRef]

Disclaimer/Publisher's Note: The statements, opinions and data contained in all publications are solely those of the individual author(s) and contributor(s) and not of MDPI and/or the editor(s). MDPI and/or the editor(s) disclaim responsibility for any injury to people or property resulting from any ideas, methods, instructions or products referred to in the content.

mathematics

MDPI

Article

Cohomology and Crossed Modules of Modified Rota–Baxter Pre-Lie Algebras

Fuyang Zhu [1] and Wen Teng [2,*]

[1] School of Mathematical Sciences, Guizhou Normal University, Guiyang 550025, China; 18030060013@gznu.edu.cn

[2] School of Mathematics and Statistics, Guizhou University of Finance and Economics, Guiyang 550025, China

* Correspondence: tengwen@mail.gufe.edu.cn

Abstract: The goal of the present paper is to provide a cohomology theory and crossed modules of modified Rota–Baxter pre-Lie algebras. We introduce the notion of a modified Rota–Baxter pre-Lie algebra and its bimodule. We define a cohomology of modified Rota–Baxter pre-Lie algebras with coefficients in a suitable bimodule. Furthermore, we study the infinitesimal deformations and abelian extensions of modified Rota–Baxter pre-Lie algebras and relate them with the second cohomology groups. Finally, we investigate skeletal and strict modified Rota–Baxter pre-Lie 2-algebras. We show that skeletal modified Rota–Baxter pre-Lie 2-algebras can be classified into the third cohomology group, and strict modified Rota–Baxter pre-Lie 2-algebras are equivalent to the crossed modules of modified Rota–Baxter pre-Lie algebras.

Keywords: pre-Lie algebra; modified Rota–Baxter operator; cohomology; deformation; abelian extension; pre-Lie 2-algebra; crossed module

MSC: 17A01; 17B30; 17B10; 17B38; 17B56

1. Introduction

Cayley [1] first introduced pre-Lie algebras (also called left-symmetric algebras) in the context of rooted tree algebras. Independently, Gerstenhaber [2] also introduced pre-Lie algebras in the deformation theory of rings and algebras. Pre-Lie algebras arose from the study of affine manifolds, affine structures on Lie groups and convex homogeneous cones [3], and then appeared in geometry and physics, such as integrable systems, classical and quantum Yang–Baxter equations [4,5], quantum field theory, Poisson brackets, operands, complex and symplectic structures on Lie groups and Lie algebras [6]. Also see [7–18] for some interesting related studies about pre-Lie algebras.

Rota–Baxter operators on associative algebras were first introduced by Baxter [19] in his study of probability fluctuation theory, and then it was further developed by Rota [20]. The Rota–Baxter operator has been widely used in many fields of mathematics and physics, including combinatorics, number theory, operands and quantum field theory [21]. The cohomology and deformation theory of Rota–Baxter operators of weight zero have been studied on various algebraic structures; see [22–26]. Recently, Wang and Zhou [27] and Das [28] studied Rota–Baxter associative algebras of any weight using different methods. Inspired by Wang and Zhou's work, Das [29] considered the cohomology and deformations of weighted Rota–Baxter Lie algebras. The authors in [30,31] developed the cohomology, extensions and deformations of Rota–Baxter 3-Lie algebras with any weight. In [32], Chen, Lou and Sun studied the cohomology and extensions of Rota–Baxter Lie triple systems. See also [33] for weighted Rota–Baxter Lie supertriple systems.

The term modified Rota–Baxter operator stemmed from the notion of the modified classical Yang–Baxter equation, which was also introduced in the work of Semenov-Tian-

Shansky [34] as a modification of the operator form of the classical Yang–Baxter equation. Recently, Jiang and Sheng the established cohomology and deformation theory of modified r-matrices in [35]. Inspired by the modified r matrix [34,35], due to the importance of pre-Lie algebras, we naturally study modified Rota–Baxter pre-Lie algebras. More precisely, we introduce the notion of a modified Rota–Baxter pre-Lie algebra and its bimodule. We define a cochain map, Υ, and then the cohomology of modified Rota–Baxter pre-Lie algebras with coefficients in a bimodule is constructed. Finally, as applications of our proposed cohomology theory, we consider the infinitesimal deformations and abelian extensions of a modified Rota–Baxter pre-Lie algebra in terms of second cohomology groups. In addition, we further classify skeletal modified Rota–Baxter pre-Lie 2-algebras using the third cohomology group of a modified Rota–Baxter pre-Lie algebra, and show that strict modified Rota–Baxter pre-Lie 2-algebras are equivalent to crossed modules of modified Rota–Baxter pre-Lie algebras.

This paper is organized as follows. In Section 2, we introduce the concept of modified Rota–Baxter pre-Lie algebras, and give its bimodules. In Section 3, we establish the cohomology theory of modified Rota–Baxter pre-Lie algebras with coefficients in a bimodule, and apply it to the study of infinitesimal deformation. In Section 4, we discuss an abelian extension of the modified Rota–Baxter pre-Lie algebras in terms of our second cohomology groups. Finally, in Section 5, we classify skeletal modified Rota–Baxter pre-Lie 2-algebras using the third cohomology group. Then, we introduce the notion of crossed modules of modified Rota–Baxter pre-Lie algebras, and show that strict modified Rota–Baxter pre-Lie 2-algebras are equivalent to crossed modules of modified Rota–Baxter pre-Lie algebras.

Throughout this paper, $\mathbb{K}$ denotes a field of characteristic zero. All the vector spaces and (multi)linear maps are taken over $\mathbb{K}$.

2. Bimodules of Modified Rota–Baxter Pre-Lie Algebras

In this section, we introduce the notion of modified Rota–Baxter pre-Lie algebras and give some examples. Next, we propose the bimodule of modified Rota–Baxter pre-Lie algebras. Finally, we establish a new modified Rota–Baxter pre-Lie algebra and give its bimodule.

First, let us recall some definitions and results of pre-Lie algebra and its bimodules from [2,8].

Definition 1 ([2]). *A pre-Lie algebra is a pair $(\mathcal{P}, \bullet)$ consisting of a vector space, $\mathcal{P}$, and a binary operation, $\bullet, \mathcal{P} \times \mathcal{P} \to \mathcal{P}$, such that for all $a, b, c \in \mathcal{P}$, the associator:*

$$(a, b, c) = (a \bullet b) \bullet c - a \bullet (b \bullet c),$$

is symmetric in a, b, i.e.,

$$(a, b, c) = (b, a, c), \text{ or equivalently, } (a \bullet b) \bullet c - a \bullet (b \bullet c) = (b \bullet a) \bullet c - b \bullet (a \bullet c). \quad (1)$$

Given a pre-Lie algebra $(\mathcal{P}, \bullet)$, the commutator, $[a, b]^c = a \bullet b - b \bullet a$, defines a Lie algebra structure on $\mathcal{P}$, which is called the sub-adjacent Lie algebra of $(\mathcal{P}, \bullet)$, and we denote it by $\mathcal{P}^c$.

Inspired by the modified r-matrix [34,35], we propose the notion of a modified Rota–Baxter operator on pre-Lie algebras.

Definition 2. *(i) Let $(\mathcal{P}, \bullet)$ be a pre-Lie algebra. A modified Rota–Baxter operator on $\mathcal{P}$ is a linear map, $M : \mathcal{P} \to \mathcal{P}$, subject to the following:*

$$Ma \bullet Mb = M(Ma \bullet b + a \bullet Mb) - a \bullet b \text{ for all } a, b \in \mathcal{P}. \quad (2)$$

Furthermore, the triple $(\mathcal{P}, \bullet, M)$ is called a modified Rota–Baxter pre-Lie algebra, simply denoted by $(\mathcal{P}, M)$.

(ii) A homomorphism between two modified Rota–Baxter pre-Lie algebras $(\mathcal{P}_1, M_1)$ and $(\mathcal{P}_2, M_2)$ is a pre-Lie algebra homomorphism, $F : \mathcal{P}_1 \to \mathcal{P}_2$, such that $F \circ M_1 = M_2 \circ F$. Furthermore, F is called an isomorphism from $(\mathcal{P}_1, M_1)$ to $(\mathcal{P}_2, M_2)$ if F is bijective.

Example 1. *Let $(\mathcal{P}, \bullet)$ be a pre-Lie algebra. Then, $(\mathcal{P}, \bullet, \mathrm{id}_{\mathcal{P}})$ is a modified Rota–Baxter pre-Lie algebra, where $\mathrm{id}_{\mathcal{P}} : \mathcal{P} \to \mathcal{P}$ is an identity mapping.*

Example 2. *Let $(\mathcal{P}, \bullet)$ be a two-dimensional pre-Lie algebra and $\{\epsilon_1, \epsilon_2\}$ be a basis, whose nonzero products are given as follows:*

$$\epsilon_1 \bullet \epsilon_2 = \epsilon_1, \quad \epsilon_2 \bullet \epsilon_2 = \epsilon_2.$$

Then, the triple $(\mathcal{P}, \bullet, M)$ is a two-dimensional modified Rota–Baxter pre-Lie algebra, where $M = \begin{pmatrix} 1 & k \\ 0 & -1 \end{pmatrix}$, for $k \in \mathbb{K}$.

Example 3. *Let $(\mathcal{P}, \bullet)$ be a pre-Lie algebra. If a linear map, $M : \mathcal{P} \to \mathcal{P}$, is a modified Rota–Baxter operator, then $-M$ is also a modified Rota–Baxter operator.*

Definition 3 ([16]). *Let $(\mathcal{P}, \bullet)$ be a pre-Lie algebra. A Rota–Baxter operator of weight-1 on $\mathcal{P}$ is a linear map, $R : \mathcal{P} \to \mathcal{P}$, subject to the following:*

$$Ra \bullet Rb = R(Ra \bullet b + a \bullet Rb - a \bullet b) \text{ for all } a, b \in \mathcal{P}.$$

Then, the triple $(\mathcal{P}, \bullet, R)$ is called a Rota–Baxter pre-Lie algebra of weight-1.

Proposition 1. *Let $(\mathcal{P}, \bullet)$ be a pre-Lie algebra. If a linear map, $R : \mathcal{P} \to \mathcal{P}$, is a Rota–Baxter operator of weight -1, then the map, $2R - \mathrm{id}_{\mathcal{P}}$, is a modified Rota–Baxter operator on $\mathcal{P}$.*

Proof. For any $a, b \in \mathcal{P}$, we have the following:

$$\begin{aligned}
&(2R - \mathrm{id}_{\mathcal{P}})a \bullet (2R - \mathrm{id}_{\mathcal{P}})b \\
&= (2Ra - a) \bullet (2Rb - b) \\
&= 4Ra \bullet Rb - 2Ra \bullet b - 2a \bullet Rb + a \bullet b \\
&= 4R(Ra \bullet b + a \bullet Rb - a \bullet b) - 2Ra \bullet b - 2a \bullet Rb + a \bullet b \\
&= (2R - \mathrm{id}_{\mathcal{P}})\big((2R - \mathrm{id}_{\mathcal{P}})a \bullet b + a \bullet (2R - \mathrm{id}_{\mathcal{P}})b\big) - a \bullet b.
\end{aligned}$$

The proposition follows. □

Recall from [16] that a Nijenhuis operator on a pre-Lie algebra $(\mathcal{P}, \bullet)$ is a linear map, $N : \mathcal{P} \to \mathcal{P}$, that satisfies the following,

$$Na \bullet Nb = N(Na \bullet b + a \bullet Nb - N(a \bullet b)),$$

for all $a, b \in \mathcal{P}$. The relationship between the modified Rota–Baxter operator and Nijenhuis operator is as follows, which proves to be obvious.

Proposition 2. *Let $(\mathcal{P}, \bullet)$ be a pre-Lie algebra and $N : \mathcal{P} \to \mathcal{P}$ be a linear map. If $N^2 = \mathrm{id}_{\mathcal{P}}$, then N is a Nijenhuis operator if, and only if, N is a modified Rota–Baxter operator.*

Definition 4 ([8]). *Let $(\mathcal{P}, \bullet)$ be a pre-Lie algebra and V a vector space. A bimodule of $\mathcal{P}$ on V consists of a pair $(\bullet_l, \bullet_r)$, where $\bullet_l : \mathcal{P} \times V \to V$ and $\bullet_r : V \times \mathcal{P} \to V$ are two linear maps satisfying the following:*

$$\begin{aligned}
&a \bullet_l (b \bullet_l u) - (a \bullet b) \bullet_l u = b \bullet_l (a \bullet_l u) - (b \bullet a) \bullet_l u, \\
&a \bullet_l (u \bullet_r b) - (a \bullet_l u) \bullet_r b = u \bullet_r (a \bullet b) - (u \bullet_r a) \bullet_r b \text{ for all } a, b \in \mathcal{P}, u \in V.
\end{aligned}$$

Definition 5. *A bimodule of the modified Rota–Baxter pre-Lie algebra* $(\mathcal{P}, \bullet, M)$ *is a quadruple* $(V; \bullet_l, \bullet_r, M_V)$ *such that the following conditions are satisfied:*
(i) $(V; \bullet_l, \bullet_r)$ *is a bimodule of the pre-Lie algebra* $(\mathcal{P}, \bullet)$ *;*
(ii) $M_V : V \to V$ *is a linear map satisfying the following equations,*

$$Ma \bullet_l M_V u = M_V(Ma \bullet_l u + a \bullet_l M_V u) - a \bullet_l u, \tag{3}$$
$$M_V u \bullet_r Ma = M_V(M_V u \bullet_r a + u \bullet_r Ma) - u \bullet_r a, \tag{4}$$

for $a \in \mathcal{P}$ *and* $u \in V$*. In this case, the quadruple* $(V; \bullet_l, \bullet_r, M_V)$ *is also called a representation over* $(\mathcal{P}, \bullet, M)$*.*

Example 4. $(\mathcal{P}; \bullet_l = \bullet_r = \bullet, M)$ *is an adjoint bimodule of the modified Rota–Baxter pre-Lie algebra* $(\mathcal{P}, \bullet, M)$*.*

Next, we construct the semidirect product of the modified Rota–Baxter pre-Lie algebra.

Proposition 3. *The quadruple* $(V; \bullet_l, \bullet_r, M_V)$ *is a bimodule of a modified Rota–Baxter pre-Lie algebra* $(\mathcal{P}, \bullet, M)$ *if, and only if,* $\mathcal{P} \oplus V$ *is a modified Rota–Baxter pre-Lie algebra with the following maps,*

$$(a + u) \bullet_\ltimes (b + v) := a \bullet b + a \bullet_l v + u \bullet_r b,$$
$$M \oplus M_V(a + u) = Ma + M_V u,$$

for $a \in \mathcal{P}$ *and* $u \in V$*. In the case, the modified Rota–Baxter pre-Lie algebra* $\mathcal{P} \oplus V$ *is called a semidirect product of* $\mathcal{P}$ *and* V*, denoted by* $\mathcal{P} \ltimes V = (\mathcal{P} \oplus V, \bullet_\ltimes, M \oplus M_V)$*.*

Proof. Firstly, it is easy to verify that $(\mathcal{P} \oplus V, \bullet_\ltimes)$ is a pre-Lie algebra. In addition, for any $a, b \in \mathcal{P}$ and $u, v \in V$, via Equations (2)–(4), we have

$$\begin{aligned}
&M \oplus M_V(a + u) \bullet_\ltimes M \oplus M_V(b + v) \\
&= (Ma + M_V u) \bullet_\ltimes (Mb + M_V v) \\
&= Ma \bullet Mb + Ma \bullet_l M_V v + M_V u \bullet_r Mb \\
&= M(Ma \bullet b + a \bullet Mb) - a \bullet b + M_V(Ma \bullet_l u + a \bullet_l M_V u) - a \bullet_l u \\
&\quad + M_V(M_V u \bullet_r b + u \bullet_r Mb) - u \bullet_r b \\
&= M \oplus M_V((a + u) \bullet_\ltimes M \oplus M_V(b + v) + M \oplus M_V(a + u) \bullet_\ltimes (b + v)) - (a + u) \bullet_\ltimes (b + v),
\end{aligned}$$

which means that $(\mathcal{P} \oplus V, \bullet_\ltimes, M \oplus M_V)$ is a modified Rota–Baxter pre-Lie algebra. □

Proposition 4. *Let* $(\mathcal{P}, \bullet, M)$ *be a modified Rota–Baxter pre-Lie algebra. Define a new operation as follows:*

$$a \bullet_M b = Ma \bullet b + a \bullet Mb \ \text{ for all } a, b \in \mathcal{P}. \tag{5}$$

Then, (i) $(\mathcal{P}, \bullet_M)$ *is a pre-Lie algebra. We denote this pre-Lie algebra as* $\mathcal{P}_M$*.*
(ii) $(\mathcal{P}_M, M)$ *is a modified Rota–Baxter pre-Lie algebra.*

Proof. (i) For any $a, b, c \in \mathcal{P}$, according to Equations (1) and (2), we have the following:

$$\begin{aligned}
&(a \bullet_M b) \bullet_M c - a \bullet_M (b \bullet_M c) \\
&= M(Ma \bullet b + a \bullet Mb) \bullet c + (Ma \bullet b + a \bullet Mb) \bullet Mc - Ma \bullet (Mb \bullet c + b \bullet Mc) \\
&\quad - a \bullet M(Mb \bullet c + b \bullet Mc) \\
&= M(Mb \bullet a + b \bullet Ma) \bullet c + (Mb \bullet a + b \bullet Ma) \bullet Mc - Mb \bullet (Ma \bullet c + a \bullet Mc) \\
&\quad - b \bullet M(Ma \bullet c + a \bullet Mc) \\
&= (b \bullet_M a) \bullet_M c - b \bullet_M (a \bullet_M c).
\end{aligned}$$

Thus, $(\mathcal{P}, \bullet_M)$ is a pre-Lie algebra.

(ii) For any $a, b \in \mathcal{P}$, according to Equation (2), we have

$$\begin{aligned}
Ma \bullet_M Mb =& M^2a \bullet Mb + Ma \bullet M^2b \\
=& M(M^2a \bullet b + Ma \bullet Mb) - Ma \bullet b + M(Ma \bullet Mb + a \bullet M^2b) - a \bullet Mb \\
=& M(Ma \bullet_M b + Ma \bullet_M b) - a \bullet_M b.
\end{aligned}$$

Hence, $(\mathcal{P}_M, M)$ is a modified Rota–Baxter pre-Lie algebra. □

Proposition 5. *Let $(V; \bullet_l, \bullet_r, M_V)$ be a bimodule of the modified Rota–Baxter pre-Lie algebra, $(\mathcal{P}, \bullet, M)$. Define two bilinear maps, $\bullet_l^M : \mathcal{P} \times V \to V$ and $\bullet_r^M : V \times \mathcal{P} \to V$, via the following:*

$$a \bullet_l^M u := Ma \bullet_l u - M_V(a \bullet_l u), \tag{6}$$

$$u \bullet_r^M a := u \bullet_r Ma - M_V(u \bullet_r a) \quad \text{for all } a \in \mathcal{P}, u \in V. \tag{7}$$

Then, $(V; \bullet_l^M, \bullet_r^M)$ is a bimodule of a pre-Lie algebra $\mathcal{P}_M$. Moreover, $(V; \bullet_l^M, \bullet_r^M, M_V)$ is a bimodule of a modified Rota–Baxter pre-Lie algebra $(\mathcal{P}_M, M)$.

Proof. First, by direct verification, we determine that$(V; \bullet_l^M, \bullet_r^M)$ is a bimodule of the pre-Lie algebra $\mathcal{P}_M$. Further, for any $a \in \mathcal{P}$ and $u \in V$, according to Equation (3), we have the following:

$$\begin{aligned}
&Ma \bullet_l^M M_V u \\
&= M^2a \bullet_l M_V u - M_V(Ma \bullet_l M_V u) \\
&= M_V(M^2a \bullet_l u + Ma \bullet_l M_V u) - Ma \bullet_l u - M_V^2(Ma \bullet_l u + a \bullet_l M_V u) + M_V(a \bullet_l u) \\
&= M_V(M^2a \bullet_l u + Ma \bullet_l M_V u - M_V(Ma \bullet_l u + a \bullet_l M_V u)) - (Ma \bullet_l u - M_V(a \bullet_l u)) \\
&= M_V(Ma \bullet_l^M u + a \bullet_l^M M_V u) - a \bullet_l^M u.
\end{aligned}$$

Similarly, according to Equation (4), there is also $M_V u \bullet_r^M Ma = M_V(M_V u \bullet_r^M a + u \bullet_r^M Ma) - u \bullet_r^M a$. Hence, $(V; \bullet_l^M, \bullet_r^M, M_V)$ is a bimodule of $(\mathcal{P}_M, M)$. □

Example 5. *$(\mathcal{P}; \bullet_l^M, \bullet_r^M, M)$ is an adjoint bimodule of the modified Rota–Baxter pre-Lie algebra $(\mathcal{P}_M, M)$, where*

$$\begin{aligned}
a \bullet_l^M b &:= Ma \bullet b - M(a \bullet b), \\
a \bullet_r^M b &:= a \bullet Mb - M(a \bullet b),
\end{aligned}$$

for any $a, b \in \mathcal{P}$.

3. Cohomology of Modified Rota–Baxter Pre-Lie Algebras

In this section, we develop the cohomology of a modified Rota–Baxter pre-Lie algebra with coefficients in its bimodule.

Let us recall the cohomology theory of pre-Lie algebras in [17]. Let $(\mathcal{P}, \bullet)$ be a pre-Lie algebra and $(V; \bullet_l, \bullet_r)$ be a bimodule of it. Denote the $n-$cochains of $\mathcal{P}$ with coefficients in representation V via the following:

$$C^n_{\text{PLie}}(\mathcal{P}, V) := \text{Hom}(\mathcal{P}^{\otimes n}, V).$$

The coboundary operator $\delta : C^n_{\text{PLie}}(\mathcal{P}, V) \to C^{n+1}_{\text{PLie}}(\mathcal{P}, V)$, for $a_1, \cdots, a_{n+1} \in \mathcal{P}$ and $g \in C^n_{\text{PLie}}(\mathcal{P}, V)$, as follows:

$$\begin{aligned}
&\delta g(a_1, \ldots, a_{n+1}) \\
=&\sum_{i=1}^{n}(-1)^{i+1} a_i \bullet_l g(a_1, \ldots, \widehat{a_i}, \cdots, a_{n+1}) + \sum_{i=1}^{n}(-1)^{i+1} g(a_1, \ldots, \widehat{a_i}, \ldots, a_n, a_i) \bullet_r a_{n+1} \\
&- \sum_{i=1}^{n}(-1)^{i+1} g(a_1, \ldots, \widehat{a_i}, \ldots, a_n, a_i \bullet a_{n+1}) + \sum_{1 \le i < j \le n} (-1)^{i+j} g([a_i, a_j]^c, a_1, \ldots, \widehat{a_i}, \ldots, \widehat{a_j}, \ldots, a_{n+1}).
\end{aligned} \tag{8}$$

Then, it is proven in [17] that $\delta^2 = 0$. Let us denote, via $H^*_{\text{PLie}}(\mathcal{P}, V)$, the cohomology group associated to the cochain complex $(C^*_{\text{PLie}}(\mathcal{P}, V), \delta)$.

We first study the cohomology of the modified Rota–Baxter operator.

Let $(\mathcal{P}, \bullet, M)$ be a modified Rota–Baxter pre-Lie algebra and $(V; \bullet_l, \bullet_r, M_V)$ be a bimodule of it. Recall that Proposition 4 and Proposition 5 give a new pre-Lie algebra, $\mathcal{P}_M$, and a new bimodule, $V_M = (V; \bullet^M_l, \bullet^M_r)$, over $\mathcal{P}_M$. Consider the cochain complex of $\mathcal{P}_M$ with coefficients in V_M:

$$(C^*_{\text{PLie}}(\mathcal{P}_M, V_M), \delta_M) = (\oplus_{n=1}^{\infty} C^n_{\text{PLie}}(\mathcal{P}_M, V_M), \delta_M).$$

More precisely, $C^n_{\text{PLie}}(\mathcal{P}_M, V_M) := \text{Hom}(\mathcal{P}_M^{\otimes n}, V_M)$ and its coboundary map, $\delta_M : C^n_{\text{PLie}}(\mathcal{P}_M, V_M) \to C^{n+1}_{\text{PLie}}(\mathcal{P}_M, V_M)$, for $a_1, \cdots, a_{n+1} \in \mathcal{P}_R$ and $f \in C^n_{\text{PLie}}(\mathcal{P}_M, V_M)$, are given as follows:

$$\begin{aligned}
&\delta_M f(a_1, \ldots, a_{n+1}) \\
=&\sum_{i=1}^{n}(-1)^{i+1}\Big(Ma_i \bullet_l f(a_1, \ldots, \widehat{a_i}, \cdots, a_{n+1}) - M_V\big(a_i \bullet_l f(a_1, \ldots, \widehat{a_i}, \cdots, a_{n+1})\big)\Big) \\
&+ \sum_{i=1}^{n}(-1)^{i+1}\Big(f(a_1, \ldots, \widehat{a_i}, \ldots, a_n, a_i) \bullet_r Ma_{n+1} - M_V\big(f(a_1, \ldots, \widehat{a_i}, \ldots, a_n, a_i) \bullet_r a_{n+1}\big)\Big) \\
&- \sum_{i=1}^{n}(-1)^{i+1} f(a_1, \ldots, \widehat{a_i}, \ldots, a_n, Ma_i \bullet a_{n+1} + a_i \bullet Ma_{n+1}) \\
&+ \sum_{1 \le i < j \le n} (-1)^{i+j} f(Ma_i \bullet a_j + a_i \bullet Ma_j - Ma_j \bullet a_i - a_j \bullet Ma_i, a_1, \ldots, \widehat{a_i}, \ldots, \widehat{a_j}, \ldots, a_{n+1}).
\end{aligned} \tag{9}$$

In particular, for $n = 1$,

$$\begin{aligned}
&\delta_M f(a_1, a_2) \\
&= Ma_1 \bullet_l f(a_2) - M_V(a_1 \bullet_l f(a_2)) + f(a_1) \bullet_r Ma_2 - M_V(f(a_1) \bullet_r a_2) - f(Ma_1 \bullet a_2 + a_1 \bullet Ma_2).
\end{aligned}$$

Definition 6. *Let $(\mathcal{P}, \bullet, M)$ be a modified Rota–Baxter pre-Lie algebra and $(V; \bullet_l, \bullet_r, M_V)$ be a bimodule of it. Then, the cochain complex $(C^*_{\text{PLie}}(\mathcal{P}_M, V_M), \delta_M)$ is called the cochain complex of the modified Rota–Baxter operator, M, with coefficients in V_M, denoted by $(\mathcal{C}^*_{\text{MRBO}}(\mathcal{P}, V), \delta_M)$. The cohomology of $(\mathcal{C}^*_{\text{MRBO}}(\mathcal{P}, V), \delta_M)$, denoted by $\mathcal{H}^*_{\text{MRBO}}(\mathcal{P}, V)$, is called the cohomology of modified Rota–Baxter operator M with coefficients in V_M.*

In particular, when $(\mathcal{P}; \bullet^M_l = \bullet^M_r = \bullet^M, M)$ is the adjoint bimodule of $(\mathcal{P}_M, M)$, we denote $(\mathcal{C}^*_{\text{MRBO}}(\mathcal{P}, \mathcal{P}), \delta_M)$ as $(\mathcal{C}^*_{\text{MRBO}}(\mathcal{P}), \delta_M)$ and call it the cochain complex of modified

Rota–Baxter operator M, denote $\mathcal{H}^*_{\mathrm{MRBO}}(\mathcal{P},\mathcal{P})$ as $\mathcal{H}^*_{\mathrm{MRBO}}(\mathcal{P})$ and call it the cohomology of modified Rota–Baxter operator M.

Next, we will combine the cohomology of pre-Lie algebras and the cohomology of modified Rota–Baxter operators to construct a cohomology theory for modified Rota–Baxter pre-Lie algebras.

Let us construct the following cochain map. For any $n \geq 1$, we define a linear map, $\Upsilon : C^n_{\mathrm{PLie}}(\mathcal{P},V) \to \mathcal{C}^n_{\mathrm{MRBO}}(\mathcal{P},V)$, via the following:

$$\begin{aligned}&(\Upsilon f)(a_1,\ldots,a_n)\\&=\sum_{i=1}^{\lfloor\frac{n}{2}\rfloor+1}\Big(\sum_{1\leqslant j_1<\cdots<j_{2i-2}\leqslant n} f(a_1,\ldots,Ma_{j_1},\ldots,Ma_{j_{2i-2}},\ldots,a_n)\\&\quad-\sum_{1\leqslant j_1<\cdots<j_{2i-3}\leqslant n} M_V f(a_1,\ldots,Ma_{j_1},\ldots,Ma_{j_{2i-3}},\ldots,a_n)\Big),\text{ if } n \text{ is an even,}\end{aligned}\tag{10}$$

$$\begin{aligned}&(\Upsilon f)(a_1,\ldots,a_n)\\&=\sum_{i=1}^{\lfloor\frac{n}{2}\rfloor+1}\Big(\sum_{1\leqslant j_1<\cdots<j_{2i-1}\leqslant n} f(a_1,\ldots,Ma_{j_1},\ldots,Ma_{j_{2i-1}},\ldots,a_n)\\&\quad-\sum_{1\leqslant j_1<\cdots<j_{2i-2}\leqslant n} M_V f(a_1,\ldots,Ma_{j_1},\ldots,Ma_{j_{2i-2}},\ldots,a_n)\Big),\text{ if } n \text{ is an odd,}\end{aligned}\tag{11}$$

Among them, when the subscript of j_{2i-3} is negative, f is a zero map. For example, when $n = 1$, according to Equation (11), the map $\Upsilon : C^1_{\mathrm{PLie}}(\mathcal{P},V) \to \mathcal{C}^1_{\mathrm{MRBO}}(\mathcal{P},V)$ is as follows:

$$(\Upsilon f)(a_1) = f(Ma_1) - M_V f(a_1).\tag{12}$$

Lemma 1. *Map* Υ *is a cochain map, i.e.,* $\Upsilon\circ\delta = \delta_M\circ\Upsilon$. *In other words, the following diagram is commutative:*

$$\begin{array}{ccccccc}
C^1_{\mathrm{PLie}}(\mathcal{P},V) & \xrightarrow{\delta} & C^2_{\mathrm{PLie}}(\mathcal{P},V) & \cdots\cdots & C^n_{\mathrm{PLie}}(\mathcal{P},V) & \xrightarrow{\delta} & C^{n+1}_{\mathrm{PLie}}(\mathcal{P},V) \;\cdots\cdots\\
\downarrow{\scriptstyle\Upsilon} & & \downarrow{\scriptstyle\Upsilon} & & \downarrow{\scriptstyle\Upsilon} & & \downarrow{\scriptstyle\Upsilon}\\
\mathcal{C}^1_{\mathrm{MRBO}}(\mathcal{P},V) & \xrightarrow{\delta_M} & \mathcal{C}^2_{\mathrm{MRBO}}(\mathcal{P},V) & \cdots\cdots & \mathcal{C}^n_{\mathrm{MRBO}}(\mathcal{P},V) & \xrightarrow{\delta_M} & \mathcal{C}^{n+1}_{\mathrm{MRBO}}(\mathcal{P},V) \;\cdots\cdots .
\end{array}$$

Proof. It can be proven by using similar arguments to those in Appendix A in [31]. Here, we only prove the case of $n = 1$. For any $f \in C^1_{\mathrm{PLie}}(\mathcal{P},V)$ and $a,b \in \mathcal{P}$, according to Equations (2)–(10) and (12), we have the following:

$$\begin{aligned}&\Upsilon(\delta f)(a,b)\\&=(\delta f)(Ma,Mb)-M_V\big((\delta f)(Ma,b)+(\delta f)(a,Mb)\big)+(\delta f)(a,b)\\&=Ma\bullet_l f(Mb)+f(Ma)\bullet_r Mb-f(Ma\bullet Mb)-M_V\big(Ma\bullet_l f(b)+f(Ma)\bullet_r b-f(Ma\bullet b)\\&\quad+a\bullet_l f(Mb)+f(a)\bullet_r Mb-f(a\bullet Mb)\big)+a\bullet_l f(b)+f(a)\bullet_r b-f(a\bullet b)\end{aligned}\tag{13}$$

and

$$\begin{aligned}&\delta_M(\Upsilon f)(a,b)\\&=Ma\bullet_l\big(f(Mb)-M_V f(b)\big)-M_V\big(a\bullet_l(f(Mb)-M_V f(b))\big)+\big(f(Ma)-M_V f(a)\big)\bullet_r Mb\\&\quad-M_V\big((f(Ma)-M_V f(a))\bullet_r b\big)-f(Ma\bullet Mb+a\bullet b)+M_V f(Ma\bullet b+a\bullet Mb)\end{aligned}\tag{14}$$

Further comparing Equations (13) and (14), we have (13) = (14). Therefore, $\Upsilon\circ\delta = \delta_M\circ\Upsilon$. □

Definition 7. *Let $(\mathcal{P}, \bullet, M)$ be a modified Rota–Baxter pre-Lie algebra and $(V; \bullet_l, \bullet_r, M_V)$ be a bimodule of it. We attribute the cochain complex $(\mathcal{C}^*_{\mathrm{MRBPLie}}(\mathcal{P}, V), \partial)$ of a modified Rota–Baxter pre-Lie algebra $(\mathcal{P}, \bullet, M)$ with coefficients in $(V; \bullet_l, \bullet_r, M_V)$ to the negative shift in the mapping cone of Υ, that is, let*

$$\mathcal{C}^1_{\mathrm{MRBPLie}}(\mathcal{P}, V) = C^1_{\mathrm{PLie}}(\mathcal{P}, V) \text{ and } \mathcal{C}^n_{\mathrm{MRBPLie}}(\mathcal{P}, V) := C^n_{\mathrm{PLie}}(\mathcal{P}, V) \oplus \mathcal{C}^{n-1}_{\mathrm{MRBO}}(\mathcal{P}, V) \text{ for } n \geq 2,$$

The coboundary map $\partial : \mathcal{C}^1_{\mathrm{MRBPLie}}(\mathcal{P}, V) \to \mathcal{C}^2_{\mathrm{MRBPLie}}(\mathcal{P}, V)$ is given by the following:

$$\partial(f) = (\delta f, -\Upsilon f) \text{ for all } f \in \mathcal{C}^1_{\mathrm{MRBPLie}}(\mathcal{P}, V);$$

For $n \geq 2$, the coboundary map $\partial : \mathcal{C}^n_{\mathrm{MRBPLie}}(\mathcal{P}, V) \to \mathcal{C}^{n+1}_{\mathrm{MRBPLie}}(\mathcal{P}, V)$ is given by the following:

$$\partial(f, g) = (\delta f, -\delta_M g - \Upsilon f) \text{ for all } (f, g) \in \mathcal{C}^n_{\mathrm{MRBPLie}}(\mathcal{P}, V).$$

The cohomology of $(\mathcal{C}^*_{\mathrm{MRBPLie}}(\mathcal{P}, V), \partial)$, denoted by $\mathcal{H}^*_{\mathrm{MRBPLie}}(\mathcal{P}, V)$, is called the cohomology of the modified Rota–Baxter pre-Lie algebra $(\mathcal{P}, \bullet, M)$ with coefficients in $(V; \bullet_l, \bullet_r, M_V)$. In particular, when $(V; \bullet_l, \bullet_r, M_V) = (\mathcal{P}; \bullet_l = \bullet_r = \bullet, M)$, we just denote $(\mathcal{C}^*_{\mathrm{MRBPLie}}(\mathcal{P}, \mathcal{P}), \partial)$ and $\mathcal{H}^*_{\mathrm{MRBPLie}}(\mathcal{P}, \mathcal{P})$ by $(\mathcal{C}^*_{\mathrm{MRBPLie}}(\mathcal{P}), \partial)$, $\mathcal{H}^*_{\mathrm{MRBPLie}}(\mathcal{P})$, and call them the cochain complex and the cohomology of the modified Rota–Baxter pre-Lie algebra $(\mathcal{P}, \bullet, M)$, respectively.

It is obvious that there is a short exact sequence of cochain complexes:

$$0 \to \mathcal{C}^{*-1}_{\mathrm{MRBO}}(\mathcal{P}, V) \longrightarrow \mathcal{C}^*_{\mathrm{MRBPLie}}(\mathcal{P}, V) \longrightarrow C^*_{\mathrm{PLie}}(\mathcal{P}, V) \to 0.$$

This induces a long exact sequence of cohomology groups:

$$\cdots \to \mathcal{H}^n_{\mathrm{MRBPLie}}(\mathcal{P}, V) \to H^n_{\mathrm{PLie}}(\mathcal{P}, V) \to \mathcal{H}^n_{\mathrm{MRBO}}(\mathcal{P}, V) \to \mathcal{H}^{n+1}_{\mathrm{MRBPLie}}(\mathcal{P}, V) \to H^{n+1}_{\mathrm{PLie}}(\mathcal{P}, V) \to \cdots.$$

At the end of this section, we use the established cohomology theory to characterize infinitesimal deformations of modified Rota–Baxter pre-Lie algebras.

Definition 8. *An infinitesimal deformation of the modified Rota–Baxter pre-Lie algebra $(\mathcal{P}, \bullet, M)$ is a pair $(\bullet_t, M_t)$ of the following forms,*

$$\bullet_t = \bullet + \bullet_1 t, \quad M_t = M + M_1 t,$$

such that the following conditions are satisfied:
(i) $(\bullet_1, M_1) \in \mathcal{C}^2_{\mathrm{MRBPLie}}(\mathcal{P})$;
(ii) $(\mathcal{P}[[t]], \bullet_t, M_t)$ is a modified Rota–Baxter pre-Lie algebra over $\mathbb{K}[[t]]$.

Proposition 6. *Let $(\mathcal{P}[[t]], \bullet_t, M_t)$ be an infinitesimal deformation of modified Rota–Baxter pre-Lie algebra $(\mathcal{P}, \bullet, M)$. Then, $(\bullet_1, M_1)$ is a 2-cocycle in the cochain complex $(\mathcal{C}^*_{\mathrm{MRBPLie}}(\mathcal{P}), \partial)$.*

Proof. Suppose $(\mathcal{P}[[t]], \bullet_t, M_t)$ is a modified Rota–Baxter pre-Lie algebra. Then, for any $a, b, c \in \mathcal{P}$, we have

$$\begin{aligned}(a \bullet_t b) \bullet_t c - a \bullet_t (b \bullet_t c) =& (b \bullet_t a) \bullet_t c - b \bullet_t (a \bullet_t c), \\ M_t a \bullet_t M_t b =& M_t(M_t a \bullet_t b + a \bullet_t M_t b) - a \bullet_t b.\end{aligned}$$

Comparing coefficients of t^1 on both sides of the above equations, we have

$$\begin{aligned}&(a \bullet_1 b) \bullet c + (a \bullet b) \bullet_1 c - a \bullet (b \bullet_1 c) - a \bullet_1 (b \bullet c) \\ &= (b \bullet_1 a) \bullet c + (b \bullet a) \bullet_1 c - b \bullet_1 (a \bullet c) - b \bullet (a \bullet_1 c), \\ &M_1 a \bullet Mb + Ma \bullet M_1 b + Ma \bullet_1 Mb \\ &= M(M_1 a \bullet b + Ma \bullet_1 b + a \bullet M_1 b + a \bullet_1 Mb) + M_1(Ma \bullet b + a \bullet Mb) - a \bullet_1 b.\end{aligned}$$

Therefore, $\partial(\bullet_1, M_1) = (\delta\bullet_1, -\delta_M M_1 - \Upsilon\bullet_1) = 0$, that is, $(\bullet_1, M_1)$ is a 2-cocycle. □

Definition 9. *The 2-cocycle $(\bullet_1, M_1)$ is called the infinitesimal of the infinitesimal deformation $(\mathcal{P}[[t]], \bullet_t, M_t)$ of the modified Rota–Baxter pre-Lie algebra $(\mathcal{P}, \bullet, M)$.*

Definition 10. *Let $(\mathcal{P}[[t]], \bullet_t, M_t)$ and $(\mathcal{P}[[t]], \bullet'_t, M'_t)$ be two infinitesimal deformations of a modified Rota–Baxter pre-Lie algebra $(\mathcal{P}, \bullet, M)$. An isomorphism from $(\mathcal{P}[[t]], \bullet'_t, M'_t)$ to $(\mathcal{P}[[t]], \bullet_t, M_t)$ is a linear map, $\varphi_t = \mathrm{id} + t\varphi_1$, where $\varphi_1 : \mathcal{P} \to \mathcal{P}$ is a linear map, such that:*

$$\varphi_t \circ \bullet'_t = \bullet_t \circ (\varphi_t \otimes \varphi_t), \tag{15}$$

$$\varphi_t \circ M'_t = M_t \circ \varphi_t. \tag{16}$$

In this case, we say that the two infinitesimal deformations $(\mathcal{P}[[t]], \bullet_t, M_t)$ and $(\mathcal{P}[[t]], \bullet'_t, M'_t)$ are equivalent.

Proposition 7. *The infinitesimals of two equivalent infinitesimal deformations of $(\mathcal{P}, \bullet, M)$ are in the same cohomology class in $\mathcal{H}^2_{\mathrm{MRBPLie}}(\mathcal{P})$.*

Proof. Let $\varphi_t : (\mathcal{P}[[t]], \bullet'_t, M'_t) \to (\mathcal{P}[[t]], \bullet_t, M_t)$ be an isomorphism. By expanding Equations (15) and (16) and comparing the coefficients of t^1 on both sides, we have

$$\bullet'_1 - \bullet_1 = \bullet \circ (\varphi_1 \otimes \mathrm{id}) + \bullet \circ (\mathrm{id} \otimes \varphi_1) - \varphi_1 \circ \bullet = \delta\varphi_1,$$
$$M'_1 - M_1 = M \circ \varphi_1 - \varphi_1 \circ M = -\Upsilon\varphi_1,$$

that is, we have the following:

$$(\bullet'_1, M'_1) - (\bullet_1, M_1) = (\delta\varphi_1, -\Upsilon\varphi_1) = \partial(\varphi_1) \in \mathcal{B}^2_{\mathrm{MRBPLie}}(\mathcal{P}).$$

Therefore, $(\bullet'_1, M'_1)$ and $(\bullet_1, M_1)$ are cohomologous and belong to the same cohomology class in $\mathcal{H}^2_{\mathrm{MRBPLie}}(\mathcal{P})$. □

4. Abelian Extensions of Modified Rota–Baxter Pre-Lie Algebras

In this section, we prove that any abelian extension of a modified Rota–Baxter pre-Lie algebra has a bimodule and a 2-cocycle. It is further proven that they are classified by the second cohomology, as one would expect of a good cohomology theory.

Definition 11. *Let $(\mathcal{P}, \bullet, M)$ be a modified Rota–Baxter pre-Lie algebra and $(V, \bullet_V, M_V)$ be an abelian modified Rota–Baxter pre-Lie algebra with the trivial product $\bullet_V$. An abelian extension $(\hat{\mathcal{P}}, \hat{\bullet}, \hat{M})$ of $(\mathcal{P}, \bullet, M)$ by $(V, \bullet_V, M_V)$ is a short exact sequence of morphisms of modified Rota–Baxter pre-Lie algebras,*

$$0 \longrightarrow (V, \bullet_V, M_V) \xrightarrow{\ \mathbf{i}\ } (\hat{\mathcal{P}}, \hat{\bullet}, \hat{M}) \xrightarrow{\ \mathbf{p}\ } (\mathcal{P}, \bullet, M) \longrightarrow 0$$

such that $\hat{M}u = M_V u$ and $u \hat{\bullet} v = 0$, for $u, v \in V$, i.e., V is an abelian ideal of $\hat{\mathcal{P}}$.

Definition 12. *A section of an abelian extension $(\hat{\mathcal{P}}, \hat{\bullet}, \hat{M})$ of $(\mathcal{P}, \bullet, M)$ by $(V, \bullet_V, M_V)$ is a linear map, $\mathbf{s} : \mathcal{P} \to \hat{\mathcal{P}}$, such that $\mathbf{p} \circ \mathbf{s} = \mathrm{id}_{\mathcal{P}}$ and $\mathbf{s} \circ M = \hat{M} \circ \mathbf{s}$.*

Definition 13. *Let* $(\hat{\mathcal{P}}_1, \hat{\bullet}_1, \hat{M}_1)$ *and* $(\hat{\mathcal{P}}_2, \hat{\bullet}_2, \hat{M}_2)$ *be two abelian extensions of* $(\mathcal{P}, \bullet, M)$ *by* $(V, \bullet_V, M_V)$*. They are said to be equivalent if there is an isomorphism of modified Rota–Baxter pre-Lie algebras,* $F : (\hat{\mathcal{P}}_1, \hat{\bullet}_1, \hat{M}_1) \to (\hat{\mathcal{P}}_2, \hat{\bullet}_2, \hat{M}_2)$ *such that the following diagram is commutative:*

$$\begin{array}{ccccccccc} 0 & \longrightarrow & (V, \bullet_V, M_V) & \xrightarrow{\mathbf{i}_1} & (\hat{\mathcal{P}}_1, \hat{\bullet}_1, \hat{M}_1) & \xrightarrow{\mathbf{p}_1} & (\mathcal{P}, \bullet, M) & \longrightarrow & 0 \\ & & \Big\| & & {\scriptstyle F}\Big\downarrow & & \Big\| & & \\ 0 & \longrightarrow & (V, \bullet_V, M_V) & \xrightarrow{\mathbf{i}_2} & (\hat{\mathcal{P}}_2, \hat{\bullet}_2, \hat{M}_2) & \xrightarrow{\mathbf{p}_2} & (\mathcal{P}, \bullet, M) & \longrightarrow & 0. \end{array} \tag{17}$$

Now for an abelian extension $(\hat{\mathcal{P}}, \hat{\bullet}, \hat{M})$ of $(\mathcal{P}, \bullet, M)$ by $(V, \bullet_V, M_V)$ with a section, $\mathbf{s} : \mathcal{P} \to \hat{\mathcal{P}}$, we define two bilinear maps, $\bullet_l : \mathcal{P} \times V \to V, \bullet_r : V \times \mathcal{P} \to V$, by

$$a \bullet_l u = \mathbf{s}(a) \hat{\bullet} u, u \bullet_r a = u \hat{\bullet} \mathbf{s}(a) \ \text{ for all } a \in \mathcal{P}, u \in V.$$

Proposition 8. *With the above notations,* $(V; \bullet_l, \bullet_r, M_V)$ *is a bimodule of the modified Rota–Baxter pre-Lie algebra* $(\mathcal{P}, \bullet, M)$ *and does not depend on the choice of* $\mathbf{s}$.

Proof. First, for any other section, $\mathbf{s}' : \mathcal{P} \to \hat{\mathcal{P}}$, for any $a \in \mathcal{P}$, we have the following:

$$\mathbf{p}(\mathbf{s}(a) - \mathbf{s}'(a)) = \mathbf{p}(\mathbf{s}(a)) - \mathbf{p}(\mathbf{s}'(a)) = a - a = 0.$$

Thus, there exists an element, $u \in V$, such that $\mathbf{s}'(a) = \mathbf{s}(a) + u$. Note that V is an abelian ideal of $\hat{\mathcal{P}}$; this yields the following:

$$\mathbf{s}'(x) \hat{\bullet} u = (\mathbf{s}(x) + v) \hat{\bullet} u = \mathbf{s}(x) \hat{\bullet} u, \ \ u \hat{\bullet} \mathbf{s}'(x) = u \hat{\bullet} (\mathbf{s}(x) + v) = u \hat{\bullet} \mathbf{s}(x).$$

This means that $\bullet_l, \bullet_r$ does not depend on the choice of $\mathbf{s}$.

Next, for any $a, b \in \mathcal{P}$ and $u \in V$, V is an abelian ideal of $\hat{\mathcal{P}}$ and $\mathbf{s}(a) \hat{\bullet} \mathbf{s}(b) - \mathbf{s}(a \bullet b) \in V$; we have the following:

$$\begin{aligned} a \bullet_l (b \bullet_l u) - (a \bullet b) \bullet_l u &= \mathbf{s}(a) \hat{\bullet} (\mathbf{s}(b) \hat{\bullet} u) - \mathbf{s}(a \bullet b) \hat{\bullet} u \\ &= \mathbf{s}(a) \hat{\bullet} (\mathbf{s}(b) \hat{\bullet} u) - (\mathbf{s}(a) \hat{\bullet} \mathbf{s}(b)) \hat{\bullet} u \\ &= \mathbf{s}(b) \hat{\bullet} (\mathbf{s}(a) \hat{\bullet} u) - (\mathbf{s}(b) \hat{\bullet} \mathbf{s}(a)) \hat{\bullet} u \\ &= b \bullet_l (a \bullet_l u) - (b \bullet a) \bullet_l u. \end{aligned}$$

By the same token, there is also $a \bullet_l (u \bullet_r b) - (a \bullet_l u) \bullet_r b = u \bullet_r (a \bullet b) - (u \bullet_r a) \bullet_r b$. This shows that $(V; \bullet_l, \bullet_r)$ is a bimodule of the pre-Lie algebra $(\mathcal{P}, \bullet)$

On the other hand, according to $\hat{M}\mathbf{s}(a) - \mathbf{s}(Ma) \in V$, we have the following:

$$\begin{aligned} Ma \bullet_l M_V u =& \mathbf{s}(Ma) \hat{\bullet} M_V u = \hat{M}\mathbf{s}(a) \hat{\bullet} M_V u = \hat{M}\mathbf{s}(a) \hat{\bullet} \hat{M} u \\ =& \hat{M}(\hat{M}\mathbf{s}(a) \hat{\bullet} u + \mathbf{s}(a) \hat{\bullet} \hat{M} u) - \mathbf{s}(a) \hat{\bullet} u \\ =& M_V(\mathbf{s}(Ma) \hat{\bullet} u + \mathbf{s}(a) \hat{\bullet} M_V u) - \mathbf{s}(a) \hat{\bullet} u \\ =& M_V(Ma \bullet_l u + a \bullet_l M_V u) - a \bullet_l u. \end{aligned}$$

In the same way, there is also $M_V u \bullet_r Ma = M_V(M_V u \bullet_r a + u \bullet_r Ma) - u \bullet_r a$. Hence, $(V; \bullet_l, \bullet_r, M_V)$ is a bimodule of $(\mathcal{P}, \bullet, M)$. □

Let $(\hat{\mathcal{P}}, \hat{\bullet}, \hat{M})$ be an abelian extension of $(\mathcal{P}, \bullet, M)$ by $(V, \bullet_V, M_V)$ and $\mathbf{s} : \mathcal{P} \to \hat{\mathcal{P}}$ be a section of it. Define the maps $\omega : \mathcal{P} \times \mathcal{P} \to V$ and $\chi : \mathcal{P} \to V$ by the following, respectively:

$$\begin{aligned} \omega(a, b) &= \mathbf{s}(a) \hat{\bullet} \mathbf{s}(b) - \mathbf{s}(a \bullet b), \\ \chi(a) &= \hat{M}\mathbf{s}(a) - \mathbf{s}(Ma) \ \text{ for all } a, b \in \mathcal{P}. \end{aligned}$$

We transfer the modified Rota–Baxter pre-Lie algebra structure on $\hat{\mathcal{P}}$ to $\mathcal{P} \oplus V$ by endowing $\mathcal{P} \oplus V$ with a multiplication, $\bullet_\omega$, and a modified Rota–Baxter operator, M_χ, defined by the following:

$$(a+u) \bullet_\omega (b+v) = a \bullet b + a \bullet_l v + u \bullet_r b + \omega(a,b), \tag{18}$$

$$M_\chi(a+u) = Ma + \chi(a) + M_V u \quad \text{for all } a,b \in \mathcal{P},\ u,v \in V. \tag{19}$$

Proposition 9. *The triple $(\mathcal{P} \oplus V, \bullet_\omega, M_\chi)$ is a modified Rota–Baxter pre-Lie algebra if, and only if, (ω,χ) is a 2-cocycle of the modified Rota–Baxter pre-Lie algebra $(\mathcal{P}, \bullet, M)$ with the coefficient in $(V, \bullet_V, M_V)$. In this case,*

$$0 \longrightarrow (V, \bullet_V, M_V) \xrightarrow{\ \mathbf{i}\ } (\mathcal{P} \oplus V, \bullet_\omega, M_\chi) \xrightarrow{\ \mathbf{p}\ } (\mathcal{P}, \bullet, M) \longrightarrow 0$$

is an abelian extension.

Proof. The triple $(\mathcal{P} \oplus V, \bullet_\omega, M_\chi)$ is a modified Rota–Baxter pre-Lie algebra if, and only if, for any $a,b,c \in \mathcal{P}$ and $u,v,w \in V$, the following equations hold true:

$$\begin{aligned} &((a+u) \bullet_\omega (b+v)) \bullet_\omega (c+w) - (a+u) \bullet_\omega ((b+v) \bullet_\omega (c+w)) \\ &= ((b+v) \bullet_\omega (a+u)) \bullet_\omega (c+w) - (b+v) \bullet_\omega ((a+u) \bullet_\omega (c+w)), \end{aligned} \tag{20}$$

$$\begin{aligned} &M_\chi(a+u) \bullet_\omega M_\chi(b+v) \\ &= M_\chi(M_\chi(a+u) \bullet_\omega (b+v) + (a+u) \bullet_\omega M_\chi(b+v)) - (a+u) \bullet_\omega (b+v). \end{aligned} \tag{21}$$

Further, Equations (20) and (21) are equivalent to the following equations:

$$\begin{aligned} &\omega(a,b) \bullet_r c + \omega(a \bullet b, c) - a \bullet_l \omega(b,c) - \omega(a, b \bullet c) \\ &= \omega(b,a) \bullet_r c + \omega(b \bullet a, c) - b \bullet_l \omega(a,c) - \omega(b, a \bullet c), \end{aligned} \tag{22}$$

$$\begin{aligned} &Ma \bullet_l \chi(b) + \chi(a) \bullet_r Mb + \omega(Ma, Mb) \\ &= \chi(Ma \bullet b + a \bullet Mb) + M_V(\chi(a) \bullet_r b + a \bullet_l \chi(b) + \omega(Ma,b) + \omega(a,Mb)) - \omega(a,b). \end{aligned} \tag{23}$$

Using Equations (22) and (23), we have $\delta\omega = 0$ and $-\delta_M\chi - \Upsilon\omega = 0$, respectively. Therefore, $\partial(\omega,\chi) = (\delta\omega, -\delta_M\chi - \Upsilon\omega) = 0$, that is, (ω,χ) is a 2-cocycle.

Conversely, if (ω,χ) is a 2-cocycle of $(\mathcal{P}, \bullet, M)$ with the coefficient in $(V, \bullet_V, M_V)$, then we have $\partial(\omega,\chi) = (\delta\omega, -\delta_M\chi - \Upsilon\omega) = 0$, in which case Equations (20) and (21) hold true. Hence, $(\mathcal{P} \oplus V, \bullet_\omega, M_\chi)$ is a modified Rota–Baxter pre-Lie algebra. □

Proposition 10. *Let $(\hat{\mathcal{P}}, \hat{\bullet}, \hat{M})$ be an abelian extension of $(\mathcal{P}, \bullet, M)$ by $(V, \bullet_V, M_V)$ and $\mathbf{s}$ be a section of it. If the pair (ω,χ) is a 2-cocycle of $(\mathcal{P}, \bullet, M)$ with the coefficient in $(V, \bullet_V, M_V)$ constructed using the section $\mathbf{s}$, then its cohomology class does not depend on the choice of $\mathbf{s}$.*

Proof. Let $\mathbf{s}_1, \mathbf{s}_2 : \mathcal{P} \to \hat{\mathcal{P}}$ be two distinct sections; according to Proposition 9, we have two corresponding 2-cocycles, (ω_1, χ_1) and (ω_2, χ_2), respectively. Define a linear map, $\gamma : \mathcal{P} \to V$, by $\gamma(a) = \mathbf{s}_1(a) - \mathbf{s}_2(a)$. Then,

$$\begin{aligned} \omega_1(a,b) &= \mathbf{s}_1(a)\hat{\bullet}_1\mathbf{s}_1(b) - \mathbf{s}_1(a \bullet b) \\ &= (\mathbf{s}_2(a) + \gamma(a))\hat{\bullet}_1(\mathbf{s}_2(b) + \gamma(b)) - (\mathbf{s}_2(a \bullet b) + \gamma(a \bullet b)) \\ &= \mathbf{s}_2(a)\hat{\bullet}_2\mathbf{s}_2(b) - \mathbf{s}_2(a \bullet b) + \mathbf{s}_2(a)\hat{\bullet}_2\gamma(b) + \gamma(a)\hat{\bullet}_2\mathbf{s}_2(b) + \gamma(a)\hat{\bullet}_2\gamma(b) - \gamma(a \bullet b) \\ &= \mathbf{s}_2(a)\hat{\bullet}_2\mathbf{s}_2(b) - \mathbf{s}_2(a \bullet b) + a \bullet_l \gamma(b) + \gamma(a) \bullet_r b - \gamma(a \bullet b) \\ &= \omega_2(a,b) + \delta\gamma(a,b) \end{aligned}$$

and

$$\begin{aligned}\chi_1(a) &= \hat{M}\mathbf{s}_1(a) - \mathbf{s}_1(Ma)\\ &= \hat{M}(\mathbf{s}_2(a) + \gamma(a)) - (\mathbf{s}_2(Ma) + \gamma(Ma))\\ &= \hat{M}\mathbf{s}_2(a) - \mathbf{s}_2(Ma) + \hat{M}\gamma(a) - \gamma(Ma)\\ &= \chi_2(a) + M_V\gamma(a) - \gamma(Ma)\\ &= \chi_2(a) - \Upsilon\gamma(a).\end{aligned}$$

Hence, $(\omega_1, \chi_1) - (\omega_2, \chi_2) = (\delta\gamma, -\Upsilon\gamma) = \partial(\gamma) \in \mathcal{B}^2_{\mathrm{MRBPLie}}(\mathcal{P}, V)$, that is (ω_1, χ_1) and (ω_2, χ_2) form the same cohomological class in $\mathcal{H}^2_{\mathrm{MRBPLie}}(\mathcal{P}, V)$. $\square$

Next, we are ready to classify abelian extensions of a modified Rota–Baxter pre-Lie algebra.

Theorem 1. *Abelian extensions of a modified Rota–Baxter pre-Lie algebra $(\mathcal{P}, \bullet, M)$ by $(V, \bullet_V, M_V)$ are classified by the second cohomology group, $\mathcal{H}^2_{\mathrm{MRBPLie}}(\mathcal{P}, V)$.*

Proof. Assume that $(\hat{\mathcal{P}}_1, \hat{\bullet}_1, \hat{M}_1)$ and $(\hat{\mathcal{P}}_2, \hat{\bullet}_2, \hat{M}_2)$ are equivalent abelian extensions of $(\mathcal{P}, \bullet, M)$ by $(V, \bullet_V, M_V)$ with the associated isomorphism $F : (\hat{\mathcal{P}}_1, \hat{\bullet}_1, \hat{M}_1) \to (\hat{\mathcal{P}}_2, \hat{\bullet}_2, \hat{M}_2)$ such that the diagram in (17) is commutative. Let $\mathbf{s}_1$ be a section of $(\hat{\mathcal{P}}_1, \hat{\bullet}_1, \hat{M}_1)$. As $\mathbf{p}_2 \circ F = \mathbf{p}_1$, we have the following:

$$\mathbf{p}_2 \circ (F \circ \mathbf{s}_1) = \mathbf{p}_1 \circ \mathbf{s}_1 = \mathrm{id}_{\mathcal{P}}.$$

That is, $F \circ \mathbf{s}_1$ is a section of $(\hat{\mathcal{P}}_2, \hat{\bullet}_2, \hat{M}_2)$. Denote $\mathbf{s}_2 := F \circ \mathbf{s}_1$. Since F is an isomorphism of modified Rota–Baxter pre-Lie algebras such that $F|_V = \mathrm{id}_V$, we have the following:

$$\begin{aligned}\omega_2(a,b) &= \mathbf{s}_2(a)\hat{\bullet}_2\mathbf{s}_2(b) - \mathbf{s}_2(a \bullet b)\\ &= F \circ \mathbf{s}_1(a)\hat{\bullet}_2 F \circ \mathbf{s}_1(b) - F \circ \mathbf{s}_1(a \bullet b)\\ &= F(\mathbf{s}_1(a)\hat{\bullet}_1\mathbf{s}_1(b) - \mathbf{s}_1(a \bullet b))\\ &= F(\omega_1(a,b))\\ &= \omega_1(a,b)\end{aligned}$$

and

$$\begin{aligned}\chi_2(a) &= \hat{M}\mathbf{s}_2(a) - \mathbf{s}_2(Ma)\\ &= \hat{M}(F \circ \mathbf{s}_1(a)) - F \circ \mathbf{s}_1(Ma)\\ &= \hat{M}(\mathbf{s}_1(a)) - \mathbf{s}_1(M(a))\\ &= \chi_1(a).\end{aligned}$$

Thus, two isomorphic abelian extensions give rise to the same element in $\mathcal{H}^2_{\mathrm{MRBPLie}}(\mathcal{P}, V)$.

Conversely, given two 2-cocycles (ω_1, χ_1) and (ω_2, χ_2), we can construct two abelian extensions, $(\mathcal{P} \oplus V, \bullet_{\omega_1}, M_{\chi_1})$ and $(\mathcal{P} \oplus V, \bullet_{\omega_2}, M_{\chi_2})$, via Proposition 9. If they represent the same cohomology class in $\mathcal{H}^2_{\mathrm{MRBPLie}}(\mathcal{P}, V)$, then there is a linear map, $\iota : \mathcal{P} \to V$, such that

$$(\omega_1, \chi_1) - (\omega_2, \chi_2) = \partial(\iota).$$

Define a linear map, $F_\iota : \mathcal{P} \oplus V \to \mathcal{P} \oplus V$, by $F_\iota(a + u) := a + \iota(a) + u$, $a \in \mathcal{P}, u \in V$. Then, it is easy to verify that F_ι is an isomorphism of the two abelian extensions $(\mathcal{P} \oplus V, \bullet_{\omega_1}, M_{\chi_1})$ and $(\mathcal{P} \oplus V, \bullet_{\omega_2}, M_{\chi_2})$. $\square$

5. Modified Rota–Baxter Pre-Lie 2-Algebras and Crossed Modules

In this section, we introduce the notion of modified Rota–Baxter pre-Lie 2-algebras and show that skeletal modified Rota–Baxter pre-Lie 2-algebras are classified by 3-cocycles of modified Rota–Baxter pre-Lie algebras.

We first recall the notion of pre-Lie 2-algebras from [18], which is a categorization of a pre-Lie algebra.

A pre-Lie 2-algebra is a quintuple, $(\mathcal{P}_0, \mathcal{P}_1, h, l_2, l_3)$, where $h : \mathcal{P}_1 \to \mathcal{P}_0$ is a linear map, $l_2 : \mathcal{P}_i \times \mathcal{P}_j \to \mathcal{P}_{i+j}$ are bilinear maps and $l_3 : \mathcal{P}_0 \times \mathcal{P}_0 \times \mathcal{P}_0 \to \mathcal{P}_1$ is a trilinear map, such that for any $a, b, c, x \in \mathcal{P}_0$ and $u, v \in \mathcal{P}_1$, the following equations are satisfied:

$$hl_2(a,u) = l_2(a,h(u)), \tag{24}$$
$$hl_2(u,a) = l_2(h(u),a), \tag{25}$$
$$l_2(h(u),v) = l_2(u,h(v)), \tag{26}$$
$$hl_3(a,b,c) = l_2(a,l_2(b,c)) - l_2(l_2(a,b),c) - l_2(b,l_2(a,c)) + l_2(l_2(b,a),c), \tag{27}$$
$$l_3(a,b,h(u)) = l_2(a,l_2(b,u)) - l_2(l_2(a,b),u) - l_2(b,l_2(a,u)) + l_2(l_2(b,a),u), \tag{28}$$
$$l_3(h(u),b,c) = l_2(u,l_2(b,c)) - l_2(l_2(u,b),c) - l_2(b,l_2(u,c)) + l_2(l_2(b,u),c), \tag{29}$$
$$\begin{aligned} &l_2(x,l_3(a,b,c)) - l_2(a,l_3(x,b,c)) + l_2(b,l_3(x,a,c)) + l_2(l_3(a,b,x),c) - l_2(l_3(x,b,a),c) \\ &+ l_2(l_3(x,a,b),c) - l_3(a,b,l_2(x,c)) + l_3(x,b,l_2(a,c)) - l_3(x,a,l_2(b,c)) - l_3(l_2(x,a) - l_2(a,x),b,c) \\ &+ l_3(l_2(x,b) - l_2(b,x),a,c) - l_3(l_2(a,b) - l_2(b,a),x,c) = 0. \end{aligned} \tag{30}$$

Motivated by [18] and [26], we propose the notion of a modified Rota–Baxter pre-Lie 2-algebra.

Definition 14. *A modified Rota–Baxter pre-Lie 2-algebra consists of a pre-Lie 2-algebra,* $\mathfrak{P} = (\mathcal{P}_0, \mathcal{P}_1, h, l_2, l_3)$ *and a modified Rota–Baxter 2-operator* $\mathfrak{M} = (M_0, M_1, M_2)$ *on* $\mathfrak{P}$*, where* $M_0 : \mathcal{P}_0 \to \mathcal{P}_0$*,* $M_1 : \mathcal{P}_1 \to \mathcal{P}_1$ *and* $M_2 : \mathcal{P}_0 \times \mathcal{P}_0 \to \mathcal{P}_1$*, for any* $a, b, c \in \mathcal{P}_0, u \in \mathcal{P}_1$*, satisfying the following equations:*

$$M_0 \circ h = h \circ M_1, \tag{31}$$
$$hM_2(a,b) + l_2(M_0a, M_0b) = M_0(l_2(M_0(a),b) + l_2(a,M_0(b))) - l_2(a,b), \tag{32}$$
$$M_2(h(u),b) + l_2(M_1u, M_0b) = M_1(l_2(M_1(u),b) + l_2(u,M_0(b))) - l_2(u,b), \tag{33}$$
$$M_2(a,h(u)) + l_2(M_0a, M_1u) = M_1(l_2(M_0(a),u) + l_2(a,M_1(u))) - l_2(a,u), \tag{34}$$

$$\begin{aligned} &M_1l_2(a,M_2(b,c)) - l_2(M_0a,M_2(b,c)) + l_2(M_0b,M_2(a,c)) - M_1l_2(b,M_2(a,c)) \\ &- l_2(M_2(b,a),M_0c) + M_1l_2(M_2(b,a),c) + l_2(M_2(a,b),M_0c) - M_1l_2(M_2(a,b),c) \\ &+ M_2(b,l_2(M_0a,c) + l_2(a,M_0c)) - M_2(a,l_2(M_0b,c) + l_2(b,M_0c)) \\ &+ M_2(l_2(M_0a,b) + l_2(a,M_0b) - l_2(M_0b,a) - l_2(b,M_0a),c) - l_3(M_0a,M_0b,M_0c) \\ &+ M_1(l_3(a,M_0b,M_0c) + l_3(M_0a,b,M_0c) + l_3(M_0a,M_0b,c)) \\ &- l_3(M_0a,b,c) - l_3(a,M_0b,c) - l_3(a,b,M_0c) + M_1l_3(a,b,c) = 0. \end{aligned} \tag{35}$$

We denote a modified Rota–Baxter pre-Lie 2-algebra by $(\mathfrak{P}, \mathfrak{M})$.

A modified Rota–Baxter pre-Lie 2-algebra is said to be skeletal (resp. strict) if $h = 0$ (resp. $l_3 = 0, M_2 = 0$).

Example 6. *For any modified Rota–Baxter pre-Lie algebra,* $(\mathcal{P}, \bullet, M)$*,* $(\mathcal{P}_0 = \mathcal{P}_1 = \mathcal{P}, h = 0, l_2 = \bullet, M_0 = M_1 = M)$ *is a strict modified Rota–Baxter pre-Lie 2-algebra.*

Proposition 11. *Let* $(\mathfrak{P}, \mathfrak{M})$ *be a modified Rota–Baxter pre-Lie 2-algebra.*

(i) If $(\mathfrak{P},\mathfrak{M})$ is skeletal or strict, then $(\mathcal{P}_0,\bullet_0,M_0)$ is a modified Rota–Baxter pre-Lie algebra, where $a\bullet_0 b=l_2(a,b)$ for any $a,b\in\mathcal{P}_0$.

(ii) If $(\mathfrak{P},\mathfrak{M})$ is strict, then $(\mathcal{P}_1,\bullet_1,M_1)$ is a modified Rota–Baxter pre-Lie algebra, where $u\bullet_1 v=l_2(h(u),v)=l_2(u,h(v))$ for any $u,v\in\mathcal{P}_1$.

(iii) If $(\mathfrak{P},\mathfrak{M})$ is skeletal or strict, then $(\mathcal{P}_1;\bullet_l,\bullet_r,M_1)$ is a bimodule of $(\mathcal{P}_0,\bullet_0,M_0)$ where $a\bullet_l u=l_2(a,u)$ and $u\bullet_r a=l_2(u,a)$ for $a\in\mathcal{P}_0,u\in\mathcal{P}_1$.

Proof. Then, (i), (ii) and (iii) can be directly verified by Equations (24)–(29) and (31)–(34). □

Theorem 2. *There is a one-to-one correspondence between skeletal modified Rota–Baxter pre-Lie 2-algebras and 3-cocycles of modified Rota–Baxter pre-Lie algebras.*

Proof. Let $(\mathfrak{P},\mathfrak{M})$ be a skeletal modified Rota–Baxter pre-Lie 2-algebra. According to Proposition 11, we can consider the cohomology of modified Rota–Baxter pre-Lie algebra to be $(\mathcal{P}_0,\bullet_0,M_0)$ with coefficients in the bimodule $(\mathcal{P}_1;\bullet_l,\bullet_r,M_1)$. For any $a,b,c,x\in\mathcal{P}_0$, combining Equations (8) and (30), we have the following:

$$\begin{aligned}
&\delta l_3(x,a,b,c)\\
=&x\bullet_l l_3(a,b,c)-a\bullet_l l_3(x,b,c)+b\bullet_l l_3(x,a,c)+l_3(a,b,x)\bullet_r c-l_3(x,b,a)\bullet_r c+l_3(x,a,b)\bullet_r c\\
&-l_3(a,b,x\bullet_0 c)+l_3(x,b,a\bullet_0 c)-l_3(x,a,b\bullet_0 c)-l_3(x\bullet_0 a-a\bullet_0 x,b,c)+l_3(x\bullet_0 b-b\bullet_0 x,a,c)\\
&-l_3(a\bullet_0 b-b\bullet_0 a,x,c)\\
=&l_2(x,l_3(a,b,c))-l_2(a,l_3(x,b,c))+l_2(b,l_3(x,a,c))+l_2(l_3(a,b,x),c)-l_2(l_3(x,b,a),c)+l_2(l_3(x,a,b),c)\\
&-l_3(a,b,l_2(x,c))+l_3(x,b,l_2(a,c))-l_3(x,a,l_2(b,c))-l_3(l_2(x,a)-l_2(a,x),b,c)\\
&+l_3(l_2(x,b)-l_2(b,x),a,c)-l_3(l_2(a,b)-l_2(b,a),x,c)\\
=&0.
\end{aligned}$$

According to Equations (9) and (35), the following hold true:

$$\begin{aligned}
&(-\delta_M M_2-\Upsilon l_3)(a,b,c)=-\delta_M M_2(a,b,c)-\Upsilon l_3(a,b,c)\\
=&-M_0a\bullet_l M_2(b,c)+M_1(a\bullet_l M_2(b,c))+M_0b\bullet_l M_2(a,c)-M_1(b\bullet_l M_2(a,c))\\
&-M_2(b,a)\bullet_r M_0c+M_1(M_2(b,a)\bullet_r c)+M_2(a,b)\bullet_r M_0c-M_1(M_2(a,b)\bullet_r c)\\
&+M_2(b,M_0a\bullet_0 c+a\bullet_0 M_0c)-M_2(a,M_0b\bullet_0 c+b\bullet_0 M_0c)\\
&+M_2(M_0a\bullet_0 b+a\bullet_0 M_0b-M_0b\bullet_0 a-b\bullet_0 M_0a,c)-l_3(M_0a,M_0b,M_0c)\\
&+M_1(l_3(a,M_0b,M_0c)+l_3(M_0a,b,M_0c)+l_3(M_0a,M_0b,c))\\
&-l_3(M_0a,b,c)-l_3(a,M_0b,c)-l_3(a,b,M_0c)+M_1l_3(a,b,c)\\
=&-l_2(M_0a,M_2(b,c))+M_1l_2(a,M_2(b,c))+l_2(M_0b,M_2(a,c))-M_1l_2(b,M_2(a,c))\\
&-l_2(M_2(b,a),M_0c)+M_1l_2(M_2(b,a),c)+l_2(M_2(a,b),M_0c)-M_1l_2(M_2(a,b),c)\\
&+M_2(b,l_2(M_0a,c)+l_2(a,M_0c))-M_2(a,l_2(M_0b,c)+l_2(b,M_0c))\\
&+M_2(l_2(M_0a,b)+l_2(a,M_0b)-l_2(M_0b,a)-l_2(b,M_0a),c)-l_3(M_0a,M_0b,M_0c)\\
&+M_1(l_3(a,M_0b,M_0c)+l_3(M_0a,b,M_0c)+l_3(M_0a,M_0b,c))\\
&-l_3(M_0a,b,c)-l_3(a,M_0b,c)-l_3(a,b,M_0c)+M_1l_3(a,b,c)\\
=&0.
\end{aligned}$$

Thus, $\partial(l_3,M_2)=(\delta l_3,-\delta_M M_2-\Upsilon l_3)=0$, that is $(l_3,M_2)\in C^3_{\mathrm{MRBPLie}}(\mathcal{P}_0,\mathcal{P}_1)$ is a 3-cocycle of a modified Rota–Baxter pre-Lie algebra $(\mathcal{P}_0,\bullet_0,M_0)$ with coefficients in the bimodule $(\mathcal{P}_1;\bullet_l,\bullet_r,M_1)$.

Conversely, suppose that $(l_3,M_2)\in C^3_{\mathrm{MRBPLie}}(\mathcal{P},V)$ is a 3-cocycle of a modified Rota–Baxter pre-Lie algebra $(\mathcal{P},\bullet,M)$ with coefficients in the bimodule $(V;\bullet_l,\bullet_r,M_V)$. Then, $(\mathfrak{P},\mathfrak{M})$ is a skeletal modified Rota–Baxter pre-Lie 2-algebra, where $\mathfrak{P}=(\mathcal{P}_0=\mathcal{P},\mathcal{P}_1=$

$V, h = 0, l_2, l_3)$ and $\mathfrak{M} = (M_0 = M, M_1 = M_V, M_2)$ with $l_2(a,b) = a \bullet b, l_2(a,u) = a \bullet_l u, l_2(u,a) = u \bullet_r a$ for any $a, b \in \mathcal{P}_0, u \in \mathcal{P}_1$. □

Whitehead [36] introduced the notion of crossed modules in the context of homotopy theory. At the end of this section, we introduce the notion of crossed modules of modified Rota–Baxter pre-Lie algebras and show that they are equivalent to strict modified Rota–Baxter pre-Lie 2-algebras.

Definition 15. *A crossed module of modified Rota–Baxter pre-Lie algebras is a quadruple $((\mathcal{P}_0, \bullet_0, M_0), (\mathcal{P}_1, \bullet_1, M_1), h, (\bullet_l, \bullet_r))$, where $(\mathcal{P}_0, \bullet_0, M_0)$ and $(\mathcal{P}_1, \bullet_1, M_1)$ are modified Rota–Baxter pre-Lie algebras, $h : \mathcal{P}_1 \to \mathcal{P}_0$ is a homomorphism of modified Rota–Baxter pre-Lie algebras and $(\mathcal{P}_1; \bullet_l, \bullet_r, M_1)$ is a bimodule of $(\mathcal{P}_0, \bullet_0, M_0)$, for any $a \in \mathcal{P}_0, u, v \in \mathcal{P}_1$, satisfying the following equations:*

$$h(a \bullet_l u) = a \bullet_0 h(u), h(u \bullet_r a) = h(u) \bullet_0 a, \tag{36}$$

$$h(u) \bullet_l v = u \bullet_r h(v) = u \bullet_1 v. \tag{37}$$

Example 7. *Let $(\mathcal{P}, \bullet, M)$ be a modified Rota–Baxter pre-Lie algebra, $\mathcal{F}$ be its two-sided ideal—that is, $\mathcal{F}$ satisfies $\mathcal{F} \bullet \mathcal{P} \subseteq \mathcal{F}, \mathcal{P} \bullet \mathcal{F} \subseteq \mathcal{F}$ and $M(\mathcal{F}) \subseteq \mathcal{F}$—and $in : \mathcal{F} \to \mathcal{P}$ be the inclusion. Then, $((\mathcal{P}, \bullet, M), (\mathcal{F}, \bullet, M|_{\mathcal{F}}), in, (\bullet_l = \bullet_r = \bullet))$ is a crossed module of modified Rota–Baxter pre-Lie algebras. In particular, $((\mathcal{P}, \bullet, M), (\mathcal{P}, \bullet, M), \mathrm{id}_{\mathcal{P}}, (\bullet_l = \bullet_r = \bullet))$ is a crossed module of modified Rota–Baxter pre-Lie algebras.*

Example 8. *Let $F : (\mathcal{P}_1, \bullet_1, M_1) \to (\mathcal{P}_0, \bullet_0, M_0)$ be a homomorphism of modified Rota–Baxter pre-Lie algebras. Then, $\ker(F)$ is a two-sided ideal of $(\mathcal{P}_1, \bullet_1, M_1)$. Thus, according to Example 7, $((\mathcal{P}_1, \bullet_1, M_1), (\ker(F), \bullet_1, M_1|_{\ker(F)}), in, (\bullet_l = \bullet_r = \bullet_1))$ is a crossed module of modified Rota–Baxter pre-Lie algebras.*

Example 9. *Let $(V; \bullet_l, \bullet_r, M_V)$ be a bimodule over a modified Rota–Baxter pre-Lie algebra $(\mathcal{P}, \bullet, M)$. Endow V with the trivial pre-Lie algebra structure, $\bullet_V = 0$; in this case, $((\mathcal{P}, \bullet, M), (V, \bullet_V, M_V), 0, (\bullet_l, \bullet_r))$ is a crossed module of modified Rota–Baxter pre-Lie algebras.*

Theorem 3. *There is a one-to-one correspondence between strict modified Rota–Baxter pre-Lie 2-algebras and crossed modules of modified Rota–Baxter pre-Lie algebras.*

Proof. Let $((\mathcal{P}_0, \mathcal{P}_1, h, l_2, l_3 = 0), (M_0, M_1, M_2 = 0))$ be a strict modified Rota–Baxter pre-Lie 2-algebra. Define the following two operations on $\mathcal{P}_0$ and $\mathcal{P}_1$:

$$a \bullet_0 b = l_2(a, b),$$
$$u \bullet_1 v = l_2(h(u), v) = l_2(u, h(v)) \quad \text{for all } a, b \in \mathcal{P}_0, u, v \in \mathcal{P}_1.$$

It is straightforward to see that both $(\mathcal{P}_0, \bullet_0, M_0)$ and $(\mathcal{P}_1, \bullet_1, M_1)$ are modified Rota–Baxter pre-Lie algebras. l_2 also gives rise to two maps: $\bullet_l : \mathcal{P}_0 \times \mathcal{P}_1 \to \mathcal{P}_1, \bullet_r : \mathcal{P}_1 \times \mathcal{P}_0 \to \mathcal{P}_1$ by

$$a \bullet_r u = l_2(a, u), u \bullet_r a = l_2(u, a) \quad \text{for all } a \in \mathcal{P}_0, u \in \mathcal{P}_1.$$

According to (33) and (34), we deduce that $(\mathcal{P}_1; \bullet_l, \bullet_r, M_1)$ is a bimodule of $(\mathcal{P}_0, \bullet_0, M_0)$. According to Equation (26), we have

$$h(u \bullet_1 v) = hl_2(h(u), v) = l_2(h(u), h(v)) = h(u) \bullet_0 h(v),$$

which implies that h is a homomorphism of modified Rota–Baxter pre-Lie algebras. Furthermore, we have

$$h(a \bullet_l u) = hl_2(a,u) = l_2(a,h(u)) = a \bullet_0 h(u),$$
$$h(u \bullet_r a) = hl_2(u,a) = l_2(h(u),a) = h(u) \bullet_0 a,$$
$$h(u) \bullet_l v = l_2(h(u),v) = l_2(u,h(v)) = u \bullet_r h(v) = u \bullet_1 v.$$

Thus, we obtain a crossed module of modified Rota–Baxter pre-Lie algebras.

Conversely, a crossed module of modified Rota–Baxter pre-Lie algebras $((\mathcal{P}_0, \bullet_0, M_0), (\mathcal{P}_1, \bullet_1, M_1), h, (\bullet_l, \bullet_r))$ gives rise to a strict modified Rota–Baxter pre-Lie 2-algebra $((\mathcal{P}_0, \mathcal{P}_1, h, l_2, l_3 = 0), (M_0, M_1, M_2 = 0))$, in which $l_2 : \mathfrak{g}_i \times \mathfrak{g}_j \to \mathfrak{g}_{i+j}$ are given by

$$l_2(a,b) = a \bullet_0 b,$$
$$l_2(u,v) = u \bullet_1 v,$$
$$l_2(a,u) = a \bullet_l u,$$
$$l_2(u,a) = u \bullet_r a,$$

for all $a \in \mathcal{P}_0, u, v \in \mathcal{P}_1$. The crossed module equations give various equations for strict modified Rota–Baxter pre-Lie 2-algebras. The proof is completed. □

6. Conclusions

In the current research, we mainly study a modified Rota–Baxter pre-Lie algebra, which includes a modified Rota–Baxter operator and a pre-Lie algebra. More precisely, we introduce the bimodule of a modified Rota–Baxter pre-Lie algebra. We show that a modified Rota–Baxter pre-Lie algebra induces a pre-Lie algebra, and the bimodule of a modified Rota–Baxter pre-Lie algebra induces the bimodule of a pre-Lie algebra. Considering this fact, we define the cohomology of a modified Rota–Baxter operator on a pre-Lie algebra. Using the cohomology of pre-Lie algebras, we construct a cochain map, and the cohomology of modified Rota–Baxter pre-Lie algebras is defined. We study infinitesimal deformations of modified Rota–Baxter pre-Lie algebras and show that equivalent infinitesimal deformations are in the same second cohomology group. We investigate abelian extensions of modified Rota–Baxter pre-Lie algebras by using the second cohomology group. Additionally, the notion of modified Rota–Baxter pre-Lie 2-algebra is introduced, which is the categorization of a modified Rota–Baxter pre-Lie algebra. We study the skeletal modified Rota–Baxter pre-Lie 2-algebras using the third cohomology group. Finally, we introduce the notion of crossed modules of modified Rota–Baxter pre-Lie algebras, give some examples, and prove that strict modified Rota–Baxter pre-Lie 2-algebras are equivalent to crossed modules of modified Rota–Baxter pre-Lie algebras.

Author Contributions: Conceptualization, F.Z. and W.T.; methodology, F.Z. and W.T.; investigation, F.Z. and W.T.; writing—original draft preparation, F.Z. and W.T.; writing—review and editing, F.Z. and W.T.; All authors have read and agreed to the published version of the manuscript.

Funding: This research was funded by the National Natural Science Foundation of China (grant number 12261022).

Data Availability Statement: No new data were created or analyzed in this study. Data sharing is not applicable to this article.

Conflicts of Interest: The authors declare no conflicts of interest.

References

1. Cayley, A. *On the Theory of Analytic Forms Called Trees. Collected Mathematical Papers of Arthur Cayley*; Cambridge University Press: Cambridge, UK, 1890; Volume 3, pp. 242–246.
2. Gerstenhaber, M. The cohomology structure of an associative ring. *Ann. Math.* **1963**, *78*, 267–288. [CrossRef]
3. Kim, H. Complete left-invariant affine structures on nilpotent Lie groups. *J. Differ. Geom.* **1986**, *24*, 373–394. [CrossRef]

4. Etingof, P.; Soloviev, A. Quantization of geometric classical r-matrix. *Math. Res. Lett.* **1999**, *6*, 223–228. [CrossRef]
5. Etingof, P.; Schedler, T.; Soloviev, A. Set-theoretical solutions to the quantum Yang-Baxter equations. *Duke Math. J.* **1999**, *100*, 169–209. [CrossRef]
6. Andrada, A.; Salamon, S. Complex product structure on Lie algebras. *Forum Math.* **2005**, *17*, 261–295. [CrossRef]
7. Burde, D. Left-symmetric algebras, or pre-Lie algebras in geometry and physics. *Cent. Eur. J. Math.* **2006**, *4*, 323–357. [CrossRef]
8. Bai, C. Left-symmetric bialgebras and an analogue of the classical Yang-Baxter equation. *Commun. Contemp. Math.* **2008**, *10*, 221–260. [CrossRef]
9. Zhu, F.; You, T.; Teng, W. Abelian extensions of modified λ-differential left-symmetric algebras and crossed modules. *Axioms* **2024**, *13*, 380. [CrossRef]
10. Guo, S.; Qin, Y.; Wang, K.; Zhou, G. Cohomology theory of Rota-Baxter pre-Lie algebras of arbitrary weights. *arXiv* **2022**, arXiv:2204.13518.
11. Bai, C. An introduction to pre-Lie algebras. In *Algebra and Applications 1*; Coordinated by A. Makhlouf; ISTE-Wiley: London, UK, 2020; pp. 243–273.
12. Li, X.; Hou, D.; Bai, C. Rota-Baxter operators on pre-Lie algebras. *J. Nonlinear Math. Phy.* **2007**, *14*, 269–289. [CrossRef]
13. Liu, J. Twisting on pre-Lie algebras and quasi-pre-Lie bialgebras. *arXiv* **2020**, arXiv:2003.11926.
14. Liu, J.; Wang, Q. Pre-Lie analogues of Poisson-Nijenhuis structures and Maurer-Cartan equations. *arXiv* **2020**, arXiv:2004.02098.
15. Liu, S.; Chen, L. Deformations and abelian extensions of compatible pre-Lie algebras. *arXiv* **2023**, arXiv:2302.07178.
16. Wang, Q.; Sheng, Y.; Bai, C.; Liu, J. Nijenhuis operators on pre-Lie algebras. *Commun. Contemp. Math.* **2019**, *21*, 1850050. [CrossRef]
17. Dzhumaldil'daev, A. Cohomologies and deformations of right-symmetric algebras. *J. Math. Sci.* **1999**, *93*, 836–876. [CrossRef]
18. Sheng, Y. Categorification of pre-Lie algebras and solutions of 2-graded classical Yang-Baxter equations. *Theory Appl. Categ.* **2019**, *34*, 269–294.
19. Baxter, G. An analytic problem whose solution follows from a simple algebraic identity. *Pacific J. Math.* **1960**, *10*, 731–742. [CrossRef]
20. Rota, G.C. Baxter algebras and combinatorial identities I, II. *Bull. Amer. Math. Soc.* **1969**, *75*, 325–329. [CrossRef]
21. Connes, A.; Kreimer, D. Renormalization in quantum field theory and the Riemann-Hilbert problem I: The Hopf algebra structure of graphs and the main theorem. *Commun. Math. Phys.* **2000**, *210*, 249–273. [CrossRef]
22. Das, A. Deformations of associative Rota-Baxter operators. *J. Algebra* **2020**, *560*, 144–180. [CrossRef]
23. Chtioui, T.; Mabrouk, S.; Makhlouf, A. Cohomology and deformations of $\mathcal{O}$-operators on Hom-associative algebras. *J. Algebra* **2022**, **604**, 727–759. [CrossRef]
24. Tang, R.; Bai, C.; Guo, L.; Sheng, Y. Deformations and their controlling cohomologies of $\mathcal{O}$-operators. *Comm. Math. Phys.* **2019**, *368*, 665–700. [CrossRef]
25. Tang, R.; Bai, C.; Guo, L.; Sheng, Y. Homotopy Rota-Baxter operators and post-Lie algebras. *J. Noncommut. Geom.* **2023**, *17*, 1–35. [CrossRef] [PubMed]
26. Jang, J.; Sheng, Y. Representations and cohomologies of relative Rota-Baxter Lie algebras and applications. *J. Algebra* **2022**, *602*, 637–670. [CrossRef]
27. Wang, K.; Zhou, G. Deformations and homotopy theory of Rota-Baxter algebras of any weight. *arXiv* **2021**, arXiv:2108.06744.
28. Das, A. Cohomology and deformations of weighted Rota-Baxter operators. *J. Math. Phys.* **2022**, *63*, 091703. [CrossRef]
29. Das, A. Cohomology of weighted Rota-Baxter Lie algebras and Rota-Baxter paired operators. *arXiv* **2021**, arXiv:2109.01972.
30. Hou, S.; Sheng, Y.; Zhou, Y. 3-post-Lie algebras and relative Rota-Baxter operators of nonzero weight on 3-Lie algebras. *J. Algebra* **2023**, *615*, 103–129. [CrossRef]
31. Guo, S.; Qin, Y.; Wang, K.; Zhou, G. Deformations and cohomology theory of Rota-Baxter 3-Lie algebras of arbitrary weights. *J. Geom. Phys.* **2023**, *183*, 104704. [CrossRef]
32. Chen, S.; Lou, Q.; Sun, Q. Cohomologies of Rota-Baxter Lie triple systems and applications. *Commun. Algebra* **2023**, *51*, 4299–4315. [CrossRef]
33. Teng, W. Weighted Rota-Baxter Lie supertriple systems. *J. Guizhou Norm. Univ. (Nat. Sci.)* **2024**, *42*, 84–90. (In Chinese)
34. Semenov-Tyan-Shanskij, M.A. What is a classical r-matrix? *Funct. Anal. Appl.* **1983**, *17*, 259–272. [CrossRef]
35. Jiang, J.; Sheng, Y. Deformations of modified r-matrices and cohomologies of related algebraic structures. *J. Noncommut. Geom.* **2024**. [CrossRef] [PubMed]
36. Wagemann, F. On Lie algebra crossed modules. *Commun. Algebra* **2006**, *34*, 1699–1722. [CrossRef]

Disclaimer/Publisher's Note: The statements, opinions and data contained in all publications are solely those of the individual author(s) and contributor(s) and not of MDPI and/or the editor(s). MDPI and/or the editor(s) disclaim responsibility for any injury to people or property resulting from any ideas, methods, instructions or products referred to in the content.

mathematics MDPI

Article

The Ribbon Elements of the Quantum Double of Generalized Taft–Hopf Algebra

Hua Sun, Yuyan Zhang *, Ziliang Jiang, Mingyu Huang and Jiawei Hu

College of Mathematical Science, Yangzhou University, Yangzhou 225002, China; huasun@yzu.edu.cn (H.S.); jzl030430@163.com (Z.J.); h2118651743@126.com (M.H.); ohujiaweio@163.com (J.H.)
* Correspondence: o9z7circle@126.com

Abstract: Let s, t be two positive integers and $\Bbbk$ be an algebraically closed field with char $(\Bbbk) \nmid st$. We show that the Drinfeld double $D(\bigwedge_{st,t}^{*cop})$ of generalized Taft–Hopf algebra $\bigwedge_{st,t}^{*cop}$ has ribbon elements if and only if t is odd. Moreover, if s is even and t is odd, then $D(\bigwedge_{st,t}^{*cop})$ has two ribbon elements, and if both s and t are odd, then $D(\bigwedge_{st,t}^{*cop})$ has only one ribbon element. Finally, we compute explicitly all ribbon elements of $D(\bigwedge_{st,t}^{*cop})$.

Keywords: quantum double; ribbon Hopf algebra; quasi-triangular Hopf algebra

MSC: 16T05

1. Introduction

The representation category of a quasi-triangular Hopf algebra is a braided tensor category. The braiding structure of a quasi-triangular Hopf algebra can supply a solution to the Yang–Baxter equation. Recently, great progress has been made in the research of the quasi-triangular Hopf algebra. Drinfeld [1] constructed a quasi-triangular Hopf algebra from a finite-dimensional Hopf algebra, i.e., the quantum double (or Drinfeld double) of a Hopf algebra. Ribbon Hopf algebra is a quasi-triangular Hopf algebra with a ribbon element. The finite-dimensional ribbon Hopf algebra plays an important role in constructing invariants of three-manifolds [2]. Thus, researchers have paid much attention to the question of when a quasi-triangular Hopf algebra has ribbon structures. In [3], Chen and Yang gave a necessary and sufficient condition for the Drinfeld double of a finite-dimensional Hopf superalgebra to have a ribbon element. Kauffman and Radford [4] gave a necessary and sufficient condition for the Drinfeld double of a finite-dimensional Hopf algebra to admit a ribbon structure, and they proved that $(D(A_n(q)), \mathcal{R})$ is a ribbon Hopf algebra if and only if n is odd, where $D(A_n(q))$ is the Drinfeld double of n^2-dimensional Taft algebra $A_n(q)$ and $\mathcal{R}$ is the universal $\mathcal{R}$-matrix of $D(A_n(q))$. In [5], Benkart and Biswal computed the ribbon element of $(D(A_n(q)), \mathcal{R})$ explicitly when n is odd. In [6], Andruskiewitsch and Schneider constructed $u(\mathcal{D}, 0, 0)$, which is a pointed Hopf algebra of the nilpotent type. In particular, if $\mathcal{D} = (G, g^s, \chi, \mu)$, $u(\mathcal{D}, 0, 0)$ is the generalized Taft–Hopf algebra denoted by $\bigwedge_{st,t}^{*cop}$. Burciu [7] provided a sufficient condition for the quantum double of $u(\mathcal{D}, 0, 0)$ to be a ribbon Hopf algebra. If $\chi(g^s) = t$ is an odd that is coprime to three, then $D(\bigwedge_{st,t}^{*cop})$ is a ribbon Hopf algebra. Leduc and Ram [8] showed how the ribbon Hopf algebra structure on the Drinfeld–Jimbo quantum groups of types A, B, C, and D can be used to derive formulas giving explicit realizations of the irreducible representations of the Iwahori–Hecke algebras of type A and the Birman–Wenzl algebras. Centrone and Yasumura [9] extended the action of the n-th Taft–Hopf algebra H on $A = k[u]$ with $u^n = \beta$ to the Drinfeld double $D(H)$. This is used to show that, for each H-action on A, there is a unique left H-comodule algebra structure on A such that A is a Yetter–Drinfeld algebra over H. Montgomery and Schneider [10] characterized the action of a Taft algebra H_n on finite-dimensional algebras A that satisfy that every skew derivation is inner. Farsad [11] proved that the Drinfeld double $D(K_n)$ of Nichols–Hopf algebra K_n is a ribbon Hopf algebra when n is even. Chang [12] provided the explicit expression of the ribbon elements of $D(K_n)$.

In this paper, we give a sufficient and necessary condition for the Drinfeld double $D(\Lambda_{st,t}^{*cop})$ of generalized Taft–Hopf algebra $\Lambda_{st,t}^{*cop}$ to have a ribbon structure. The paper is organized as follows. In Section 2, we recall some definitions and notions and the structures of generalized Taft–Hopf algebra $\Lambda_{st,t}^{*cop}$. In Section 3, we describe the Hopf algebra structure of $(\Lambda_{st,t}^{*cop})^*$. In Section 4, we show that $(D(\Lambda_{st,t}^{*cop}), \mathcal{R})$ have ribbon elements if and only if t is odd. Finally, we compute all ribbon elements of $(D(\Lambda_{st,t}^{*cop}), \mathcal{R})$.

2. Preliminaries

Throughout, we work over an algebraically closed field $\Bbbk$ with char $(\Bbbk) \nmid st$. Unless otherwise stated, all algebras and Hopf algebras are defined over $\Bbbk$; dim and $\otimes$ denote $dim_{\Bbbk}$ and $\otimes_{\Bbbk}$, respectively. References [13–15] are basic references for the theory of Hopf algebras and quantum groups.

Let $0 \neq q \in \Bbbk$. For any non-negative integer n, define $(n)_q$ by $(0)_q = 0$ and $(n)_q = 1 + q + \cdots + q^{n-1}$ for $n > 0$. Observe that $(n)_q = n$ when $q = 1$ and

$$(n)_q = \frac{q^n - 1}{q - 1}$$

when $q \neq 1$. Define the q-factorial of n by

$$(n)!_q = \frac{(q^n - 1)(q^{n-1} - 1)\dots(q - 1)}{(q - 1)^n}$$

when $n > 0$ and $q \neq 1$. The q-binomial coefficients $\begin{pmatrix} n \\ i \end{pmatrix}_q$ are defined inductively as follows for $0 \leq i \leq n$:

$$\begin{pmatrix} n \\ 0 \end{pmatrix}_q = 1 = \begin{pmatrix} n \\ n \end{pmatrix}_q, \ for\ n \geq 0,$$

$$\begin{pmatrix} n \\ i \end{pmatrix}_q = q^i \begin{pmatrix} n-1 \\ i \end{pmatrix}_q + \begin{pmatrix} n-1 \\ i-1 \end{pmatrix}_q, \ for\ 0 < i < n.$$

It is well-known that $\begin{pmatrix} n \\ i \end{pmatrix}_q$ is a polynomial in q with integer coefficients and with the value at $q = 1$ equal to the usual binomial coefficient $\begin{pmatrix} n \\ i \end{pmatrix}$ and that

$$\begin{pmatrix} n \\ i \end{pmatrix}_q = \frac{(n)!_q}{(i)!_q (n-i)!_q}$$

when $(n-1)!_q \neq 0$ and $0 < i < n$.

Next, we use the sigma notation: for $x \in H$, H being a coalgebra,

$$\Delta(x) = \sum x_1 \otimes x_2.$$

Suppose that H is a bialgebra over $\Bbbk$. The left and right H-module actions defined on H^* by

$$< a \rightharpoonup p, b > = < p, ba > = < p \leftharpoonup b, a >,$$

respectively, for $a, b \in H$ and $p \in H^*$ give H^* an A-bimodule structure. Likewise, the left and right H^*-modules actions on H by

$$p \rightharpoonup a = \sum a_1 < p, a_2 >, \ a \leftharpoonup p = \sum < p, a_1 > a_2,$$

respectively, for $p \in H^*$ and $a \in H$ give H a H^*-bimodule structure.

2.1. Generalized Taft–Hopf Algebra

In this subsection, we recall the structure of generalized Taft–Hopf algebra $\Lambda_{st,t}^{*cop}$.

Let $s \geq 2$, $t \geq 1$, and let $p \in \Bbbk$ be a primitive t-th root of unity. The generalized Taft–Hopf algebra $\Lambda_{st,t}^{*cop}$ is generated as an algebra by g and x subject to the following relations:

$$g^{st} = 1, \ x^t = 0, \ xg = pgx.$$

The comultiplication Δ, counit ε, and antipode S are given, respectively, by

$$\Delta(x) = x \otimes g + 1 \otimes x, \ \varepsilon(x) = 0, \ S(x) = -xg^{-1},$$

$$\Delta(g) = g \otimes g, \ \varepsilon(g) = 1, \ S(g) = g^{-1} = g^{st-1}.$$

Note that $\dim(\Lambda_{st,t}^{*cop}) = st^2$, and $\Lambda_{st,t}^{*cop}$ has a $\Bbbk$-basis $\{g^i x^j | 0 \leq i \leq st-1, 0 \leq j \leq t-1\}$. In case $s = 1$, then $\Lambda_{st,t}^{*cop} = \Lambda_{t,t}^{*cop}$ is the t^2-dimensional Taft–Hopf algebra. For this reason, $\Lambda_{st,t}^{*cop}$ is called a generalized Taft algebra. For details, one can refer to [16]. In the following, we denote $\Lambda_{st,t}^{*cop}$ by $\mathcal{T}$.

2.2. Ribbon Hopf Algebra

In this subsection, we recall the definition of the quasi-triangular Hopf algebra and ribbon Hopf algebra [5] (Section 3.1).

Definition 1. *Let H be a Hopf algebra. If there exists an invertible element $\mathcal{R} \in H \otimes H$, such that*

$$\begin{aligned}
&\mathcal{R}\Delta(x) = \Delta^{op}(x)\mathcal{R}, \ for \ all \ x \in H,\\
&(\Delta \otimes id)\mathcal{R} = \mathcal{R}_{13}\mathcal{R}_{23},\\
&(id \otimes \Delta)\mathcal{R} = \mathcal{R}_{13}\mathcal{R}_{12},
\end{aligned}$$

then H is called a quasi-triangular Hopf algebra. Here, $\Delta^{op}(x)$ has the tensor factors in $\Delta(x)$ interchanged, and $\mathcal{R} = \sum_i x_i \otimes y_i, \mathcal{R}_{12} = \sum_i x_i \otimes y_i \otimes 1, \mathcal{R}_{13} = \sum_i x_i \otimes 1 \otimes y_i, \mathcal{R}_{23} = \sum_i 1 \otimes x_i \otimes y_i$. Let $\mathcal{R}^{op} = \sum_i y_i \otimes x_i$. For instance, both Radford–Hopf algebra and generalized Taft algebra are a quasi-triangular Hopf algebra.

We assume $\mathcal{R} = \sum_i x_i \otimes y_i$ as above and use the antipode S to define

$$u = \sum_i S(y_i)x_i \in H. \tag{1}$$

Then, the following expressions hold

$$uxu^{-1} = S^2(x) \ for \ all \ x \in H \ and \ \Delta(u) = (\mathcal{R}^{op}\mathcal{R})^{-1}(u \otimes u).$$

Definition 2. *Let H be a quasi-triangular Hopf algebra. If there exists an invertible element v (the ribbon element) in the center of H such that*

$$v^2 = uS(u), \ S(v) = v, \ \varepsilon(v) = 1, \ \Delta(v) = (\mathcal{R}^{op}\mathcal{R})^{-1}(v \otimes v), \tag{2}$$

where u is as in (1), then $(H, \mathcal{R}, v)$ is called a ribbon Hopf algebra. For example, at^2-dimensional Taft–Hopf algebra is a ribbon Hopf algebra (see [4]).

3. The Structure of $\mathcal{T}^*$

In this section, we describe the Hopf algebra structure of $\mathcal{T}^*$.

Let $\{\overline{g^i x^j} | 0 \le i \le st-1, 0 \le j \le t-1\}$ be the basis of Hopf algebra $\mathcal{T}^*$ such that $\overline{g^i x^j}(g^i x^j) = 1$ and $\overline{g^i x^j}(g^{i'} x^{j'}) = 0$ for $(i', j') \neq (i, j)$, $0 \le i, i' \le st-1$, $0 \le j, j' \le t-1$.

Lemma 1. *Let $0 \le i, k \le st-1$ and $0 \le j, l \le t-1$. Then,*

$$\overline{g^i x^j} * \overline{g^k x^l} = \begin{cases} 0, & \text{if } k \neq i+j (\text{mod } st) \text{ or } l+j \ge t, \\ \begin{pmatrix} l+j \\ j \end{pmatrix}_p \overline{g^i x^{j+l}}, & \text{otherwise.} \end{cases}$$

Proof. By the coalgebra structure of $\mathcal{T}$, we have $\Delta(g^a x^b) = (g^a \otimes g^a)(x \otimes g + 1 \otimes x)^b = \sum_{u=0}^{b} \begin{pmatrix} b \\ u \end{pmatrix}_p g^a x^{b-u} \otimes g^{a+b-u} x^u$, where $0 \le a \le st-1, 0 \le b \le t-1$. If $0 \le i, k \le st-1$, $0 \le j, l \le t-1$, then $(\overline{g^i x^j} * \overline{g^k x^l})(g^a x^b) = \sum_{u=0}^{b} \begin{pmatrix} b \\ u \end{pmatrix}_p \overline{g^i x^j}(g^a x^{b-u}) \overline{g^k x^l}(g^{a+b-u} x^u)$. Hence, $(\overline{g^i x^j} * \overline{g^k x^l})(g^a x^b) \neq 0$ if and only if $a = i, b = l+j, j+l < t$ and $k \equiv i+j (\text{mod } st)$. Obviously, $(\overline{g^i x^j} * \overline{g^k x^l})(g^a x^b) = \begin{pmatrix} l+j \\ j \end{pmatrix}_p$. □

Obviously, $\sum_{i=0}^{st-1} \overline{g^i} = \varepsilon$ is the identity of the algebra $\mathcal{T}^*$.

Let $\omega \in \Bbbk$ be a primitive st-th root of unity with $\omega^s = p$. Put $\alpha = \sum_{i=0}^{st-1} \omega^i \overline{g^i}$ and $\beta = \sum_{i=0}^{st-1} \overline{g^i x}$.

Lemma 2. *$\mathcal{T}^*$ is generated as an algebra by α and β.*

Proof. Obviously, $\alpha, \beta \in \mathcal{T}^*$. Let A be a subalgebra of $\mathcal{T}^*$ generated by α and β. It follows from Lemma 1 that $\beta^j = (j)!_p(\overline{x^j} + \overline{g x^j} + \cdots + \overline{g^{st-1} x^j}), 1 \le j \le t-1$, and

$$\begin{aligned} \alpha &= \overline{1} + \omega \overline{g} + \omega^2 \overline{g^2} + \cdots + \omega^{st-1} \overline{g^{st-1}}, \\ \alpha^2 &= \overline{1} + \omega^2 \overline{g} + \omega^4 \overline{g^2} + \cdots + \omega^{2(st-1)} \overline{g^{st-1}}, \\ &\cdots \\ \alpha^{st-1} &= \overline{1} + \omega^{st-1} \overline{g} + \omega^{2(st-1)} \overline{g^2} + \cdots + \omega^{(st-1)(st-1)} \overline{g^{st-1}}. \end{aligned} \tag{3}$$

Then, we have

$$\begin{aligned} \frac{1}{(j)!_p} \alpha \beta^j &= \overline{x^j} + \omega \overline{g x^j} + \omega^2 \overline{g^2 x^j} + \cdots + \omega^{st-1} \overline{g^{st-1} x^j}, \\ \frac{1}{(j)!_p} \alpha^2 \beta^j &= \overline{x^j} + \omega^2 \overline{g x^j} + \omega^4 \overline{g^2 x^j} + \cdots + \omega^{2(st-1)} \overline{g^{2(st-1)} x^j}, \\ &\cdots \\ \frac{1}{(j)!_p} \alpha^{st-1} \beta^j &= \overline{x^j} + \omega^{st-1} \overline{g x^j} + \omega^{2(st-1)} \overline{g^2 x^j} + \cdots + \omega^{(st-1)(st-1)} \overline{g^{st-1} x^j}, \\ \frac{1}{(j)!_p} \alpha^{st} \beta^j &= \overline{x^j} + \overline{g x^j} + \overline{g^2 x^j} + \cdots + \overline{g^{st-1} x^j}. \end{aligned}$$

The coefficient determinant of (3) is $|B| = \begin{vmatrix} 1 & \omega & \omega^2 & \cdots & \omega^{st-1} \\ 1 & \omega^2 & \omega^4 & \cdots & \omega^{2(st-1)} \\ & \cdots & & & \\ 1 & \omega^{st-1} & \omega^{2(st-1)} & \cdots & \omega^{(st-1)(st-1)} \end{vmatrix}$ $= \prod_{0\leq i<j\leq st-1}(\omega^i - \omega^j) \neq 0$.

Therefore, by Cramer's Rule, we have $\overline{g} \in A$. Similarly, one can prove that $\overline{g^i x^j} \in A$ for $0 \leq i \leq st-1, 0 \leq j \leq t-1$. □

Proposition 1. *In $\mathcal{T}^*$, we have*

$$\alpha^{st} = \varepsilon,\ \beta^t = 0,\ \beta\alpha = \omega\alpha\beta.$$

Proof. It follows from Lemma 1 that $\alpha^{st} = \overline{1} + \overline{g} + \overline{g^2} + \cdots + \overline{g^{st-1}} = \varepsilon$, $\beta^t = (t)!_p(\overline{x^t} + \overline{gx^t} + \cdots + \overline{g^{st-1}x^t}) = 0$, and $\beta\alpha = (j)!_p(\omega\overline{x} + \omega^2\overline{gx} + \cdots + \omega^{st}\overline{g^{st-1}x}) = \omega\alpha\beta$. This completes the proof. □

Proposition 2. *The comultiplication, the counit, and the antipode of $\mathcal{T}^{*cop}$ are given by*

$$\Delta(\alpha) = \alpha \otimes \alpha,$$

$$\Delta(\beta) = \beta \otimes 1 + \alpha^s \otimes \beta,$$

$$\varepsilon(\alpha) = 1,\ \varepsilon(\beta) = 0,$$

$$S(\alpha) = \alpha^{st-1},\ S(\beta) = -\alpha^{-s}\beta.$$

Proof. We only consider the formula of $\Delta(\alpha)$ since the proof for $\Delta(\beta)$ is similar. Suppose that $\Delta(\overline{g^t}) = \sum_{j=0}^{st-1}\sum_{k=0}^{t-1}\theta_{j,k,j',k'}\overline{g^jx^k} \otimes \overline{g^{j'}x^{k'}}$, where $\theta_{j,k,j',k'} = \overline{g^t}(g^jx^kg^{j'}x^{k'})$. One can prove that $\theta_{j,k,j',k'} = 1$ if an only if $j + j' \equiv t (mod\ st), k = k' = 0$. Consequently, in $\mathcal{T}^{*cop}$, we have $\Delta(\overline{g^t}) = \sum_{i+j\equiv t(mod\ st)} \overline{g^i} \otimes \overline{g^j}$, then we have $\Delta(\alpha) = \alpha \otimes \alpha$. Similarly, one can show the formulas of the counit ε and antipode S of $\mathcal{T}^{*cop}$. □

Definition 3 ([13] (Definition IX.4.1)). *The quantum double $D(\mathcal{T})$ of Hopf algebra $\mathcal{T}$ is the bicrossed product of $\mathcal{T}$ and of $\mathcal{T}^{*cop}$.*

$$D(\mathcal{T}) = \mathcal{T}^{*cop} \bowtie \mathcal{T}.$$

By Proposition 3 and Lemma 2, one knows that $D(\mathcal{T})$ is generated as an algebra by $\varepsilon \bowtie g$, $\varepsilon \bowtie x$, $\alpha \bowtie 1$, and $\beta \bowtie 1$.

Lemma 3 ([13] (Lemma IX.4.2)). *The multiplication, comultiplication, and counit in $D(\mathcal{T})$ are given by*

$$(f \bowtie a)(g \bowtie b) = \sum_{(a)} f(a_1 \rightharpoonup g \leftharpoonup s^{-1}(a_3)) \bowtie a_2 b,$$

$$\varepsilon(f \bowtie a) = \varepsilon(a)f(1),$$

$$\Delta(f \bowtie a) = \sum_{(a)(f)} (f_1 \bowtie a_1)(f_2 \bowtie a_2),$$

$$\begin{aligned} S(f \bowtie a) &= \sum(S(a_2) \rightharpoonup S(f_1)) \bowtie (f_2 \rightharpoonup S(a_1)) \\ &= \sum(S(f_2) \leftharpoonup a_1) \bowtie (S(a_2) \leftharpoonup S(f_1)), \end{aligned}$$

where $f, g \in \mathcal{T}^{*cop}$ and $a, b \in \mathcal{T}$, $\sum f_1(x)f_2(y) = f(yx)$ for all $x, y \in \mathcal{T}$.

4. The Ribbon Elements of $(D(\mathcal{T}), \mathcal{R})$

In this section, we recall some results about quasi-triangular Hopf algebras, and then, we investigate the ribbon elements of $(D(\mathcal{T}), \mathcal{R})$.

4.1. Universal R-Matrix of $D(\mathcal{T})$

In this subsection, we determine the universal R-matrix of $D(\mathcal{T})$.

By [13] (Lemma IX.4.2), the universal $\mathcal{R}$-matrix of the quantum double has an explicit formula:

$$\mathcal{R} = \sum_{i \in I} (1 \bowtie e_i) \otimes (e^i \bowtie 1),$$

where $\{e_i\}_{i\in I}$ is a basis of the vector space H and $\{e^i\}_{i\in I}$ is its dual basis in $(H^{op})^* = (H^*)^{cop}$.

Lemma 4. *For any $0 \le i \le st-1$, $0 \le j \le t-1$, set*

$$y_{i,j} = \frac{1}{st}\frac{1}{(j)!_p}\sum_{k=0}^{st-1} \omega^{-ik}\alpha^k\beta^j$$

in $\mathcal{T}^*$. Then, $y_{i,j}(g^{i_1}x^{j_1}) = \delta_{i,i_1}\delta_{j,j_1}$ for all any $0 \le i, i_1 \le st-1$, $0 \le j, j_1 \le t-1$.

Proof. For $0 \le i \le st-1$, $0 \le j \le t-1$, let $\delta_{i,j}$ be the Kronecker symbol, then we have

$$\begin{aligned}
&y_{i,j}(g^{i_1}x^{j_1})\\
=&\frac{1}{st}\frac{1}{(j)!_p}(\sum_{k=0}^{st-1} \omega^{-ik}\alpha^k\beta^j)(g^{i_1}x^{j_1})\\
=&\frac{1}{st}\frac{1}{(j)!_p}(j)!_p(\beta^j + \omega^{-1}\alpha\beta^j + \cdots + \omega^{-(st-1)i}\alpha^{st-1}\beta^j)(g^{i_1}x^{j_1})\\
=&\frac{1}{st}(\sum_{v=0}^{st-1}\overline{g^v x^j} + \omega^{-i}\sum_{v=0}^{st-1}\omega^v\overline{g^v x^j} + \cdots + \omega^{-(st-1)i}\sum_{v=0}^{st-1}\omega^{(st-1)v}\overline{g^v x^j})(g^{i_1}x^{j_1})\\
=&\frac{1}{st}(1 + \omega^{(i_1-i)} + \cdots + \omega^{(i_1-i)(st-1)})\delta_{j,j_1}\\
=&\delta_{i,i_1}\delta_{j,j_1}.
\end{aligned}$$

□

By Lemma 4, one can easily know that the $\mathcal{R}$-matrix of $D(\mathcal{T})$ is

$$\begin{aligned}
\mathcal{R} &= \sum_{i,j}(1 \bowtie g^i x^j) \otimes (y_{i,j} \bowtie 1)\\
&= \frac{1}{st}\sum_{i,j,k}\frac{1}{(j)!_p}\omega^{-ik}(1 \bowtie g^i x^j) \otimes (\alpha^k\beta^j \bowtie 1).
\end{aligned}$$

4.2. The Existence of Ribbon Elements

In this subsection, we review some facts about the integral and quasi-ribbon element for a finite-dimensional Hopf algebra H. For $h \in H$ and α in the dual space H^*, we define

$$\langle \alpha, h \rangle := \alpha(h) \in \Bbbk.$$

The following results on the integral can be found in [14] (Chapter 2):

- A left integral element in H is an element t in H such that $ht = \varepsilon(h)t$, $\forall h \in H$. A right integral element in H is an element t' in H such that $t'h = \varepsilon(h)t'$, $\forall h \in H$.

$\int_H^l$ denotes the subspace of left integrals in H, and $\int_H^r$ denotes the subspace of right integrals in H. H is called *unimodular* if $\int_H^l = \int_H^r$.

- Let H be a finite-dimensional Hopf algebra. Then, we have the following:
  (1) $\int_H^l$ and $\int_H^r$ are each one-dimensional.
  (2) The antipode S of H is bijective, and $S(\int_H^l) = \int_H^r$, $S(\int_H^r) = \int_H^l$.
- Suppose $t \in \int_H^l$ and $T \in \int_{H^*}^r$. Notice that the left integrals for H form a one-dimensional ideal of H. Hence, there is a unique $\tilde{\alpha} \in G(H^*)$ such that $th = \langle \tilde{\alpha}, h \rangle t$ for all $h \in H$. The condition that H is unimodular is equivalent to $\tilde{\alpha} = \varepsilon$.

Likewise, there is a unique $\tilde{g} \in H$ such that $qT = \langle q, \tilde{g} \rangle T$, for all $q \in H^*$. We call $\tilde{\alpha}$ and $\tilde{g}$ the *distinguished group-like elements* of H^* and H, respectively.

As above, assume the R-matrix is $\mathcal{R} = \sum_i x_i \otimes y_i$, and define

$$g_{\tilde{\alpha}} = \sum_i x_i \tilde{\alpha}(y_i), \ and \ h_{\tilde{\alpha}} = g_{\tilde{\alpha}} \tilde{g}^{-1}, \tag{4}$$

where $\tilde{\alpha}$ is the distinguished group-like element of H^* and $\tilde{g}$ is the distinguished group-like element of H.

A *quasi-ribbon* element of Hopf algebra H is an element satisfying all the ribbon conditions in (2), except for the requirement that it is central. Our approach to finding an explicit formula for the ribbon element of $D(\mathcal{T})$ is to use the following results from quasi-ribbon elements.

Theorem 1 ([4] (Theorem 1)). *Let $(H, \mathcal{R})$ be a finite-dimensional quasi-triangular Hopf algebra over a field $\Bbbk$. Suppose $h'_{\tilde{\alpha}}$ is any element of H such that $(h'_{\tilde{\alpha}})^2 = h_{\tilde{\alpha}}$, i.e., $h'_{\tilde{\alpha}}$ is any square root of the element $h_{\tilde{\alpha}}$ in (4). Then, $v = uh'_{\tilde{\alpha}}$ is a quasi-ribbon element, where u is as in (1). Moreover, $v = uh'_{\tilde{\alpha}}$ is a ribbon element of $(H, \mathcal{R})$ if and only if $S^2(a) = (h'_{\tilde{\alpha}})^{-1} a h'_{\tilde{\alpha}}$ for all $a \in H$.*

Theorem 2 ([4] (Theorem 3)). *Suppose that H is a finite-dimensional Hopf algebra with antipode S over a field $\Bbbk$. Let $\tilde{g}$ and $\tilde{\alpha}$ be the distinguished group-like elements of H and H^*, respectively. Then, we have the following:*

(1) $(D(H), \mathcal{R})$ has a quasi-ribbon element if and only if there are $h \in G(H)$ and $\gamma \in G(H^*)$ such that $h^2 = \tilde{g}$ and $\gamma^2 = \tilde{\alpha}$.

(2) $(D(H), \mathcal{R})$ has a ribbon element if and only if there are $h \in G(H)$ and $\gamma \in G(H^*)$ as in part (1) such that

$$S^2(y) = h(\gamma \rightharpoonup y \leftharpoonup \gamma^{-1})h^{-1}$$

for all $y \in H$.

Corollary 1 ([4] (Proposition 3)). *Let $\mathcal{S}$ be the antipode of $D(H)$, and set $\mathcal{U} = \sum \mathcal{S}(y_i)x_i$. Then,*

$$(\gamma, h) \mapsto \mathcal{U}(\gamma^{-1} \otimes h^{-1})$$

defines a one-to-one correspondence between those pairs $(\gamma, h) \in G(H^*) \times G(H)$ such that $h^2 = \tilde{g}$ and $\gamma^2 = \tilde{\alpha}$ and the quasi-ribbon elements of $(D(H), \mathcal{R})$. The ribbon elements correspond to those pairs (γ, h), which further satisfy $S^2(y) = h(\gamma \rightharpoonup y \leftharpoonup \gamma^{-1})h^{-1}$, for all $y \in H$.

By [17], $D(\mathcal{T})$ is unimodular, so that $\alpha_D = \varepsilon_D$, where α_D and ε_D are the distinguished group-like element and the counit of $(D(\mathcal{T}))^*$, respectively.

Lemma 5. *(1) $\sum_{i=0}^{st-1} \omega^{(t-1)i} \alpha^i \beta^{t-1}$ is a right integral in $\mathcal{T}^*$, and the distinguished group-like element of $\mathcal{T}$ is g^{1-t}.*

(2) $\sum_{i=0}^{st-1} g^i x^{t-1}$ is a left integral in $\mathcal{T}$, and the distinguished group-like element of $\mathcal{T}^*$ is α^{-s}.

Proof. Let $\lambda = \sum_{\substack{0 \le i \le st-1 \\ 0 \le j \le t-1}} a_{ij}\alpha^i\beta^j$. We use the definition of a right integral of $\mathcal{T}^*$:

$$\lambda \in \int_{\mathcal{T}^*}^{r} \Leftrightarrow \lambda h^* = \varepsilon(h^*)\lambda,$$

for all $h^* \in \mathcal{T}^*$. Let $h^* = \beta$; we have

$$\sum_{\substack{0 \le i \le st-1 \\ 0 \le j \le t-1}} a_{ij}\alpha^i\beta^{j+1} = 0.$$

Since $\{\alpha^i\beta^k | 0 \le i \le st-1, 0 \le j \le t-1\}$ is the basis of $\mathcal{T}^*$, and $\beta^t = 0$, we obtain

$$\lambda = \sum_{i=0}^{st-1} a_{i,t-1}\alpha^i\beta^{t-1}.$$

Let $h^* = \alpha$. We have

$$\sum_{i=0}^{st-1} a_{i,t-1}\omega^{t-1}\alpha^{i+1}\beta^{t-1} = \sum_{i=0}^{st-1} a_{i,t-1}\alpha^i\beta^{t-1},$$

Then, $a_{i,t-1}\omega^{t-1} = a_{i+1,t-1}$. Moreover, $\int_{\mathcal{T}^*}^{r}$ is one-dimensional. Therefore, $\lambda = \sum_{i=0}^{st-1} \omega^{(t-1)i}\alpha^i\beta^{t-1}$.

Let $\tilde{g} = \sum_{\substack{0 \le k \le st-1 \\ 0 \le l \le t-1}} b_{kl}g^kx^l$ be the distinguished group-like element of $\mathcal{T}$. Then, we have

$$h^*\lambda = h^*(\tilde{g})\lambda.$$

Let $h^* = \alpha^j$. We have

$$\sum_{\substack{0 \le i \le st-1 \\ 0 \le j \le t-1}} \omega^{(t-1)i}\alpha^{i+j}\beta^{t-1} = \langle \sum_{\substack{0 \le i \le st-1 \\ 0 \le j \le t-1}} \omega^{ij}\overline{g^i}, \sum_{\substack{0 \le k \le st-1 \\ 0 \le l \le t-1}} b_{kl}g^kx^l\rangle \sum_{i=0}^{st-1} \omega^{(t-1)i}\alpha^i\beta^{t-1}.$$

Thus, $\sum_{k=0}^{st-1} \omega^{kj}b_{k0} = \omega^{(1-t)j}$, $0 \le j \le st-1$. By Cramer's Rule and the Vandermonde determinant, we have

$$b_{k0} = \begin{cases} 1, & k = st+1-t, \\ 0, & \text{otherwise.} \end{cases}, \ \textit{where}\ 0 \le k \le st-1.$$

Let $h^* = \alpha^j\beta^z$, $0 \le j \le st-1$, $1 \le z \le t-1$. We have

$$\langle (z)!_p \sum_{k=0}^{st-1} \omega^{jk}\overline{g^kx^z}, \sum_{\substack{0 \le k \le st-1 \\ 0 \le l \le t-1}} b_{kl}g^kx^l\rangle \sum_{i=0}^{st-1} \omega^{(t-1)i}\alpha^i\beta^{t-1} = 0.$$

Since $\{\alpha^i\beta^k | 0 \le i \le st-1, 0 \le j \le t-1\}$ is the basis of $\mathcal{T}^*$, we have

$$\langle (z)!_p \sum_{k=0}^{st-1} \omega^{jk}\overline{g^kx^z}, \sum_{\substack{0 \le k \le st-1 \\ 0 \le l \le t-1}} b_{kl}g^kx^l\rangle = (z)!_p \sum_{k=0}^{st-1} \omega^{jk}b_{kz} = 0.$$

By Cramer's Rule and the Vandermonde determinant, we have

$$b_{kl} = 0,\ 0 \le k \le st-1,\ 1 \le l \le t-1.$$

Consequently, $\tilde{g} = g^{1-t}$. Similarly, we can prove part (2). $\square$

Theorem 3. *(1)* $(D(\mathcal{T}),\mathcal{R})$ *has quasi-ribbon elements if and only if t is odd.*
(2) $(D(\mathcal{T}),\mathcal{R})$ *has unique ribbon element if and only if both s and t are odd.*
(3) $(D(\mathcal{T}),\mathcal{R})$ *has two ribbon elements if and only if s is even and t is odd.*

Proof. (1) By part (1) of Theorem 2, $(D(\mathcal{T}),\mathcal{R})$ has a quasi-ribbon element if and only if there exist $h = g^j \in G(\mathcal{T})$, $\gamma = \alpha^k \in G(\mathcal{T}^*)$, *where* $j,\ k \in \mathbb{Z}$, such that $(g^j)^2 = g^{1-t}$, $\alpha^{2k} = \alpha^{-s}$, which implies $st \mid (2j+t-1)$ and $st \mid (2k+s)$. Since, when t is even, $2j+t-1$ is odd, st is even, which contradicts $st \mid (2j+t-1)$. However, when t is odd, no matter whether s is even or odd, there exist $j = \frac{2st+1-t}{2}$, $k = \frac{st-s}{2} \in \mathbb{Z}$ such that $st \mid (2j+t-1)$, $st \mid (2k+s)$. Thus, one knows that $(D(\mathcal{T}),\mathcal{R})$ has quasi-ribbon elements if and only if t is odd.

(2) By part (2) of Theorem 2, $(D(\mathcal{T}),\mathcal{R})$ has ribbon elements if and only if there exist $\gamma = \alpha^k \in G(\mathcal{T}^*)$, $h = g^j \in G(\mathcal{T})$, which satisfy

$$
\begin{aligned}
&h^2 = g^{1-t},\ \gamma^2 = \alpha^{-s},\\
&S^2(x) = h(\gamma \rightharpoonup x \leftharpoonup \gamma^{-1})h^{-1},\\
&S^2(g) = h(\gamma \rightharpoonup g \leftharpoonup \gamma^{-1})h^{-1},
\end{aligned}
\tag{5}
$$

where x and g are the generators of $\mathcal{T}$, $k, j \in \mathbb{Z}$ and γ, h are given in part (1).

It follows $S^2(x) = \omega^{-s}x$, $h(\gamma \rightharpoonup x \leftharpoonup \gamma^{-1})h^{-1} = g^j(\omega^k x)g^{-j} = \omega^{k-sj}x$, $S^2(g) = g$, $h(\gamma \rightharpoonup g \leftharpoonup \gamma^{-1})h^{-1} = g^j g g^{-j} = g$ that $(D(\mathcal{T}),\mathcal{R})$ has ribbon elements if and only if there exist pairs $(\gamma, h) = (\alpha^k, g^j)$ such that

$$
\begin{aligned}
&g^{2j} = g^{1-t},\ \alpha^{2k} = \alpha^{-s},\\
&\omega^{-s}x = \omega^{k-sj}x.
\end{aligned}
$$

Since the order of α is st and the order of g is st, $(D(\mathcal{T}),\mathcal{R})$ has ribbon elements if and only if there exist pairs $(\gamma, h) = (\alpha^k, g^j)$ such that

$$st \mid (2j+t-1), st \mid (2k+s), st \mid (ks-sj).$$

$\Leftrightarrow$

$$j = \frac{stu+1-t}{2} \in \mathbb{Z}, k = \frac{stv-s}{2} \in \mathbb{Z}, v - su = 2w - 1, \tag{6}$$

where $u, v, w \in \mathbb{Z}$.

By part (1), one knows that, if $(D(\mathcal{T}),\mathcal{R})$ has ribbon elements, then t must be odd. If v is odd, then $\alpha^k = \alpha^{\frac{stv-s}{2}} = \alpha^{\frac{s(t-1)}{2}}$; if v is even, $\alpha^k = \alpha^{\frac{stv-s}{2}}$, $k = \frac{stv-s}{2} \in \mathbb{Z}$, which implies that s must be even. If u is odd, $j = \frac{stu+1-t}{2} \in \mathbb{Z}$, which implies s must be even, then we have $g^j = g^{\frac{stu+1-t}{2}} = g^{\frac{st+1-t}{2}}$; if u is even, then $g^j = g^{\frac{stu+1-t}{2}} = g^{\frac{1-t}{2}}$. If both t and s are odd, u is even, v is odd or u is odd, and v is even since $v - su = 2w - 1$. Moreover, $j = \frac{stu+1-t}{2} \in \mathbb{Z}$ and $k = \frac{stv-s}{2} \in \mathbb{Z}$ imply that u is even and v is odd, then there exists a unique pair $(\gamma, h) = (\alpha^{\frac{s(t-1)}{2}}, g^{\frac{1-t}{2}})$ satisfying (5). If t is odd and s is even, v must be odd since $v - su = 2w - 1$. In this case, no matter whether p is odd or even, $j = \frac{stu+1-t}{2} \in \mathbb{Z}$ and $k = \frac{stv-s}{2} \in \mathbb{Z}$. Thus, there exist two pairs $(\gamma_1, h_1) = (\alpha^{\frac{s(t-1)}{2}}, g^{\frac{1-t}{2}})$ and $(\gamma_2, h_2) = (\alpha^{\frac{s(t-1)}{2}}, g^{\frac{(s-1)t+1}{2}})$ satisfying (5). Consequently, by Corollary 1, $(D(\mathcal{T}),\mathcal{R})$ has a unique ribbon element if and only if both s and t are odd; $(D(\mathcal{T}),\mathcal{R})$ has two ribbon elements if and only if s is even and t is odd. □

4.3. Computation of the Ribbon Elements of $D(\mathcal{T})$

Throughout this subsection, assume t is an odd integer. Notice that $\tilde{\alpha} = \alpha^{-s}$ and $\tilde{g} = g^{1-t}$ are the distinguished group-like elements in $\mathcal{T}^*$ and $\mathcal{T}$, respectively. By the description about the distinguished group-like element of the Drinfeld double of a finite-dimensional quasi-triangular Hopf algebra in [17], the distinguished group-like element in $D(\mathcal{T})$ is $\tilde{\alpha} \bowtie \tilde{g}$.

Recall the universal R-matrix of $D(\mathcal{T})$ given in Section 4.1:

$$\mathcal{R} = \frac{1}{st} \sum_{i,j,k} \frac{1}{(j)!_p} \omega^{-ik} (1 \bowtie g^i x^j) \otimes (\alpha^k \beta^j \bowtie 1). \tag{7}$$

Theorem 4. *Assume that t is an odd integer:*

(1) When s is odd, the unique ribbon element in $D(\mathcal{T})$ is

$$v = u(\alpha^{\frac{s(t+1)}{2}} \bowtie g^{\frac{t-1}{2}}),$$

$$\text{where } u = \frac{1}{st} \sum_{\substack{0 \le i,k \le st-1 \\ 0 \le j \le t-1}} (-1)^j \frac{1}{(j)!_p} \omega^{-(i+j)k - \frac{j(j-1)s}{2}} (\alpha^{-sj-k} \beta^j \bowtie g^i x^j).$$

(2) When s is even, the ribbon elements in $D(\mathcal{T})$ are

$$v_1 = u(\alpha^{\frac{s(t+1)}{2}} \bowtie g^{\frac{t-1}{2}}),\ v_2 = u(\alpha^{\frac{s(t+1)}{2}} \bowtie g^{\frac{t(s+1)-1}{2}}),$$

$$\text{where } u = \frac{1}{st} \sum_{\substack{0 \le i,k \le st-1 \\ 0 \le j \le t-1}} (-1)^j \frac{1}{(j)!_p} \omega^{-(i+j)k - \frac{j(j-1)s}{2}} (\alpha^{-sj-k} \beta^j \bowtie g^i x^j).$$

Proof. (1) We adopt the previous conventions and set $g_{\alpha_D} = g_{\varepsilon_D}$ (which holds as $D(\mathcal{T})$ is unimodular). By (4) and (7), we have

$$\begin{aligned} g_{\varepsilon_D} &= \frac{1}{st} \sum_{\substack{0 \le i,k \le st-1 \\ 0 \le j \le t-1}} \frac{1}{(j)!_p} \omega^{-ik} \varepsilon(\alpha^k \beta^j \bowtie 1)(1 \bowtie g^i x^j) \\ &= \frac{1}{st} \sum_{\substack{0 \le i,k \le st-1 \\ 0 \le j \le t-1}} \frac{1}{(j)!_p} \omega^{-ik} \varepsilon(1) \alpha^k \beta^j(1)(1 \bowtie g^i x^j). \end{aligned}$$

Since $\beta^j(1) = 0$ when $j \neq 0$ and ε_D is an algebra homomorphism, only the terms with $j = 0$ survive, and therefore,

$$\begin{aligned} g_{\varepsilon_D} &= \frac{1}{st} \sum_{\substack{0 \le i,k \le st-1 \\ 0 \le j \le t-1}} \omega^{-ik} (1 \bowtie g^i) \\ &= \frac{1}{st} \sum_{i=0}^{st-1} (\sum_{k=0}^{st-1} \omega^{-ik})(1 \bowtie g^i). \end{aligned}$$

Observe that

$$\sum_{k=0}^{st-1} \omega^{-ik} = \frac{1 - (\omega^{-i})^{st}}{1 - \omega^{-i}} = 0$$

unless $i = 0$, in which case $\sum_{k=0}^{st-1} \omega^{-ik} = st$. Therefore, $g_{\varepsilon_D} = 1_{D(E)}$.

By the discussion above, the distinguished group-like element in $D(\mathcal{T}) \simeq \mathcal{T}^* \otimes \mathcal{T}$ is $\hat{g} = \alpha^{-s} \bowtie g^{1-t}$.

By (4), $h_{\varepsilon_D} = g_{\varepsilon_D}(\hat{g})^{-1} = (\alpha^{-s} \bowtie g^{1-t})^{-1} = \alpha^s \bowtie g^{t-1}$. When s and t are both odd, the square root h'_{ε_D} of h_{ε_D} is unique, because h_{ε_D}, and therefore, h'_{ε_D} has odd order. Thus,

$$h'_{\varepsilon_D} = \alpha^{\frac{s(t+1)}{2}} \bowtie g^{\frac{t-1}{2}},$$

$$v = uh'_{\varepsilon_D} = u(\alpha^{\frac{s(t+1)}{2}} \bowtie g^{\frac{t-1}{2}}).$$

By Theorem 1, the quasi-ribbon element v is the unique ribbon element of $D(\mathcal{T})$.

(2) When s is even and t is odd, h_{ε_D} has four square roots:

$$h'_{\varepsilon_{D1}} = \alpha^{\frac{s(t+1)}{2}} \bowtie g^{\frac{t-1}{2}},\ h'_{\varepsilon_{D2}} = \alpha^{\frac{s}{2}} \bowtie g^{\frac{t-1}{2}},$$

$$h'_{\varepsilon_{D3}} = \alpha^{\frac{s(t+1)}{2}} \bowtie g^{\frac{t(s+1)-1}{2}},\ h'_{\varepsilon_{D4}} = \alpha^{\frac{s}{2}} \bowtie g^{\frac{t(s+1)-1}{2}}.$$

By Theorem 1,

$$S^2(\varepsilon \bowtie g) = (h'_{\varepsilon_{Di}})^{-1}(\varepsilon \bowtie g)h'_{\varepsilon_{Di}},\ S^2(\varepsilon \bowtie x) = (h'_{\varepsilon_{Di}})^{-1}(\varepsilon \bowtie x)h'_{\varepsilon_{Di}},$$

$$S^2(\alpha \bowtie 1) = (h'_{\varepsilon_{Di}})^{-1}(\alpha \bowtie 1)h'_{\varepsilon_{Di}},\ S^2(\beta \bowtie 1) = (h'_{\varepsilon_{Di}})^{-1}(\beta \bowtie 1)h'_{\varepsilon_{Di}},$$

where $i = 1, 3$ and $\varepsilon \bowtie g, \varepsilon \bowtie x, \alpha \bowtie 1, \beta \bowtie 1$ are the generators of $D(\mathcal{T})$.

Therefore, quasi-ribbon elements

$$v_1 = uh'_{\varepsilon_{D1}} = u(\alpha^{\frac{s(t+1)}{2}} \bowtie g^{\frac{t-1}{2}}) \text{ and } v_2 = uh'_{\varepsilon_{D3}} = u(\alpha^{\frac{s(t+1)}{2}} \bowtie g^{\frac{t(s+1)-1}{2}})$$

are the ribbon elements of $D(\mathcal{T})$.

It remains to show that u has the expression in (1). Recall that $u = \sum_i S(y_i)x_i$, where

$$\mathcal{R} = \frac{1}{st}\sum_{i,j,k} \frac{1}{(j)!_p}\omega^{-ik}(1 \bowtie g^i x^j) \otimes (\alpha^k \beta^j \bowtie 1).$$

Therefore,

$$\begin{aligned} u &= \frac{1}{st}\sum_{\substack{0\le i,k\le st-1\\ 0\le j\le t-1}} \frac{1}{(j)!_p}\omega^{-ik}S(\alpha^k\beta^j \bowtie 1)(1 \bowtie g^i x^j) \\ &= \frac{1}{st}\sum_{\substack{0\le i,k\le st-1\\ 0\le j\le t-1}} \frac{1}{(j)!_p}\omega^{-ik}((-\alpha^{-s}\beta)^j(\alpha^{st-1})^k) \bowtie 1)(1 \bowtie g^i x^j) \\ &= \frac{1}{st}\sum_{\substack{0\le i,k\le st-1\\ 0\le j\le t-1}} (-1)^j\frac{1}{(j)!_p}\omega^{-ik-jk-\frac{j(j-1)s}{2}}(\alpha^{-sj-k}\beta^j \bowtie 1)(1 \bowtie g^i x^j) \\ &= \frac{1}{st}\sum_{\substack{0\le i,k\le st-1\\ 0\le j\le t-1}} (-1)^j\frac{1}{(j)!_p}\omega^{-(i+j)k-\frac{j(j-1)s}{2}}(\alpha^{-sj-k}\beta^j \bowtie g^i x^j). \end{aligned}$$

Finally, we know that, when s is odd, $v = u(\alpha^{\frac{s(t+1)}{2}} \bowtie g^{\frac{t-1}{2}})$ is the unique ribbon element of $D(\mathcal{T})$. When s is even, $v_1 = u(\alpha^{\frac{s(t+1)}{2}} \bowtie g^{\frac{t-1}{2}})$ *and* $v_2 = u(\alpha^{\frac{s(t+1)}{2}} \bowtie g^{\frac{t(s+1)-1}{2}})$ are the ribbon elements of $D(\mathcal{T})$. □

Remark 1. *The generalized Taft algebra is a special rank-one pointed Hopf algebra of the nilpotent type. We have provided a necessary and sufficient condition for the quantum double of generalized Taft algebra $\Lambda_{st,t}^{*cop}$ to be a ribbon Hopf algebra. Besides, we computed all ribbon elements of $D(\Lambda_{st,t}^{*cop})$. Further research is required to obtain the necessary and sufficient condition for the quantum double of all pointed Hopf algebras of the nilpotent type.*

Author Contributions: Funding acquisition, J.H.; methodology, H.S.; supervision, Z.J. and M.H.; visualization, J.H.; writing—original draft, Y.Z.; writing—review and editing, H.S. and Y.Z. All authors will be informed about each step of manuscript processing including submission, revision, revision reminder, etc., via emails from our system or assigned Assistant Editor. All authors have read and agreed to the published version of the manuscript.

Funding: This work was financially supported by the Natural Science Foundation of Jiangsu Province (No. BK20210783).

Data Availability Statement: The original contributions presented in the study are included in the article, further inquiries can be directed to the corresponding author.

Conflicts of Interest: The authors declare no conflicts of interest.

References

1. Drinfeld, V.G. Quantum groups. In Proceedings of the International Congress of Mathematicians, Berkeley, CA, USA, 3–11 August 1986; pp. 798–820.
2. Reshetikhin, N.; Turaev, V.G. Inviriants of 3-manifolds via link polynomials and quantum groups. *Invent. Math.* **1991**, *103*, 547–597. [CrossRef]
3. Chen, J.L.; Yang, S.L. Ribbon Hopf Superalgebras and Drinfel'd Double. *Chin. Ann. Math. Ser. B* **2018**, *39*, 1047–1064. [CrossRef]
4. Kuaffman, L.H.; Radford, D.E. A necessary and sufficient condition for a finite-dimensional Drinfel'd double to be a ribbon Hopf algebra. *J. Algebra* **1993**, 159, 98–114. [CrossRef]
5. Benkart, G.; Biswal, R.; Kirkman, E.; Nguyen, V.C.; Zhu, J. Tensor Representations for the Drinfeld Double of the Taft Algebra. *arXiv* **2020**, arXiv:2012.15277. [CrossRef]
6. Andruskiewitsch, N.; Schneider, H.J. On the classification of finite-dimensional pointed Hopf algebras. *Ann. Math.* **2010**, *171*, 375–417. [CrossRef]
7. Burciu, S. A class of Drinfeld doubles that are ribbon algebras. *J. Algebra* **2008**, *320*, 2053–2078. [CrossRef]
8. Leduc, R.; Ram, A. A ribbon Hopf algebra approach to the irreducible representations of centralizer algebras: The Brauer, Birman-Wenzl, and type A Iwahori-Hecke algebras. *J. Algebra* **1993**, *159*, 98–114. [CrossRef]
9. Centrone, L.; Yasumura, F. Actions of Taft's algebras on finite dimensional algebras. *J. Algebra* **2020**, *560*, 725–744. [CrossRef]
10. Montgomery, S.; Schneider, H.-J. Skew derivations of finite-dimensional algebras and actions of the double of the Taft–Hopf algebra. *Tsukuba J. Math.* **2001**, *25*, 337–358. [CrossRef]
11. Farsad, V.; Gainutdinov, A.M.; Runkel, I. The symplectic fermion ribbon quasi-Hopf algebra and the $SL(2,\mathbb{Z})$-action on its centre. *Adv. Math.* **2022**, *400*, 108247. [CrossRef]
12. Chang, L.; Wang, Z.H.; Zhang, Q. Modular data of non-semisimple modular categories. *arXiv* **2024**, arXiv:240409314.
13. Kassel, C. *Quantum Groups*; Springer: New York, NY, USA, 1995.
14. Montgomery, S. *Hopf Algebras and Their Actions on Rings*; CBMS Series in Math; American Mathematical Soc.: Providence, RI, USA, 1993; Volume 82.
15. Erdmann, K.; Green, E.L.; Snashall, N.; Taillefer, R. Representation theory of the drinfeld doubles of a family of hopf algebras. *J. Pure Appl. Algebra* **2006**, *204*, 413–454. [CrossRef]
16. Sweedler, M.E. *Hopf Algebras*; Benjamin: New York, NY, USA, 1969.
17. Radford, D.E. Minimal quasitriangular Hopf algebras. *J. Algebra* **1993**, *157*, 285–315. [CrossRef]

Disclaimer/Publisher's Note: The statements, opinions and data contained in all publications are solely those of the individual author(s) and contributor(s) and not of MDPI and/or the editor(s). MDPI and/or the editor(s) disclaim responsibility for any injury to people or property resulting from any ideas, methods, instructions or products referred to in the content.

MDPI AG
Grosspeteranlage 5
4052 Basel
Switzerland
Tel.: +41 61 683 77 34

Mathematics Editorial Office
E-mail: mathematics@mdpi.com
www.mdpi.com/journal/mathematics

Disclaimer/Publisher's Note: The title and front matter of this reprint are at the discretion of the Guest Editor. The publisher is not responsible for their content or any associated concerns. The statements, opinions and data contained in all individual articles are solely those of the individual Editor and contributors and not of MDPI. MDPI disclaims responsibility for any injury to people or property resulting from any ideas, methods, instructions or products referred to in the content.

www.ingramcontent.com/pod-product-compliance
Lightning Source LLC
Chambersburg PA
CBHW061614210926
51850CB00009B/2320
* 9 7 8 3 7 2 5 8 7 4 8 6 6 *